Healthcare Management in India

Healthcare Management in India

Psycho-Social and Neurological Aspects of HIV/AIDS and Other Physical and Mental Disorders *Including Case Studies*

Edited by

S.K. Srivastava, Vipin Kumar and Veena Katyal

New Century Publications
New Delhi, India

NEW CENTURY PUBLICATIONS
4800/24, Bharat Ram Road,
Ansari Road, Daryaganj,
New Delhi – 110 002 (India)

Tel.: 011-2324 7798, 4358 7398, 6539 6605
Fax: 011-4101 7798
E-mail: indiatax@vsnl.com • info@newcenturypublications.com
www.newcenturypublications.com

Editorial office:
LG–7, Aakarshan Bhawan
4754-57/23, Ansari Road, Daryaganj,
New Delhi – 110 002

Tel.: 011-4356 0919

First Published: **July 2010**

ISBN: **978-81-7708-244-9**

Published by New Century Publications and printed at Salasar Imaging Systems, New Delhi

Designs: Patch Creative Unit, New Delhi

PRINTED IN INDIA

About the Book

Healthcare is fundamental to national progress in any sphere. In terms of resources for economic development, nothing can be considered of higher importance than the health of the people which is a measure of their energy, capacity and potential for productive work. Health is a positive state of well being in which the harmonious development of physical and mental capacities of the individual lead to the enjoyment of a rich and full life. It is not a negative state of mere absence of disease. Health further implies complete adjustment of the individual to his total environment, physical and social.

Considerable achievements have been made since Independence in 1947 to improve health standards in the country. Nevertheless, problems abound. India has to deal with rising costs of healthcare and growing expectations of the people. The challenge of quality health services in remote rural regions has to be urgently met.

AIDS, cancer, diabetes, cardiovascular disease (CVD) and stroke are not only serious health problems but also pose formidable development issues on account of their potential adverse impact on productivity and hence socio-economic development.

The present volume comprises 26 research papers—contributed by psychologists, psychiatrists, home scientists, AIDS counsellors, social workers and human resources (HM) experts—which provide deep psycho-social and neurological insights into various dimensions of healthcare challenges being faced by India. Out of 26 papers, 15 papers deal with the pressing problem of HIV/AIDS and the remaining 11 with other physical and mental disorders including cancer, diabetes, depression, inhalant abuse, sleep problems, examination stress and sexually transmitted infections (STIs). These well-researched papers provide valuable information on management of healthcare problems in India.

Profiles of Editors

Dr. S.K. Srivastava is presently Professor in the Department of Psychology, Gurukul Kangri University, Haridwar. He received his Ph.D. Degree in Psychology from I.I.T. Roorkee. He has completed 4 research projects sponsored and financed by Indian Council of Social Science Research (ICSSR), New Delhi and University Grants Commission (UGC), New Delhi. He has contributed more than 125 research papers and articles to various national and international journals of repute. Dr. Srivastava has been a member of the Executive Committee of International Association for Peace Psychology (IAPP).

Dr. Vipin Kumar is a faculty member in the Department of Psychology, Gurukul Kangri University, Haridwar. He obtained his Doctoral Degree from the same University. He has published 4 research papers in reputed journals. His field of specialization is Clinical and Health Psychology.

Dr. Veena Katyal is presently working as a psychologist/counsellor at Lord International School, Alwar (Rajasthan). She obtained her M.A. and Ph.D. degrees in Psychology from M.J.P. Rohilkhand University, Bareilly. She is the recipient of Gold Medal for her academic excellence in Master Degree. She has published 7 empirical and 2 theoretical papers in professionally recognised journals.

Contents

Part II: Psycho-Social and Neurological Aspects of Physical and Mental Diseases

Contributors

Ira Das Professor of Psychology, Faculty of Social Sciences, Dayalbagh Educational Institute, Agra.

Suman Mishra Research Scholar, Department of Psychology, Faculty of Social Sciences, Dayalbagh Educational Institute, Agra.

Irfat Ara Khan Ph.D. Student in Psychology, Gurukul Kangri University, Haridwar.

S.K. Srivastava Professor of Psychology, Gurukul Kangri University, Haridwar.

R. Kannappan Associate Professor in Clinical Psychology, Vinayaka Missions Medical College Hospital, Salem, Tamil Nadu.

Manisha Dasgupta Lecturer, Department of Psychology, University of Calcutta, Kolkata.

Anand Prakash Assistant Professor in Clinical Psychology, Department of Psychology, University of Gondar, Gondar, Ethiopia.

N.V.V.S. Narayana Department of Psychology and Parapsychology, Andhra University, Visakhapatnam.

Nidhi Kotwal Post-graduate Department of Home Science (CRM&E) GCW Parade, Jammu.

Bharti Prabhakar Project Officer, Centre for Adult and Continuing Education and Extension, University of Jammu, Jammu.

Surila Agarwala Professor and Head, Department of Psychology, Dayalbagh Educational Institute, Agra.

Satya Satvir Singh Research Scholar, Department of Psychology, Faculty of Social Science, Dayalbagh Educational Institute, Agra.

Ameesha Research Student, Department of Psychology, Lady Shri Ram College for Women, University of Delhi, Delhi.

Priti S. Dhawan Associate Professor, Department of Psychology, Lady Shri Ram College for Women, University of Delhi, Delhi.

Shahzadi Malhotra Clinical Psychologist, Department of Clinical Psychology, Institute of Human Behaviour and Allied Sciences (IHBAS), Delhi.

Gaurav Rajender Senior Resident, Department of Psychiatry, University College of Medical Sciences and GTB Hospital, Delhi.

T.B. Singh Professor and Head, Department of Clinical Psychology, Institute of Human Behaviour and Allied Sciences (IHBAS), Delhi.

Yogita Rai Research Scholar, Department of Psychology, Banaras Hindu University, Varanasi.

Tanusree Dutta Lecturer, Department of Psychology, MMV, BHU, Varanasi.

Sarika Jaiswal Lecturer of Home Science, C.R.D. Arya Women's Post-graduate College, Gorakhpur.

Smita Jaiswal Senior Lecturer in Psychology, D.V. Post-graduate College, Orai, Jalaun.

Sonal Sharma AIDS Counselor Distt. (M.) Hospital, Hamirpur.

Deapti Mishra Assistant Professor, Clinical Psychology, Gwalior Manasik Arogyashala, Gwalior, Madhya Pradesh.

Ranjeet Kumar Assistant Professor, Clinical Psychology, Gwalior Manasik Arogyashala, Gwalior, Madhya Pradesh.

J. Mathto Professor, Clinical Psychology, Post-graduate Institute of Behavioural and Medical Sciences, Raipur.

S.N. Sahu Professor, Psychiatric Social Work, Post-graduate Institute of Behavioural and Medical Sciences, Raipur.

Manoranjan Tripathi Post-graduate Student, Department of Psychology, Gurukul Kangri University, Haridwar.

Archana Dutta Lecturer, HR, Globsyn Business School, Ahmedabad.

Sheenu Research Scholar, Department of Psychology, Faculty of Social Sciences, Dayalbagh Educational Institute, Agra.

Roshan Lal Zinta Senior Lecturer, Department of Psychology, Himachal Pradesh University, Summer Hill, Shimla.

Meera Manjul Ph.D. Student in Psychology, H.P. University, Shimla.

S.P. Sinha Professor Emeritus, Department of Psychology, Dayalbagh Education Insitute, Agra.

Shraddha Sharma Research Scholar, Department of Psychology, Dayalbagh Education Insitute, Agra.

A.V.S. Madnawat Associate Professor, Department of Psychology, University of Rajasthan, Jaipur.

V.K. Bhardwas Research Fellow, Department of Psychology, University of Rajasthan, Jaipur.

Anubhuti Dubey Department of Psychology, D.D.U. Gorakhpur University, Gorakhpur.

Dhananjay Kumar Department of Psychology, D.D.U. Gorakhpur University, Gorakhpur.

Kailash Chandra Barmola Student of Psychology, Gurukul Kangri University, Haridwar.

Priyanka Behrani Faculty Member, Department of Psychology, The M.S. University of Baroda, Vadodara.

Nitu Singh Bhadouria Counselor, Vikas Jyot Trust, Baroda.

Namitesh Gupta Lecturer, Home Science, CRD P.G. College, Gorakhpur.

Preface

Healthcare is fundamental to national progress in any sphere. In terms of resources for economic development, nothing can be considered of higher importance than the health of the people which is a measure of their energy, capacity and potential for productive work. Health is a positive state of well being in which the harmonious development of physical and mental capacities of the individual lead to the enjoyment of a rich and full life. It is not a negative state of mere absence of disease. Health further implies complete adjustment of the individual to his total environment, physical and social. Health involves primarily the application of medical science for the benefit of the individual and of society. However, many other factors, social, economic and educational have an intimate bearing on the .health of the community. Health is thus a vital part of a concurrent and integrated programme of development of all aspects of community life.

Considerable achievements have been made since Independence in 1947 to improve health standards in the country. Nevertheless, problems abound. Malnutrition affects a large proportion of the population especially women and children. An unacceptably high proportion of the population continues to suffer and die from new diseases apart from the existing ones. There is a strong link between poverty and ill-health. Ill health creates immense stress even among those who are financially secure. Onset of a long and expensive illness can drive the economically well-off into poverty. The importance of public provisioning of quality healthcare to enable access to affordable and reliable heath services cannot be underestimated. This is particularly so in the context of preventing the non-poor from entering into poverty and reducing the suffering of those who are already below poverty line.

India has to deal with rising costs of healthcare and growing expectations of the people. The challenge of quality health services in remote rural regions has to be urgently met. Given the magnitude of the problem, there is the need to transform public healthcare into an accountable, accessible and affordable system of quality services. Special attention needs to be given to the health of vulnerable groups like adolescent girls, women, children, older persons, disabled and primitive tribal groups. The contribution of the private sector in providing primary, secondary and tertiary services should be enhanced through various measures including partnership with the Government.

Rising income levels and the emergence of health insurance has facilitated the growth of high quality healthcare sector in India although the capacity to pay for health services remains limited to middle and high income brackets. With the opening of the insurance market in 2000 to private players, health and medical insurance has shown significant growth. Cashless claim facilities offered by many players have led to a significant rise in health insurers.

The public healthcare system is not able to meet the growing demands for healthcare facilities. The gap between demand and supply has to be bridged by the private players, and this has facilitated the growth of the corporate healthcare industry in India. Although emergence of strong corporate players in healthcare is not a substitute for expansion of public sector health facilities yet it has led to professionalization of the industry, better hospital management and higher investments in infrastructure facilities.

Adolescent Health

Adolescents in India represent nearly one-third of the population. The last two decades have witnessed a rapid increase in their population. Some of the public health challenges for adolescents include pregnancy, excess risk of maternal and infant mortality, sexually transmitted infections, reproductive tract infections and the rapidly rising incidence of HIV. The use of health services by adolescents is limited due to poor knowledge and lack of awareness. Pregnancy is associated with significantly higher obstetric risk in adolescent girls. Many of them suffer from malnutrition and anaemia. This combined with poor antenatal care leads not only to increased morbidity in the mother but also to high incidence of low birth weight and prenatal mortality. Poor childrearing practices add to the morbidity and under-nutrition in infants, thus perpetuating the inter-generational cycle of under-nutrition and ill health. Thus, ill health during adolescence has profound implications for maternal and infant morbidity and mortality. The urgent need for appropriate nutrition and health education for adolescents should be met by advocacy for delay in age at marriage and optimum health and nutrition interventions during pregnancy.

Older Persons

An area of growing importance and demanding attention is the health of older persons. It requires comprehensive care providing preventive, curative and rehabilitative services. Unlike developed countries, India does not have a Geriatric Health Service. According to the 2001 Census, there were 76.6 million people over the age of 60, constituting about 7.4 percent of the total population. Life expectancy has been increasing and the proportion of older persons in India will rise in the next few decades. The health services need to be responsive to the special needs of older persons in the following areas: (a) provision of specialtybased clinics, (b) counselling, (c) long-term care, (d) community-based rehabilitation and (e) medical care facilities.

HIV/AIDS

AIDS is not only a serious health problem but also a major development issue on account of its potential impact on productivity and economic growth within the country. A nation-wide HIV sentinel surveillance conducted by National AIDS Control Organization in all States/UTs has indicated that HIV infection is prevalent in all States/UTs. Six States have emerged as high incidence States where HIV prevalence rate is recorded to be 1 percent and above, viz. Karnataka, Tamil Nadu, Andhra Pradesh, Maharashtra, Manipur and Nagaland. The National AIDS Control Programme (NACP) Phase II (1999-2004) was implemented with an estimated outlay of Rs. 1,425 crore with funding by World Bank and USAID.

The focus of this programme was to reduce HIV transmission among the poor and marginalised high-risk groups by adopting following measures:

- Condom promotion.
- Reduction in blood-borne transmission.
- Voluntary testing and counselling.
- Developing capacity for community-based low cost care for people living with HIV/AIDS.
- Strengthening implementation capacity at the National, State and Panchayat levels.
- Forging inter-sectoral linkages between public, private and voluntary sectors.

Nearly 20,408 AIDS cases were reported in 2007, out of which, 87.4 percent of the infections were transmitted through the sexual route and pre-natal transmission accounted for 4.7 percent of infections. About 1.8 percent and 1.7 percent of infections were acquired through injecting drug use and contaminated blood and blood products respectively.

During the Eleventh Five Year Plan (2007-12), the National AIDS Control Programme (NACP) Phase III has set the goal to halt and reverse the epidemic in India over the next 5 years by integrating programmes for prevention, care, support and treatment and also addressing the human rights issues specific to people living with HIV/AIDS. The specific objectives are to reduce new infections by 60 percent in high prevalence States so as to obtain reversal of the epidemic and by 40 percent in the vulnerable States so as to stabilize the epidemic.

In order to achieve the objectives, the following strategies will be adopted:

- Preventing new infections in high risk groups and general population through (a) saturation of coverage of high risk groups with targeted interventions and (b) scaled up interventions in the general population.
- Increasing the proportion of people living with HIV/AIDS who receive care, support and treatment.
- Strengthening the infrastructure, system and human resource in prevention, care support and treatment programmes at the district and national levels.
- Enacting and enforcing national legislation prohibiting discrimination against people living with HIV/AIDS and their families in health facilities, schools, places of employment and other institutions.
- Including mechanisms for victims and their guardians to lodge complaints and receive quick redressal.
- Ensuring that women and children living with HIV/AIDS receive medical care, including antiretroviral treatment and use all possible means to remove barriers to their receiving care.
- Strengthening a nation-wide strategic information management system.
- Advancing research and development of vaccines suitable for the strains of HIV prevalent in India.

National Cancer Control Programme (NCCP)

During the Tenth Five Year Plan (2002-07), a Taskforce comprising of experts from across the country was constituted. Based on the recommendations of the Taskforce a comprehensive NCCP will be implemented during the Eleventh Five Year Plan. The main activities during the Plan will be as follows:

- Establishing new Regional Cancer Centres.
- Upgradation of the existing Regional Cancer Centres based on their performance and linkages with other cancer organizations in the region.
- Creating skilled human resources for quality cancer care services.
- Training healthcare providers for early detection of cancers at primary and secondary level.
- Increasing accessibility and availability of cancer care services.
- Providing behavioural change communication along with provision of cost effective screening techniques and early detection services at the door step of community.
- Propagating self-screening of common cancers (oral, breast).
- Upgrading Oncology Wings in Government Medical Colleges.
- Creating and upgrading cancer detection and surgical and medical treatment facilities in District/Charitable/NGO/Private Hospitals.

- Promoting research on effective strategies of prevention, community-based screening, early diagnosis, environmental and behavioural factors associated with cancers and development of cost effective vaccines.
- Creating Palliative Care and Rehabilitation Centres.
- Monitoring, Evaluation and Surveillance.

National Programme for Prevention and Control of Diabetes, Cardiovascular Disease (CVD) and Stroke

Common risk factors for both CVD and diabetes are unhealthy diet, physical inactivity and obesity. There is evidence-based information that non-communicable diseases (NCDs) are preventable through integrated and comprehensive interventions. Cost effective interventions exist and have worked in many countries. The most successful ones have employed a range of population wide approaches combined with interventions for the individuals. Eleventh Five Year Plan aims to prevent and control common risk factors through an integrated approach and to reduce premature morbidity and mortality from diabetes, CVD and stroke. During the Plan, the objectives of the programme would be as follows:

- Primary prevention of major NCDs through health promotion.
- Surveillance of NCDs and their risk factors in the population.
- Capacity enhancement of health professionals and health systems for diagnosis and appropriate management of NCDs and their risk factors.
- Reduction of risk factors in the population.
- Establishment of National guidelines for management of NCDs.
- Development of strategies and policies for prevention by inter-sectoral coordination.
- Community empowerment for prevention of NCDs.

National Mental Health Programme (NMHP)

A multi-pronged strategy to raise awareness about issues of mental health and persons with mental illness with the objective of providing accessible and affordable treatment, removing ignorance, stigma and shame attached to it and to facilitate inclusion and acceptance for the mentally ill is the basis of NMHP. Its main objective is to provide basic mental health services to the community and to integrate these with the National Rural Health Mission. The programme envisages a community and more specifically family-based approach to the problem.

Recognizing the importance of mental health care, Eleventh Five Year Plan would provide counselling, medical services and establish helplines for people affected by calamities, riots, violence (including domestic) and other traumas. The Plan has envisaged strengthening District Mental Health Programme (DMHP) and enhancing its visibility at grassroots level by promoting greater family and community participation and creating para-professionals equipped to address the mental health needs of the community from within. The Plan aims to fill up human resource gap in the field of psychiatry, psychology, psychiatric social work and DMHP. The Plan will strive to incorporate mental health modules into the existing training of health personnel.

The present volume comprises 26 research papers—contributed by psychologists, psychiatrists, home scientists, AIDS counsellors, social workers and human resources (HM) experts—which provide deep psycho-social and neurological insights into various dimensions of healthcare challenges being faced by India. Out of 26 papers, 15 papers deal with the pressing problem of HIV/AIDS and the remaining 11 with other physical and mental disorders including cancer, diabetes, depression, inhalant abuse, sleep problems, examination stress and sexually transmitted infections (STIs).

The editors place on record their deep appreciation and gratefulness to all the contributors for their scholarly and well-researched papers which will undoubtedly provide valuable information on management of healthcare problems in India.

Haridwar
June 10, 2010

S.K. Srivastava
Vipin Kumar
Veena Katyal

Part I

Psycho-Social and Neurological Aspects of HIV/AIDS

1

HIV/AIDS in India

Ira Das and Suman Mishra

Introduction

India has the world's third largest population suffering from AIDS, after South Africa and Nigeria. However, the estimated number of human immunodeficiency virus (HIV) infections in India has declined drastically in recent years from 5.5 million in 2005 to below 2.5 million in 2007. These new figures are supported by the World Health Organization and UNAIDS. Despite being home to the world's third largest population suffering from AIDS, the AIDS prevalence rate in India is relatively lower.

In 2007, India's AIDS prevalence rate stood at approximately 0.30 percent the 89th highest in the world. The spread of HIV in India is primarily restricted to the southern and north-eastern regions of the country and India has also been praised for its extensive anti-AIDS campaign. The US$ 2.5 billion National AIDS Control Plan III was set up by India in 2007 and received support from UNAIDS. The apex Government of India body for HIV surveillance is the National AIDS Control Organization (NACO). The majority of HIV surveillance data collected by the NACO is done through annual unlinked anonymous testing of prenatal clinic (or antenatal clinics) and sexually transmitted infection clinic attendees.

History of HIV/AIDS in India

India's first cases of HIV were diagnosed among sex workers in Chennai, Tamil Nadu. Most of the initial cases had occurred through heterosexual sex; but at the end of the 1980s, a rapid spread of HIV was observed among injecting drug users in Manipur, Mizoram and Nagaland.

In 1987, a National AIDS Control Programme was launched to coordinate national responses. Its activities covered surveillance, blood screening and health education. In 1992, the government set up NACO (National AIDS Control Organisation), to oversee the formulation of policies, prevention work and control programs related to HIV and AIDS. In 2001, the government adopted the National AIDS Prevention and Control Policy. NACP III was launched formally on 6th July 2007.

The main factors which have contributed to India's large HIV-infected population are extensive labour migration, low literacy level in certain rural areas resulting in lack of awareness and gender disparity. The Government of India has also raised concerns about the role of intravenous drug use and prostitution in spreading AIDS, especially in north-east India and certain urban pockets. A recent study published in the British medical journal "The Lancet" in (2006) reported an approximately 30 percent decline in HIV infections among young women aged 15 to 24 years attending prenatal clinics in selected southern states of India from 2000 to 2004 where the epidemic is thought to be concentrated.

Incidence: According to UNICEF, 30,000 babies are born HIV positive each year in India. According to the NFHS 3 survey data in 2006 estimated population of HIV are 2.1 to 3.1 million people but its reliability some critics are questioning and claiming 5.1 to 5.3 millions. These are only estimates and there is no true cases reflecting data available.

Some Facts

- In 1986 first case of HIV in female sex worker in Chennai.
- In 1986 first report of AIDS in Mumbai.
- In 1991 NACP was launched.
- In 2000-01 PMTCT feasibility studies initiated by NACO.
- In 2001 ART drugs are manufactured at considerable price reduction.

Prevalence: The HIV prevalence is greater among the males (0.43) than among the females (0.29). For every 100 people living with HIV/AIDS (PLHAs), 61 are men and 39 women (taking into account the fact that the total number of men is greater than to 0.30 percent women as elucidated by the sex ratio). Prevalence is also high in the 15-49 age group (88.7 percent of all infections), indicating that AIDS still threatens the cream of society, those in the prime of their working life. Between 2005 and 2006, prevalence has fallen in some major states—Maharashtra from 0.80 to 0.74 percent, in Tamil Nadu from 0.47 to 0.39 percent—for instance. Yet, new areas of concern have emerged. In West Bengal, prevalence has gone up from 0.21 and in Rajasthan from 0.12 to 0.17 percent. And the HIV adult prevalence is more in the urban (0.4) compared to rural (0.3).

The prevalence rate is high in illiterate when compared to literate ANC and also the prevalence rate is more in ANC with spouse in driving occupation.

While adult HIV prevalence among the general population is 0.36 percent, high-risk groups, inevitably, show higher numbers. Among Injecting Drug Users (IDUs), it is as high as 6.92 percent, while it is 6.41 percent and 4.9 percent among Men who have Sex with Men (MSM) and Female Sex Workers (FSWs), respectively.

People Living with HIV/AIDS (PLHA): The total number of people living with HIV/AIDS in the country estimated 2.47 million. The highest numbers of PLHA are in Andhra Pradesh, Maharastra, Tamil Nadu and Karnataka contributes 63 percent of all the PLHA in the country.

Trends in HIV Epidemic: The prevalence rate in adults is decreasing from 0.45 to 0.36 percent and also there is considerable decrease in total PLHA from 2.73 to 2.47 millions, but in female LHAs it is almost around 0.99 percent.

Some Specific Characters of the Disease: Caused by a RNA virus, man is the only reservoir in the form of cases and sub clinical cases, and got a very long incubation period making the disease surveillance a big problem.

Awareness Regarding HIV/AIDS Status

Eighty-six percent of the Indian population is unaware of their HIV status. Only 57 percent of the general population and 80 percent of commercial sex workers are aware of preventive methods.

Interventions: National AIDS Control Programme was launched in 1987. Since then, the National HIV Programme has moved through three phases. 1986-1992, Denial of the Threat of HIV: This was a period that saw the beginning of a largely research-based programme. Surveillance activities were launched in 55 cities in three states. 1992-97, First Acceleration of the Programme: Backed by World Bank funding and strong WHO GPA (Global Programme on AIDS) support, this phase saw the creation of the National AIDS Control Organization (NACO).

1998-2001, focus on Targeted Intervention: Building on the experience of the first phase, there was a twin drive to focus on coverage among high risk groups like sex workers, truck drivers and injecting drug users. Make the programme multi-sectoral. It has resulted in a strongly decentralized programme with the responsibility of implementation vested with the states. Flexible State AIDS Societies were formed with stronger mechanisms for state level programme management.

An innovative approach for providing technical support by establishing a network of 12 Technical Resource Groups (TRGs), covering different thematic areas of the epidemic and mandated was set up to provide technical support to states. These include building capacities to implement the strategies of prevention and building a genuinely multi-scrotal response that is sustainable. It also involves mobilizing and coordinating a considerable range of partners, including the private sector.

National Family Health Survey 2005-2006, HIV Statistics

The National Family Health Survey conducted between 2005 and 2006 measured HIV prevalence among the general adult population of India, as presented in Table 1.1. The survey found the rate among men to be considerably higher than that among women.

Table 1.1: HIV Prevalence among General Adult Population of India

	HIV prevalence (percent)		
Age group	Male	Female	*Total*
15-19	0.01	0.07	*0.04*
20-24	0.19	0.17	*0.18*
25-29	0.43	0.28	*0.35*
30-34	0.64	0.45	*0.54*
35-39	0.53	0.23	*0.37*
40-44	0.41	0.19	*0.30*
45-49	0.48	0.17	*0.33*
Total age 15-49	*0.36*	*0.22*	*0.28*

The National Family Health Survey, which tested more than 100,000 people for HIV, also found prevalence to be higher in urban areas (0.35 percent) than in rural areas (0.25 percent).

HIV Statistics, 2007

NACO releases HIV figures each year based on data gathered from HIV Sentinel Surveillance sites. In 2007 surveillance was conducted at 1134 sites and 358,797 samples were tested for HIV. The sites carry out tests among the high-risk groups and among antenatal clinic attendees. Data gathered from the antenatal clinics are then used as a surrogate for the general population.

Across India HIV prevalence appears to be low among the general population, but disproportionately high among high-risk groups, such as injecting drug users (IDUs), female sex workers (FSW), men who have sex with men (MSM) and sexually transmitted disease (STD) clinic attendees.

The average HIV prevalence among women attending antenatal clinics in India is 0.48 percent. Much higher rates are found among people attending STD clinics (3.6 percent), female sex workers (5.1 percent), injecting drug users (7.2 percent) and men who have sex with men (7.4 percent). As Table 1.2 shows, the rates among different groups vary widely between states.

Some areas report an HIV prevalence rate of zero in antenatal clinics. This does not necessarily mean HIV is absent from the area, as some states report the presence of the virus at STD clinics and amongst injecting drug users. In some states and territories the average antenatal HIV prevalence is based on reports from only a small number of clinics.

Table 1.2: HIV Rates among Different Groups in States of India

State/Union Territory	Antenatal clinic HIV prevalence 2007 (percent)	STD clinic HIV prevalence 2007 (percent)	IDU HIV prevalence 2007 (percent)	MSM HIV prevalence 2007 (percent)	*Female sex worker HIV prevalence 2007 (percent)*
A & N Islands	0.25	1.33	...	...	...
Andhra Pradesh	1.00	17.20	3.71	17.04	*9.74*
Arunachal Pradesh	0.00	0.00	0.00	...	...
Assam	0.00	0.50	2.41	2.78	*0.44*
Bihar	0.25	0.40	0.60	0.00	*3.40*
Chandigarh	0.25	0.42	8.64	3.60	*0.40*
Chhattisgarh	0.25	3.33	...	...	*1.43*
D&N Haveli	0.50	...	...	...	...
Daman & Diu	0.13	...	...	...	...
Delhi	0.25	5.20	10.10	11.73	*3.15*
Goa	0.18	5.60	...	7.93	...
Gujarat	0.25	2.40	...	8.40	*6.53*
Haryana	0.13	0.00	0.80	5.39	*0.91*
Himachal Pradesh	0.00	0.00	...	0.00	*0.87*
Jammu & Kashmir	0.00	0.20	...	...	...
Jharkhand	0.00	0.40	...	...	*1.09*
Karnataka	0.50	8.40	2.00	17.60	*5.30*
Kerala	0.38	1.60	7.85	0.96	*0.87*
Lakshadweep	0.00	0.00	...	...	...
Madhya Pradesh	0.00	1.72	...	...	*0.67*
Maharashtra	0.50	11.62	24.40	11.80	*17.91*
Manipur	0.75	4.08	17.90	16.40	*13.07*

Contd...

Meghalaya	0.00	2.21	4.17	...	...
Mizoram	0.75	7.13	7.53	...	*7.20*
Nagaland	0.60	3.42	1.91	...	*8.91*
Orissa	0.00	1.60	7.33	7.37	*0.80*
Pondicherry	0.00	3.22	...	2.00	*1.30*
Punjab	0.00	1.60	13.79	1.22	*0.65*
Rajasthan	0.13	2.00	...	...	*4.16*
Sikkim	0.09	0.00	0.47	...	*0.00*
Tamil Nadu	0.25	8.00	16.80	6.60	*4.68*
Tripura	0.25	0.40	0.00	...	...
Uttar Pradesh	0.00	0.48	1.29	0.40	*0.78*
Uttaranchal	0.00	0.00	...	...	...
West Bengal	0.00	0.80	7.76	5.61	*5.92*

Outlook

There is no cure for HIV infection. People with AIDS lived only for a couple of years. Fortunately, medications have substantially improved the outlook and survival rates. Prevention efforts have sharply reduced HIV infection in young children and have the potential to sharply limit new infections in other populations. Medications have extended the average life expectancy, and many people can expect to live for decades with proper treatment. An increasing number have a normal life expectancy if they adhere carefully to medication regimens. Medications help the immune system recover and fight infections and prevent cancers from occurring. Eventually, the virus may become resistant to the available drugs, and the manifestations of AIDS may develop. Drugs used to treat HIV and AIDS do not cure the infection. It is important for the person to remember that he or she is still contagious. Intensive research efforts are being focused on developing new and better treatments. Although currently there is no promising vaccine, work continues on this front.

References

Aarogya AIDS Support Group.

CIA World Factbook Publication - AIDS Prevalence Rates.

Ekstrand Maria, Garbus Lisa and Marseille Elliot (2003) 'HIV/AIDS in India', AIDS Research Institute: AIDS Policy Research Centre, University of California, San Francisco, August. http://ari.ucsf.edu/ari/policy/countries.html.

HIV/AIDS in India from wikipedia, the free encyclopaedia http://www.articlesbase.com/diseases-and-conditions-articles/hiv-aids-in-india-a- review-808158.html.

India HIV Caseload Seen Dramatically Lower, *Reuters*, Jul 4, 2007.

Marfatia, Y.S., Sharma, A. and Modi, M. (2007). Overview of HIV/AIDS in India (Review Article). *Indian Journal of Sexually Transmitted Diseases*, 28 (1), 1-5. DOI: 10.4103/0253-

7184.35702.

National AIDS Control Organization (NACO) (2006). 'Sentinel Surveillance and HIV Estimation in India'.

National AIDS Control Organization (NACO) (2007). 'HIV Sentinel Surveillance and HIV Estimation in India: A Technical Brief'.

National Family Health Survey (NFHS-3) 2005-06, September 2007.

New York Times (2007). "2.5 million people in India living with Aids, according to new estimates". http://data.unaids.org/pub/PressRelease/2007/070706_indiapressrelease_en.pdf. Retrieved 2007-06-08.

UNAIDS (2007) 'Press release: 2.5 million people in India living with HIV', according to new estimates'.

UNAIDS (2004) Report on the Global AIDS Epidemic.

UNPAN (2003) National AIDS Prevention and Control Policy (India).

World Health Organization (2005) 'India: Summary Country Profile for HIV/AIDS Treatment Scale-up'.

World Heath Organization (2007). "2.5 million people in India living with HIV, according to new estimates". http://www.who.int/mediacentre/news/releases/2007/pr37/en/index.html. Retrieved 2007-06-08.

Website

http://www.aids-free-india.org

http://www.emedicinehealth.com/hivaids/glossary_em.htm

http://www.google.com

http://www.lifepositive.com/Body/body-holistic/AIDS/aids.asp

http://www.unpan.org

2

HIV/AIDS: Major Health Endangering Behaviours of Life

Irfat Ara Khan and S.K. Srivastava

Introduction

The threat of AIDS has become a fact of life around the world. In just the past decade, over one-quarter of a million Americans has been diagnosed as having AIDS and as many as two million more have been infected with HIV, the virus that leads to AIDS. An estimated 75,000 of these Americans are adolescents (St. Lawrence, 1998). Currently, the majority of those affected in the United States are male, but the ratc for female is doubling every year or two (Ickovics and Roddin, 1999). Unsafe sex- especially having sex without having a condom greatly increases the risk of contracting HIV, yet many American adolescents and adults continue this dangerous practice (Catania etal, 2000). Like smoking and many other health- threatening behaviours, unprotected sex is disproportionately common among low-income individuals, many of whom are members of ethnic minority groups (St. Lawrence, 1998). Among African-American men the risk of contracting AIDS is three times greater than for European-American men; the risk for African-American women is fifteen times higher than for European-American women (USDHHS, 2002). Health psychologists are deeply involved in the fight against the spread of HIV and AIDS (Kiecolt- Glaser and Glaser, 1998; Kelly and Murphy, 1998).

The AIDS virus is spread by blood or semen (Catania etal, 1990). Some victims, most notably hemophiliacs, have acquired the virus in transfusions of contaminated blood. Heroin addicts can acquire it by sharing hypodermic needles with infected addicts. The virus can also be transmitted through sexual activity, including anal sex and vaginal sex. Even infants born to mothers with AIDS are at high risk of developing the disease. Transmission of the virus from infected dental or medical personnel to their patients, or from infected patients to dental or medical personnel, is much less likely. There is no evidence that the virus is spread by kissing, simple touching, food handling, or other casual kinds of contact.

Because AIDS is, so for, inevitably fatal, its prevention is crucial. One of the primary means of prevention is educating people to avoid risky behaviours. Foremost among the suggestions has been to practice "safe sex" (or at least "safer sex"). In regard to AIDS, the safest sex is abstinence or limiting oneself to an uninfected partner. Many people choose not to abstain, however, and may have a series of partners, so the next best suggestions are to use condoms and reduce the number of one's sex partners. Efforts to reduce risky behaviours have achieved some success. Through elsewhere in the world AIDS is more prevalent among heterosexuals, in North America it has been more prevalent among homosexual men. This has been attributed to the common practice of unprotected anal sex. The 10 percent of heterosexuals who practice anal sex are also at increased risk of contracting AIDS (Voeller, 2006). Because it has so ravaged the North America homosexual community, the earliest anti-AIDS programs have been aimed at homosexuals. Cities with large homosexual and bi-sexual men. Such programs have been effective. For example, survey of homosexual men in San Francisco, where there is a high level of AIDS education, found a significant increase in their use of condoms (Catania etal, 2002).

Scope of the Problem

First identified in 1981, AIDS has emerged as the most serious infectious epidemic of modern times. Indeed, it has been compared with the Black Plague of the Middle Ages. By mid-1992, 150,000 people in the United States had died from complications from the disease and between one and 1.5 million were HIV-positive (carrying the virus that causes AIDS; Sarngadharan et al., 2000). There were also 206,000 documented living cases of AIDS. The U.S. Centres for Disease Control estimate that by the end of 1993, as many as 170,000 more Americans will have died from AIDS; thus the total number of fatalities in the United States would be as high as 320,000. Another way to portray the spreading epidemic is to note that every thirteen minutes someone in the United States becomes infected with the human immunodeficiency virus (HIV).

Figures like these can be so numbing that it is instructive to put them in perspective. The Vietnam War, the morality and casualties of which have been constantly debated in this country, claimed about 58,000 lives in the ten years of American involvement (1964 to 1973). The analogous ten-year figure for AIDS is 150,000, or two and a half times higher. But since the worst fatality figures are yet to come, the magnitude of the loss of human life in the United States alone is going to be many times greater than U.S deaths in Vietnam.

The prevalence of AIDS among African-American and Hispanics is more than double the percentages of these groups in the U.S population—about 40 percent of U.S. AIDS cases are members of these minorities (Centres for Disease

Control, 1989; Foreyt, 1999). The imbalance is even greater for women; most women with AIDS are intravenous (IV) drug users or have had sexual contact with IV drug users. In 162 countries reporting data to the World Health Organization, close to 350,000 cases have been isolated, but his figure is believed to be a gross underestimate because detection and reporting of cases lag in many countries (underreporting in Africa may be as high as 90 percent). Perhaps even more daunting are future estimates of the number of people in the world believed to be HIV positive but not yet diagnosed as having AIDS (e.g., Earvin "Magic" Johnson, formerly of the Los Angeles Lakers basketball team): according to the World Health Organization, as of 1991 as many as 10 million people throughout the world were HIV- positive and about one-third of these will have developed AIDS by 1993 (Wright, 2000).

AIDS was first proclaimed in this country to be a disease of homosexuals. As of the late 1980s, almost three-quarters of AIDS patients were homosexual men, with intravenous drug users accounting for approximately 20 percent. Before blood screening began in 1985, many hemophiliacs received contaminated blood transfusions that ultimately resulted in their contracting AIDS. But AIDS never was homosexual disease at all, and there are signs that the disease is increasing among heterosexuals, both men and women (Centres for Disease Control, 1989). Indeed, in Africa and parts of Latin America, AIDS is found primarily among heterosexuals, and throughout the world, infected women are giving birth to babies who are HIV- positive. Even in parts of the world in which AIDS is not yet a significant health problem, it is likely to become one.

Description of the Disease

Although the medical intricacies of AIDS are beyond the scope of this paper, it is important to understand a few fundamentals. AIDS is a disease in which the body's immune system is severely compromised, putting the individual at high risk for opportunistic disease, such as Kaposi's sarcoma, rare forms of lymph cancer, and a wide range of dangerous fungal, viral, and bacterial infections. Medical authorities suspect AIDS when an otherwise healthy person presents with an illness that he or she would not likely have with a properly functioning immune system. (People who have had an organ transplant, for example, are at risk for such opportunistic diseases because they are given drugs that suppress the immune system so that the body will not reject the new organ. In a sense, the AIDS patient is someone who presents similarly, without having taken the anti-rejection, immunosuppressant medication. The big difference, of course, is that the transplant patient is kept in an antiseptic intensive care hospital environment while his or her immune system is being artificially and temporarily compromised). Strictly speaking, people do not die of AIDS as much as they die of fatal infectious diseases that AIDS makes them vulnerable to.

The HIV-infection may also attack the central nervous system directly (Nurnberg, Prudic, Fiori, and Freedman, 2001), sometimes leading to problems in memory and concentration many months before an AIDS-related illness appears. One study (Navia, Cho, Petito and Price, 2005) found that of seventy AIDS patients autopsied at death fewer than 10 percent had normal brains and most of them had exhibited what has come to be called AIDS dementia complex, a deterioration in memory, thought, judgment, and motor coordination that is believed to be caused directly by the AIDS virus prior to the suppression of the immune system that is the hallmark of AIDS. However, many studies fail to show this direct damaging effect of the HIV infection).

If a person tests positive for HIV, the body has produced antibodies to the AIDS virus. AIDS is diagnosed when the virus has destroyed a large number of T-4 or helper T lymphocytes, cells that are at the core of the body's immune system, the system that fights off the many infections that humans are exposed to daily but resist rather routinely most of the time. All people who test HIV-positive develop AIDS, usually within eight years, but some first develop AIDS-related complex, ARC, which is less severe than AIDS and which develops into AIDS, usually within a year (Redfield, Wright, and Tramat, 2004).

Spread of the Disease

The AIDS crisis is exacerbated by the fact that many untested HIV-positive people feel healthy and are unaware of their illness. Though little talked about in the media, there is an illness called acute HIV syndrome, characterized by flu-like symptoms such as fever, night sweats, and headaches, that occurs about a month after infection and lasts two or three weeks (Glasner and Kaslow, 2004).

HIV positive individuals can infect others, in the ways described below, and contribute to what some have called a ticking time bomb in the health of the human race. Complicating efforts to control transmission of HIV is the fact that the most widely employed tests detect antibodies to infection, and these antibodies do not appear in most infected people until several months following infection (McCutchan, 2006). Thus even if a test is negative, a person recently exposed to an infected individual may have HIV.

Once diagnosed with AIDS, drugs such as AZT can bring about some improvement and perhaps even prolong life, but available data offer little encouragement that lives can be saved over the long haul (and "long" is seldom more than a few years"). Although millions are being spent on developing a vaccine against HIV, the focus is now squarely on behavioural science research and practice for prevention and control.

The core of the problem is risky sexual practices, not sexual orientation. HIV is present only in blood, semen and vaginal secretions and can be transmitted only when infected liquids get into the bloodstream. AIDS cannot be caught through casual social contact or even by living with an AIDS or HIV-positive person, provided that reasonable care is taken to avoid contact with blood. Unprotected receptive anal intercourse (i.e. having a penis inserted into one's anus) is the riskiest of sexual practices (Kingsley et al., 2004). Considerably less risky but still chancy is vaginal intercourse without a condom, and probably also unprotected oral-genital contact and finger or hand insertion into the anus or vagina. The other category of risky behaviour is found among intravenous drug users who share unsterilized needles and thus can introduce HIV-carrying blood into the bloodstream of another. The use of alcohol and drugs during sex increases the probability of risky sexual practices (Stall et al., 2007). Perhaps the most tragic victims are infants born to HIV-positive mothers, for the virus can cross the placental barrier and infect the developing fetus. The virus can also be transmitted through breast-feeding.

Prevention of the Disease

The primary focus in prevention of sexually transmitted AIDS is on changing sexual practices. Exposure can of course be eliminated by being in a monogamous relationship with a partner who tests negative for HIV. However, monogamous relationships are very rare among young people, and are not invariably found among married people or those in other committed relationships. Prevention is best directed at encouraging sexually active people to use condoms which are about 90 percent effective in preventing HIV infection. Employing sophisticated probability modelling techniques, Reiss and Leik (2002) demonstrated that risk is far more significantly reduced by using condoms—even though they are less than 100 percent effective—than by reducing the number of partners with whom a person has sex. Of course, the safest strategy would be to use condoms in a monogamous relationship, a tack that is probably unrealistic and that is also contrary to the strictures of some religious groups (since condoms are a form of birth control). More prevalent in the public health arena, however is advocacy of monogamous relationships, a recommendation that is based more on morality than on data.

People are also urged to explore the pleasures of low-risk sex, such as mutual masturbation and frottage (body rubbing without insertion of the penis into vagina, mouth or anus of the partner). Note that for the most part this advice holds for same or opposite sexed partners. Prevention for IV drug users includes the aforementioned measures, but should also include the use of new or sterilized needles. The best precaution would be getting off drugs altogether.

In cities where AIDS is less of a problem than it is in centres like New York and San Francisco, high risk behaviour is much more common. Perhaps there is a (mistaken) sense of personal invulnerability when there is not an epidemic in one's immediate vicinity (St. Lawrence, et al., 1998). This certainly seems to be the case, especially among young heterosexuals (both male and female) who continue to see the problem as mostly limited to gays and drug users and who perhaps wish to distance themselves from a disease that bears the social stigma of those whom it affects the most at the present time. There is, then, little evidence that high-risk behaviour among heterosexuals has markedly changed, especially among African-Americans and Hispanics (Thomas, Gilliam, and Iwrey, 2001), whose attitudes toward the use of condoms are quite negative. Adolescents in general see AIDS as a personal threat less than do people in their twenties and beyond. These facts pose a serious problem, because the most prudent judgment for people to make regardless of sexual orientation – when they consider having sexual relations, particularly with a new partner, is that their partner could be HIV-positive.

But how can changes be brought about, especially (at least for heterosexuals) in a generation of sexually active people for whom the pill marked a welcome liberation from the need to use condoms? Also daunting is the challenge of changing the attitudes and practices of adults for whom the 1960s ushered in a period of sexual liberation, restrained to be sure by the danger of herpes and other venereal diseases but not by the certainty of dying. Kelly and St. Lawrence (2001) draw on social psychological and behaviour therapy theory and research to suggest principles that can form the basis of effective interventions. Educational messages should (1) emphasize the risk of certain behaviours; (2) make clear the vulnerability of people who engage in such behaviours; (3) demonstrate how changes in behaviour can reduce risk; and (4) persuade the person that the benefits of making behavioural changes outweigh any inconvenience and loss of satisfaction. The information needs to be presented so that people know exactly what they should be doing and why; and communication has to be frequent and conveyed in a supportive, optimistic (yet realistic) way by respected persons with whom the audience can identify. Also important are social support and encouragement.

Interventions implementing these principles lead to reductions in unprotected anal intercourse and increased use of condoms in gay and bisexual men. Such efforts are having a positive impact in reducing the spread of HIV infection among gays.

Such cognitive-behavioural approaches to prevention might, we believe, benefit from some social psychological research inspired by Milton Rokeach's work on values (1973; Ball-Rokeach and Rokeach, 2004). Rokeach held that human behaviour is controlled in important ways by values, for example, involvement in civil rights is associated with a person valuing equality more than freedom of choice. In a technique he called value self-confrontation, Rokeach and others have shown that if one confronts an individual with a discrepancy between the values held by those whom the person wishes to emulate and the values the person currently holds, one can influence the individual to change his or her behaviour in an enduring fashion.

What might be the implications for AIDS prevention? It is possible—and remains to be researched—that people who are successful in changing from high to low risk sexual practices differ in their values from those who do not. For example, they may value wisdom more than short term pleasure. If this is the case, then informing HIV-negative people of this fact may encourage them to change their own values (or maintain them if they match those of successful behaviour changers) and thereby regard their sexuality in a way that promotes more healthful, less risky behaviour in the interests of a long term benefit. Research inspired by Rokeach would seem to be of particular importance to social scientists concerned with behavioural risk reduction in AIDS, because, to be meaningful, any behavioural changes brought about need to be enduring ones. Cognitive change aimed at a deep level, such as a change in values, is likely to be superior to a more superficial change.

Therapy for HIV-positive and AIDS Patients

What can mental health professionals offer HIV-positive people and those afflicted with AIDS? Anxiety and depression are common, as is a sense of outrage that Nature has perpetrated such as sick joke on humankind.

Psychological stress can have a negative impact on the immune system. Alleviating such stress can have positive benefits (Kielcolt-Glaser et al., 2000). This kind of work is being applied to therapy for HIV-positive and AIDS patients because the infection results in a suppression of the immune system. For example, there is some promising evidence that, in the early stages of HIV infection, aerobic exercise can increase T-4 cell levels and reduce anxiety and depression (Antoni et al., 2007). A possible mechanism for these preliminary gains may be an enhanced sense of control and well-being.

For those with full-blown AIDS, therapy entails supporting the person in seeking available and acceptable experimental medical treatments and helping the person make contact with AIDS support groups in the area. Stress management approaches can also be beneficial, though one cannot and should not deny the objective gravity of the situation. What also seems in our view to be emerging in the clinical literature is the appropriateness of an existential approach that encourages examination of the meaning of one's life and of one's impending death and the importance of achieving some manner of resolution, including making out a will, saying goodbye, in short, doing what has long been believed to be useful and meaningful as one confronts his or her mortality and obligations to those about to be left behind. No doubt a religious belief in an afterlife can bring comfort both to the patient and to his or her loved ones. Social support from family and friends and from other AIDS sufferers is also beneficial. Since many terminal AIDS patients have been estranged from their families because of their sexual orientation, drug use, or family members fears of contagion, concerted efforts are needed to effect what can sometimes be remarkable and bolstering reconciliations.

The fact that most of those dying of AIDS are young and in what would have been their most productive years underscores the personal and social tragedy. Those who test HIV-positive but do not yet have AIDS or ARC are under stress as they face the knowledge that they will almost certainly contract AIDS. With such individuals Kely and St. Lawrence advise encouragement of healthful practices such as exercise, decreased alcohol consumption, and good nutrition, all of which may have positive effects on the immune system. Indeed, since little is known about the biological and psychological factors that may determine when an HIV-positive individual will develop AIDS, there is much research to be done in hopes of buying time.

AIDS and Public Policy

Any discussion of AIDS prevention is fraught with moral, political, and public policy implications. In the early 1990s we are witnessing heated debate about how much information to convey to children and young adults in elementary and secondary school. Most young people in the United States have had intercourse by the time they enter high school (Hofferth and Hayes, 2007) and perhaps as few as 15 percent of sexually active teenagers use condoms. Should society distribute free condoms to junior high school children? Or should abstinence from sexual intercourse be advocated? At what age do we believe that people should become sexually active? If condoms are sold or distributed gratis in secondary schools, does this condone premarital teenage sex? Or does it represent a realistic and humane confrontation with the real world?

Should we distribute free clean needles to intravenous drug users, or does this, too, condone a pattern of behaviour that can be regarded as harmful, both to the abuser and to society?

Should we require mandatory testing and of whom should we require it? Is it health care workers only? If so, are we prepared to protect those who test positive for the AIDS virus from job discrimination and quarantine? And if we do not offer legal protection, will that not undermine voluntary testing? And isn't that undesirable, given that such testing could reduce the spread of the virus and might also prolong life in infected individuals by enabling them to make choices for drubs, like AZT, which if begun in the early stages of infection can improve the quality and length of life.

Also critical for society to face are the attitudes and practices of health care providers. Although the risks of contagion from treating HIV-infected or AIDS patients are known, very small, and eminently controllable, many workers are still reluctant to treat such patients. It is also the case that recruitment and training of physicians and other health care workers to care for AIDS patients are not keeping pace with the growing needs and the ultimate impact of this epidemic has not even yet been felt.

As the world is affected more and more by AIDS, we will all ultimately have to confront our values and our prejudices, our deepest fears and most urgent desires, as we negotiate a period of uncertainty and threat that few of us have ever had to face.

Role of NGOs in Promoting Guidance and Counselling on HIV/AIDS

Non-Governmental organizations (NGOs) have emerged as an important element of contemporary Indian society. They have been variously described as the third sector, civil society, non-profits, voluntary sectors etc. The very diversity of social information included under the rubric of NGOs makes all these descriptions accurate at various movements. Here, however attempt on one element of NGOs that remain invisible NGOs as place of work particularly in promoting HIV/AIDS guidance, communication, counselling to the target population such as young population, High Risk behaviour group, HIV-positive and AIDS patients.

The advent of HIV/AIDS gave an extraordinary significance to the concept of counselling. NGOs promoting AIDS guidance and counselling is considered important in the present day context of high incidences of AIDS cases. In the absence of a preventive vaccine against HIV, or a cure for AIDS, the single most important way to halt the pandemic is through preventive guidance, communication and counselling, however urgent action is required from the Government and NGOs to increase counselling centres such as voluntary confidential counselling and testing centres (VCCTCS) and AIDS counselling centres and counselling services.

Information, education, communication counselling (IECS) are essential to prevent and control of HIV/AIDS and bringing great awareness among the population. Counselling includes information, education and psychological support and allows individuals to make decisions that facilitate coping and preventive behaviour, guidance and counselling is necessary for having accurate information about human sexuality, safe and protected sex, reproductive health and STD/HIV/AIDS including eliminating myths and misconceptions.

Conclusions and Recommendations

Providing conclusion on the psychological aspects of HIV is a difficult task, as HIV/AIDS continues to change. New information about treatments may cause significant shifts in many relationships as this is a rapidly changing area. There is a need to continue to examine the role of gender in social aspects of HIV/AIDS. Women and men are clearly affected by HIV/AIDS differently, from coping strategies to media images. Demographic finding related to HIV/AIDS can also be overlooked in attempts to see patterns or similarities on HIV-infected person. Cultural differences are also not well understood in HIV infection generally. Psychiatric disorder and distress is common in HIV positive subjects. Use of psychiatric medications in people with HIV disease is complex and demanding. Issues of potential drug interactions and the need for careful planning and coordination of therapeutic efforts make providing psychiatric care and stabilization difficult.

As we have come to recognize that adherence is one of the keys to antiretroviral success, that HIV prevention efforts must be improved, and that patient's quality of life depends in large part on their psychological health, the issues of psychiatric disorders and maximizing psychiatric and overall well-being are be coming increasingly important to physicians treating persons living with HIV infection. Mental health professional can provide valuable assistance to medical care providers to improve health outcomes for these patients. With new treatment for HIV/AIDS changing rapidly, it seems imperative that therapists, health care workers, community organisation personnel, and massage designers work more closely together to address emerging challenges. These issues could include compliance with medical regimens, symptoms management, and the need for new disease prevention strategies. Therapists could be invaluable resources for health care workers as they struggle with client compliance. Healthcare workers could, in turn, to providers of important information to public health campaign strategists. In essence, new challenges ahead could be faced more adequately if interests and knowledge of the perspectives were more closely aligned. The time for separate, field-specific work has clearly passed.

Another area where professional cross-fertilisation of ideas will become important is in the development of prevention strategies. For too long, relationships of HIV-infected people have been ignored: the emphasis has been on prevention and treatment. Future research on HIV/AIDS must incorporate factors such as gender and race in explaining the effects of new treatments. This is an area where more research would be especially useful. If HIV-infected people will be living longer, healthier lives, then the importance of understanding social aspects of the disease become even more pressing. In future, the task is to confront the fear based messages and biased social attitudes in order to reduce the discrimination and stigma of people who are living with HIV/AIDS. The fear and prejudice that lies at the core of the HIV/AIDS discrimination heed to be tackled at the community and national level and a more enabling environment needs to be created to increase the visibility of people with HIV/AIDS as a 'normal' part of any society should be recommended. It was suggested that the key determinant of effective HIV- prevention and AIDS-care is the existence of a humane and supportive environment for people with AIDS.

References

Antoni, I. (2007). Evidence of HIV infection aerobic exercise increased T-4 cell levels and reduce anxiety and depression. *Psychosomatic Medicine,* 69(1), 74-80.

Catania, A., (1990). High risk of developing the AIDS involvement in contaminated blood. A cognitive and electrophysiological study. *Journal of community Health Nursing*, 24(1), 49-64.

Catania, A., (2002) Survey of Homosexual men in San Francisco. *AIDS Public Policy Journal*, 20 (1-2), 40-50.

Catania, C. (2000). Understanding HIV/AIDS stigma. A theoretical and methodological analysis. Cape Town: *Human Sciences Research Council.*

Cutchan, M. (2006). Models for understanding transmission of HIV. *Journal of Communicable Disease*, 38(1), 57-69.

Glasner, R. and Kaslow, W. (2004). Stigma directed towards chronic illness is resistant to change through education and exposure. *Psychological Reports*, 90, 1161-1173.

Hofferth, H. and Hayes, S. (2007). AIDS. A comparative study on young people enter high school in United States: its contexts and potential intervention Strategies. *AIDS Public Policy Journal*, 20(1-2), 25-39.

Ickovics S, Roddin, F. (1999) Rutio of AIDS among males and females in United States. *Western Journal of Medicine*, 175 (5), 332-335.

Kelly, Y. and Lawrence, St. (2001). Social psychological Foundations and Behavioural therapy. *Journal of Health and Social Behaviour*, 41 (1), 50-67.

Kiecolt, C. Glaser, G., Kelly, K., and Murphy, M., (1998). Fight against AIDS/HIV. *Journal of Health Psychology*. 68(2), 92-5.

Kielcolt, T. and Geaser, R. (2002) AIDS. in Fink G (Editor-in-Chief), Encyclopaedia of Stress, 2nd edn. Amsterdam: Elseiver, 1, 108-114.

Kingsley, Y. G. (2004). Knowledge and beliefs of patients regarding risky sexually transmitted infection and HIV/AIDS in U.S. *Journal of American Medical Association*, 68(2), 92-5.

Lawrence, S.T. (1998). Knowledge and beliefs of adolescents regarding sexually transmitted infections and HIV/AIDS in America. *Western Journal of Medicine*, 57 (1), 8-11.

Navia, A., Cho, O., Petito, O. and Price, E. (2005). Psychosocial functioning of patients with AIDS and HIV infection: review of the literature from a socio-ecological framework. *Journal of Developmental Behaviour in Psychiatrics*, 28(1), 58-69.

Nurnberg, G, Prudic, C., Fiori, I and Freedman, N. (2001). Nervous system involvement in asymptomatic HIV Selopositive individuals: A cognitive and electrophysiological study. *Neurology India,* 57, 466-9.

Redfield, D., Wright. R and Tramat, T. (2004). Disclosure of HIV status and sexual orientation independently predicts increased absolute CD4 cell counts over time for Psychiatric Patients *Psychosomatic Medicine,* 69 CD, 74-80.

Reiss, S. and Leik, K. (2002). Demonstrated that risk reduced by condoms. *Indian Journal of Medical Research*, 121, 45-467.

Rokeach, B. (2004). Technique Self-Confrontation and Social support as determinants of quality of life in HIV/AIDS. AIDS Care, 8, 15-32.

Sarngadharan, S., (2000). HIV Ratio rate of the HIV- positive in United States: A comparison of its impact on the self of person with HIV/AIDS. *Journal of Health and Social Behaviour*, 4(1), 50-67.

Stall, L. (2007). Intravenous drug injecting in U.S. Psychological, Neuropsychiatric and substance abuse aspects of AIDS. Bridge, T.P. Mirsky, A.F:, Goodwin, F.K. (eds). *New York: Raven Press*, 85-94.

Thomas, S., Gieliam, S . and Iwrey, Y. (2001). Dynamics of knowledge and attitudes about AIDS among the educated in African-Americans. *AIDS Care*, 9(3), 319-330.

USDHHS (2002) Report on the Global AIDS epidemic, the impact of AIDS on people and societies. *USDHHS; Geneva.*

Voller, V., (2006). AIDS identify and community. The HIV epidemic and lesbian gay men. Thousand Oaks: Sage.

Wright, R., (2000). AIDS Knowledge and attitudes in U.S population: an epidemiological study. *W.H.O. Public Health* 5, 95.

3

Counselling and Psycho-social Care of HIV Positive Patients

R. Kannappan

Introduction

Mood influences much on a patient's outlook and perception of self and others and his environment. He experiences abnormally depressed mood which is a pervasive emotional tone. The symptoms affect all areas of functioning as they occur with history of a long term stress. The onset of depressive disorder begins in the ages of 30 years and the disorder may or may not have the psychotic symptoms of delusion and hallucination. The depressive disorder is a chronic disorder and is persistently present most of the days. The symptoms become worse when the day progresses on. It is commonly seen in women rather men with insidious attack (Kaplan and Sadock, 1999). The patients can be sarcastic, nihilistic, brooding, demanding, and complaining with resistance of therapeutic interventions. The patients have changes in appetite and sleep patterns, low self esteem, loss of energy, psychomotor retardation, decreased sexual drive, and obsessive preoccupation with health matters (Gelder, Gath, et al., 1996; Hales, Yudofsky, and Talbott, 1999; Kaplan, and Sadock, 1999).

Moore, Vosvick, and Amey, (2006) reported that care giving demand, role captivity, and job conflict were positively associated with self-reported depression and suggested that work-related strains and role strains were associated with depression levels among caregivers. The present study attempts to incorporate psycho social care of family members for the remission of depressive disorder in the patient.

Objective: They were to use counselling strategy for the management of depressive disorder in HIV positive patient and to assess depression at follow up.

Design: The patient who was tested positive for HIV suffering from symptoms of severe depression for 2 months came to the hospital. Antidepressants and anti-anxiety drugs were administered and then it was decided that phased counselling would be suitable to treat the patient. The duration of the counselling was 15 sessions, each for 50 minutes session. Self report and family members' report were collected to understand the changing behaviour of the patient specially increased confidence, practice of healthy habits and nutrition and depression.

Description of the Scales: Zing's Depressive Status Inventory (DSI) (Zung, 1972), provides a global measure of the intensity of depressive symptoms. It is a self-rated scale consisting of 20 items. Items are rated on either a 0-4 spectrum (1=none/absent and 3= severe). The total score consists of the sum of the items of the inventory. Zung scores were interpreted as follows: <50, within normal range; 50–59, minimal to mild depression; 60–69, moderate to severe depression; >70, severe depression. A severity index may be calculated by dividing the total score by 80 (the total possible). Data were collected before, after and follow-up by using the scale to measure the level of depression. Before, after and follow-up scores were 71, 59 and 56 respectively. There had been remarkable reduction in depression in the patient.

Sample

The patient Mr. M. who had the symptoms of difficulty in breathing, fearfulness, sleep disturbance, feeling of hopelessness, not able to do work, loss of appetite, fear about future, suicidal ideas and palpitation, came to the hospital for treatment. He was a dhobi of 46 years old, and had two wives. His first wife had one daughter who got married. Second wife had two sons and they lived separately after their marriages. He also had multi-partner high risk sex behaviour. He reported of unsafe sexual practices. The patient developed initially fever, and tiredness. He also had loss of sleep and his appetite was also decreased markedly. He was advised by his friends to get tested for HIV and the test results showed positive status. After this, he developed problems which hindered his normal routine life. He started hopeless, helpless and worthless feelings. He had crying spells and suicidal ideas. He developed fear of death and stigma towards the disease. He did not have a similar episode in his remote past.

Personal history revealed that his developmental milestones were normal. His marriages were a non- consanguineous and arranged one and the second one was consanguineous. He had extramarital affairs and the habits of drinking alcohol and smoking. No history of mental illness, suicide, epilepsy, asthma, diabetes, and head injury, was reported in his family.

On mental status examination, he was aesthetic build, and fairly clean and tidy. He was cooperative while interviewing him. His talk was relevant and coherent with low tone. He had a fearful and depressed mood and a retarded psychomotor activity. He did not have the psychotic syndromes of delusion and hallucination. He had orientation to time, place, and persons. He had good immediate and long term memories but he had disturbed short term memory. He did not have the disturbances of judgment and insight. He had a good rapport with the therapist and the doctor. The diagnosis was done as HIV with depressive disorder because the symptoms met the criteria of depressive disorder [DSM-IV TR] (Kaplan and Sadock, 1999).

The drugs -Cap. Prodep 20mg 1-0-0, Tab. Dothip 50mg 0-0-1, Tab. Rivotril 0.5mg 0-0-1- were given to the patient for the entire period of treatment.

Psychological Management

Besides taking drugs, psychosocial care was given to the patient. It was a short term program oriented to the current problems and their resolution. To begin with, reading material on coping with depression was given. The focus of the therapist was to recognize the nature of the dysfunctional thinking. During the counselling/therapy session, mood shift helped the therapist to identify the automatic thoughts. Observing strong emotions such as irritability, anxiety and depression, the patient was asked to describe the thoughts that went through his mind just prior to mood shifts. He was instructed to recognize schemas (core belief or basic assumptions) on his own for psycho-education was used to explain the concept of schemas and their linkage to superficial automatic thoughts (Beck, 1995). After identifying schema, he had to do pro and cons analysis; it induced his to doubt the validity of the schema and to start think of alternative explanations. Modifying schema included examining evidence, listing advantage and disadvantage, generating alternatives and cognitive rehearsals. In cognitive rehearsal, he had to imagine various steps in meeting and mastering a challenging task and to rehearse various steps of it.

The counselling session helped the patient to understand meaning of HIV positive and positive living. Behavioural intervention used to change dysfunctional patterns of behaviour (e.g. hopelessness) to reduce troubling symptoms (e.g. intrusive thoughts) and to assist in identifying and modifying maladaptive cognitions (e.g. activity schedules) with mastery and pleasure when he engaged in each activity).a weekly log was employed in which he recorded what he did during each hour of the day and rated each activity for mastery and pleasure. The patient was found to gain confidence when he understood the benefit of getting diagnosed for HIV at the earliest and also developed hope to live positively. He reviewed the data in the next session with the therapist. In graded task assignment, a behavioural goal was broken down into small steps that could be taken one at a time to solve a part of the problem.

The sessions focused on safe behaviour practices. Importance of condom after becoming positive was shared and the patient accepted that he should not infect others and also he had to take care of his viral load count. Further nutritional counselling was given to him to make him understand how nutrition plays a vital role in disease progression. The patient's myths on nutritious food were addressed and he was advised to start of low cost of nutritious food habits. He was instructed to stop dysfunctional behaviours e.g. crying spells and diverted them from intrusive thoughts by engaging activities such as play, physical activity. Role play was used as it could be a particularly powerful and useful technique to elicit automatic thoughts and to learn new behaviour (Kendell and Panichelli-Mindel, 1995). The present research confirms the findings of earlier researches of Patrick, Andrea, et al., (2004); Kovacs, Rush, and Bech, (1981).

Report of the Patient

The patient was able to eat and sleep well and to do work. he did not make the complaints of difficulty in breathing, fearfulness, and sleep disturbance. He involved in pleasurable activities and handled situations successfully with out much worry.

Report of the Family Members

His sad emotion disappeared remarkably. Irritability that he showed with the family members and friends had changed. He had good relationship with others. He did not worry much and he was alert and energetic. He functioned effectively in social and occupational areas when compared to his past.

Conclusion

The counselling sessions helped him to come out of his fear of death and his worries about his illness and family. Changes in his cognition and behaviour helped him lowered his level of depressive disorder.

References

Beck, J.S. (1995). *Cognitive Therapy: Basics and Beyond.* New York: Guilford.

D'Cruz, P. (2004). The family context of care in HIV/AIDS: A study from Mumbai, India. *The Qualitative Report,* 9(3), 413-434.

Gelder M, Gath D. Mayou, R. and Cowen, P. (1996). *Text book of psychiatry,* New York: Oxford University Press.

Hales, R.E. Yudofsky, S.C., and Talbott, J.A. (1999). *Textbook of Psychiatry,* New Delhi: Jaypee Brothers.

Kaplan, H.I. and Sadock, B.J. (1999). *Concise Textbook of Clinical Psychiatry.* London: Williams and Wilkins.

Kendell, P.C. and Panchelli-Meindel, S.M. (1995). Cognitive behavioural treatment, *Journal of Abnormal Psychology,* 23, 107.

Kovacs, M. Rush, and A.J. Bech, A.T. (1981).Depressed outpatients' treatment with cognitive therapy or pharmacotherapy: a one year follow-up. *Archives of General Psychiatry,* 38, 33-39.

Moore, A.R., Vosvick, M.and Amey, F.K. 2006 Stress, social support and depression in informal caregivers to people with HIV/AIDS in Lome, Togo. *International Journal of Sociology and Social Policy,* 26, (1/2), 63 – 73.

Patrick, P., Andrea B, H., Gunter, G, and Martin, H. (2004). School-Based Prevention of Depressive Symptoms in Adolescents: A 6-Month Follow-up, *Journal of the American Academy of Child and Adolescent Psychiatry,* 43 (8), 1003-1010.

Zung WWK: The depression status inventory: an adjunct to the Self-Rating Depression Scale. *Journal of Clinical Psychology* 28:539–543, 1972.

4

HIV/AIDS and Cancer Patients: A Comparative Study

Manisha Dasgupta

Introduction

Mankind is adorned by sparkling achievements in varied spectrums in the current century of technology-rimmed globalization. Yet human adaptive functioning loses its vitality and staggers with different degrees in the face of deadly terminal diseases. As such, man has to bow down generously before Mother Nature and the varied forms of existential platters that it poses. HIV/AIDS and Cancer are such deadly halts posed by life that leave the "prisoned being" shackled all over by "perceived defeats"—the reactions to which may be varied, depending on one's temperamental frame. The shattered self calls forth a deep "mental struggle" at the detection of the disease. The self now prepares to cruise over the remaining days by means of differing coping strategies that one imbibes. The present research is a journey into the psychosocial facades of such clients in their coping endeavour to trace the differences and similarities, if any, among each other in a comparative parlance with normal controls. The research would help identify the vulnerable aspects of personality, which get influenced by the terminal diseases. This would help quicken the provision of appropriate interventions to patients suffering from HIV/AIDS and cancer, thereby giving some relief and improving their quality of life (QOL), at least temporarily.

Before launching the research formally, the magnitude of the problem posed by HIV/AIDS and Cancer at the national and global level and its associated features require mentioning.

HIV/AIDS Epidemic: Global and National Overview

Acquired Immuno Deficiency Syndrome (AIDS) represents the late clinical stage of infection with human immuno deficiency virus (HIV). It is diagnosed when there is evidence of severe immuno-suppression in an HIV/-infected person (defined by a CD4 T-lymphocyte count of less than 200 cells/ml or less than 14 percent of total lymphocytes) or the presence of pulmonary tuberculosis, recurrent pneumonia, or invasive cervical cancer (Kazdin, 2000). The virus is spread by unprotected sexual intercourse with an infected person, by needle-sharing among injection drug users or through transfusions of infected blood or blood clotting factors. Babies born to HIV-infected women may also become infected before or during birth, or shortly after birth through breast-feeding (Straub, 2007).

AIDS has crossed geographic borders around the world, within Asia and nations and has turned out to be an epidemic (Joshi, 2006). HIV/AIDS is currently endemic at varying but usually high prevalence levels are seen among men who have sex with men (MSM) in most regions of the world. Explosive spread of HIV still occurs within pockets of susceptible injecting drug users (IDU) populations world-wide and sexual transmission occurs throughout the world among both males and females who have unprotected sex with multiple partners (Joshi, 2006).

In India, the HIV epidemic has become generalized in six Indian states: (Sharma, 2006)

- Maharashtra,
- Tamil Nadu,
- Karnataka,
- Andhra Pradesh,
- Manipur, and
- Nagaland.

Two different types of HIV epidemic have been seen in India. In north-eastern India, the epidemic is mainly among IDU whereas it is mainly spread through the heterosexual route in the rest of the country (Sharma, 2006). India's epidemic seems to be following the so-called Type 4 pattern, first described in Thailand. The epidemic shifts from the highest risk groups (commercial sex workers, drug users) to bridge populations (clients of sex workers, STD patients, partners of drug users) and then to the general population (Joshi, 2006).

Interplay of Factors Driving Sexual Transmission

There is evidence from around the world that many factors play a role in kick-starting a sexually transmitted HIV epidemic or driving it to higher levels.

Behavioural and Social Factors:

- Little or no condom use;
- Large proportions of the adult population with multiple sexual partners;
- Overlapping sexual partnerships – Individuals are highly infections when they first acquire HIV and thus more likely to infect any concurrent partners;
- Large sexual networks;
- "Age-mixing", typically between older men and young women or girls;

- Women's economic dependence on marriage or prostitution, robbing them off control over the circumstances of safe sex.

Biological Factors:

- High rates of STD, especially those causing genital ulcers, low rates of male circumcision;
- High viral load-HIV levels in the bloodstream.

Diagnosis of AIDS:

The WHO Case Definition for AIDS Surveillance envisages the existence of at least two major signs associated with at least one minor sign.

Major Signs:

- Weight loss $\geq$ 10 percent of body weight
- Chronic diarrhoea for more than 1 month
- Prolonged fever for more than 1 month (intermittent or constant)

Minor Signs:

- Persistent cough for more than 1 month
- Generalized pruritic dermatitis
- History of herpes zoster
- Oral-pharyngeal candidiasis
- Chronic progressive or disseminated herpes simplex infection
- Generalized lymphadenopathy.

HIV and AIDS carry with them a diverse array of psychological processes that can be studied, some being prejudice; loss, grieving, and associated sequelae; stress and coping; and empowerment, volunteerism and thereby impairing quality of life (QOL).

The next fold of the discourse will attempt to highlight the nature of cancer in relation to key psychosocial variables.

Nature of Cancer

The human cost of cancer is staggering. It is a significant medical problem, having its varied types, that affects the health status of millions of people worldwide. Cancer involves continual, uncontrolled production of cells that have no benefit to the organism. It develops when cells in a part of the body begin to grow out of control.

As such, cancer is accompanied by the occurrence of stress resulting in lowered quality of life that comes with diagnosis and treatment. Consequently, it leads to negative health behaviours owing to low mood states (e.g. Alcohol drinking, appetite disturbances etc.), affecting immunity in the long run. Besides, stress sets in motion important biological effects involving the autonomic, endocrine and immune systems, thereby making the system vulnerable to pathogens and facilitating the course of the disease.

Living-Dying Interval: A Challenge to Cancer Patients

Having one's disease classified as terminal does not necessarily mean that death is immediately forthcoming. Some clients must learn to live with the knowledge that they will die sooner rather than later, but not in the very near future. When patients learn that their cancer is terminal, this knowledge of their death forces them to recognize that they do not have as much time left as they had thought. This time between learning one's illness is terminal and the actual time of death is sometimes referred to as the living-dying interval (Pattison, 1977; 1978).

Psychological Issues Associated with Cancer

Death Anxiety and the Meaning of Death: For most patients, awareness that their cancer is terminal leads to an acute crisis characterized by intense death anxiety. This anxiety is a response to the recognition that death is a reality – that one will soon cease to exist and that there is nothing that can be done to change the situation. The usual methods of problem-solving are then inadequate (Ketel and Kopala, 2000).

Strong religious beliefs help many to find meaning in life and death by providing solace and helping them to derive meaning as they move through the death process. Similarly, some others who do not have strong religious beliefs may find that the process of dying provides an opportunity for human growth and that one can achieve a greater understanding of him/ herself and his/ her life by engaging in the process (Keitel and Kopala, 2000).

Physical Status and Age: How an individual responds to the terminal diagnosis may be influenced by his/ her physical status and age. An individual who has lived fully may have concerns about dying with dignity or about being a burden to the family. On the contrary, a younger patient may feel great terror at the thought of dying before he/ she has had a chance to participate fully in living.

Pattison (1978) suggests that the terminal phase of living-dying interval "is not precise and is roughly thought to begin when the dying person starts to withdraw into him/herself and respond to those internal bodily signals that tell him/her he/she must now conserve his/her energy" (Pattison, cited in Rando, 1984, p. 222).

This calls forth the crucial role of the psychologist, who needs to adopt the psycho-ontological approach aimed at providing palliative care to such clients (Sanyal and Dasgupta, 2005; Barraclough, 2001). It can be fostered by encouraging:

- Social support;
- Emotional expression;
- Detoxifying dying by processing existential concerns;
- Reorganizing life priorities and living in the present;
- Enhancing family support;
- Improving communication with physicians;
- Symptoms control.

Role of Proactive Coping in Terminal Diseases

Proactive coping incorporates a confirmatory and positive approach to dealing with stressors, and thereby the integral elements of positive psychology, by focusing on improved quality of life. It is a coping strategy that is multi-dimensional and forward-looking. It integrates processes of personal quality of life-management with those of self-regulatory goal-attainment (Greenglass, 2002). It can be considered as an effort to build up general resources that facilitate promotion toward challenging goals and personal growth. It combines autonomous goal-setting with self-regulatory goal-attainment cognitions (Greenglass, Schwarzer and Taubert, 1999).

Coping strategies play a critical role in an individual's physical and psychological well-being when faced with challenges, negative events, and stress (imposed by different diseases), with coping being of different types; some being reactive coping, anticipatory coping, preventive coping and proactive coping. In fact, coping strategies and behaviours at work involving mastery or problem-solving are associated with more positive outcomes and decreased distress than are "escape" or more passive forms of coping (Leiter, 1991; Armstrong-Stasson, 1994).

Spirituality and Mood States in Relation to Terminal Diseases

Spirituality is a complex, multi-dimensional part of human existence. It has cognitive, experiential and behavioural aspects. The cognitive or philosophic aspect includes the search for meaning, purpose and truth in life, and belief and value by which an individual lives (Quinn, 2008; Vachon, 2008). The experiential and emotional aspects involve feelings of hope, love, connection, inner peace, comfort and support, which get reflected in an individual's inner resources as well as the type of relationships and connections that exist within the self, the community, the environment, nature and the transcendent (Lane, 2008; Cotton et al., 2006). The behavioural aspect of spirituality involves the way a person externally manifests individual spiritual belief and inner spiritual state.

The issue of meaning in life and spirituality are of particular importance, given the threat of a serious illness like HIV/AIDS and cancer, and the confrontation with the finiteness of one's life. Thus, addressing cues of spiritual domains have been identified as essential by health-care professionals. Theoretical models for the understanding, development and adoption of concepts and interventions addressing meaning and spirituality in the terminally-ill are offered by the philosophical tradition of existentialism and logo therapy. Meaning-cantered interventions have been developed in recent years primarily within the context of palliative care. These are intended to support patients to find meaning in life in the face of serious illnesses and to experience their lives as fulfilled.

Moreover, recent research suggests that moods are strongly influenced by illnesses (Kaplan and Sadock, 1998). Individuals with HIV infections are faced with an ongoing threat to their own health and well-being. Depression was found to be a common symptom in such patients, hindering their prognosis as well (Carver, Scheier, and Weintraub, 1989). Taylor et al. (2000) also found that higher levels of stress, anxiety and depression were related to the diagnosis of AIDS. In addition, Bruera and Kim (2003) found that cancer patients suffer greater extents of mood disturbances in comparison to normal individuals because of the physical pain they go through. Ahles, Blanchard and Ruckdeschel (1983) conducted a study on terminal-stage cancer patients and found that having incurable cancer led to feelings of depression and hopelessness. As such, it can be said that mood states have an important role to play in influencing the affective platter of patients suffering from HIV/AIDS and cancer thereby affecting their quality of life grossly.

With the conceptual frame having been laid, it is now time to state the objectives of the present research which are as follows:

- to determine whether patients suffering from HIV/AIDS and cancer show any difference in proactive coping and its different dimensions separately when compared to matched normal controls;
- to investigate whether HIV/AIDS and cancer patients differ in spiritual meaning individually in comparison to matched normal controls;
- to reveal whether HIV/AIDS and cancer patients differ in the different dimensions of mood states separately in comparison to normal controls;
- to determine whether HIV/AIDS and cancer patients differ among each other with respect to proactive coping and its dimensions, spiritual meaning and the dimensions of mood states;

- to find out whether gender difference exists with respect to the aforementioned variables and their dimensions; and
- to investigate whether intra-group differences exist with regard to the variables mentioned before.

Method

Participants: A total of 80 participants was selected by means of purposive sampling and divided into three groups:

1. Cancer group (N = 20; which comprised 10 males and 10 females) (M = 43.85 yrs., S.D. = 5.82 yrs.).
2. HIV/ AIDS group (N = 20; which comprised 10 males and 10 females) (M = 40.30 yrs., S.D. = 4.87 yrs.).
3. Control group (N = 40; which comprised 20 males and 20 females) (M = 41.05 yrs., S.D. = 4.72 yrs.).

The normal controls were matched to the two study groups on the basis of age, sex, religion, socio-economic status and marital status.

All the subjects ranged between the ages of 30-50 yrs., were Indian citizens, followed Hinduism as their religion, belonged to lower and middle SES, received formal education at least till Class X and were heterosexual in orientation. HIV/AIDS patients also needed to be confirmed of their medical status as tested by ELISA, and had CD4 cell count below 200. All the patients were under drug treatment during the course of the study due to ethical reason. Patients with any psychiatric illness prior to the onset and during the course of their illness or those having any organic involvement were excluded from the study. Cancer patients having genital or breast cancer were also excluded.

Measures

Self-report instruments or scales were used to obtain information from the subjects. The measures used in the study are described below:

Spiritual Meaning Scale: The 15-item scale was developed by Mascara, Rosen, and Morey (2004) to provide a measure of spiritual meaning. It involves participants to rate each item on a 5-point Likert scale ranging from 1 (totally disagree) to 5 (totally agree), which are scored 0 and 4 respectively. A sum score was found out. The scale has been found to have a coefficient alpha of 0.89 (Mascara et al., 2003).

Proactive Coping Inventory: It was developed by Greenglass, Schwarzer, Jakubiec, Fiksenbaum and Taubert (1999). It consists of seven scales and a total of 55 items, which implement on a cognitive and behavioural level, a way of coping, based on resourcefulness, responsibility and vision. Its different scales are:

- Proactive Coping
- Reflective Coping
- Strategic Planning
- Preventive Coping
- Instrumental Support Seeking
- Emotional Support Seeking
- Avoidance Coping

It involves subjects to respond to each of the statements on the basis of four alternatives:

"Not at all true" (1), "Barely true" (2), "Somewhat true" (3), and "Completely true" (4).

Anti-trait items are reversed and the responses are then summed with respect to the different sub-scales. High scores in a domain indicate high level of coping with respect to that dimension/ strategy. The scale has high internal consistency as seen in reliability measures (alpha) of 0.85 and 0.80, good item-total correlation and acceptable skewness as an indicator of symmetry around the mean. The individual scales have also been reported to have good validity (Taubert, 1999). Construct validity has been found to be appreciable.

Profile of Mood States: It has been developed by McNair, Lorr and Droppleman (1971). It consists of 37 items measuring mood disturbance. Items on the scale are rated using a 5-point Likert scale from 0 (not at all) to 4 (extremely). Participants are asked to rate how they have been feeling during the past one week. The scale consists of 6 mood factors:

- Tension-anxiety
- Depression-dejection
- Anger-hostility
- Vigour-activity
- Fatigue-inertia
- Confusion-bewilderment

Scoring involves first calculating each mood factor by summing the responses defining the factor. The total mood disturbance score is obtained by summing the score on the six mood factors, with vigour-activity weighted negatively. Internal consistency of the scale has been found to be high and test-retest reliability has been found to be adequate. Internal consistency was found to range from 0.87 to 0.95 for males and 0.84 to 0.95 for females. The scale has been also found to be highly valid on clinical as well as normal population.

Procedure

All the questionnaires were translated into Bengali version and checked by five raters for their approval, to be used as standardized tools for the present study. The participants were administered with the questionnaires one at a time, for their completion in a single session. The sequence of the administration followed a pre-determined schedule:

1. Information Schedule.
2. Spiritual Meaning Scale.
3. Profile of Mood States.
4. Proactive Coping Inventory.

Analysis and Results

Attempts were made to test the significance of difference between the means of HIV/AIDS, Cancer and control groups for each of the variables under consideration along with their different dimensions. Besides, it was also examined whether there was any gender difference for the respective variables for which two-way analysis of variance (ANOVA) was computed. Student's t-test was also computed so as to ascertain the general trend of the significance of difference between the different groups.

Table 4.1 describes the F-values obtained from two-way analysis of variance (ANOVA) showing the significance of groups, gender and their interaction on spirituality, mood states and proactive coping dimensions. The results suggest that spirituality, mood states and the different dimensions of proactive coping differed among the three different groups, namely, cancer patients, HIV/AIDS patients and normal controls except for the dimension of avoidance coping. The effect of gender and interaction of group and gender was not found to be significant for any of the variables.

Table 4.2 represents the combined descriptive data for each variable and the significance of the difference between pairs of groups (namely, cancer, HIV/AIDS and normal controls). The results suggest that both the clinical groups have significantly lowered:

- Spirituality
- Emotional support seeking, and
- Instrumental support seeking.

In comparison to normal controls, they also have significantly higher:

- Mood disturbance (tension-anxiety, depression-dejection, anger-hostility, fatigue-inertia, and confusion-bewilderment), when compared to normal counterparts.

Cancer patients also have significantly lower:

- Proactive coping
- Avoidance coping
- Strategic planning
- Preventive coping

Table 4.1: F-values Obtained from Two-way Analysis of Variance (ANOVA) Showing the Significance of Groups, Gender and Their Interaction on Selected Variables

Variables	Sources of Variance	*F values*
1. Spirituality	Between groups	*6.69***
	Between gender	*0*
	Interaction	*0.025*
2. Mood states	Between groups	*131.75***
	Between gender	*1.37*
	Interaction	*0.58*
3a. Proactive coping	Between groups	*5.079***
	Between gender	*1.22*
	Interaction	*1.05*
3b. Reflective coping	Between groups	*16.48***
	Between gender	*0.60*
	Interaction	*1.35*
3c. Strategic planning	Between groups	*3.93***
	Between gender	*0.55*
	Interaction	*0.62*
3d. Emotional Support Seeking	Between groups	*27.59***
	Between gender	*3.77*
	Interaction	*2.50*
3e. Preventive coping	Between groups	*23.63***
	Between gender	*0.712*
	Interaction	*3.018*
3f. Avoidance coping	Between groups	*2.11*
	Between gender	*0.07*
	Interaction	*2.93*
3g. Instrumental support seeking	*Between groups*	*29.98***
	Between gender	*1.71*
	Interaction	*2.01*

*p<0.05; **p<0.01

Table 4.2: Means (M), Standard Deviations (S.D.) and t-values Showing the Significance of the Difference between the Means of the Total Scores Obtained by Different Groups for the Selected Variables

Variables	HIV/AIDS Patients (1)		Cancer Patients (2)		Normal Controls (3)		t between 1 and 3	t between 2 and 3	t between 1 and 2
	M	S.D.	M	S.D.	M	S.D.			
Spirituality	47.35	7.56	47.40	3.47	53	7.49	2.74**	3.17**	0.027
Mood states	110.90	15.26	68.85	24.54	35.70	12.60	20.28**	6.94**	6.50**
Proactive coping	40.95	6.20	38.45	6.79	44.10	6.96	1.71	2.98**	0.405
Reflective coping	31.7	6.19	27.00	5.11	42.5	47.16	1.02	1.46	2.62*
Strategic planning	11.55	2.01	10.55	2.89	12.62	2.94	1.47	2.59**	1.27
Emotional Support Seeking	4.65	4.97	10.50	4.47	16.27	2.77	6.65**	6.16**	0.57
Preventive coping	32.75	3.90	23.60	6.69	32.40	4.76	0.29	5.87**	5.28**
Avoidance coping	5.40	2.23	4.35	2.03	5.50	2.17	0.17	1.97*	1.55
Instrumental support seeking	15.40	5.24	14.90	4.48	24.02	5.44	5.86**	6.33**	0.31

*$p<0.05$; **$p<0.01$

Besides, the typical profile of HIV/AIDS patients in comparison to cancer patients involves the former to have significantly higher:

- Mood disturbances (tension-anxiety, depression-dejection, anger-hostility, fatigue-inertia, vigour-activity, and confusion-bewilderment),
- Reflective coping, and
- Preventive coping, in comparison to the latter.

Discussion

In the discussion fold, results on spirituality had been selected as the first to be focussed. The basic indication is that hopelessness and helplessness of both sets of clients bring out their cry regarding their death anxiety and total loss of faith of spiritualistic support. Their emotional tune seems to be "God, why did you do it to me? What did I do?" The wish is enjoyment of existential elements, the fear is "I am forced to leave all these." Hence, the other selected variables would be discussed thereafter, having the findings on reaction to spirituality.

Table 4.3: Means (M), Standard Deviations (S.D.) and t-values Showing the Significance of the Difference between the Means of the Total Scores for Different Dimensions of Mood States

Dimensions of mood states	HIV/AIDS Patients (1)		Cancer Patients (2)		Normal Controls (3)		t between 1 and 3	t between 2 and 3	t between 1 and 2
	M	S.D.	M	S.D.	M	S.D.			
Tension-anxiety	17.50	2.64	10.10	5.10	5.20	4.01	12.39**	4.06**	5.75**
Depression-dejection	25.00	3.95	13.80	7.12	4.65	4.10	3.66**	6.28**	6.15**
Anger-hostility	22.00	4.55	13.80	5.05	4.82	3.48	16.21**	8.66**	5.39**
Vigour-activity	15.50	3.59	11.80	4.09	13.20	4.41	2.02*	1.18	3.03**
Fatigue-inertia	15.90	3.18	10.40	3.39	3.85	2.59	15.75**	8.38**	5.24**
Confusion-bewilderment	15.35	3.40	9.00	4.15	3.95	3.08	13.00**	5.30**	5.28**

*p<0.05; **p<0.01

Inter-group Comparison with Respect to Spirituality

Members of both the clinical groups (HIV/AIDS and cancer) were found to have significantly impaired spiritual meaning in comparison to normal counterparts (Tables 4.1 and 4.2). The probable reason appears to be the diagnoses of the deadly diseases make patients, in general, to loose all hopes for recovery, owing to their shattered sense of self.

Such deadly terminal diseases challenge patients' belief system, resulting in high levels of spiritual distress. As such, their relationship to the schema of death, hope of life after death, through identifications, and through assurance of cosmic order get impaired in comparison to normal counterparts (Pevev, Jones and Yarber, 2009; Phelps et al., 2009).

Moreover, patients of both the clinical groups tend to succumb to greater extents of hopelessness, worthlessness and hence depression, on the average, owing to the knowledge of the detection of the disease. This is often associated with significantly lowered spirituality, being inversely proportional (Mystakidou et al., 2008). As such, attributed meanings to the illnesses in the form of different categories of "positive meaning", "natural acceptance", "negative acceptance", "search for meaning" and "regret and sorrow" are likely to be affected. Patients of both the clinical groups, being significantly low in spiritual meaning, tend to attribute their illnesses to "regret and sorrow", and "search for meaning" (Ando, Morita, Lee and Okamoto, 2008; Lissoni et al., 2008; Quinn, 2008).

Individuals can be considered being-in-relationships, and illness can be considered a disruption in biological relationships that, in turn, affects all the other relational aspects of the person. Spirituality concerns a person's relationship with transcendence (Sanyal, 2009). Therefore, genuinely, holistic health care must address the totality of patient's relational existence-physical, psychological, social and spiritual-which naturally get affected, owing to the shattering detection of the deadly terminal diseases (Sulmasy, 2002). Hence the needs of seriously ill patients need to be addressed in a holistic manner in order to better understand and empathize with them (Woll, Hinshaw and Pawlik, 2008; Sanyal, 2009). In fact, Schulz et al. (2008) revealed that spirituality plays a strong role in cancer coping and survivorship. Spirituality may address a human need for certitude in crisis. Further support in this line have been offered by Lane (2008), Pedersen and Zachariae (2008). Thus, it appears that members of both the clinical samples have significant impairment in quality of life (QOL), thereby affecting psychological, social and physiological well-being in the long run (Tuck, McCain and Elswick, 2001; Fitzpatrick et al., 2007). Poorer health status and perceptions, less social support and lower spiritual well-being and self-transcendence are likely to be related to significant depressive loadings, that "block" their affective spree (Yi et al., 2006; Ramer, Johnson, Chan and Barrett, 2006; Szaflarski et al., 2006; Lorenz, Hays, Shapiro, Cleary, Ash and Wenger, 2005).

Hence, spiritual beliefs and religious practices appear to play a role in end-of-life decisions. Discussions about end-of-life decisions may be facilitated by a patient's belief in a forgiving God and impeded by a patient's interpretation of HIV infection as punishment (Kaldjian, Jekel and Friedland, 1998; Hall, 1997). Thus it appears that clinical education interventions should focus on raising awareness among clinicians about the importance of spirituality in HIV/AIDS and cancer so as to incorporate them into discussions about terminal care.

However, when the two clinical samples were compared, the two did not significantly differ from each other, indicating their relative homogeneity with respect to their impairment in spirituality.

Inter-group Comparison with Respect to Mood States

Members of both the clinical samples had significantly higher scores on mood states indicating higher mood disturbances in all the dimensions in comparison to normal counterparts, namely, tension-anxiety, depression-dejection, anger-hostility, fatigue-inertia, confusion-bewilderment and vigour-activity (Tables 4.1, 4.2 and 4.3). It highlights the presence of emotional distress among them, serving as a deteriorating factor in coping with the disease(s). This may be because of the relative loss of meaning in life for which they loose all hopes in life (Julkunen and Ahlstrom, 2006).

The findings of the present research are supported by those of Julkunen, Gustavsson-Lilius and Hietanen (2009), who revealed that cancer patients often succumb to relatively higher anger-expression, which affects their quality of life. They tend to experience feelings of hopelessness and diminished optimism, owing to their highly morbid conditions (Gustavsson-Lilius, Julkunen and Hietanen, 2007; Julkunen and Ahlstrom, 2006). Thus, such patients are likely to have a high degree of perceived stress, high anger-in and anger-out, which may lead to depression in the long run (Lee, Sohn, Lee, Park, and Park, 2005; Angerer et al., 2000; Iwamitsu et al., 2005; Uchitomi et al., 2003).

In line with the present research, Lin, Lai and Ward (2003) revealed that pain intensity was significantly correlated with performance status and mood states among cancer patients with pain. Pain interference with daily life was significantly correlated with performance status, mood state and level of hope. Pain intensity and pain interference were significantly correlated with each mood state as well as with total mood disturbance. As such, quality of life among both cancer and HIV/AIDS patients is likely to be grossly affected (Molassiotis, Chan, Yam, and Chan, 2000; Suzuki et al., 1998). They tend to be characterized by greater negative affect (Kalichman and Weinhardt, 2001; Crepaz and Marks, 2001) as revealed from the present research as well. In addition, both the clinical groups are characterized by significantly higher score on fatigue component of mood states, probably owing to their physical debility (Wagner and Rabkin, 2000; Ferrando et al., 1998). Thus, fatigue appears to be a chronic symptom that is associated with depressed mood, major depressive disorder, physical limitations and disability. They also tend to have greater somatic symptoms and avoidance coping responses in comparison to normal controls (Fukunishi, Havashi, Matsumoto, Negishi, Hosaka, and Moriva, 1997; Perkins et al., 1995).

When the two clinical groups were separately taken into consideration, HIV/AIDS patients were found to show significant higher impairments in all the dimensions of mood states in comparison to their cancer counterparts (Tables 4.2 and 4.3). This may be attributed to the presence of relatively high guilt-orientation among HIV/AIDS patients, owing to the social stigma associated with itself; it being a life-style disorder (Straub, 2007). This may affect the extent of social support that they receive in contrast to cancer patients who are usually reciprocated with sympathy and support from significant care-givers. Thus, the society appears to cushion the distress among such patients unlike those suffering from HIV/AIDS, though the grave scenario is having transitions these days.

Inter-Group Comparison with Respect to Proactive Coping

Results reveal that members of both the clinical groups have significantly impaired scores on the different dimensions of proactive coping (Tables 4.1 and 4.2).

Both the clinical groups have significantly impaired emotional support-seeking and instrumental support-seeking in contrast to normal controls. Thus, they have deficit in seeking emotional support from nearby relations, and instead, withdraw into their own selves. They also have deficits in obtaining advice, information and feedback from people in one's social network while dealing with stressors (Greenglass, 1999). Thus, they are likely to show impairments in problem-solving skills (Malcarne, Banthia, Varni, Sadler, Greenbergs and Ko, 2002).

Besides, cancer patients show significant deficits in proactive coping, strategic planning and preventive coping strategies in comparison to normal partners. This hints at the presence of impaired coping strategies leading to subsequent lowered quality of life as explained earlier (Danhauer, Crawfor, Farmer, and Avis, 2009; Phelps et al., 2009). Thus, it appears that emotional support-focussed nursing interventions have a part in increasing psychosocial adjustment of patients. (Gumus and Cana, 2008; Filazoglu and Griva, 2008). The significantly higher score on avoidance-seeking of normal controls in comparison to cancer patients may be attributed to the fact that probably normal controls are better apt to cope with a stressor by delaying their responses, owing to their relatively higher sense of controllability (Heth and Somer, 2002).

When the two clinical groups are considered together, cancer patients were found to have significantly impaired strategic planning and preventive coping (Table 4.2). This highlights their weakness in the process of generating goal-oriented schedule of action in which extensive tasks are broken down into manageable components (Greenglass, 1999). They also lack the ability to anticipate potential stressors and so cannot initiate preparation before stressors develop fully. It may also be attributed to the overall uncontrollability of the disease, resulting in disengagement coping (Gonzalez, Solomon, Zvolensky and Miller, 2009; Kremer, Ironson and Kaplan, 2009; Moskowitz, Hult, Bussolari and Acree, 2009).

Thus, it appears that more attention should be paid to social environment of individuals diagnosed with HIV/AIDS and cancer so as to uplift the quality of social relationships (Mavandedi, Zanjani, Ten Have and Oslin, 2009).

Highlights of the Study

The chief findings of the present research appear to converge at the following:

- HIV/AIDS and cancer patients have significantly lowered spirituality compared to normal counterparts.
- Both the clinical samples have significantly higher mood disturbances, with impairment in all the dimensions (tension-anxiety, depression-dejection, anger-hostility, fatigue-inertia, and confusion-bewilderment except for vigour-activity for cancer patients) when compared to normal partners. Cancer patients have significantly greater deficits than HIV/ AIDS patients in all the dimensions of the construct.
- Both the clinical samples show significant deficits in emotional support-seeking and instrumental support-seeking in comparison to normal controls. Cancer patients also have significantly lower proactive coping, strategic planning, avoidance coping and preventive coping than normal subjects. Additionally, cancer patients have significantly lower reflective and preventive coping than HIV/AIDS partners.

Conclusion

The study, with its limited sphere, has brought out a distressing aspect of life amidst so many others. The killing diseases, HIV/AIDS and Cancer, are not only physically killing; they are responsible for totally destroying the mental flares of even general people to have the survival spirit. This is fact, no doubt, but something needs to be done and that is why research attempts are there. The humble urge of this present work is to pinpoint that the fading-away process of these patients is obvious and inevitable; but can we, psychologists, help them a bit, in terms of early intervention, palliative care and offering tender love and support with all our individual might?

References

Ahles T.A., Blanchard E.B. and Ruckdeschel J.C. (1983). Multidimensional nature of cancer pain. *Pain.*; *17:* 277–288. doi: 10.1016/0304-3959 (83) 90100-8.

Anderson, B.L., Kiecolt-Glaser, J.K., and Glaser, R. (1994). A bio-behavioural model of cancer stress and disease course. *American Psychologist,* 49, 389-404.

Ando M, Morita T, Lee V, Okamoto T. (2008). A pilot study of transformation, attributed meanings to the illness, and spiritual well-being for terminally-ill cancer patients. *Palliat Support Care, 6(4)*:335-40.

Angerer P, Siebert U, Kothny W, Mühlbauer D, Mudra H, von Schacky C. (2000). Impact of social support, cynical hostility and anger expression on progression of coronary atherosclerosis. *Journal of the American College of Cardiology, 15; 36(6)*:1781-8.

Armstrong-Stassen, M. (1994). Coping with transition: A study of layoff survivors. *Journal of Organizational Behaviour, 15,* 597-621.

Barraclough, J. (Ed.) (2001), "*Integrated Cancer Care: Holistic, Complementary and Creative Approaches*". Oxford University Press.

Bruera E, Kim HN. (2003). Cancer pain. *Journal of American Medical Association.*; 290: 2476–2479. doi: 10.1001/ jama.290.18.2476.

Carver, C.S., Scheier, M.F., and Weintraub, J.K. (1989). Assessing coping strategies: A theoretically-based approach. *Journal of Personality and Social Psychology,* 56, 267-283.

Cotton S, Puchalski CM, Sherman SN, Mrus JM, Peterman AH, Feinberg J, Pargament KI, Justice AC, Leonard AC, Tsevat J. (2006). Spirituality and religion in patients with HIV/ AIDS. *Journal of General Internal Medicine;* 21 Suppl. *5*:S5-13.

Crepaz N, Marks G. (2001). Are negative affective states associated with HIV sexual risk behaviours? A meta-analytic review. *Health Psychology; 20(4):*291-9.

Danhauer SC, Crawford SL, Farmer DF, Avis NE. (2009). A longitudinal investigation of coping strategies and quality of life among younger women with breast cancer. *Journal of Behavioural Medicine,* March 24.

Ferrando S, Evans S, Goggin K, Sewell M, Fishman B, Rabkin J. (1998). Fatigue in HIV illness: Relationship to depression, physical limitations and disability. *Psychosomatic Medicine; 60(6):*759-64.

Filazoglu G, Griva K. (2008). Coping and social support and health-related quality of life in women with breast cancer in Turkey. *Psychol Health Med.; 13(5)*:559-73.

Fitzpatrick AL, Standish LJ, Berger J, Kim JG, Calabrese C, Polissar N. (2007). Survival in HIV-1- positive adults practicing psychological or spiritual activities for one year. *Alternative Therapies in Health and Medicine;13(5):*18-20, 22-4.

Fukunishi I, Hayashi M, Matsumoto T, Negishi M, Hosaka T, Moriya H. (1997). Liason psychiatry and HIV infection (I): Avoidance coping responses associated with depressive symptoms accompanying somatic complaints. *Psychiatry and Clinical Neurosciences; 51(1)*:1-4.

Gonzalez A, Solomon SE, Zvolensky MJ, Miller CT. (2009). The interaction of Mindful-based Attention and Awareness and Disengagement Coping with HIV/ AIDS-related stigma in regard to Concurrent Anxiety and Depressive Symptoms among Adults with HIV/ AIDS. *Journal of Health Psychology; 14(3):*403-13.

Greenglass, E. R. (2002). Proactive coping. In E. Frydenberg (Ed.), *Beyond Coping: Meeting Goals, Vision, and Challenges.* London: Oxford University Press, pp. 37-62.

Greenglass, E. R., Schwarzer, R., and Taubert, S. (1999). *The Proactive Coping Inventory (PCI): A Multidimensional Research Instrument.* [online publication].

Greenglass, E. R., Schwarzer, R., Jakubiec, D., Fiksenbaum, L., and Taubert, S. (1999). *The Proactive Coping Inventory (PCI): A Multidimensional Research Instrument.* Paper presented at the 20th International Conference of the Stress and Anxiety Research Society (STAR), Cracow, Poland, July 12-14.

Gumus AB, Cam O. (2008). Effects of emotional support-focussed nursing interventions on the psychosocial adjustment of breast cancer patients. *Asian Pacific Journal of Cancer Prevention.; 9 (4)*:691-7.

Gustavsson-Lilius M, Julkunen J, Hietanen P. (2007). Quality of life in cancer patients: The role of optimism, hopelessness, and partner support. *Quality of Life Research. 16(1):*75-87.

Hall BA. (1997). Spirituality in terminal illness: An alternative view of theory. *Journal of Holistic*

Nursing; 15(1):82-96.

Heth, J.T., and Somer, E. (2002). Characterizing stress tolerance: Preliminary results from a new approach to controllability and its relationship to perceived stress and reported health. *Personality and Individual Differences, 33(6),* 883-895.

Iwamitsu Y, Shimoda K, Abe H, Tani T, Okawa M, Buck R. (2005). The relation between negative emotional suppression and emotional distress in breast cancer diagnosis and treatment. *Health Communication; 18(3)*:201-15.

Joshi, P.L. (2006). Global and National Overview of HIV/AIDS epidemic. In Sharma, V.K. (ed.), *Sexually Transmitted Diseases and AIDS;* Viva Books Private Ltd., New Delhi, pp. 59-76.

Julkunen J, Ahlström R. (2006). Hostility, anger and sense of coherence as predictors of health-related quality of life. Results of ASCOT sub-study. *Journal of Psychosomatic Research; 61(1)*:33-9.

Julkunen J, Gustavsson-Lilius M, Hietanen P. (2009). Anger expression, partner support, and quality of life in cancer patients. *Journal of Psychosomatic Research; 66(3)*:235-44.

Kaldjian LC, Jekel JF, Friedland G. (1998). End-of-life decisions in HIV-positive patients: The role of spiritual beliefs. *AIDS (London, England); 12(1)*:103-7.

Kalichman SC, Weinhardt L. (2001). Negative affect and sexual risk behaviour: Comment on Crepaz and Marks (2001). *Health Psychology; 20(4)*:300-1.

Kaplan, H.I., and Sadock, B.J. (1998). *Synopsis of Psychiatry: Behavioural Sciences/Clinical Psychiatry.* 8th Edition, Williams and Wilkins, USA.

Kazdin, A.E. (2000). *Encyclopaedia of Psychology,* Vol. 1, American Psychological Association, Oxford University Press.

Keitel, M.A., and Kopala, M. (2000). *Counselling Women with Breast Cancer: A Guide for Professionals.* Sage Publications.

Kremer H, Ironson G, Kaplan L. (2009). The fork in the road: HIV as a potential positive turning point and the role of spirituality. *AIDS Care; 21(3)*:368-77.

Lane MR. (2008). Spirit-body healing II: A nursing intervention model for spiritual/creative healing. *Cancer Nursing; 31(3)*:E24-31.

Lee P.S., Sohn J.N., Lee Y.M., Park E.Y., Park J.S. (2005). A correlational study among perceived stress, anger expression, and depression in cancer patients. *Taehan Kanho Hakhoe Chi.; 35(1)*:195-205.

Leiter, M. P. (1991). Coping patterns as predictors of burnout: The function of control and escapist coping patterns. *Journal of Organizational Behaviour,* 12, 123-144.

Lin CC, Lai YL, Ward SE. (2003). Effect of cancer pain on performance status, mood states and level of hope among Taiwanese cancer patients. *Journal of Pain and Symptom Management. 25(1)*:29-37.

Lissoni P, Messina G, Parolini D, Balestra A, Brivio F, Fumagalli L, Vigore L, Rovelli F. (2008). A spiritual approach in the treatment of cancer: Relation between faith score and response to chemotherapy in advanced non-small cell lung cancer patients. *In Vivo;* 22(5), 577-81.

Lorenz KA, Hays RD, Shapiro MF, Cleary PD, Asch SM, Wenger NS. (2005). Religiousness and spirituality among HIV-infected Americans. *Journal of Palliative Medicine; 8(4)*: 774-81.

Malcarne VL, Banthia R, Varni JW, Sadler GR, Greenbergs HL, Ko CM. (2002). Problem-solving skills and emotional distress in spouses of men with prostrate cancer. *Journal of Cancer Education. The Official Journal of the American Association for Cancer Education; 17(3)*:150-4.

Mascaro, N., Rosen, D.H. and Morey, L.C. (2004). The development, construct validity and clinical utility of the spiritual meaning scale. *Personality and Individual Differences, 37,* 845-860.

Mavandadi S, Zanjani F, Ten Have TR, Oslin DW. (2009). Psychological well-being among individuals aging with HIV: The value of social relationships. *Journal of Acquired Immune Deficiency Syndromes,* Mar 11. [Epub ahead of print].

McNair, D., Lorr, M., and Droppleman, L. (1971). *POMS Manual for the Profile of Mood States.* San Diego: Educational and Industrial Testing Service.

Molassiotis A, Chan CW, Yam BM, Chan SJ. (2000). Quality of life in Chinese women with gynaecological cancers. *Supportive Care in Cancer. ; 8(5):*414-22.

Moskowitz JT, Hult JR, Bussolari C, Acree M. (2009). What works in coping with HIV? A meta-analysis with implications for coping with serious illness. *Psychological Bulletin;* 135(1):121-41.

Mystakidou K, Tsilika E, Prapa E, Smyrnioti M, Pagoropoulou A, Lambros V. (2008). Predictors of spirituality at the end of life. *Can Fam Physician;* 54 (12): 1720-1721.e5.

Pattison, E.M., (1977). *The Experience of Dying.* Englewood Cliffs, New Jersey: Prentice Hall.

Pattison, E.M., (1978). The living-dying process. In C.A. Garfield (Ed.), *Psycho-social Care of the Dying Patient.* New York: McGraw-Hill.

Pedersen CG, Zachariae B. (2008). The importance of spiritual well-being for cancer patients' quality of life. *Ugeskrift for Laege; 170(10):*847-9.

Perkins DO, Leserman J, Stern RA, Baum SF, Liao D, Golden RN, Evans DL. (1995). Somatic symptoms and HIV infection: Relationship to depressive symptoms and indicators of HIV disease. *The American Journal of Psychiatry;* 152 (12):1776-81.

Pevey CF, Jones TJ, Yarber A. (2009). How religion comforts the dying: A qualitative inquiry. *Omega (Westport);* 58(1): 41-59.

Phelps AC, Maciejewski PK, Nilsson M, Balboni TA, Wright AA, Paulk ME, Trice E, Schrag D, Peteet JR, Block SD, Prigerson HG. (2009). Religious coping and use of intensive life-prolonging care near death in patients with advanced cancer. JAMA. *The Journal of American Medical Association,* 18;301 (11):1140-7.

Quinn B. (2008). Spirituality in cancer care. *European Journal of Cancer Care (England); 17(5):* 422.

Ramer L, Johnson D, Chan L, Barrett MT. (2006). The effect of HIV/ AIDS disease progression on spirituality and self-transcendence in a multi0cultural population. *Journal of Transcultural Nursing: Official Journal of Transcultural Nursing Society; 17(3):*280-9.

Rando, T.A. (1984). *Grief, dying and death: Clinical interventions for caregivers.* Champaign, IL: Research Press.

Sanyal, N. (2009). Psychotherapy: An unaware act of spiritual journey. In Husain, A. (Ed.) *Twenty-first Century Psychology: Spirituality, Behaviour and Wellness,* 1st Edition, (2009), Global Vision Publishing House. New Delhi, pp. 115-130.

Sanyal, N. and Dasgupta, M. (2005). Psychological intervention for oncological patients: A psycho-oncological approach. *Journal of Psychometry,* Vol. XIX., No. 1, pp. 1-13.

Schulz E, Holt CL, Caplan L, Blake V, Southward P, Buckner A, Lawrence H. (2008). Role of spirituality in cancer coping among African American: A qualitative examination. *Journal of Cancer Survivorship: Research and practice; 2 (2):*104-15.

Sharma, V.K. (2006). *Sexually Transmitted Diseases and AIDS,* Viva Books Private Ltd., New Delhi.

Straub, R.O. (2007). *Health Psychology: A Biopsychosocial Approach,* Second Edition, Worth

Publishers, New York.

Sulmasy DP. (2002). A biopsychosocial-spiritual model for the care of patients at the end of life. *Gerontologist; 42 Spec No 3*:24-33.

Suzuki R, Hirao M, Miyo T, Nagashima G, Fujimoto T, Ooshima A, Higuchi T (1998). Changes in QOL in patients with brain tumours measures by mood changes during and after treatment. *No Shinkei Geka: Neurological Surgery*; *26(9)*:795-801.

Szaflarski M, Ritchey PN, Leonard AC, Mrus JM, Peterman AH, Ellison CG, McCullough ME, Tsevat J. (2006). Modelling the effects of spirituality/ religion on patients' perceptions of living with HIV/ AIDS. *Journal of General Internal Medicine, Suppl 5*: S28-38.

Taubert, S. (1999). *Development and validation of a psychometric instrument for the assessment of proactive coping*. Unpublished diploma thesis, Freie Universitat Berlin, Germany.

Taylor, S.E., Klein, L. Lewis, B.P., Gruenwald, T.L., Gurung, R.A., and Updegraff, J.A.(2000). Bio-behavioural responses to stress in females: Tend-and befriend, not fight-or-flight. *Psychological Review, 107*, 411-429.

Tuck I, McCain NL, Elswick RK Jr. (2001), Spirituality and psychosocial factors living with HIV. *Journal of Advanced Nursing;* 33 (6):776-83.

Uchitomi Y, Mikami I, Nagai K, Nishiwaki Y, Akechi T, Okamura H. (2003). Depression and psychological distress in patients during the year after curative resection of non-small-cell lung cancer. *Journal of Clinical Oncology, 1; 21(1)*:69-77.

Vachon ML. (2008). Meaning, spirituality and wellness in cancer survivors. *Seminars in Oncology Nursing; 24(3)*: 218-25.

Wagner GJ, Rabkin R. (2000). Effects of dextroamphetamine on depression and fatigue in men with HIV: A double-blind, placebo-controlled trial. *Journal of Clinical Psychiatry; 61(6)*: 436-40.

Woll ML, Hinshaw DB, Pawlik TM. (2008). Spirituality and religion in the care of surgical oncology patients with life-threatening or advanced illnesses. *Annals of Surgical Oncology; 15(11)*:3048-57.

Yi MS, Mrus JM, Wade TJ, Ho ML, Hornung RW, Cotton S, Peterman AH, Puchalski CM, Tsevat J. (2006). Religion, spirituality and depressive symptoms in patients with HIV/AIDS. *Journal of General Internal Medicine*.

5

Co-morbidity in Children and Adolescents with HIV/AIDS

Anand Prakash

Introduction

According to a report co-morbidity is increasing in India particularly among women (Godbole and Mehendale, 2005). Many symptoms are associated with inception, development and complications of HIV/AIDS affecting health of patients in several ways regardless of their developmental stage. The HIV-related co-morbidity and pain remains a clinically challenging condition despite recent advances in treatment modalities. The existing data demonstrate a high prevalence and significant negative impact on health-related quality of life, and alarmingly inadequate assessment and management (Douaihy et al., 2007, part-1 and part-2). These symptomatic complexities may impact the patients' ability to seeking and complying medical treatment and over all quality of life of entire family because usually the family members are deeply involved in proper and adequate care.

Some of these symptoms are required to be intervened by the means of psychological techniques along with medical treatment, e.g. anorexia, weight loss, cognitive impairment, fatigue, sleep disturbances, and pain etc. The behavioural interventions for HIV-infected persons have been a promising approach to facilitate positive adjustment (Brown and Vanable, 2008). The incorporation of psychological intervention along with medical and other non-medical treatment are effective in brining about positive changes in perceived stress, depression, anxiety, global psychological functioning, social support, and quality of life (Brown and Vanable, 2008) as it is positively correlated with CD_4 counts especially in women (Kohli and Sane et al., 2005). These interventions promote survival through lessening the physical and mental agony in fighting with the disease syndrome comparatively for a long period. Hence, in this chapter, a Special focus has been given to psychological assessment issues, behavioural and psychotherapeutic approaches and important indication to an integrated, flexible, and interdisciplinary team approach for treating HIV/AIDS.

Anorexia and Weight loss

Anorexia is characterized by loss of appetite and decreased food intake resulting into refusal to maintain normal body weight. Weight loss is involuntary loss of body weight comprising loss of body fat and cell mass (indicating cell number and cell size). These are always seen in persons with HIV/AIDS including all age-groups due to syndromal complications as well as related psychological consequences. The salient contents of psychological assessment in anorexia and weight loss include medical complications, inadequate nutrition (as in case of 25 percent of weight loss hospitalization is must), related cognitive changes, emotional feelings associated with loss of control over eating behaviour, history of physical and emotional abuse, reasons of stopping normal eating, eating rituals, side effects of medicines, family dynamics and problem situations (Agras et al., 1974; Arwood and Chester, 1987). The relevant behavioural and psychological interventions could b as follows:

- Psycho-education in relation to importance of nutrition, weight gain and supporting immune system.
- Encourage honest and appropriate emotional expression, positive self-statement.
- Provision for fresh air activities stimulating appetite.
- Relaxation techniques and Developing assertiveness if relevant.
- Facilitating personal care and appropriate self-perception.
- Developing realistic expectations and encouraging appropriate grieving for loss of control.
- Challenging or modifying negative talks, over generalizations and absolute thinking.
- Encouraging participation in problem-solving, and identifying personal growth- related activities.
- Teaching to separate and maintain their own emotions fro others' feelings.
- Supporting the person in effective dealing with emotional feelings.
- Facilitating acknowledgement of hunger and eating in response to internal cues of hunger.
- Identifying role of the person as well as the family in recovery.
- Family members are required to be honest, affectionate, and supportive with confident, calming and assertive posture. They should neither demand weight gain, blame, criticize the patient for having anorexia nor demand the person eating with them or allowing the patient's eating problem to dominate the family's eating schedules or use of kitchen. Once the patient is involved in treatment regardless of improvement, the family should not be directly

involved with the issues of weight gain rather they should contact the clinician after seeing any change in appearance of the patients.

- Decisions regarding intervention for weight gain should clearly define in terms of short-term and long-term goals. The family should be necessarily involved in such decisions as they have to bear the burden and be able to support the scientific intervention.
- If possible, the patients should be involved in meal preparation, food shopping and arranging table. However, it is also relevant to mention here that in typical psychological psychiatric case of anorexia this method may not be recommendable as it puts the patient in a nurturing role allowing him or her to deny their own need for food by feeding and serving others.

Cognitive Impairment

The cognitive dysfunction in children, adolescents and adults is caused by progression of HIV/AIDS and often observed secondary to physical and psychological problems and difficulties (Meehan and Brush, 2001; Ungvarski et al., 2000). Its main causes include bacterial, fungal and viral infections, cerebrovascular disease, cancerous impact on central nervous system, metabolic dysfunctions, side effects of medication and undoubtedly psychological stress also. These processes damage white matter of the brain, nerve tracks, cause cerebral atrophy, ventricular enlargements, and some other damages in brain (Belman et al., 1988; Mintz, 1999; Mitchell, 2001) leading to sensory impairment, poor brain growth, language-related impairment, loss of developmental milestones, deficits in memory, motor dysfunctions, executive functions like problem-solving, planning, visuo-spatial skills, social-emotional regulatory functions etc (Belman,1997; Bisiacchi et al., 2000; Wachsler-Feller and Golden, 2002). The psychological assessment of such cognitive impairment comprise assessment of developmental milestones, motor disturbances including communication skills, scholastic or educational performance, other cognitive impairments like dysfunctional attention, concentration, articulation, judgment making, difficulty in completing class- or home works, executive functioning, visuo-spatial and perceptual abilities, problem-solving, socio-emotional behaviour, assessment of family environment, safety assessment at home, support system etc. After completing comprehensive psychological and neuropsychological assessment an adequate, timely and consistent psychological intervention is required for better survival of the patient, prevention or lessening intensity of disease progression and familial stress as well. The behavioural and psychological interventions for cognitive impairment in HIV/AIDS should essentially include the following points:

- Psycho-education in relation to cognitive impairment due to HIV and its prevention in children, adolescents and adults must be provided to the family and relevant care takers.
- Intervention to the cognitive impairment is an interdisciplinary service. Therefore, each area of cognitive dysfunction should be carefully examined by relevant professional like clinical psychologist, neuropsychologist, speech pathologist, neurologist, physiologist etc to determine current level of functioning and intervention to be provided. It should not be forgotten to repeat the assessment from time to time as the disease progresses.
- Family should be taught to monitor patient's safety issues and use of conspicuous communication along with support with advanced directives, wills, trust, referral for assisted living and other relevant legal issues before the progression of disease (Bachanas, 2003).
- For intervening scholastic problems children less than three years of age are required to be referred for early intervention. Other children and adolescents can be referred to special schooling and an individualized educational programme. Some sort of non-academic support like short period of schooling due to fatigue, classes in nearby locations to reduce walking, transportation and facility of elevators may also be required.
- For adequate self care encouragement is to be given to independent living with proper supervision in areas, e.g., bathing, cleaning and grooming hair, brushing teeth, proper dressing etc.
- In order to improve sensory-perceptual co-ordination, attention and concentration, environmental stimuli are to be decreased and reality testing to be assisted. Discouragement to pattern stabilization of false ideas should be given by talking to the person about real people and situations. The care taker should facilitate reality testing when the patient demonstrates inaccurate sensory perception.
- To improve cognitive functions, care takers should facilitate patient's orientation to day, date, time, place, person, situations etc. They can be assisted by providing memory aids like calendars, timer alarm, medicine kit etc. The family should offer simple explanation to any matter, talk face to face with slow volume, and speed the patient up to increase effective communication skills.
- Low self-esteem can be treated through encouraging honest expression of emotional feelings related to loss and deterioration in psycho-social functioning. Focus should be given on abilities and accomplishments rather

than loss and decrement. Prompt and possible feedbacks are given in reinforcing accurate reality testing.

- Sometimes violent behaviour to self and others are also likely in HIV/AIDS. Therefore, level of agitation and anger, related thought processes, and indicative violent behaviours as well as acting-out behaviours must be assessed. Minimum environmental stimuli are kept in patient's surrounding and all dangerous objects are removed. The caregivers are advised to be calm and cool with the patient, and evaluation of need for higher level of care is conducted with the help of the clinicians.
- At last, the family and significant caregivers are advised to take some precaution while caring patient with HIV infection, especially adolescents and adults. The care providers should remain in close proximity of the patient for proper monitoring. The household and other required objects in room of the patient should be placed as per their use, function and safety in mind. Sometimes, padding of certain objects may be felt necessary. The caregivers should always be reminded on safety and management related matters.
- Delirium which is especially found in the elderly, characterized by disturbances in conscious and alteration in cognitive domain developing over a short span of time. Patients with this problem in HIV are characterized by varying mental alertness, e.g., agitation particularly at night, lethargies, stupor or coma; abrupt disturbance in pattern of sleep; impaired memory, orientation, executive functions, decreased speech fluency and frequency, hallucinations and delusion, hyperactivity, labile affect, nystagmus, ataxia etc Its behavioural and psychological interventions include teaching family members in relation to its care, effects of medication and providing orientation to the patient, providing safe and consistent environment with proper and regular supervision, clear communication using simple words and terms to avoid misperceptions, attempt to ensuring patient's undisturbed sleep at night, correcting underlying conditions leading to delirium, e.g., metabolic abnormalities, illicit drug abuse etc. (New York state Department of health AIDS Institute, 2001).

Fatigue

Fatigue must be considered as a legitimate complaint to the person living with HIV, public and professional community which appears silent, invisible, and is often missed to be acknowledged, and understood by the health professionals, families, friends and other relevant caretakers (Jenkin, Koch, and Kralik, 2006). The problem of fatigue could be attributable to several factors such as poor nutrition particularly deficiency of magnesium (Skurnick et al., 1996), testosterone (Groopman, 1998), endocrinal dysfunction especially hypothalamic, pituitary and adrenal malfunctioning (Clerici et al., 1997; Stolarczyk et al., 1998), liver disease, medication and pain, depression (Barroso, 1999,2001; Rabkin et al., 1999), anxiety (Barroso, 2001; Wessely et al., 1998)). Thankfully, to assess HIV-related fatigue a scale has been developed, i.e. HIV-Related Fatigue Scale (Barroso and Lynn, 2002) containing 56 items which emphasizes to examine intensity of fatigue, its duration and status over last week, situation factors making it worse and better, its consequences on daily activities, individual's pattern of fatigue and ability to think, work and socialize; adequacy of individual's sleep and drug abuse. In addition to such tool-based assessment, a comprehensive interview must be conducted to listen, understand and consider the complexities of the personal experience of the patient, and its wider social aspects of life (Jenkin, Koch, and Kralik, 2006). The psychological intervention to fatigue aims at knowing characteristics of fatigue based on the assessment, determining its causes, maintaining or restoring optimally functioning abilities as well as finding out sources of help and coping for the patient. To accomplish the purpose:

- Underlying medical complications like opportunistic infections, diarrhoeas etc are examined.
- Benefits of medication against its side effects are also assessed.
- Proper nutrition has to be provided as per the clinical guidelines and the underlying depression (if any), must be treated.
- Sometimes, the support system should know about suicidal nature of the patient, and always accompany the patient so the extent and intensity of suicidal thoughts into action could be avoided.
- Patients should be encouraged to keep necessarily a diary to track individual pattern of fatigue and plan own daily activities the best way possible so that strenuous activities could be completed at the highest level of energy.
- Having a nap and support in reducing strenuous activities can also be quite helpful (Van Servellen et al., 1998). In addition, the patient can be referred to community intervention centre (if available) for relevant assistance, e.g., house keeping, routinely activities etc, as well as involvement of occupational therapy can teach the techniques of energy conservation and strengthening exercises to the patient.

Sleep Disturbances

This is characterized by insufficient non-restorative sleep (i.e., insomnia), restless leg syndrome involving creepy, crawly, unpleasant sensing, burning and itching often between ankles and knees (Rothenberg, 1997); hypersomnia featuring breathing during sleep, periodic disorder of organ movement, narcolepsy; and parasomnia which implies nocturnal seizure, behavioural disorder related to Rapid Eye Movement (REM) and somnambulism. It may be caused by anxiety, depression, HIV-related infections, and other related symptoms like fever, and nocturnal sweating etc. In addition, limitation of financial means and support, hospitalization and unstable family and housing could be significant social and environmental determinants. It causes poor quality of life (Phillip and Skelton, 2001). In case of children, assessment of adequate rest, respite and sleep of entire family may be required. Because often children experience interrupted sleep increasing fatigue, loss of energy and disturbance in routine of the family as a whole. Parents of children with HIV do feel difficulty in setting bedtime and other limits for children and themselves due to guilt-feeling, lack of organization, fear, worries and irregularity in life. They themselves don't get proper and adequate rest as being occupied with the patient child in several responsibilities from feeding to toileting. Its assessment includes nature and extent of sleep disturbance, sleep latency (time required in falling asleep after going to bed which may indicate problem in sleep is crossing 30 minutes), problem in restoration in sleep, problem of deep sleep, associated medical complication, nature and degree of psycho-social support, types and pattern of nutritional fulfilment etc. The psycho-social and behavioural intervention may require following points:

- Establishing a regular time-table for going to bed without any inconsistency. One should not go to bed too early or too late.
- Bed should be used only for sleeping, and avoiding other practices like reading, writing, eating etc. The room temperature and bed should be comfortable.
- Any physical and psychological stimulation at sleeping time by any means (e.g., strife, tea, coffee, alcohol etc) should be avoided. Ideally, stimulants should be taken after 5-6 p.m.
- Napping is not advisable at all.
- Dinner should be light like snacks, rather than a heavy diet.
- Thinking time can be scheduled in hours of early evening and the bed time worriers can prepare a list of problems and programmes of tomorrow before going to bed.
- Regular exercise and bathing with warm water in evening could be practiced.
- Failure in falling asleep within 15-30 minutes after going to bed should not be

substituted by another activity, e.g. reading completing pending works, rather practice of paradoxical intention must be incorporated and practiced.

Depression

Depression is a kind of mood disorder which is characterized by dysphoric mood, loss of interest, changes in psycho-motor behaviour, biogenic motives, sense of worthlessness, suicidal tendency alike. For diagnostic purpose, these symptoms are not considered as reactions to any incident or accident and impact of substance abuse which must persist leastways for two weeks and above. Such clinical features often result in impairment in socio-occupational functioning. It is worth mention here that despite having similar feature, bereavement is not an episode of depression unless the clinical features are sustaining over two months of period. Normal grief may also sustain as a self-limiting situation beyond six months (Bonanno and Kaltman, 1999). Other symptoms of depression are guilt-feeling, tearfulness, revival memories, brooding, fatigue, decreased attention and concentration etc (American Psychiatric Association, 2000a). In the context of HIV/AIDS the rate of prevalence of depression can vary from 2-35 percent (Morrison et al., 2002) and mostly women are affected by the depressive syndrome. The psychological assessment of depression in persons with HIV/AIDS includes global functioning, mental status examination, level of depression and suicidal thoughts, danger to self and others due to depressive features, ineffective problem solving; dysfunctional thinking, grieving and coping strategies; self-esteem, dysfunctional personality features, family environment etc. Here, serious and immediate need for attention, assessment and intervention may be toward suicidal thoughts, personal and impersonal dangers as these thoughts may contain homicidal thinking also. In order to such comprehensive assessment clinicians can opt for scientific tool like Beck-Depression Inventory (BDI), Family Environment Scale, Global Assessment Functioning Scale, Bell's Adjustment Inventory, Rorschach Psycho-diagnostics, 16 PF, Hamilton Depression Rating Scale, Brief Psychiatric rating Scale and alike. The psychological intervention can be aimed at supporting feelings of acceptance (as they feel isolated usually) in family through personal and family counselling, minimizing sense o worthlessness, isolation and loss facilitating effective problem-solving and adequate coping. The following behavioural and psychological techniques could be helpful in achieving goals of intervention:

- Providing safe and secured environment including removal of harmful or harm-inducing objects to be used in self-harm, medication, firearms etc. The patient must be provided flexible and extended time of meeting to ventilate their emotions, and agreeing initiation of steps toward effective problem-solving (Farewell, 1993).

- Adequate coping, social and interpersonal skills should be provided. Facilitating how to prioritize different issues within limitations, encouragement and positive feedback in decision making could be very helpful.
- Distraction techniques and activity scheduling including mild exercise everyday could be useful in minimizing or modifying psycho-motor retardation, ruminated thinking and increasing positive feelings.
- For nourishing self-esteem, individual's strengths and accomplishments should be focused while ignoring, reconceptualizing or neutralizing past failures as a part of learning and experience in life. Encouragement should be provided for independent efforts, initiating taking responsibilities and successful gradual accomplishments. They can be taught that living with responsibilities is linked with active life style, healthy self-esteem and meaningful existence.
- If grief is present, relevant counselling strategies could be required. Firstly, nature and level o current grief should be assessed prior to counselling. Expression of feeling, empathic support and care should be facilitated. The clinicians and care takers can educate the patient of different stages of grief and normalize or neutralize appropriate emotional feelings, e.g., guilt, anger, dejection. People can support in removing or decreasing patient's idealized perception and getting accepting pros and cons of their source or object of loss. Lastly, incorporation of empty chair technique or writing something to the lost object for facilitating resolution process, and talking and exploring spiritual matters and support could also be useful (James and Cherry, 1988).
- Distorted thinking can be modified through identifying dysfunctional thinking, educating positive self-talk, reinforcing reality based thinking, thought stopping and logical confrontation (if possible).
- Biological motives or physiological functioning (e.g., hunger, sleep) can be treated by proper activity scheduling, psycho-education including importance of nutrition and side effects of medication also, relaxation training and additional herbal and traditional medicinal treatment.
- Teaching risks and benefits of appropriate exercise may be undertaken by those living with HIV/AIDS with the help of healthcare providers. Often these are effective and safe enhancing and improving the overall outcome for adults living with HIV and the effectiveness of HIV intervention. Researches indicated that performing constant or interval aerobic exercise, or a combination of constant aerobic exercise and progressive resistive exercise

for at least 20 minutes, and three times per week for four weeks appears to be safe and may lead to significant reductions in depressive symptoms and potentially clinically important improvements in cardiopulmonary fitness (Nixon, O'Brien, Glazier, Tynan, 2005).

Anxiety Disorders

The anxiety disorders are quite common among persons with HIV/AIDS, across its infections and sufferings. The prevalence rate of these disorders is almost similar to depression in HIV infections. The salient features of anxiety disorders include anxiety, apprehension, distress, worries, self-defeating cognitive and behavioural rituals, physical symptoms like bodily tension, decreased sleep and appetite; feeling of lack of control, and difficulty in effective coping. The types of anxiety commonly found in HIV infected people are generalized anxiety disorder, panic disorder, phobias, obsessive-compulsive disorders, somatoform disorder, post traumatic stress disorder. Sometimes, anxiety may exist with depression creating difficulties in assessment and intervention. Since both of these disorders have common feature of general distress (e.g. guilt, anger, tearfulness, sadness, disgust etc., their overlapping can be differentiated by identifying two more but separate group of clinical features-absence of positive affect (presumably associated with depression) and physiological arousability characterized by palpitations, feeling shortness in breathing, increased sweating or cold sweating, muscular tension, restlessness, shakiness, abdominal distress etc. which are chiefly associated with anxiety rather than depression. These mutually exclusive clinical features of anxiety and depression often don't fully meet the criteria of full-fledged separate diagnosis. The psychological assessment of anxiety-related disorders include chief complaints, history of present psychological problem, type and level of its severity, socio-occupational history, post medical history and stressful experiences, physical symptoms, support system, personality features, cognitive assessment etc. The behavioural and psychological interventions of anxiety disorders in HIV/AIDS include the following points:

- Psycho-education regarding the anxiety-related problem, its causes and intervention, side effects of medication and role of support system.
- Training on relaxation techniques including differential relaxation and deep breathing also.
- Teaching self-care methods including proper nutrition, activity scheduling, time management and positive self-talks etc.
- To alleviate or remove feelings of anxiety sources and reasons of anxiety are

identified and logical validation to the patient's emotional feelings is provided.

- Systematic desensitization to irrational fears could be used and developing alternative coping strategies must be taught to the patient. In addition, clarifications of reality of the fear base as well as venting of the relevant feelings are to be encouraged.
- Reality testing, distraction techniques, and exposure and response prevention can be used in obsessive-compulsive disorders. It can be accompanied by positive feedback, reinforcement for accomplishment and cognitive restructuring toward effective coping.
- To improve problem-solving, relevant skills and steps must be taught and secondary gain inhibiting progress toward change should be identified, modified and challenged.
- Feeling of lacking control over personal and impersonal issues and situations can be intervened by breaking down simple behaviours of necessary tasks into several manageable steps in ascending order of the severity of the problem. The techniques of shaping toward successive approximation and relevant positive reinforcement can also be incorporated.
- Modification of dysfunctional thinking can be accomplished by identifying negative thoughts, statements and connection between self-talk and anxiety; reality-based counterstatement and substitute thoughts, distraction techniques, logical challenges to dysfunctional and negative thinking.
- Assertiveness training may also be required. In addition, encouraging self-esteem through logical and realistic setting o goals, expectations and limitations as well as overcoming negative attitude toward self may also be necessary.
- Alleviating anger may include validation and encouraging venting off underlying feeling of anger, role play for appropriate expression of anger, developing commitment to change for improving quality of life, keeping delay in reacting through distraction and seeking possible an pleasurable activities, broadening choices, resources and support system, accepting by the patient and letting it go that failure is a part of life and perfection in not attainable.

Substance Abuse

The substance abuse including drug addiction and alcoholism accounts for more than one-third percentage of the HIV/AIDS cases (Lucas, 2001; Bing et al., 2001). The relationship between substance abuse and risk for HIV infection is multi-fold. Psychologically, the Freudian theory of psycho-sexual development hypothesized that aberration in psycho-sexual development leads to fixation (regarding alcoholism, the fixation occurs in oral stage) which is, in turn, significant in substance abuse, especially alcoholism and other oral cravings like smoking. Such substance abuse stimulates sexual urges getting an individual occupied in multiple sexual acts with several partners and thus increasing vulnerability to HIV infections. Secondly, difficulties surrounding sexual preference may also be regarded as a significant factor of substance abuse and related vulnerability to HIV infection. Because conflicts over undesirable or denied homosexual preference may create discomfort to be alleviated drug or alcohol. Alternatively, choosing homosexual orientation may give rise to stress to be treated by alcohol (Cox, 1987). Thus substance abuse, homosexuality and HIV infection are deeply related with each other. Thirdly, sexual status, behaviour and experience have been frequently found associated with substance abuse among women than men counterparts, where alcoholic women have been promiscuous (Karpman,1948), or frigid (Levine, 1955). Furthermore, seller of alcohol and drugs, smugglers and sex workers are more prone to substance abuse.

All these factors and situations increase individuals' risk toward HIV infections, mental disorders and, so much so, toward a combination of HIV and psychological disorders. Thus, substance abuse among persons with HIV is not uncommon, and a need for psychological intervention must be felt and provided along with medical and psychiatric treatment as per the following guidelines:

- Firstly, the problem of substance abuse must be properly examined by a qualified professional or a group of professionals including psychiatrist and clinical psychologist. Thereafter, the relevant treatment programme should b followed accordingly.
- While dealing with denial, conveying a non-rejecting or non-judgmental attitude is desirable. It can be confronted with current impact of substance abuse and education to correct misconceptions. The patient's use of other defence mechanisms to avoid reality should not be accepted and ignored.
- Intervention for lacking self-control requires facilitating individual's analysis of pattern of substance abuse and its monitoring and related sense of responsibility. Besides, identification of relationship between substance abuse and personal problems, situations, people, related beliefs and emotional feelings are also important. Preparation and planning for anticipated difficult situations for coping, participation in group intervention and other self-care measures require adequate and regular facilitation.
- Training for relaxation, assertiveness and verbal communication must be

provided. In addition, standing up for patient's rights with the help of family members and teaching how to deal with being left out, group pressure and fear could also be tremendously helpful.

- Dysfunctional family interaction and irrational thinking can be dealt with family therapy and cognitive-behaviour therapy respectively. Education for positive self-statement to challenge negative self-statements and beliefs with factual and logical information could also be added necessarily.
- Programme for holistic day treatment including support groups could be advantageous in stabilizing the patient and compliance to treatment.

Pain Management

Pain is defined as 'an unpleasant sensory and emotional experience associated with actual or potential damage, or described in terms of that damage (International Association for the Study of Pain, 1979). John Loeser (1989) has proposed a model for understanding and evaluating pain which includes four components as follow:

- **Nociception:** This is the first stage of pain related to experience of tissue damage and activation of A-delta and C-fibers. The 'A' and 'C' fibers convey information of pain from skin to spinal cord and through other nerve structures to brain. The 'A' fibers (myelinated fibers) has two types: *'A' beta and 'A' delta*. The 'A' beta fibers are large fibers in the spinal cord inhibiting transmission of pain where as the 'A' delta fibers are small fibers facilitating the transmission of pain. The 'C' fibers are small, unmyelinated conducting impulse slowly and give diffuse sensation of pain.
- **Pain:** This is the second stage which includes the perception of tissue damage.
- **Suffering:** This is a negative emotional response to the tissue damage realizing severe pain.
- **Pain behaviour:** It includes actions reflecting presence of the tissue damage.

However, pain necessarily does not undergo all these stages or levels. In the context of HIV/AIDS, the incidence and severity of pain depend on progression of disease as well as co- morbidity. It is of two types: *acute and chronic pain*. The acute pain is a short-term pain related to tissue damage comprising sharp, localized, intense pain, resulted restlessness, agitation, perspiration, muscular tension; increased blood pressure,, pulse rate and respiration. The patient generally avoids physical contact with others while focusing and guarding the area of pain. On the contrary, the chronic pain sustains for, more than six months causing chronic pathological processes (Bonica, 1990; Casey et al., 1996). Often this nature of pain is associated with psychological features of depression, anxiety, disabilities, adverse physical effects as well as changes in personality also. Some important neurological sources of pain are meningitis, hyper tonicity, spasticity, peripheral neuropathy due to medication, post herpetic neuropathy, musculoskeletal pain, body pain (all in children particularly); headache, central nervous system related toxoplasmosis, syphilis, histoplasmosis, tuberculosis, multi-focal leukoencephalopathy,, migraine, spinal abscess etc (all in adolescents and adults particularly).

The assessment of pain aims at evaluating duration and frequency of pain, fear and prior experience o pain, related other symptoms and feelings, impact of pain, socio-economico-spiritual well-being, use of street- and self-prescribed drugs (Holzemer et al., 1998), culture-specific meaning and expression of pain, behavioural measures being taken by the client during and avoiding pain as well, support system etc. It is also important mention here that the relevance of culture should not at all be ignored or undermined in such assessment and intervention, because cultures or subcultures of the individual with HIV are often stigmatized by adverse psycho-social and economic conditions, and thus causing additional burden of the disease. In fact, individuals of such cultures often have long history of rejection which is potentially enough to replace or damage honesty and trust between the patient and clinician. As a result, communication gap and hiding important information on the part of the patient emerge worsening the condition of pain and suffering. Therefore, it is advisable to focus on patient's indigenous culture, attitudes, beliefs, practices, views and values in assessment and intervention.

Such assessment and intervention could be difficult in case of children for several reasons. Generally, clinical care for children focuses on controlling the virus of HIV/AIDS rather than treating pain and symptoms. The children may not communicate properly about their pain felt which can be misconstrued that they don't experience such pain like adults. Sometimes, it is also found that assistant clinicians lack adequate education, knowledge, skills and may mistake considering the child's pain as attention-seeking behaviour, however, the reverse is true. In addition, often children opt for play activity to distract themselves from pain and fall asleep when get exhausted in such activities even during pain. Thus, it should not be concluded that children don't feel pain while playing and sleeping. Therefore, proper and comprehensive assessment of pain in case of children must include some important behavioural signs like listlessness in usual enjoyable activities, crying, mood change or fluctuation, pattern of sleep, playfulness, decreasing attention and concentration, wincing etc. A separate behavioural and psychological care for children, adolescents and adults must be considered as per the following guidelines.

Intervention for Children

- Psycho-education to family in relation to pain and other symptoms resulting from HIV infections. Such symptoms include fever, severe cough, fast or difficult breathing, poor weight gain or decreasing weight, white patches or sores in the mouth persistent diaper rashes, blood in diaper or bowel movements, vomiting, diarrhoea, contact with a person with measles, chicken pox, tuberculosis and other contagious diseases, swelling in neck (around lymph glands), under the arms and diaper area, itching skin rashes, frequent lung' infections, ENT infections, otherwise inability in sitting, crawling, walking etc.
- Sufficient time should be taken in teaching children and care takers about programmes and procedure of intervention to be employed. Parents must be encouraged to participate.
- Techniques of diaphragmatic breathing and muscular relaxation should be taught.
- Methods of distraction from pain can be employed like blowing bubbles, looking at 'magic wands', singing, telling stories etc. The techniques of guided imagery could also be helpful in minimizing pain.

Intervention for Adolescents and Adults

- There must be individualized treatment programme for each patient during custodial or hospitalized care in relation to pain control.
- Teaching and training for relaxation techniques, imagery, bio-feedback, meditation and yoga etc could also be very helpful.
- Exercise is another key management strategy advised and used by health care professionals to address impairments (problems with body function or structure as a significant deviation or loss such as pain or weakness), activity limitations (i.e. difficulties in executing activities such as inability to walk) and participation restrictions (i.e. problems in life situations such as inability to work) of persons with HIV/AIDS. Exercise may also be useful in this population to address changes in weight and body composition. For example, aerobic exercise could support improvements in strength, cardiovascular function, and psychological status. Researches have emphasized that aerobic exercise interventions appear to be safe and lead to improvements in cardiopulmonary fitness in HIV/AIDS. An another kind of exercise which is known as Progressive resistive exercise alone, or a combination of

progressive resistive exercise and aerobic exercise appear to be safe and beneficial for adolescents and adults with HIV/AIDS in improving strength and psychological status (O'Brien, Nixon, Glazier, Tynan, 2004).

- Sometimes, prayer could also be relieving.
- Stress management (e.g. stress inoculation technique, participation in pleasurable behaviours, time management, adequate nutrition and regular exercise etc.) and cognitive restructuring in course of gradual relief (e.g., educating regarding the impact of negative thinking and self-talks, focus on capabilities rather than disabilities, compartmentalizing, realistic confrontation).
- To deal with body image and other related issues, encouragement to grieving for any loss related to bodily functioning is given as it affects personal identity and adjustment. In addition, encouragement and positive feedback can benefit in self acceptance or acknowledgement of realistic perception of body.
- Facilitating effective coping may include validation of individual's experience of pain, identification and resolution of related secondary gain, encouraging venting of anxiety and fears, dealing with precipitating stressors, encouraging compliance to time contingent programme of medical treatment rather than pain contingent (means, taking medication as prescribed rather than as required of felt taking the same).
- To be realistic without being fatalistic and avoiding making judgments related to coping strategies could also be advantageous.

Care for Dying and Death Issues of Children and Adolescents with HIV/AIDS

Death can be defined as a final phase of dying characterized by cessation of all physiological functions as a result of acute health problems of slow chronic deterioration of body due to sudden and acute illness, accidents or even HIV/AIDS. Similar to the process of birth, labour also occurs in dying stage preceding actual death and classifying the process of end of life in three stages:

- **Preactive Dying**: It is characterized by decreased eating and drinking, increased level of pain and sensitivity to sensory functions, changes in respiration, weakness and confusion, crying and withdrawal, fear of loneliness, depression, agitation, planning for funeral etc.
- **Active Dying:** Its salient characteristics are skin cooling, temperature fluctuation in body, changes in skin colour, irregular breathing, decrease in control over bladder and bowels, deterioration in orientation and awareness,

restlessness, calm acceptance, fear, intensity of sense of spiritual sources etc.

- **Death:** It is characterized by termination of all bodily functions, changes in skin colour as gray, mouth and eye may close or remain open, may have involuntary loss of stool and urine.

The impact of death often and obviously leads to bereavement in family and other significant people to which three types of response are found:

- **Denial:** This is the first stage of response in bereavement due to death. It is not accepted that the person has died of HIV/AIDS (or due to any reason). This is a shocking stage which may continue for few days. The bereaved person/s feels numbness as if in unreal or dream-like state.
- **Stage of Sadness:** It begins after completion of all the rites and rituals of funeral when the bereaved people are back to normal and routinely life. The dead person is missed a lot and the family is surrounded by sadness and despair. Some people may hear their names being called by the lost person or blame the dead for their agony. Besides, decreased sleep, loss of interest in activities and frequent crying spells are also common.
- **Stage of Reorganization:** This is the last and final stage of bereavement which is characterized by recuperation fro the loss in bereaved family members, relatives and friends. The loss of the person is accepted as a part of life; however, the lost person is still remembered now and then. But their sadness does not interfere with enjoying delightful moments in life as well as a future with hope without the loved person.

Thus, these processes of death and bereavement clearly indicate that care for dying and death duly include the aspects related with the dying person with HIV, e.g., disclosure of diagnosis, assessment of needs and supportive intervention for the dying child or adolescent as well as issues related with the bereaved people. Though willingness for disclosure of diagnosis of HIV infection to the child or adolescent differs from family to family, however, there are few strategies for coping with disclosure-related matters relevant to the young or minor patient and his or her family. In fact, affirmation of the positive nature of diagnosis of the terminal disease like HIV could provide a deep insight to the dying child or adolescent for better coping (Kuber-Ross, 1983). But, sometimes the family is reluctant to disclose the diagnosis to the young patient. In such situations, it's better to motivate the child to ask questions regarding the current health problems which could be answered indirectly along with encouraging him or her to communicate personal feelings, fantasies, aims, longings to be reciprocated. While assessing need of the child and family is it important to discuss their level of comfort with impending death. The dying child's willingness and requirements should be respected for his/her own satisfaction as well as family's comfort and successful coping. For example, the child may ask to see somebody, may have some toys and other articles to be gifted to another friend or sibling. S/he may be afraid of being forgotten which must be clarified warmly supported. It could also be quite helpful to explore their unfinished works to be completed by the family.

Intervention to the dying child is very crucial but quite difficult as family members are shocked by the clinical information of the diagnosis of HIV. Therefore, first of all it is clarify clinician's information to the child and family, as well as their beliefs about the condition o the child and whether it can be altered or reversed with intervention. It may also be useful to find out alternative methods and viewpoints regarding care and treatment of the child based on previous experience, health beliefs, culture and practice in case of controversy or disagreement among the family, child and clinical team of treatment. Above all, discuss death as a part of natural course of life allowing the suffering child or adolescent for living as per their will and modifying false beliefs that disclosure of diagnosis and discussions over the issue of end of life will hasten death.

The tangible and personalized care for the dying child should include all senses, i.e. vision, audition, olfaction, gustation, and kinesthetics as each of these sensory functions remains working until last breath. The personalized care related to these functions can include gathering of patient's choice of children, adults, and food activities; pictures of family and friends containing shared time together, spiritual books alleviating fear, soothing music etc. The caretaker's effort to make time for each person to be alone with the dying child could be pacifying.

In addition, quiet sitting beside the patient, gentle touch of forehead or face along with empathic and honest feeling and expression of impending loss could also be included. The gentle touch could be important between isolation and feeling of shame as well as a sense of acceptance and sympathy. The voice of loved one's makes a great difference in comfort of the dying person, especially young people. The desires of the dying ward and his/her boundaries must be honoured, and the family should be guided by them. The clinicians and other health care professionals should overcome their own fear in patients and increase home visits in such situations (Whitecar et al., 2000). The surrounding environment should be kept peaceful and comfortable. Since, hearing ability is found as acute during the dying state, therefore, the dying people do feel relaxed after hearing the voice of the loved one. Lastly, visualizations for pain relief, release of grief, and meditation also assist the dying person and caretakers as well (Levine, 1982).

Conclusions and Suggestions

The chapter has provided a comprehensive description of psychological co-morbidity in persons with HIV/AIDS with special emphasis on psychological assessment and intervention in collaboration with medical treatment to minimize its complications and facilitate patient's survival. However, the psychological aspects of some more health problems which are simultaneously present in HIV have to be studied to extend and strengthen the health services in this context. For example, presence of disability prior and post HIV infection has differential impact on the patient. It should not be considered equal for forthcoming psychological impact, diagnosis and intervention in HIV. In addition, the sensory and motor impairments affect differentially the male and female patients. This is highly relevant in the context of our Indian subcontinent. Since girls with disabilities are trapped more for sexual abuse and thus, are at stake toward HIV-related health problems, therefore, an special preventive programme should be initiated at large scale with particular inclusion of rural people and societies where such vulnerabilities is highly likely due to lack o orientation and information among the public in relation to HIV and sources of its infection. The inclusion of psychological intervention could be advantageous in sexual abuse as well as transmission of HIV in such situations. Furthermore, different techniques and approaches are implicated to be developed for persons with co-morbidity of different types of disabilities in HIV/AIDS.

Similarly, whether the cognitive impairment has occurred prior in an elderly or it is due to the progression of HIV, has to be clarified and its impact to be studied in relation to psychological intervention. Lastly, one more aspect of the prospective study can be included, i.e., divorce and HIV. Presently the rate of divorce is increasing in our Indian society and causing extra-marital relationships making people vulnerable to HIV as most of the cases of divorce occurring in young an fertile age-groups. There could be two possibilities of study o divorce and its relationship with HIV. The divorce due to extra-marital relationship and resulted HIV infections may have different psychological impact than post-divorce cohabitation and promiscuous relationship with resulted HIV. Thus, such differential consequences o life events could provide distinct dynamics to its relationships with HIV-related disease, and the programme for psychological intervention can be developed accordingly. Researches on these aspects of co-morbidity I HIV and relevant psychological interventions are highly welcomed.

References

Agras WS, Barlow TH, Chapin HN, Abel GG, Leitenberg H(1974). Behavioural modification of anorexia nervosa. Archives of General Psychiatry, 30, 279-86.

American Psychiatric Association (2000a). Diagnostic and statistical manual of mental disorders (4th ed.). Washington, DC.

Arwood J, Chester R (1987). Treatment techniques for common mental disorders. New Jersey. Jason Aronson, Inc.

Bachanas PJ (2003). Cognitive Impairment and developmental Delay. In Carl Kirton [Ed], ANAC's Coe Curriculum for HIV/AIDS Nursing. Thousand Oaks, USA. Sage Publications.

Barroso J (1999). A review of fatigue in people with HIV infection. Journal of the Association of Nurses in AIDS care, 10(5), 42-49.

Barroso J (2001). "Just worn out": A qualitative study of HIV related fatigue. In S.G. Funk E.M Tornquist, J. Leeman, M.S. Miles and J.S. Harrell [Eds.], Key aspects of preventing and managing chronic illness(pp. 183-194). New York. Springer.

Barroso J, Lynn MR (2002). Psychometric properties of the HIV-Related Fatigue Scale. Journal of the Association of Nurses in AIDS Care, 13(1), 66-75.

Belman AL (1997). Pediatric neuro-AIDS. Neuroimaging Clinics of North America, 7(3), 593-613.

Belman AL, Diamond G, Dickson D, Horoupian D, Llena J, Lantos G et al. (1988). Pediatric acquired immunodeficiency syndrome. American Journal of Diseases of Children, 142, 29-35.

Bing EG, Burnnam MA, Longshore D, Fleishman JA, Sherbourne CD, London AS, et al. (2001). Psychiatric disorders and drug use among human immunodeficiency virus-infected adults in the United States. Archives of General Psychiatry, 58(8), 721-28.

Bisiacchi PS, Suppiej A, Laverda A (2000). Neuropsychological evaluation of neurologically asymptomatic HIV-infected children. Brain and Cognition, 43, 49-52.

Bonica J (1990). The management of pain. Pliladelphia. Lea and Febiger.

Bonnano G, Kaltman S (1999). Toward an integrated perspective on bereavement. Psychological Bulletin, 125, 760-76.

Brown JL, Vanable PA (2008). Cognitive-behavioural stress management interventions for persons living with HIV: a review and critique of the literature. Ann Behav Med, Feb; 135(1), 26-40.

Casey KM, Cohen F, Hughes A [Eds]. (1996). ANAC's core curriculum for HIV/AIDS nursing. Philadelphia. Nursecom, Inc.

Clerisi M, Trabattoni D, Piconi S, Fusi ML, Ruzzante S, Clerisi C et al. (1997). A possible role for the cortisol/anticortisol imbalance in the progression of human immunodeficiency virus. Psychoneuroendocrinology, 22(suppl. 1), 27-31.

Cox W Miles [Ed]. (1987). Treatment and Prevention of Alcohol Problems. Orlando, USA. Academic Press, Inc.

Douaihy AB, Stowell KR, Kohnen S, Stoklosa JB, Breitbart WS (2007). Psychiatric aspects of co-morbid HIV/AIDS and pain- Part1. AIDS read, Jun; 17(6), 310-14.

Fawcell JMD (1993). Predicting and preventing suicide. Psychiatric Anals, 23.5.

Garcia J, Altman RD (1997). Chronic pain states: pathophysiology and medical therapy. Seminars in Arthritis and Rheumatism, 27(1), 1-16.

Godbole S, Mehendale S (2005). HIV/AIDS epidemic in India: risk factors, risk behaviour and strategies for prevention and control. Indian Journal of Medical Research, 121(4), 356-68.

Groopman JE (1998). Fatigue in cancer and HIV/AIDS. Oncology, 12, 335-41.

Holzemer WL, Henry SB, Reilly CA (1998). Assessing and managing pain in AIDS care: the patient perspective. Journal of Association of Nurses in AIDS Care, 9(1), 22-30.

International Association for the Study of Pain. Subcommittee on taxonomy (1979). Pain terms: A list of definitions and notes on usage. Pain, 6(3), 248-52.

James J, Cherry F (1988). The grief recovery handbook. New York. Harper and Row.

Jenkin P, Koch T, Kralik D (2006). The experience of fatigue for adults living with HIV. J Clin Nurs, Sep; 15(9), 1123-31.

Karpman B (1948). Alcoholic women. Washington, DC. The Linacre Press.

Kohli RM, Sane S, Kumar K, Paranjape RS, Mehendale SM (2005). Assessment of quality of life among HIV-infected persons in Pune, India. Quality of Life Research, 14(6), 1641-47.

Kuber-Ross E (1983). On children and death. New York. Macmillan.

Levine J (1955). The sexual adjustment of alcoholics: A clinical study of a selected sample. Quarterly Journal of studies on Alcohol, 16, 675-80.

Levine S (1982). Who dies? Garden City, NY. Anchor.

Loeser JD (1989). Chronic pain. In FC Seitz, JE Carr and M. Covey [Eds], Issues in Behavioural medicine (pp. 16-20). Bozeman MT. Clinical Management Consultants.

Lucas GM (2001). Management of HIV infection in injecting drug users. Retrieved January 18,2003, from www.medscape.com/view article/418652_print.

Meehan RA, Brush JA (2001). An overview of AIDS dementia complex. American Journal of Alzheimer's Disease, 16 (4), 225-29.

Mintz M (1999). Clinical features and treatment interventions for human immunodeficiency virus-associated neurologic disease in children. Seminars in Neurology, 19, 165-76.

Mitchell W (2001). Neurological and developmental effects of HIV and AIDS in children an adolescents. Mental Retardation and Developmental Disabilities Research Review, 7, 211-16.

Morrison MF, Pettito JM, Have TT, Gettes DR, Chiappini MS, Weber AL et al. (2002). Depressive and anxiety disorders in women with HIV infection. American Journal of Psychiatry, 159(5), 789-96.

New York State Department of health AIDS Institute (2001). Mental health care for people with HIV infection: HIV clinical guidelines for the primary care practitioners. New York.

Nixon S, O'Brien K, Glazier RH, Tynan AM (2005). Aerobic exercise interventions for adults living with HIV/AIDS. Cochrane database Syst Rev, April; 18(2), CD 001796.

O'Brien K, Nixon S, Glazier RH, Tynan AM (2004). Progressive resistive exercise interventions for adults living with HIV/AIDS. Cochrane database Syst Rev, Oct; 18(4), CD004248.

Phillips K, Skelton W (2001). Effects of individualized acupuncture on sleep quality in HIV disease. Journal of the Association of Nurses in AIDS Care, 12(1), 27-39.

Rabkin JG, Wagner GJ, Rabkin R (1999). Fluoxetine treatment for depression in patients with HIV/AIDS: A randomized placebo controlled trial. American Journal of Psychiatry, 156, 101-07.

Rothenberg S (1997). Introduction to sleep disorders. in M. Pressman W Orr [Eds], Understanding sleep: The evaluation and treatment of sleep disorders (pp. 57-72). Washington, DC. American Psychological Association.

Skurnick JH, Bogden JD, baker H, Kemp FW, Sheffet A, Quattrone G et al. (1996). Micronutrient profile in HIV-1-infected heterosexual adults. Journal of Acquired Immune Deficiency Syndromes and Human Retrovirology, 2, 75-83.

Stolarczyk R, Rubio SI, Smolyar D, Young IS, Poretsaky L (1998). Twenty-four-hour urinary free cortisol in patients with acquired immunodeficiency syndrome. Metabolosm, 47, 690-94.

Ungvarski PJ, Trzcianowska H (2000). Neurocognitive disorders seen in HIV disease. Issues in Mental Health Nursing, 21, 51-70.

Van Servellen G, Sarna L, Jablonski KJ (1998). Women with HIV: Living with symptoms. Western Journal of Nursing Research, 20, 448-64.

Wachsler-Felder JL, Golden CJ (2002). Neuropsychological consequences of HIV in children: A review of the current literature. Clinical Psychology review, 22(3), 441-62.

Wessely S, Hotopf M, Sharpe M (1998). Chronic fatigue and its syndromes. Oxford, UK. Oxford University Press.

Whitecar PS, Jonas AP, Clasen ME (2000). Managing pain in the dying patient. Am Fam Physician, Feb 1; 61(3), 755-64.

Some Other Useful References

Ackerman R, Michael J (1990). Recovery source guide (4th edition).Deer field Beach, FL. Health Communication.

Agras WS (1965). An investigation in the decrements of anxiety response during systematic desensitization therapy, Behav. Res. Ther., 2, 267-70.

Alexander JF, Parsons BV (1982). Functional family therapy. Monterey, CA. Brooks/Cole.

Altmaier EM, Ross SL, Leary MR, Thornborugh M (1982). Matching stress inoculation's treatment components to client's anxiety mode. Journal of Counselling Psychology, 29, 331-34.

Anderson PK (1988). Adult children of alcoholics: Coming home. Seattle. Glen Abbey Books.

Aranoff GM, Wagner JM, Spangler AS (1986). Chemical intervention for pain. Journal of Consulting and Clinical Psychology.

Beck A, Rush J, Emery G (1979). Cognitive therapy of depression. New York. Guilford Press.

Beck AT (1976). Cognitive therapy and emotional disorders. New York. International Universities Press.

Bellak AS, Hersen M, Himmelhoch J (1981). Social skill training, pharmacotherapy, and psychotherapy for unipolar depression. American Journal of Psychiatry, 138, 1562.

Bellak L, Small L (1965). Emergency psychotherapy and brief psychotherapy. New York. Grune and Stratton.

Bepko C, Krestan JA (1985). The responsibility trap: A blueprint for training the alcoholic family. New York. The Free Press.

Berman A (1991). Adolescent suicide: Assessment and intervention. Washington, DC. American Psychological Association.

Brown S (1988). Treating adult children alcoholics: A developmental perspective. New York. Wiley.

Chiauzzi E (1991). Preventing relapse in the addictions: A biopsychosocial approach. New York. Pergamon Press.

Daigle B, Lasch K, McCluskey C, Wancho B [Eds]. (2000). HIV Homecare Handbook. Chennai, India. All India Publishers and Distributors.

Daley D (1989). A psycho-educational approach to relapse prevention. Journal of Chemical Dependency Treatment, 2(2), 105-24.

Daley D, Sproule C (1991). Adolescent relapse prevention workbook. Holmes Beach, FL. Learner Publications.

Dewitt KN (1984). Adjustment disorder. In HH Goldman [Ed], Review of general psychiatry, Los Altos, CA. Lange Medical Publications.

Everstine DS, Everstine L (1983). People in crisis; Strategic therapeutic interventions. New York. Brunner/Mazel.

Flor H, Kerns RD, Turk DC (1987). The role of spousal reinforcement, perceived pain and activity level of chronic pain patients. Journal of psychosomatic research, 31(2), 251-59.

Fordyce WE (1976). Behavioural concepts in chronic pain and illness. In PO Davison [ed.], Behavioural management of anxiety, depression and pain. New York. Brunner/Mazel.

Hackett G, Horan JJ (1980). Stress inoculation for pain: What is really going on? Journal of Counselling Psychology, 27, 107-16.

Hay WM, Hay LR, Nelson PO (1977). The adaptation of covert modelling procedures to the treatment of chronic alcoholism and obsessive-compulsive behaviour. Behavioural Therapy, 8, 70-76.

Horowitz MJ (1976). Stress response syndrome. New York. Aronson.

Hoyt MF (1979). Aspects of termination in a brief time-limited psychotherapy. Psychiatry, 42, 208-19.

Hoyt MF (1995). Brief therapy and managed care: Readings form contemporary practice. San Francisco. Jossey-Bass.

Johnson S (1997). Therapist's Guide to Clinical Intervention. London. Academic Press.

Kandal D, Faust R (1975). Sequence and stages in pattern of adolescent drug use. Archives of General Psychiatry, 32, 923-32.

Keefe FJ, Williams DA (1989). New direction in pain assessment and treatment. Clinical Psychology Review, 549-68.

Kirton C [Ed]. (2003). ANAC's Core curriculum for HIV/AIDS Nursing (2nd ed.). Thousand Oaks, CA. Sage Publications.

Kubler-Ross E (1969). On death and dying. New York. Macmillan.

Lewinsohn PM (1974). A behavioural approach to depression. In RJ Friedman and MM Katz [Eds], The psychology of depression. Washington, DC. VH Winston and Sons.

Linton S (1994). Chronic back pain: Integrating psychological and physical therapy- an overview. Behavioural Medicine, 20, 101-04.

Mann J (1973). Time-limited psychotherapy. New York. McGraw-Hill.

Marlott GA, Gordon JR [Eds.]. (1985). Relapse prevention: Maintenance strategies in treatment of addictive behaviours. New York. Guilford Press.

Mash E, Barkley R (1989). Treatment of childhood disorders. New York. Guilford Press.

McKay M, Fanning P (1992). Self-esteem. Oakland, CA. New harbinger Publications.

Meichenbaum DH (1976). A cognitive-behaviour modification approach to assessment. In M Hersen and AS Bellack [Eds.], Behavioural assessment: A practical handbook. New York. Pergamon Press.

Meichenbaum DH, Turk D (1976). The cognitive-behavioural management of anxiety, anger, and pain. In PO Davidson [Ed], The behavioural management of anxiety, depression, and pain. New York. Brunner/Mazel.

Miller W (1989). Matching individuals with interventions: Handbook of alcoholism treatment approaches. New York. Pergamon Press.

Mirin S, Weiss R (1983). Substance abuse. In E Bassuk, S Schoonover and A. Gelenberg [Eds.], The practitioner's guide to psychoactive drugs (pp. 221-90). New York. Plenum Press.

Monti PM, Abrams DB, Kadden RM, Cooney NL (1989). Treating alcohol dependence: A coping skills training guide. New York. Guilford Press.

Patsiokas AJ et al. (1979). Cognitive characteristics of suicidal attempts. Journal of Consulting and Clinical Psychology, 47, 478-484.

Pruder RS (1988). Age analysis of cognitive behavioural group therapy for chronic pain patients.

Psychology and aging, 3(2), 204-07.
Psychotherapy of anorexia nervosa and developmental obesity. In RK Goldstein [Ed], Eating and weight disorders. New York. Springer.
Sifnios P (1972). Short-term psychotherapy and emotional crisis. Cambridge, MA. Harvard University Press.
Simos BG (1979). A time to grieve: Loss as a universal human experience. New York. Family Services Association of America.
Small L (1979). The briefer psychotherapies. New York. Brunner/ Mazel.
Turk D, Genest M (1979). Regulation of pain: The application of cognitive and behavioural techniques for prevention of remediation. In P Kendall and S Holon [Eds.], Cognitive-Behavioural interventions: Theory, research and procedures. New York. Academic Press.
Washton AM (1979). Psychotherapy and substance abuse: A practitioners' handbook. New York. Guilford Press.
Wernick RL (1983). Stress inoculation in the management of clinical pain: Application to burn pain. New York. Norton.
Wetzel RD (1976). Hopelessness, depression and suicidal intent.
Wexler D (1991). The adolescent self: Strategies for self-management, self-soothing, and self-esteem in adolescents. New York. Norton.
Wooten V (1994). Medical causes of insomnia. In MH Kryger, T Roth, and WC Dement [Eds.], Principles and practice for sleep medicines (2nd ed) (pp. 509-22). Philadelphia. Saunders.
Yapko M (1990). When living hurts: Directives for treating depression. New York. Brunner/Mazel.
Zorick F (1994). Overview of insomnia. In MH Kryger, T Roth, and WC Dement [Eds.], Principles and practice for sleep medicines (2nd ed) (pp. 483-85). Philadelphia. Saunders.
Zweben JE (1992). Issues in the treatment of the dual diagnosis patient. In BC Wallace [Ed], The chemically dependent: Phases of treatment and recovery. New York. Brunner/Mazel.

6

Effects of Counselling on HIV/AIDS Patients

N.V.V.S. Narayana

Introduction

AIDS is considered one of the most serious public health problems in modern history. AIDS stands for acquired immune deficiency syndrome. The disease is caused by a virus known as the human immunodeficiency virus (HIV). The first reported AIDS related fatalities occurred in 1981 (Altman, 1981), and in 1982, scientist began to use the term, "Acquired Immunodeficiency Syndrome (AIDS)".

A person can be infected with HIV without developing AIDS. The virus can remain in a person's body for many years without causing serious health problems. During this period, the virus is said to be latent, or inactive. Eventually, however, most people who are infected with HIV do develop AIDS. By definition, "AIDS is the end-stage disease manifestation of an infection with a virus called the human immunodeficiency virus (HIV).

HIV infects mainly two systems in the body, the Immune system and the central nervous system, and disease manifestation are consequent on damage to these two systems" (Schoub, 1999). As a result, HIV-positive persons might face a chronic disease that is typically characterized by having an uncertain course, lead to progressive physical decline, and cause increased dependency on medical interventions (Lutgendorf, Antoni, Schneiderman, and Fletcher, 1994). Treatment of HIV patients involves trying to slow or stop the virus from spreading in the body's cells and treating or preventing diseases that develop when a person's immune system has been damaged by the virus.

Route of Transmission

This virus may be passed from one person to another when infected blood, infected hypodermic needle, semen, or vaginal secretions come in contact with an uninfected person's broken skin or mucous membranes. And also the infected pregnant women can pass HIV to their baby during pregnancy or delivery, as well as through breast-feeding. People with HIV have what is called HIV infection.

Epidemiology

AIDS is a far worse problem in some parts of the world than it is in others. Two forms of HIV are now recognized: HIV-1, which causes most cases of AIDS in Europe, North and South America, and most parts of Africa. HIV-2 type virus is more prevalent in Western Africa.

HIV/AIDS is a significant cause of death and disability, especially in low- and middle-income countries. The World Health Organization (WHO, 2007) estimated that 32.2 million adults and 1.2 million children worldwide were infected with HIV/AIDS as of 1998. Most of these cases occur in the developing countries of Asia and Africa.

HIV/AIDS Prevalence in India

India has a population of more than 1 billion people. India stands second most affected Country in the world after South Africa. More than 4.5 million of the population was recognized as HIV/AIDS positive.

However, in terms of percentage about 0.7 percent of India's population is infected with HIV. This epidemic is fast spreading; mainly in the southern and western states of the country. The epidemic in the western and southern states is primarily heterosexual. The north-eastern states of India, being in geographical proximity to the Golden Triangle of Asia, initially experienced HIV in the injection drug user population and their sexual partners, but spread to the heterosexual population has been increasing.

At present, the northern states, which are the most densely populated, appear to remain largely unaffected by the HIV epidemic. India's socio-economic status, traditional social ills, cultural myths on sex and sexuality and a huge population of marginalized people has made India extremely vulnerable to the HIV/AIDS epidemic. Antiretroviral drugs are manufactured in the country and exported elsewhere, and the government of India has announced free provision of ART drugs to all who need it from 2004.

HIV and Mental Health Issues

The World Health Organization (WHO) estimates that 450 million people live with a mental illness or behavioural disorder worldwide. Mental health and HIV/AIDS are closely interlinked; mental health problems, including substance-use disorders, are associated with increased risk of HIV infection and AIDS and interfere with their treatment, and conversely some mental disorders occur as a direct result of HIV infection. Studies have demonstrated a high prevalence of HIV infection in people with serious chronic mental illnesses.

Prevalence of HIV in mentally ill inpatients and outpatients have been reported to be between 5 percent and 23 percent, compared with a range of 0.3 percent to 0.4 percent in the general population in the United States of America over comparable time periods. Some studies have reported behavioural risk factors for transmission of HIV in between 30 percent and 60 percent of people with severe mental illnesses. These risks include high rates of sexual contact with multiple partners, injecting drug use, sexual contact with injecting drug users, sexual abuse (in which women are particularly vulnerable to HIV (infection), unprotected sex between men and low use of condoms. Besides these behavioural risks, mental disorders may also interfere with the ability to acquire and/or use information about HIV/AIDS and thus to practice safer behaviours or increase the likelihood of situations occurring in which risk behaviours are more common.

HIV/AIDS imposes a significant psychological burden. People with HIV often suffer from depression and anxiety as they adjust to the impact of the diagnosis of being infected and face the difficulties of living with a chronic life-threatening illness, for instance shortened life expectancy, complicated therapeutic regimens, stigmatization, and loss of social support, family or friends. HIV infection can be associated with high risk of suicide or attempted suicide. The psychological predictors of suicidal ideation in HIV-infected individuals include concurrent substance-use disorders, past history of depression and presence of hopelessness.

Apart from psychological impact, HIV infection has direct effects on the central nervous system, and causes neuropsychiatric complications including HIV encephalopathy, depression, mania, cognitive disorder, and frank dementia, often in combination. Infants and children with HIV infection are more likely to experience deficits in motor and cognitive development compared with HIV negative children.

The expansion of AIDS treatment initiatives in resource poor settings provides an opportunity for integrating mental health care into HIV treatment. The WHO recommends that attention to the psychosocial needs of people with AIDS should be an integral part of HIV care. This includes assistance with employment, income, housing, spouse HIV status, coping with stigma and discrimination, and prevention and treatment of mild and serious mental health problems. Mental health care has been integrated into HIV programs in rich countries for many years as a result of substantial evidence of linkages between mental health and HIV.

North American and European studies suggest that people with HIV often suffer from depression and anxiety disorders as they adjust to the diagnosis, struggle with the meaning of a positive HIV test result, adapt to life with a chronic, life-threatening illness, anticipate and receive news of the disease's advance, and witness the death of friends and family. Bing et al. found a 36 percent 1-year prevalence of depression and 16 percent prevalence of anxiety among a large national sample of HIV-positive men and women in the United States. A meta-analysis of studies comparing HIV-positive and HIV-negative samples showed that major depressive disorder occurred nearly twice as often among HIV-positive than HIV-negative patients.

Anxiety in HIV Positives

Anxiety is a common symptom in HIV-infected patients. When anxiety symptoms are severe or persistent in HIV patients may have an anxiety disorder. These disorders include panic disorder, generalized anxiety disorder, obsessive-compulsive disorder, and post-traumatic stress disorder (PTSD). Anxiety-like symptoms may also be caused by mental health disorders other than anxiety disorders. It may be difficult to distinguish depression with agitation from an adjustment disorder with anxious mood which is characterized by insomnia, diminished appetite, diurnal variation in mood, loss of pleasure/interest, feelings of guilt, fatigue, and attention and concentration problems.

HIV/AIDS is one disease that does not exist in isolation. It impacts not just the physical but also the psychological and emotional well-being of the person with HIV/AIDS as well as the family system. A number of studies have shown that a HIV positive diagnosis often results in stigma and fear of death, both of which can lead to depression, anxiety, somatic complaints, and suicidal ideations (Jacobson, Perry, and Hirsch, 1990).

Quality of Life (QoL) of HIV Positives

Vital issues like QOL have come to limelight with a booming increase in HIV/AIDS cases in these countries. WHO has defined QOL as "Individual's perception of their position in life in the context of the culture and value systems in which they live and in relation to their goals, expectations, standards, and concerns".

Social support is another aspect of the disease that directly impacts the quality of living, and the mental health of people and families living with HIV/AIDS. It is widely believed that social support buffers the impact of a wide variety of stressful life-events including chronic illnesses (Cohen and Wills, 1985).

Counselling in HIV/AIDS

Counselling is a helping process where; one person explicitly and purposefully, gives his/her time, attention and skills to assist a client to explore his/her situation, identify and act upon solutions within the limitations of the given environment.

Counselling provides psychosocial support and strengthens the sense of individual responsibility needed if people are to build on new information and modify their life styles. This involves helping people to define for themselves the nature of the problems they are facing and then make realistic decisions about what they can do to reduce the impact of these problems on themselves and their family and friends. Therefore, helping people to achieve the confidence to bring about positive changes in their life style is an integral part of the counselling relationship.

Nurses undoubtedly play an important role as counsellor in health care. All of us are aware that in a hospital as well as community setting the client requires cure and care. The American Nurses' Association defines "Care" as providing comfort and support in times of anxiety, loneliness and helplessness. As caring people, nurses are perceived as reliable sources of health information and people often feel more comfortable discussing personal matters with them than with others.

HIV/AIDS counselling is recommended for the following: (a) Persons who are being tested for HIV [Pre and Post-testing] (b) Persons seeking help because of past or current risk behaviour and planning their future. (c) Those not seeking help, but who practice high risk behaviour.

Types of Situation in which HIV/AIDS Counselling is of value:

1. People with AIDS or other disease related to their HIV infection.
2. People experiencing difficulties with employment, housing, finances, family etc. as a result of HIV infection.
3. People considering being tested for HIV.
4. The family and friends of people who are infected with HIV.
5. People worried that they might have become infected with HIV.
6. Health professionals who come into regular contact with people infected with HIV/AIDS.

Counselling as a process can:

- ensure passing on of correct information,
- provide support at times of crisis,
- encourage change when change is needed for the prevention or control of infection,
- help clients focus and identify for themselves their immediate and long-term needs,
- propose realistic action suitably adopted to the different clients and circumstances,

- assist clients to accept and act on information on health and well being, and
- help clients to be well informed and appreciate the technical, social, ethical and legal implications of HIV testing.

Principles of Counselling: *Counselling should*

- be tailor made to the requirement of an individual problem.
- emphasize on thinking with the individual.
- avoid dictatorial attitude.
- build relationship of trust and confidence with the client.
- Stress on client need.

Counselling skills:

A good counsellor needs to possess the following counselling skills:

1. Active listening: Listening is the most important skill the counsellor must possess. In addition to this, observing the non-verbal messages of the client, encouraging the client to talk by nodding the head and saying 'go on' is very important, counsellor should pay his total attention to what is being said,
2. Summarizing and paraphrasing: This means restating by the counsellor in his/her own words what the client has said to check whether it has been understood correctly,
3. Empathy: In empathizing with a client, the counsellor leaves aside his/her own frame of reference, and for the time being adopts the frame of reference of the client and then appreciates how the client experiences the events in his/her world. It is essential that the counsellor must communicate to the client that his/her feelings are being understood.

Importance of counselling in HIV/AIDS

Counselling in HIV/AIDS is important because:

- Infection with HIV is life-long!
- a diagnosis of HIV infection can create enormous psychological pressures and anxieties that can delay constructive change or worsen illness, especially as the HIV epidemic has given rise to fear, misunderstanding and discrimination!

Behavioural change can prevent a person from contracting HIV infection or transmitting it to others.

Functions of Counselling in HIV/AIDS

Counselling in HIV/AIDS has two main functions: (a) the provision of social and psychological support to those infected with HIV; (b) the prevention of HIV infection and its transmission to other people.

HIV/AIDS counselling should include discussions on the following:

- The primary need to prevent infection and re-infection.
- Basic information about HIV infection and associated diseases and means of transmission.
- Assessment of the level of risk of HIV infection.
- Review of possible sources of client's infection.
- Specific information on risk reduction by changing behaviour or adopting safer sexual practices.
- Information about what testing can and cannot do and assessment of consequences of having the HIV antibody test.
- Follow-up guidance after testing has been done
- How to tell others that one is HIV infected.
- Handling hostility, fear and feelings about having infection or being diagnosed as having AIDS.

When a person is diagnosed with HIV, counselling must also include:

- Supporting the process of anticipatory grief.
- Planning for continued involvement of client in self care.
- Establishing or re-establishing a support network to provide physical and emotional care during the course of disease.
- Exploring ways of taking care of survivors.
- Accepting fear of death and continuing to provide emotional support.

Finally, HIV/AIDS counselling is aimed at providing psychosocial support and preventing HIV infection. Psychosocial support is necessary because diagnosis of HIV infection confronts people with a host of emotional and practical problems.

Counselling in the context of prevention can take the form of primary prevention, intended for people at risk but not known to be infected and secondary prevention, where clients are known or thought to be infected. Primary prevention focuses on risk behaviour, while the man emphasis in secondary prevention is on preventing transmission.

Aim

To examine the effect of counselling on HIV/AIDS patients.

Sample

The study was conducted on a sample of 100 patients infected with HIV/AIDS. The researcher approached the NGO counsellors at their work place and asked them to obtain data from the patients. The sample was selected from east Godavari district.

The total sample of the study consisted of 100 HIV/AIDS infected patients. Among them 50 patients were males and 50 were females. The age range of the sample is 20 to 54 years. Average age is 31.5. Sample was stratified on the basis of Education, Income, Family type, Alcohol and Smoking habits (Table 6.1).

Table 6.1: Sample Characteristics

S.N	Characteristics	Sample Number
1	Total Sample Size	100
2	Educated Group	65
3	Uneducated Group	35
4	Male	50
5	Female	50
6	Below 30 years	59
7	Above 30 years	41
8	Average Age	31.5
9	Income Blow 1500	65
10	Income Above 1500	35
11	Nuclear Family	75
12	Joint Family	25
13	Alcoholics	32
14	Non-Alcoholics	68
15	Smokers	31
16	Non-Smokers	69

Measures

Biographical data sheet and General Health Questionnaire were used to collect the data. Biographical data sheet: It was developed by the researcher to identify the various demographic variables. These demographic variables are Age, Gender, Education, Income, Family type, Alcohol and Smoking habits.

General Health Questionnaire

The scale used in this study was developed by D.P. Gold Berg and V.H. Hiller (1979). The scale has four factors "Somatic Symptoms", "Anxiety and Insomnia", "Social Dysfunction" and "Severe Depression". The scale consists of 7 items in each factor. The responses are scores according to the weightage of 0 to 1 (much more than usual to not at all). It was translated into Telugu for the convenience of the common people.

Procedure

Sample was identified with the support of a local Non Government Organization (NGO) in East Godavari District. The participants, upon diagnosed with HIV, were initially administered General Health Questionnaire (GHQ) and Biographical Data Sheet. All the participants were provided with four sessions of counselling to cope with the psychological distress by the NGO counsellors. All these four sessions were conducted within a period of one month. After the completion of counselling sessions, all the participants were again administered GHQ and Biographical data sheet. The total procedure was done with the help of NGO's counsellors.

Analysis of Data

Data obtained from the sample was analyzed using the following statistical techniques. t-test to examine the influence of Gender, Education, Alcohol and Smoking habits, Effected Groups and Pre-test and Post-test results. SPSS 13.0 was used to analyze the data.

Results and Discussion

Table 6.2 indicates that the significance of difference between Male and Female groups on GHQ factors. It is observed that there are some significant differences on factors namely Somatic Symptoms, Anxiety and Insomnia, Social Dysfunction and Severe Depression observed. From these results it is noted that both the groups have significantly differed in GHQ dimensions. It shows the male group has more somatic symptoms, anxiety and severe depression than female group. Male group members were more social dysfunction and insomnia problems than counter group. In Indian culture most of the families would be depends on males, that is also one of the chance factor of men having this problems.

Table 6.3 indicates significance of difference in between Uneducated and Educated groups on GHQ factors. It is observed that there are some factors of GHQ, i.e., Somatic Symptoms ($t=2.358$, $p<=0.05$), Anxiety and insomnia ($t=2.520$, $p<=0.05$) and Social Dysfunction ($t=2.135$, $p<=0.05$) differed significantly in between the uneducated and educated groups. The results indicate that uneducated group has more somatic symptoms, anxiety, social dysfunction and insomniac rather than educated group. There is no significance difference is found between these two groups on the factor severe depression, but it is also observed from the mean values, that the uneducated group has more depression than educated group, because, lack of education and illiteracy, the uneducated group may need to have more understanding about HIV and sex education. They need some special education about HIV/AIDS and Reproductive Health.

Table 6.2: Significance of Differences between Male and Female Groups on GHQ Factors in Pre Test (N=100)

GHQ Factors		Male (N=50)	Female (N=50)	t value
Somatic symptoms	Mean	4.60	3.04	2.668**
	S.D.	2.871	2.976	
Anxiety and insomnia	Mean	4.26	2.76	2.488**
	S.D.	3.174	2.847	
Social dysfunction	Mean	4.22	2.58	2.770**
	S.D.	3.241	2.650	
Severe depression	Mean	4.26	2.98	2.032*
	S.D.	3.250	3.047	

*P≤0.05, **P≤0.01

Table 6.3: Significance of Differences between Uneducated and Educated Groups on GHQ Factors in Pre Test (N=100)

GHQ Factors		Uneducated (N=35)	Educated (N=65)	t value
Somatic symptoms	Mean	4.74	3.32	2.358*
	S.D.	2.780	3.037	
Anxiety and insomnia	Mean	4.51	2.97	2.520**
	S.D.	2.811	3.122	
Social dysfunction	Mean	4.26	2.94	2.135*
	S.D.	2.873	3.077	
Severe depression	Mean	4.43	3.18	1.935
	S.D.	2.953	3.264	

*P≤0.05, **P≤0.01

Table 6.4 shows the mean differences between Alcoholic and Non-alcoholic groups on GHQ factors. The results indicated that Somatic Symptoms (t=2.420. p<=0.05), Anxiety and Insomnia (t=-2.649, p<=0.05), Social Dysfunction (t=-2.909, p<=0.05), and Severe Depression (t=-2.123, p<=0.01) dimensions are differed significantly in between the Alcoholic and Non-Alcoholic groups. It can be noted that Alcoholic group differed significantly high on these factors when compared to the non-alcoholic group. It shows that the alcoholic group has more somatic symptoms, anxiety, social dysfunction, severe depression and insomniac.

Table 6.4: Significance of Differences between Non-alcoholic and Alcoholic Groups on GHQ Factors in Pre Test (N=100)

GHQ Factors		Non-Alcoholic (N=68)	Alcoholic (N=32)	t value
Somatic symptoms	Mean	3.32	4.88	-2.420*
	S.D.	2.893	3.035	
Anxiety and insomnia	Mean	2.94	4.72	-2.649**
	S.D.	2.870	3.245	
Social dysfunction	Mean	2.78	4.72	-2.909**
	S.D.	2.774	3.255	
Severe depression	Mean	3.15	4.63	-2.123*
	S.D.	3.043	3.338	

*P≤0.05, **P≤0.01

Table 6.5 shows the significance of difference between Non-smoking and smoking groups on GHQ factors. It is observed that there are some factors of GHQ, i.e., Somatic Symptoms (t=-2.076, p<=0.05) and Anxiety and Insomnia (t=-2.070, p<=0.05) differed significantly in between the non-smoking and smoking groups. The results indicate that smoking group has higher scores on these factors, shows smoking group have more somatic symptoms, anxiety and insomnia problems than non-smoking group. There is no significance difference found in between these two groups on Social dysfunction and severe depression factors. It is also observed from the mean values that the smoking group has more mean values on these factors when compared to the non-smoking group.

Table 6.5: Significance of Differences between Non-smoking and Smoking Groups on GHQ Factors in Pre Test (N=100)

GHQ Factors		Non-Smoking (N=69)	Smoking (N=31)	t value
Somatic symptoms	Mean	3.14	4.74	-2.076*
	S.D.	2.952	2.989	
Anxiety and insomnia	Mean	3.07	4.48	-2.070*
	S.D.	2.942	3.244	
Social dysfunction	Mean	3.00	4.29	-1.860
	S.D.	2.849	3.359	
Severe depression	Mean	3.30	4.32	-1.443
	S.D.	3.112	3.331	

*P≤0.05, **P≤0.01

Table 6.6 indicates significance of difference between effected groups (spouse, others) on GHQ factors. It is observed that there is one factor of GHQ, i.e., Social Dysfunction (t=-2.419, p<=0.05) differed significantly in between spouse and others groups. It can be noted that others group has more mean value than spouse group, which means other group has high social dysfunction rather than counter group. There is no significance difference in between these two groups on somatic symptoms, anxiety and insomnia and severe depression. It is also observed from the mean values, others group has more mean value on these factors then spouse group. It can be noted that those who got HIV/AIDS from others, they have more somatic symptoms, anxiety and insomnia and severe depression.

Table 6.6: Significance of Differences between Effected Groups on GHQ Factors in Pre Test (N=100)

GHQ Factors		Spouse (N=46)	Others (N=54)	t value
Somatic symptoms	Mean	3.20	4.35	-1.938
	S.D.	2.979	2.966	
Anxiety and insomnia	Mean	2.91	4.02	-1.819
	S.D.	2.858	3.218	
Social dysfunction	Mean	2.63	4.06	-2.419*
	S.D.	2.619	3.270	
Severe depression	Mean	3.24	3.94	-1.107
	S.D.	3.056	3.310	

*P≤0.05, **P≤0.01

Table 6.7 presents the results, the HIV/AIDS patients displayed decreased score on all the four factors as indicated by statistically significance of means between pre and post testing. A decrease of nearly 3.5 points on the factor 'Somatic Symptoms', an initial mean of 3.82 (SD=3.013) to a mean of 0.20 (SD=1.044; t=111.236; p<=0.01). Anxiety and Insomnia factor scores also showed a significant change, from an initial mean of 3.51 (SD=3.093) to a mean of 0.17 (SD=0.943) on this factor (t=10.120, p<=0.01). Social Dysfunction factor also showed a significant decrease, from 3.40(SD=3.058) to 0.23 (SD=1.109; t=9.407, p<=0.01). Severe Depression factor also showed a significant decrease, from 3.62(SD=3.20) to 0.17(SD=0.17; t=10.291, p<=0.01). In the above results, effect of counselling shows significant results on GHQ factors. So that we can say that counselling plays a very important role in the treatment of HIV/AIDS patients and also it helps to the patients how to lead a better life.

Table 6.7: Significance of Differences between the Pre Test and Post Test on GHQ Factors (N=100)

GHQ Factors		Pre Test	Post Test	t value
Somatic symptoms	Mean	3.82	0.20	11.236**
	S.D.	3.013	1.044	
Anxiety and insomnia	Mean	3.51	0.17	10.120**
	S.D.	3.093	0.943	
Social dysfunction	Mean	3.40	0.23	9.407**
	S.D.	3.058	1.109	
Severe depression	Mean	3.62	0.17	10.291**
	S.D.	3.200	0.995	

*P≤0.05, **P≤0.01

Conclusion

As we know infection with HIV/AIDS is life long, the diagnosis of HIV infection can create enormous psychological depression, pressures and anxieties that can delay constructive change or worsen illness, especially as the HIV epidemic has given rise to fear, misunderstanding and discrimination. Behavioural change can prevent a person from contracting HIV infection or transmitting it to others and taking care of themselves for better life. The findings of the present study indicate that counselling has significantly beneficial effects on the mental health of the individuals infected with HIV/AIDS.

References

Bennett and James (1993). Quality of life of HIV-infected patients with chronic diarrhoea. *Journal of Acquired Immune Deficiency Syndromes*, Vol. 18, 158-164.

Blalock (2001). Effect of employment on quality of life and psychological functioning in patients with HIV/AIDS. *Journal of Psychosomatics,* Vol.43, 400-404.

Broekhluzen, A. (1998). Survey of Pan European attitude to HIV. Presentation at the *12th World AIDS Conference*, Geneva (Abstract #32345).

Burke and Dennis (2002). Effects of depressive symptoms and mental health quality of life on use of highly active antiretroviral therapy among HIV-seropositive women. *Journal of Acquired Immune Deficiency Syndromes,* Vol.30(4):401-409.

Chandra, P.S., Deepti Varma, S., Jairam, K.R., and Thomas, T. (2003). Relationship of psychological morbidity and quality of life to illness-related disclosure among HIV-infected persons. *Journal of Psychosomatic Research, 54,* 199-203.

Chesney, M. A., Folkman, S. (1999). The burden on health-related quality of life associated with gender. *Journal of Sexually Transmitted Diseases*, Vol. 3, 987-992.

Chung (2000). The relationship between traumatic stress and death anxiety among community residents. *Easthope Death Studies*, Vol. 24, 689- 704.

Cohen, S. (1988). Psychological models of the role of social support in the etiology of physical diseases. *Health Psychology, 7,* 269-297.

Cohen, S., and Willis, T.A. (1985). Stress, social support and the buffering hypothesis. *Psychological Bulletin, 98,* 310-357.

Collins, P. (2006). Health-related quality of life in patients with human immunodeficiency virus infection in the United States: *The American Journal of Medicine,* Volume 108, 714-722.

D' Cruz – Grofe. (1996). Doris: Prevention of HIV infection in Developing countries. The Lancet, Vol.348, 1071-74.

Fleishman and McCaffrey, (1996). Social support and HIV, *Psychological and Socio-medical Aspects of AIDS/HIV*, Vol. 5, 87-104.

Frey, L.R., Query, J.L., Flint, L.J., and Adelman, M.B. (1998). Living together with AIDS: Social support processes in a residential facility. In V.J. Derlega and A.P. Barbee (Eds.), *HIV and social interactions* (pp. 129-146). Thousand Oaks, CA: Sage.

Friedland, J., Renwick, R., and McColl, M. (1996). Coping and social support as determinants of quality of life in HIV/AIDS. *Psychological and Socio-medical Aspects of HIV/AIDS*, Vol. 8, 15-32.

GOI (1996). HIV/AIDS: Prevention, Care and Control. Self instructional module; for pre-service and in-service Nurses and Midwives, National AIDS Control Organisation, MOHFW.

GOI (1997). HIV/AIDS in India: A status report, National AIDS Control Organisation. MOHFW.

Hays, R.B., Magee, R.H., and Chauncey, S. (1994). Identifying helpful and unhelpful behaviours of loved ones: The PWA's perspective. *AIDS Care, 6,* 379-392.

Hays, R.B., McKusick, L., Pallack, L., Hilliard, R., Hoff, C., and Coates, T.J. (1993). Disclosing HIV seropositivity to significant other. *AIDS, 7,* 425-431.

Herek, G.M., and Capitano, J.P. (1993). Public reactions to AIDS in the United States: A second decade of stigma. *American Journal of Public Health, 83,* 886-891.

Herek, G.M., and Glunt, E.K. (1988). An epidemic of stigma: Public reactions to AIDS. *American Psychologist, 43,* 886-891.

Jacobson, P., Perry, S., and Hirsch, D. (1990). Behavioural and psychological responses to HIV antibody testing. *Journal of Consulting and Clinical Psychology, 58,* 31-37.

Kelly, J.A., Murphy, D.A., Bhar, G.R., Koob, J.J., Morgan, M.G., Kalichman, S.C., Stevenson, L.Y., Brasfield, T.L., Bernstein, B.M., and St. Lawrence, J.S. (1993). Factors associated with severity of depression and high risk sexual behaviour among persons diagnosed with human immunodeficiency virus (HIV) infection. *Health Psychology, 12,* 215-219.

Koopman. C (2000). Relationships of perceived stress to coping, attachment and social support among HIV-positive persons. *Psychological and Socio-medical Aspects of AIDS/HIV*, Vol. 12, 663-672.

Leary, M.R., and Schreindorger, L.S. (1998). The stigmatization of HIV and AIDS: Rubbing salt in the wound. In V.J. Derlega and A.P. Barbee (Eds.), *HIV and Social Interactions* (pp. 12-29). Thousand Oaks, CA: Sage.

Leserman, J., Jackson, E.D., Pettitto, J.M., Golden, R.N., Silva, S.G., Perkins, D.O., Cai, J., Folds, J.D., and Evans, D.L. (1999). Progression to AIDS: The effects of stress, depressive symptoms, and social support. *Psychosomatic Medicine, 61,* 397-406.

Lutgendorf, S., Antoni, M.A., Schneiderman, N., and Fletcher, M.A. (1994). Psychosocial counselling to improve quality of life in HIV infection. *Patient Education and Counselling, 24,* 217-235.

Marks, G., Richardson, J.L., Ruiz, M.S., and Maldonado, N. (1992). Social Relations, Coping, and Psychological Distress Among Persons With HIV/AIDS: *Psychological and Socio-medical Aspects of AIDS/HIV,* Vol. 16, 62-74.

Mason, H.R.C., Simoni, J.M., Marks, G., Johnson, C.J., and Richardson, J.L. (1997). Missed opportunity? Disclosure of HIV infection and support seeking among HIV+ African-American and European-American men. *AIDS and Behaviour, 1,*155-162.

Mast and Kigozi (2004). Measuring quality of life among HIV-infected women using a culturally adapted questionnaire in Rakai district, Uganda. *Psychological and Socio-medical Aspects of AIDS/HIV*, Vol. 16, 81–94.

McDonnell and Faden (2000). Quality of life among women living with HIV: the importance violence, social support, and self care behaviours. *JAIDS Journal of Acquired Immune Deficiency Syndromes,* 32(1):38-47.

Nirmal. B (2008). Quality of life in HIV/AIDS patients: A cross-sectional study in south India, *Institute of Venereology, Madras Medical College*, Chennai, India; Vol:29, 15-17.

Nott, K., Vedhara (1995). The role of social support in HIV Infection. Journal of Psychological Medicine, Vol. 25, 971-984.

Pakenham (1994). Relationship between adjustment to HIV and both social support and coping. *Journal of Consulting and Clinical Psychology,* Vol. 62, 1194-1203.

Saxena. S. (2001). Quality of life in HIV patients: *Journal of Quality of Life Research*, Vol. 8, 711-721.

Schoub, B.D. (1999). *AIDS and HIV in perspective: A guide to understanding the virus and its consequences.* New York: Cambridge University Press.

Seals. G. (1997). The relative importance of social (social support, material resources, disclosure, and family functioning) and psychological factors in HIV patients. *Psychological and Socio-medical Aspects of AIDS/HIV*, Vol. 9, 501- 512.

Simoni, Jane M. (2006). Symptoms of posttraumatic stress and death anxiety in persons with HIV and medication adherence difficulties, *AIDS Patient Care and STDs*, Vol.17 (12), 657-664.

Simoni, Simoni, J.M., Mason, H.R.C., Marks, G., Ruiz, M.S., Reed, D., and Richardson, J.L. (1995). A longitudinal evaluation of a social support model of medication adherence among HIV-positive men and women on antiretroviral therapy. *Journal of Health Psychology,* Vol. 25(1), 74-81.

Song, Y.S., and Ingram, K.M. (2002). Unsupportive social interactions, availability of social support, and coping: Their relationship to mood disturbance among African American living with HIV. *Journal of Social and Personal Relationship, 19,* 67-71.

Steven. A. Safren (2003). Symptoms of posttraumatic stress and death Anxiety in persons with HIV. *Psychological Monograph,* Vol. 80, 61-75.

Subramanian. ,Thilakavathi (2008). Psycho-social impact and quality of life of people living with HIV/AIDS in South India. *Psychological and Socio-medical Aspects of AIDS/HIV*, Vol. 21, 473-481.

Wallston, B.S., Alagna, S.W., DeVellis, B., McE., and DeVellis, R.F. (1983). Social support and physical health. *Health Psychology, 2,* 367-391.

WHO (1993). An Orientation to HIV/AIDS Counselling; A Guide for Trainers; pp. 27-35.

7

Awareness of HIV/AIDS among School Going and School Dropout Adolescent Girls: A Case Study of Jammu City

Nidhi Kotwal and Bharti Prabhakar

Introduction

Adolescents represent a major potential human resources for the over all development of a nation. Reproductive health is an important component of general health, it is a perquisite for social and economic and imperative because human energy and creativity are the driving forces of development.

Approximately one billion people-nearly one out of every six persons on the planet are adolescents: Eighty-five percents live in developing countries. Many adolescent are sexually active (although not always by choice) and, in some regions, are many as half are married. Sexual activity puts adolescents at risk of various reproductive health challenges. Each year about 15 million adolescents aged 15-19 years give birth; as many as 4 million obtain an abortion and up to 100 million become infected with a curable sexually transmitted disease (STD). Globally, forty percent of all new human immuno deficiency virus (HIV) infections occur among 15-24 years olds; recent estimates are that 7, 000 are infected each day. These health risks are influenced by many interrelated factors, such as expectations concerning early marriage and sexual relationships access to education and employment, gender inequities, sexual violence, and the influence of mass media and popular culture.

Adolescents often lack basic reproductive health information, skills in negotiating sexual relationships and access to affordable, confidential reproductive health services concerns about privacy or the ability to pay, and real or perceived disapproval by services where they exist, as do legal barriers to information and services. Many adolescents lack strong stable relationships with parents or other adults whom they can talk to about their reproductive health concerns.

Young people tend to be at higher risk of contracting STDs, including HIV/AIDS, for several reasons, Intercourse often is unplanned or unwanted. Even when sex is consensual, adolescents often do no plan a head for condom or other contraceptive use, and inexperienced users are more unlikely to use methods incorrectly. Further more, adolescents girls are at greater risk of infection than older women because of the immaturity of their reproductive system (WHO, 1998).

Many adolescents do not have the ability or social support to resist pressure to have sexual relations, negotiate safer sex, or protect themselves against unintended pregnancy and STIs. WHO is committed to protecting the sexual and reproductive health and fights for adolescents and facilitating their healthy transition to adulthood, particularly with regard to strengthening health sector capacity to provide accurate information, high quality counselling, and adolescent friendly, comprehensive sexual and reproductive health care (UNFPA 1995).

Sexuality is a natural and intrinsic part of an individual's personality and needs to be nurtured and developed like all other facts of life. This fact is completely ignored by parents and teachers in our society, because they themselves do not feel comfortable in discussing their issues with the youngsters, and moreover they are not much knowledgeable on this subject. They have inhibition about discussing and expressing themselves on sex-related issues. They rather discourage the children from any form of sexual expression and encourage them to hide their sexuality. In the Indian socio-cultural setting sex is a taboo, and hence the society does not provide them with channels for being appropriately educated in this area. The adolescents generally do no get any advice and guidance regarding, various aspects like puberty, menarche, reproductive health, HIV/AIDS from their parents and teachers or any other groups of professionals.

With the onset of puberty and accompanying physiological changes, these adolescents are unable to cope with their increased curiosity and interest in the subject. They turn to unreliable sources for information, such as friends, poems, movies, television, cheap books, etc, which in turn may make them vulnerable to various misconceptions born out of unscientific knowledge. These myths are the cause of many sexual disorders and remain ingrained in their psyche making it difficult to eradicate subsequently.

A preliminary survey of the previous studies, discussion and experience relating to reproductive health among adolescent girls revealed various NGO's and International agencies, including WHO, UNAIDS, UNFPF, UNICEF and UNCHR and at the National Level ICDS, SNP, ANP, SEWA, CHETNA, CSWB, working on reproductive health issues. There is meagre development in the reproductive field. Hence the present study was undertaken with the following objectives.

1. To study the knowledge of adolescent girls regarding:

- Reproductive anatomy.

- Teenage pregnancy/abortions.
- AIDS/STDs/HIV.

2. To identify the sources from where they get information, source preference for acquiring further information and strategies for reproductive health education.

Methodology

The study was conducted in village Poni-Chakh and Ramgarh areas of Jammu District. Poni-Chakh is about 18 kms and Ramgarh is about 45 kms from the heart of Jammu City. Majority of the people in both villages are employed in agriculture and working as labourers. The sample comprised of 100 rural adolescent girls in the age group of 12-17 yrs. A sample of 50 adolescent girls was selected from Ponichak village and 50 adolescent girls were from Ramgarh village, of Jammu City. From each village 25 Adolescent school going and 25 adolescent dropout girls were selected by using snowball technique. An interview schedule was used for data collection. Discussion was also done with students and the School Authorities. In case of School Dropout Girls, data was collected by home visits. Data were tabulated for precise and systematic analysis for the presentation of results.

Result and Discussion

General Information: The data were collected to obtain background information about the respondents regarding their age, education, caste status, type of family and monthly income of the family.

Majority of the school going girls (90 percent) and school dropout girls (80 percent) were in the age groups of 15-17 years. The rest (10 percent) of school going and (20 percent) of school dropout girls belonged to the age group 12-17 years.

Majority of the school going girls (80 percent) were studying in 10-12th class. Most of the school dropout girls (58 percent) had education up to 7th to 9th standard and rest of the school dropout girls (42 percent) had education up to 10th to 12th class.

Majority of the school dropout girls (70 percent) belonged to joint family system, whereas most of the school going girls (58 percent) belonged to nuclear family and the rest (42 percent) belonged to joint family.

Monthly income of the family of school going girls (52 percent) and (40 percent) school dropout girls was between Rs. 5,000 to Rs. 7,000. For (24 percent) school going girls and (30 percent) school dropout girls the family income was Rs. 3,000 to Rs. 5,000.

Knowledge of Various Aspects of Reproductive Health

Reproductive Health is state of complete physical, mental and social well being and not merely the absence of reproductive disease or infirmity. It deals with the Reproductive process, functions and systems at all stages of life.

It is clear from Table 7.1 that school dropout girls had more knowledge of reproductive system as compared to school going girls but this difference in the knowledge level related to reproductive system was not significant. Knowledge of reproductive system focused on (a) Identification of reproductive system (b) Knowledge of female reproductive organs (c) Knowledge of male reproductive organs (d) conceivable age of women (e) Reproductive age of men.

- Sixty eight percent of school going girls and (74 percent) of school dropout girls could identify the reproductive system.

The areas where both School going girls and dropout girls scored low were:-

- Knowledge about female reproductive organs, of School going girls (20 percent) and school Dropout girls (30 percent).
- Knowledge of male reproductive organs, School going girls (24 percent) and school Dropout girls (16 percent).
- Knowledge about conceivable age of women, School going girls (34 percent) and School dropout girls (38 percent).
- Knowledge about reproductive age of men, School going girls (34 percent) and School dropout girls (46 percent).

Some of school going girls stated that "In Schools both students and teachers hesitated and felt shy to discuss such topics in the class because of Co-education".

Table 7.1: Knowledge of Reproductive System

Respondents	Reproductive System percent Avg. Score					Total average Scores	Mean Scores	SD	*t- Value*
	IRS	KFRO	KMRO	CAW	RAM				
School Going Girls	68%	20%	24%	34%	34%	36	1.8	1.56	*0.98*
Dropout Girls	*74%*	*30%*	*16%*	*38%*	*46%*	*40.8*	*2*	*1.3*	

IRS = Identification of Reproductive System; KFRO = Knowledge of Female Reproductive Organs; KMRO = Knowledge of Male Reproductive Organs; CAW = Conceivable Age of Women; RAM = Reproductive Age of Men.
SD = Standard Deviation.
df = 98; Tabulated value of t at 5 percent =1.99, at 1 percent = 1.66

A similar study was conducted by Mahajan and Sharma (2004) on knowledge level of adolescent girls towards reproductive system and reproductive organs.

The results of the study revealed that urban adolescent girls have comparatively better knowledge regarding reproductive system that the rural adolescent girls.

Table 7.2 depicts that the knowledge of teenage pregnancy was more among School dropout girls as compared to School going girls but this difference in the knowledge level related to teenage pregnancy was not significant. Knowledge of teenage pregnancy focused on (a) Meaning of pregnancy (b) Mode of Pregnancy (c) Right age of child bearing (d) Adverse effects of early pregnancy.

Table 7.2: Knowledge of Teenage Pregnancy

df = 98; Tabulated value of t at 5 percent = 1.99, at 1 percent = 1.66

Respondents	Knowledge regarding teenage pregnancy percent average scores				Total average scores	Mean scores	Standard deviation	t -value
	Meaning	Mode of Pregnancy	Right age of child bearing	Adverse effects of early pregnancy	49.5	1.98	1.29	1.54
School going girls	28%	54%	60%	56%				
Dropout girls	80%	82%	60%	74%	74	2.98	0.95	

Wide variations were seen in the scores of School going girls and School dropout girls.

- Majority of School dropout girls (80 percent) knew the meaning of Pregnancy.
- Majority of school dropout girls (82 percent) and school going girls (54 percent) knew about the mode of pregnancy.
- Majority of school dropout girls (60 percent) and school going girls (60 percent) had knowledge about right age of child bearing.
- Majority of dropout girls (74 percent) and school going girls (56 percent) were aware of the adverse effects of early pregnancy.

The areas where school going girls scored low were:

- Meaning of pregnancy (28 percent).

Respondents of both school going and dropout girls believed that there should be no physical relation before marriage. Some of the Respondents stated that "it is against our society."

Few of the respondents also stated that "early pregnancy leads to nutritional deficiency, weight loss of mother and sometimes leads to death of mother. Few respondents stated that it leads to adverse effects on baby like small for size, premature birth and still birth".

Bhatia (2001), conducted a study and found that majority of the girls were aware of fertility control methods. The awareness was found higher among girls who had literate mothers and whose fathers were in government and affiliated jobs. Girls from rural area had much lower level of knowledge regarding fertility control methods.

It is clear from Table 7.3 that school dropout girls had more knowledge about unsafe abortion as compared to school going respondents. The difference in the knowledge level of these two groups was significant. Knowledge of unsafe abortion focused on (a) Meaning of abortion (b) Meaning of unsafe abortion (c) Legal Abortion (d) Illegal abortion (e) Harmful effects of unsafe abortion.

Table 7.3: Knowledge of Unsafe Abortion

Respondents	Knowledge Regarding Unsafe Abortion percent Average Scores					Total Average Scores	Mean Scores	SD	t-value
	Abortion	Unsafe abortion	Legal Abortion	Illegal abortion	Harmful effects				5.23*
School going girls	8%	5%	16%	16%	3%	9.6	0.96	0.44	
Dropout girls	17%	18%	30%	36%	11%	22.4	2.32	1.80	

SD - Standard Deviation

df = 98; Tabulated value of t at 5 percent = 1.99, at 1 percent = 1.66

The areas where both school going and school dropout girls scored low were:

- Meaning of abortion - school going girls (8 percent) and school dropout girls (17 percent).
- Meaning of unsafe abortion - school going girls (5 percent) and school dropout girls (18 percent).
- Illegal abortion - school going girls (16 percent) and school dropout girls (36 percent).
- Harmful effects of unsafe abortion - school going girls (3 percent) and school dropout girls (11 percent).

Few of the respondents stated that abortion should be made legal in cases when "foetus is at risk, mother's life at risk or there is complication during pregnancy".

Table 7.4 reveals that School going girls had more knowledge about HIV but this difference was not significant. Knowledge of AIDS focused on (a) Abbreviation of the term AIDS (b) Transmission of AIDS (c) Protection from AIDS (d) Relation with AIDS (e) Biological symptoms.

- Majority of school going girls (62 percent) and (46 percent) of dropout girls knew the full form of HIV.

- Majority of school going girls (72 percent) and school dropout girls (82 percent) knew that it could be transmitted by infected blood and by having a sex with multiple partners.

Table 7.4: Knowledge of Adolescent Girls about HIV

Respondents	Knowledge of Students About HIV percent Avg. Scores					Total Average Scores	Mean Scores	Standard Deviation	t-value
	A	T	P	Relation with AIDS	BS				1.42
School going girls	62%	72%	86%	34%	38%	58.4	2.92	1.09	
Dropout girls	46%	82%	84%	8%	28%	49.5	2.46	0.82	

A = Abbreviation; T = Transmission; P = Protection; BS = Biological Symptoms
df = 98; Tabulated values of t at 5 percent = 1.99, at 1 percent =1.66

The message, that *"person with infected blood having sex with multiple partners has been filtered in the minds of adolescent girls. But they are confused about the various routes of transmission. Though the correct routes were identified many incorrect ones, like transmission by shaking hands, by kissing were also mentioned".*

Majority of school going girls (86 percent) and school dropout girls (84 percent) had the knowledge regarding protection from HIV. They stated that the only way to prevent its spread is by "precaution" — (safe sex rather than abstinence).

The areas in which both school going and school dropout girls scored low was:

- Relation of HIV with AIDS — School going girls (34 percent) and School dropout girls (8 percent).
- Biological symptoms of HIV — School going girls (38 percent) and School dropout girls (28 percent).

Sharma (2001), in a study found that very few respondents had adequate knowledge about modes of transmission and methods of prevention.

Table 7.5 reveals the school dropout girls scored more than school going girls. The difference in the knowledge level of AIDS in these two groups was significant. Knowledge of AIDS focused on (a) abbreviation of the term AIDS (b) transmission of AIDS (c) protection from AIDS (d) clinical symptoms, and (e) biological symptoms.

- Majority of school dropout girls (96 percent) and school going girls (76 percent) knew the full form of AIDS.

- Majority of both of school dropout girls and school going girls (94 percent) knew about the mode of transmission of AIDS.
- Majority of school dropout girls (90 percent) and school going girls (86 percent) knew the protection from AIDS.
- Majority of school dropout (90 percent) and school going girls (84 percent) had knowledge of biological symptoms.

Table 7.5: Knowledge of Adolescent Girls About AIDS

Respondents	Knowledge of Students About Aids percent Avg. Scores					Total Average Scores	Mean Scores	Standard Deviation	t-value
	A	T	P	CS	BS				2.22*
School going girls	76%	94%	86%	24%	84%	72.8	3.54	1.34	
Dropout girls	96%	94%	90%	14%	90%	76.8	3.86	0.85	

A = Abbreviation; T = Transmission; P = Protection; CS = Clinical Symptoms BS = Biological Symptoms
df = 98; Tabulated values of t at 5 percent = 1.99, at 1 percent =1.66

The areas where both school dropout girls and school going girls scored low were clinical symptoms of AIDS.

The results of the study are at par with the study conducted by Aggarwal and Kumar 1997. The result indicated high level of knowledge of AIDS, but misconception of transmission and prevention were present. Rural girls had significantly more knowledge as well as misconceptions regarding AIDS than urban girls.

Table 7.6 reveals that the School going girls scored more than the School dropout girls but this difference in the knowledge level regarding STD was not significant. Knowledge about STD included (a) abbreviation of the term STD (b) mode of transmission (c) protection from STD (d) relation with AIDS, and (e) biological symptoms. Not much variation was seen in the scores of school going and dropout girls.

- Most of the School going girls knew about the mode of transmission (56 percent) and protection from STD (70 percent).

The areas where both school going and school dropout girls lacked knowledge were:

- Abbreviation of STD- School going girls (46 percent) and School dropout girls (28 percent).
- Syphilis and Gonorrhoea are the most commonly occurring sexually transmitted diseases of which AIDS is now becoming a part. Since one of its

routes of transmission is via sexual intercourse, people suffering from other STDs have a greater chance of being infected with HIV. However only (6 percent) of School going girls and (6 percent) School dropout girls knew about the relation with AIDS.

- Biological symptoms of STD (28 percent) and (26 percent) respectively.

Table 7.6: Knowledge of Adolescent Girls about STD

Respondents	Knowledge of Students About Std. percent Avg. Scores					Total Average Scores	Mean Scores	Standard Deviation	t- value
	A	T	P	Relation with AIDS	BS				1
School going girls	46%	56%	70%	6%	28%	41.2	2.04	1.47	
Dropout girls	28%	28%	28%	6%	26%	23.2	1.22	1.79	

A = Abbreviation; T = Transmission; P = Protection; BS = Biological Symptoms
df = 98; Tabulated values of t at 5 percent = 1.99 at 1 percent = 1.66

Few respondents stated that a person becomes *overweight* and *pale* if he is infected with STD. Some respondents also stated that STD can be tested through *Urine test* and *X-Ray*. The low scores for STDs showed that confusions existed in the minds of the students regarding STD.

Bhan (2004), in a study on awareness regarding sex knowledge on adolescent girls (16-20 year) found that awareness regarding HIV/AIDS among adolescent girls is very low. Adolescent girls also lack adequate knowledge about sexual matters and contraception, which results in early pregnancy, increased risk of STD infections, maternal morbidity and mortality and unsafe abortions.

Source of Information

For majority of school going girls (70 percent) and school dropout girls (52 percent) their mothers provided them information regarding reproductive health. Few of the school going (22 percent) and school dropout girls (4 percent) attained information from their fathers. The rest of the respondents in both the groups stated that friends and relatives served as an important source of information for them.

Majority of the School going girls (72 percent) and school dropout girls (66 percent) stated that in print media, books served as the major source of providing knowledge on reproductive health. The media provided more authentic and reliable information and helped them in over coming the myths and misconceptions regarding such issues.

Some of the respondents in both the groups stated that they acquired information from newspaper, magazines, television.

Source References

Majority of both school going (90 percent) and dropout girls (100 percent) stated that they preferred a combination of all i.e. print-media, audio-media and audio-visual for acquiring information on reproductive health education. Respondents gave mixed responses for acquiring information. Some stated that they found print media best for acquiring information on reproductive issues. Respondents also mentioned that audio-media and audio-visual aids were the best methods for acquiring information.

Balaganesh (1997), conducted a similar study on the awareness about AIDS/STDs in Indian Communities (both rural and urban) and found out that Mass Media played an important role is providing information.

Strategies for Reproductive Health Education

Majority of both (96 percent) school going and (100 percent) dropout girls believed that group approach was the best strategy for imparting reproductive health education among youth. They believed that Reproductive health education should involve discussions about sex which otherwise is a taboo in our society. Girls had inhibitions and could not talk freely about such issues individually; hence, group approach was the best strategy to be followed. In this way girls can shed their inhibition and talk freely with each other and discuss their queries related to the topic.

While the others preferred individual approach and mass approach for such kind of education, most of the school going girls (60 percent) and school dropout girls (50 percent) felt that reproductive health education should be started at secondary school level (i.e. from 6th standard to 10th standard), because if the girls had proper knowledge of reproductive health at this age they will not be exploited.

A very few school going girls (10 percent) and school dropout girls (8 percent) said that it should start at college level.

Conclusion

Adolescent girls themselves and community at large have a negative perception of girl's health in general and reproduction health in particular. So, it is imperative to provide them authentic knowledge to help them understand the process of growing up in particular references to their reproductive health needs, to make them well equipped to cope with the problems, which they confront during the transitional phase. They need guidance, education as well as opportunities to explore life for them in order to attain a level of maturity required to make responsible decisions.

It can be concluded that the School dropout girls had more knowledge regarding identification of reproductive system and teenage pregnancy, than school going girls, but this difference was not significant. The School dropout girls also had more knowledge about unsafe abortion and Aids than the School going girls and this difference was significant. The school going girls on the other hand had more knowledge regarding HIV and STD than their counterparts, but the difference was insignificant.

The areas where both school going girls and school dropout girls scored low were:

- Female reproductive organs, conceivable age and reproductive age of men.
- Lack of knowledge of teenage pregnancy and mode of pregnancy (in school going girls).
- Unsafe abortion, legal and illegal abortion and its harmful effects.
- Clinical symptoms and biological symptoms of AIDS and the relationship between AIDS/HIV/STD's.

The School dropout girls had more knowledge, than school going girls because these girls had attended many intervention programmes on HIV/AIDS conducted by various NGO's and Aganwadi Workers. Whereas the teachers of the school hesitated to discuss such issues in the class and often presented untrue facts, which may have lead to the development of false concepts among the school going girls.

For majority of school going girls (70 percent) and school dropout girls (52 percent) mothers were the major source for providing information on reproductive health. Both school going (90 percent) and dropout girls (100 percent) preferred a combination of print-media, audio-media and audio-visual for acquiring information on reproductive health education. They believed that this media provided more authentic and reliable information and helped in over coming the myths and misconceptions regarding such issues.

According to them group approach was the best strategy for imparting reproductive health education among youth. Most of the school going girls (60 percent) and school dropout girls (50 percent) felt that reproductive health education should be imparted from secondary school level onwards because if the girls had proper knowledge of reproductive health at this age they will not be exploited.

Suggestions

Instead of laying emphasis only on selected issues concerning reproductive health, a wholesome approach encompassing all the aspects is the need of the hour. A positive attitude in bringing about social justice appears to be the key to bring about the fundamental shift in values.

- Parents, especially mothers should freely talk to their daughters about sexuality and HIV/AIDs. They should initiate, encourage and participate in discussions with the girls, which would prevent development of false concepts.
- Parent and teachers should not snub their children on asking questions related to HIV / AIDS.
- Parents and teachers should try to establish healthy relationships with their children.
- Teachers should encourage their students to ask questions related to reproductive health issues.
- Seminars, symposiums and group discussions regarding these issues should be organized in the vocational skills training institutes as well in order to make school dropout aware about the same.
- Leaflets, folders and pamphlets with information regarding HIV/AIDs and STD should be distributed among the students.
- Teachers especially in rural areas should provide health and sex education with open mind to their students, as they are the only trusted sources of information and role model for the students.
- School teacher play a key role in bringing about this desirable change and socially acceptable approaches to sex education. Such as letter box approach may be used for providing scientific knowledge about sex and related issues.
- Effort should be made to change the negative attitude of rural parents towards girl's education.
- The participating of voluntary agencies and NGO's in rural education development activities should be promoted.
- Confidence should be developed among the rural girls.
- Awareness campaigns regarding AIDS, (STD, HIV, Sexual abuse be organ these should target not only the youth but also their families and society at large.
- Sensitive programmes for development and rehabilitation of adolescent who are physically and mentally challenged to be started in rural as well as in urban areas.
- The school should also include such courses in their curriculum so that the

doubts are cleared and a better sense of responsibility prevails among the adolescent girls.

- In the process of discovering their sexuality adolescent girls rely heavily on mass media entertainment radio, television, films, magazines, books and more. Media often present in adequate information. Instead media should project clear and heal concept relating to reproductive so that the girls may not become victims of wrong information.

References

Aggarwal, A. K., and Kumar, R. (1997). Awareness of AIDS among school children in Haryana. In O. P. Aggarwal, A.K. Sharma, and A. Indrayan (Eds.), HIV-AIDS Research In India (pp. 195-207). New Delhi: NACO, Ministry of Health and Family Welfare, GOI.

Balaganesh, G., Chandrasekhar, V., Sia, T. S. .R, Babu, V. S. (1997). Survey of Public Awareness on AIDS in Rural South Indian Community. In O. P. Aggarwal, A. K. Sharma, A. Indrayan (Eds), HIV/ AIDS Research In India (Pp. 119-122). New Delhi: NACO, Ministry Health and Family Welfare, GOI.

Bhan, N.B., Mahajan, P. and Sondhi M. (2004) : Awareness Regarding Sex Knowledge Among Adolescent Girls (16-20 years) The journal of Anthropologist, 6 (2):101-103.

Bhatia, V. Swami, H.M. and Malhotra, S.(2001) : Menstruation Among Adolescent Girls In India. Journal Of Medical Associations 40(24):46-48.

Mahajan, P.; and Sharma, N. (2004): Awareness level of Adolescent Girls Regarding HIV/ AIDS (a comparative study of rural and urban areas of Jammu). Human Ecology 17 (4):313-314.

Sharma, A.K.; Gupta, A.; and Aggarwal, O.P. (2001): HIV / AIDS Related Knowledge risk perceptions, attitude and sexual behaviour of working women staying in hostels. Indian Journal of Dermatol Venereol Leprol.

UNFPA (1995): Guidelines on Reproductive Health. http: // WWW. Piere @ unfpa. org.

WHO (1998 : Programming For Adolescent Health And Development. Report of The WHO/UNFPA/UNICEF. In: Anonymous (1998): Adolescent Reproductive Health: Making A Difference. Outlook, 16(3):1-10.

8

AIDS Related Stigma: A Challenge for Humanity

Surila Agarwala and Satya Satvir Singh

Introduction

In ancient times usage of stigma referred to the cluster of wounds manifested by Catholic saints, which corresponded to the wounds of the crucified Jesus. These stigmata were said to appear regularly, sometimes bleeding, in conjunction with important religious feast days. Religious stigmata signified holiness, but in recent times stigma more commonly has had a thoroughly negative connotation. Taken literally, it refers to a visible marking on the body, usually made by a branding iron or pointed instrument. But the "mark" could also be a non-physical condition or attribute as in case of people suffering from AIDS. In recent times it is clear that vulnerability to becoming infected with HIV derives directly from stigma and discrimination (and, more broadly, violations of human rights and dignity) occurring within each society. AIDS related stigma represents a set of shared values, attitudes, and beliefs that can be conceptualized at both cultural and individual levels. At the cultural level, AIDS related stigma is manifested in laws, policies, popular discourse, and the social conditions of persons with HIV and those at risk for infection.

At the individual level, it takes the form of behaviours, thoughts and feelings that express prejudices against persons infected with HIV. Such prejudices can be found among persons with HIV as well those who are uninfected. AIDS-related stigma and discrimination refers to prejudice, negative attitudes, abuse and maltreatment directed at people living with HIV and AIDS. They can result in being shunned by family, peers and the wider community; poor treatment in healthcare and education settings; an erosion of rights; psychological damage; and can negatively affect the success of testing and treatment.

Why is there Stigma Related to HIV and AIDS?

According to United Nations AIDS Report (2008), fear of contagion coupled with negative, value-based assumptions about people who are infected leads to high levels of stigma surrounding HIV and AIDS. The stigma attached to an undesirable condition tends to be more intense when that condition is understood to be the bearer's responsibility. An illness is likely to be stigmatized if it is perceived as having been contracted through voluntary and avoidable behaviours, especially behaviours that evoke social disapproval. Such an illness tends to evoke responses of anger and moralism rather than pity or empathy. Because the common routes of HIV include male-male sex, illicit sex and behaviours associated with injecting drug use, it is not surprising that people with HIV are regarded by a significant portion of the public as responsible for their condition and consequently are stigmatized. Indeed, research consistently reveals hierarchies of stigma associated with HIV according to who gets infected and how. Gay and bisexual men with AIDS are more stigmatized than heterosexual women with the disease. People who contracted AIDS through sex with multiple partners or sharing needles receive the most hostile reactions, with the least negative evaluations going to those who were infected through receiving contaminated blood products.

Second, greater stigma is associated with conditions that are lethal and incurable. AIDS has been widely perceived to be a fatal condition since the earliest days of the epidemic. Although new drug regimens now offer realistic hope that HIV disease may be transformed from a fatal malady to a chronic illness, these regimens are not effective for everyone who takes them and many with HIV cannot tolerate them or do not have access to them. For the foreseeable future, therefore, most of the public will probably continue to perceive AIDS as invariably fatal.

Third, greater stigma is associated with a condition when it is perceived to pose a risk to others. More negative attitudes are directed at a stigmatized person to the extent that others believe they can be physically, socially, or morally tainted by interacting with him or her. Perceptions of danger and fears of contagion have surrounded AIDS since the beginning of the epidemic, and are evident in general public continuing overestimation of the transmission risks posed by casual social contact. Some important factors that contribute to HIV/AIDS-related stigma are:

- HIV/AIDS is a life-threatening disease, and therefore people react to it in strong ways.
- HIV infection is associated with behaviours (such as homosexuality, drug addiction, prostitution or promiscuity) that are already stigmatized in many societies.
- Most people become infected with HIV through sex which often carries moral baggage.
- There is a lot of inaccurate information about how HIV is transmitted, creating irrational behaviour and misperceptions of personal risk.

- HIV infection is often thought to be the result of personal irresponsibility.
- Religious or moral beliefs lead some people to believe that being infected with HIV is the result of moral fault (such as promiscuity or 'deviant sex') that deserves to be punished.

Effects of Aids Related Stigma

According to the International Centre for Research on Women (ICRW, 2005), "The epidemic of fear, stigmatization and discrimination has undermined the ability of individuals, families and societies to protect themselves and provide support and reassurance to those affected. This hinders, in no small way, efforts at stemming the epidemic. It complicates decisions about testing, disclosure of status, and ability to negotiate prevention behaviours, including use of family planning services."

AIDS-related stigma has had a profound effect on the epidemic's course. The World Health Organization (WHO, 2008) cites fear of stigma and discrimination as the main reason why people are reluctant to be tested, to disclose HIV status or to take antiretroviral drugs. One study found that participants who reported high levels of stigma were more than four times more likely to report poor access to care (Sayles, 2009). These factors all contribute to the expansion of the epidemic (as a reluctance to determine HIV status or to discuss or practice safe sex means that people are more likely to infect others) and a higher number of AIDS-related deaths. An unwillingness to take an HIV test means that more people are diagnosed late, when the virus has already progressed to AIDS, making treatment less effective and causing early death.

Research by the ICRW (2005) found the possible consequences of HIV-related stigma to be:

- Loss of income/livelihood.
- Loss of marriage and childbearing options.
- Poor care within the health sector.
- Withdrawal of care giving in the home.
- Loss of hope and feelings of worthlessness.
- Loss of reputation.

Some of these consequences refer to 'internal stigma' or 'self-stigma'. Internal stigma refers to how people living with HIV regard themselves, as well as how they see public perception of people living with HIV. Self-stigma and fear of a negative community reaction can hinder efforts to address the AIDS epidemic by perpetuating the wall of silence and shame surrounding the epidemic.

AIDS related stigma and discrimination exist worldwide, although they manifest themselves differently across countries, communities, religious groups and individuals. They occur alongside other forms of stigma and discrimination, such as racism, homophobia or misogyny and can be directed towards those involved in what are considered socially unacceptable activities such as prostitution or drug use. The problem of AIDS related stigma is inextricably bound to issues of health, human rights, and the law. Such stigma translates into feelings of fear and hostility directed at people with HIV. It finds expression in avoidance and ostracism of people with HIV, discrimination and violence against them, and public support for punitive policies and laws that restrict civil liberties while hindering AIDS prevention efforts. Being the target of stigma inflicts pain, isolation, and hardship on many people with HIV, while the desire to avoid it deters some from being tested for HIV, seeking treatment, or practicing risk-reduction.

AIDS Related Stigma and Prevention

AIDS related stigma interferes with effective prevention efforts. Fears of stigma represent an impediment to disclosure by persons with HIV of their serostatus to others, including sexual partners, which can interfere with effective risk reduction. In addition, the experience of stigma may represent an ongoing source of psychological distress that may make effective risk reduction more difficult for persons with HIV. It also appears that fears of AIDS related stigma can deter people at risk for HIV from being tested and from seeking information and assistance for risk reduction. Delays in testing increase the likelihood that infected individuals will transmit the virus to their sexual partners, to those with whom they share needles, and to their offspring. Internalized stigma and fear of stigma from others also may be associated with adverse responses to receiving a positive HIV test result which, in turn, may increase the likelihood of continuing that transmit HIV.

Responding to AIDS Related Stigma

How can we best respond to AIDS related stigma? Historically, the stigma associated with some diseases declined dramatically when the disease etiology was understood and cures or effective treatments were developed. This is illustrated in Charles Rosenberg's account of three nineteenth century cholera epidemics in United States Between the 1832 and 1866 epidemics, Americans progressed from regarding cholera as a moral punishment for sinners to understanding its connections with poor sanitation and public health practices in recent times. Cholera is no longer considered a social stigma or punishment for ones sins.

The story of cholera offers some hope for combating HIV/AIDS related stigma. We do not yet have a cure for AIDS but we understand how HIV is transmitted, and this understanding should help to reduce stigma. WHO (2003) claimed that, "As HIV/AIDS becomes a disease that can be both prevented and treated, attitudes will change, and denial, stigma and discrimination will rapidly be reduced."

Progress can be made in overcoming this stigma and discrimination. A certain amount can be achieved through the legal process. In some countries people living with HIV lack knowledge of their rights in society. They need to be educated, so they are able to challenge the discrimination, stigma and denial that they encounter. Institutional and other monitoring mechanisms can enforce the rights of people with HIV and provide powerful means of mitigating the worst effects of discrimination and stigma.

According to Ban Ki moon (Secretary-General of The United Nations Organization, 2008), "We can fight stigma. Enlightened laws and policies are key. But it begins with openness, the courage to speak out. Schools should teach respect and understanding. Religious leaders should preach tolerance. The media should condemn prejudice and use its influence to advance social change, from securing legal protections to ensuring access to health care."

However, no policy or laws can alone combat HIV/AIDS related discrimination. Stigma and discrimination will continue to exist so long as societies as a whole have a poor understanding of HIV and AIDS and the pain and suffering caused by negative attitudes and discriminatory practices. The fear and prejudice that lie at the core of the HIV/AIDS discrimination need to be tackled at the community and national levels, with AIDS education playing a crucial role. A more enabling environment needs to be created to increase the visibility of people with HIV/AIDS as a 'normal' part of any society. The presence of treatment makes this task easier; where there is hope, people are less afraid of AIDS; they are more willing to be tested for HIV, to disclose their status, and to seek care if necessary. In the future, the task is to confront the fear-based messages and biased social attitudes, in order to reduce the discrimination and stigma of people living with HIV and AIDS.

Another approach to stigma reduction has been to encourage people with HIV to disclose their serostatus to others. The hope is that uninfected individuals will be less likely to stigmatize people with HIV if they personally know someone who is infected. HIV infection is concealable, which makes it possible for many with HIV to "pass" as uninfected in routine social interactions. Controlling who knows that they are infected not only helps them to avoid the stigma associated with AIDS and related statuses (e.g., being gay), but also allows them to preserve their privacy and maintain a sense of normalcy in their own lives. Passing, however, is often stressful. Keeping important information about oneself a secret can have negative consequences for one's mental and physical health. The demands of passing can disrupt relationships, requiring those with HIV to create distance from others in order to avoid disclosing their diagnosis. This may prevent them from receiving much needed social support. Moreover, hiding their diagnosis may reinforce a sense of shame about being infected, or may cause them to feel inauthentic - that they are living a lie.

On the other hand, people with HIV have legitimate concerns about personal rejection, discrimination, and even violence if others know their serostatus. It is understandable, then, if the admonition to people with HIV to disclose to others—not only sexual partners, but also family, friends, co-workers, and even strangers—meets with resistance. It is appropriate that they should want to know that "coming out of the closet", i.e. disclosing their serostatus will have a positive effect or, at the least, will not cause them harm.

The use of the phrase "coming out" to describe self-disclosure of HIV status intentionally invokes the metaphor used by gay men and lesbians to describe the process whereby they reveal their sexual orientation to others. The expectation that coming out as an HIV-positive person will help to reduce AIDS-related stigma is based to a significant extent on the experiences of gay and lesbian people in various nations. Indeed, the public's attitudes toward homosexuality have moderated during the past few decades and one likely reason is that increasing numbers of heterosexual public now know that they have a gay or lesbian friend or close relative.

A related strategy that is often advocated for reducing AIDS stigma is to encourage famous people who are HIV-infected to publicly disclose their serostatus. The underlying assumption is that members of the public will be affected by such an announcement in much the same way that they would be affected by learning that a close friend is infected. The difference between the two situations, of course, is that people have direct contact with friends but most have only vicarious contact with celebrities.

Expectations about the beneficial effects of vicarious contact with a famous person with HIV were discussed extensively in the United States when basketball star Earvin "Magic" Johnson revealed his HIV infection in 1991. The president of one AIDS organization commented on the effect of Johnson's announcement: "The main thing that raises awareness of HIV or AIDS is to know someone who has it. Now everybody in America knows someone with HIV." In similar fashion, a Sports Illustrated writer compared Johnson's disclosure to the shock of learning that a member of one's own family has AIDS. Social scientists also speculated that the effect of Johnson's announcement on those without AIDS would be similar to that of having personal contact with someone who did have the disease. Magic Johnson's announcement provided an unusual opportunity to study the effects of celebrity disclosure on AIDS stigma.

Public disclosure by other celebrities with HIV may well have a different impact. However, given Magic Johnson's prominence, the public's high regard for him, and the way in which he disclosed (e.g. the fact that he revealed his serostatus while still in apparent good health), public reactions to his disclosure may well be as positive as we are likely to see in response to any celebrity disclosure. If this is true, the potential for reducing stigma through vicarious contact with people with HIV is probably limited.

AIDS stigma is a worldwide phenomenon. People with HIV in different nations are subjected to varying degrees of personal rejection, social ostracism, discrimination, violence, and, in many countries, laws and policies that deprive them of basic human rights. Stigma and discrimination are the enemies of public health not only because they inflict suffering on people with HIV and undermine efforts to prevent the further spread of HIV, but also because they heighten vulnerability to HIV infection among individuals and groups. We need to change the law and public policy so that they censure AIDS stigma rather than sanction it. At the same time, we must change individual attitudes and behaviours so that people understand that HIV is a virus, not a moral judgment, and that those who contract it are human beings, not symbols. Thus, institutional and individual change must be central objectives of any anti-stigma project.

"AIDS is a war against humanity. We need to break the silence, banish the stigma and discrimination and ensure total inclusiveness within the struggle against AIDS. If we discard the people living with HIV/AIDS, we can no longer call ourselves human". — Nelson Mandela

References

Ban Ki-moon. 2008. *The sigma factor*, The Washington Times.

International Centre for Research on Women (ICRW, 2005). *'HIV-related stigma across contexts: common at its core'.*

Sayles J. 2009. 'The Association of Stigma with Self-Reported Access to Medical Care and Antiretroviral Therapy Adherence in Persons Living With HIV/AIDS.' *Journal of General Internal Medicine, 24*(10).

The World Health Organization Strategy (2003) 'Treating 3 Million by 2005: Making it Happen'

United Nations, AIDS 2008 Report on the Global AIDS Epidemic.

World Health Organization (2008). 'Towards Universal Access: Scaling up priority HIV/AIDS interventions in the health sector: Progress Report 2008'.

9

Social Support and Coping Styles for HIV+ Individuals: A Psycho-social Study

Ameesha and Priti S. Dhawan

Introduction

With the growing incidents of HIV positive cases coming into light, and governments taking various actions to combat the stigma, it has become important to look into the psychosocial adjustment of HIV infected individuals. The ability to cope with change is related to the nature of the change, availability of social support, and personal factors. Social support can offer practical help, provide information, or help to contain and deal with strong emotions. The extent to which people feel in control of their lives varies according to individuals, and active coping strategies that enhance a feeling of control, such as task-focused coping or positive reframing, are beneficial (Gibson and Swartz, 2002).

Persons who receive a diagnosis of HIV or AIDS often react with a mixture of emotions, including shock, depression, hopelessness, grief, anger, and fear. Psychosocial factors such as coping and social support may affect both disease progression and quality of life. For example, a study of 736 individuals with AIDS by Fleishman and Vogel, 1994, noted that these individuals practiced a variety of coping behaviours categorized as positive coping, social support seeking, and avoidance coping. The coping behaviours were associated with health behaviours, affect, and disease progression in both cross-sectional and longitudinal analyses. Similar findings were reported in a phenomenological pilot study conducted by Russell and Smith (1999) explored the experiences of five HIV-infected African American women. Audio taped interviews from these women were examined. Twelve themes emerged from the data: violence, addiction, it couldn't happen to me, shock and denial, education, time, uncertainty, cycles, secretive nature of their lives, someone, survival, and children. It is evident, even from this small pilot study, that these individuals have complex experiences and that the complexities of stress has an effect on coping and psychological well being.

The present study tried to focus on the relationship between perceptions of social support and coping strategies, where perceived social support was affected by 'onset controllability'.

Onset Controllability was here referred to as whether the individuals think that they could have controlled the acquiring of the infection. If yes, it is internal and if no, then it is external. This term coincides with Weiner's projection of locus of control. External onset controllability is generally the result of contracting the virus through blood transfusion or accidental needle usage. Internal onset controllability generally resulted from the contraction of infection through unsafe sex and intravenous drug use. Weiner (1980a, 1980b), hypothesized that the perceived controllability of another person's need would influence pity and anger directly, which in turn would directly influence decisions to help. In this model, he posited that if the cause of another person's need is perceived as controllable (i.e., if the person is thought to be responsible for his or her need), help is more likely to be withheld than when the cause is perceived to be uncontrollable. Thus, people's judgement of responsibility of one's infection can in turn decrease or increase the amount of social support one receives.

Perceived Social Support and Onset Controllability: Social support refers to a social network's provision of psychological and material resources intended to benefit an individual's ability to cope with stress. It is often differentiated in terms of three types of resources: instrumental, informational, and emotional. Instrumental support involves the provision of material aid, for example, financial assistance or help with daily tasks. Informational support refers to the provision of relevant information intended to help the individual cope with current difficulties and typically takes the form of advice or guidance in dealing with one's problems. Emotional support involves the expression of empathy, caring, reassurance, and trust and provides opportunities for emotional expression and venting. Perceived social support refers to the belief that helping behaviour would be provided when needed (Barrera, 1986).

It is important here to differentiate between perceived and received social support. Received social support is the amount of social support one has received in reality, however perceived social support is the belief that support would be provided. Perceived social support links up with onset controllability because both are seen from the view point of the individual in question. Thus, one's own guilt and responsiveness might influence perception of supportive behaviour or in the other case; the knowledge of internal/ external controllability can have an effect on the support provided by people thus resulting in lower social support.

Coping Strategies

According to Lazarus's model of coping, process of coping begins with appraisal of challenge, and of one's ability to handle it. Coping strategies fall into two main categories—problem focussed (engagement) coping which aims at managing the external environmental aspects of the stressor, and emotion-focussed (disengagement) coping which regulates the internal effective consequences of the stressor. Research generally suggests that emotion-focussed coping has negative impact on the adjustment, while problem-focussed coping has a positive effect. When faced with a stimulus, the person analyses its menacing potential. If he feels it is dangerous, he will assess the resources he can tap on in order to cope with it and will face the situation either successfully (adaptively) or unsuccessfully (non-adaptively). Should coping not be successful, the menacing situation will still be there and the person will remain under stress.

Research has shown that social and emotional support available to the person helps him/her to effectively cope with the stress. Persons maintaining close interpersonal relationships with friends and families are able to use more approach strategies. Social support includes both material support (providing resources) and emotional support (listening to the person and encouraging him/her). However, studies have shown that unsolicited support may have negative consequences.

The present study was designed to:

- To find out the effect of onset controllability on Perceived Social Support of HIV positive individuals.
- To find out the effect of onset controllability on Coping Strategies of HIV positive individuals.

Keeping in mind the above objectives, two hypotheses were formulated.

- Some extent of difference is likely to exist in the levels of perceived social support of HIV positive individuals with different onset controllability.
- And, some extent of difference is likely to exist in the ways of coping of HIV positive individuals with different onset controllability.

Method

The study was done by using a non-probability purposive sample. The sample comprised of two groups.

- The first group consisted of HIV+ individuals who have acquired the infection via the mode of blood transfusion, accidental needle infection or single sex. Since the onset of the infection was attributed to external event, the group is called external onset controllability group.
- The second group consisted of HIV+ individuals who have acquired the infection via the mode of multiple sex, intra venous drug use or homosexual

contact. Since the onset of the infection was attributed to internal factors, the group is called internal controllability group.

A total sample of 46 HIV positive individuals was collected from SAHARA care, a NGO in Delhi and X Nursing Home, Mathura. These individuals varied with respect to age, gender, educational qualifications, socio-economic status, marital status and event controllability. Number of people in condition1 where onset controllability is external was 19 and in condition 2 where onset controllability is internal was 27.

Onset controllability was measured using by asking them information about their seropositive status along with other demographic variables such as age, gender, education, and employment status. Perceived Social Support was measured by using Norbeck Social Support Questionnaire (1995 revised) which gave multiple components of social support including functional properties of social support (e.g. emotional and tangible support) and network properties (e.g. stability of relationships, frequency of contact), as well as eliciting descriptive data about recent losses of supportive relationships.

Ways of Coping questionnaire by Folkman and Lazarus (1980) was used to investigate the determinants of coping. The *ways of coping* was designed to identify the thoughts and actions an individual has used to cope with a specific encounter. It measured, the following coping strategies: confrontive coping, distancing, self-controlling, seeking social support, accepting responsibility, planful problem solving, escape-avoidance, and positive reappraisal.

Results

In order to find out whether significant difference exists between HIV positive individuals with external onset controllability and internal onset controllability, Wilcoxon Mann Whitney test was applied, with degree of freedom at 0.05, on

- perceived social support of HIV+ individuals with external and internal onset controllability, and
- coping strategies of HIV+ individuals with external and internal onset controllability.

Those HIV+ who consider that they could not have controlled the acquiring of infection perceived significantly greater amounts of informational, tangible and emotional support than those HIV+ who think that they could have controlled the onset of infection. On the other hand, those people who blamed chance for their infection engaged in building greater network of social support, but those who blamed themselves for their infection seems to have lesser number of people available when support is required.

Table 9.1: Mean Scores and Standard Deviation of Perceived Social Support for People with Internal and External Onset Controllability

	Total functional		Total network	
	MEAN	SD	MEAN	SD
External	158.63	7.427	80.95	5.57
Internal	99.48	6.428	49.85	4.497

Results were also analyzed with respect to onset controllability and coping strategies employed. People in external onset controllability group confronted situation more than those in internal onset controllability group.

Table 9.2: Mean Scores and SD of Coping Strategies of HIV+ Individuals with Internal and External Onset Controllability

Onset controllability		Conf	Dist	Self-ctrl	Seek SS	Acc Res	Esc-Avoi	PPS	*PR*
Internal	Mean	12.37	11.58	14.21	13.21	7.84	12.89	12.84	*14.16*
	SD	1.99	1.775	1.428	1.533	1.4	1.777	1.63	*1.698*
External	Mean	8.7	12.25	11.48	10.07	6.55	16.77	10.78	*11.81*
	SD	*1.915*	*1.676*	*1.876*	*1.89*	*1.66*	*2.294*	*1.905*	*2.011*

Table 9.3: Wilcoxon Mann Whitney Test for Total Function of Social Support for HIV+ With External and Internal Onset Controllability

	Total Function	*Total Network*
Z	3.457	*3.647*
P	*0.0003**	*0.00032**

* $p < (0.05)$

Those who acquired infection via uncontrollable means used distancing as a coping strategy equally as those who acquired the infection via controllable means. HIV+ who acquired infection through uncontrollable means put more restrain on their behaviour, feelings and desires than those who think that they could have controlled the infection's onset. This indicates that people in external onset controllability group seek more social support when compared with those in internal onset controllability group.

Those who acquired infection via uncontrollable means made use of accepting responsibility as a coping strategy to the equal extent when compared with those who acquired the infection via controllable means. When confronted with stressful situation, those with internal onset controllability preferred to escape from the situation than people with external onset controllability.

Table 9.4: Wilcoxon Mann Whitney Test for Coping Strategies of Individuals with External and Internal Onset Controllability

	conf	dist	Self-ctrl	Seek SS	Acc Res	Esc-Avoi	PPS	*PR*
Z	2.88	1.653	2.619	2.886	1.466	2.722	1.799	*2.514*
P	*0.004**	*0.099*	*.0088**	*0.024**	*0.072*	*0.003**	*0.734*	*0.012**

* $p < (0.05)$

When confronted with stressful situation, those with internal onset controllability prefer to positively reappraise the situation than people with external onset controllability.

Discussion

When the mode of acquisition of infection is viewed as uncontrollable or external by others, helping judgments whether direct or indirect are more favourable than when mode of acquisition is viewed as controllable or internal (Weiner et al., 1989). But in the present research, the results show that when onset controllability of HIV positive individual was perceived by oneself as chance blame or external or uncontrollable, the belief that people will help when needed or perceived social support is relatively high for both qualitative and quantitative perceived social support.

A relationship is a two way process. What one gives in a relationship and what one gets effects what the other gives and gets. This interrelationship is contingent on behaviour, feelings and understanding of each one equally.

When one comes to know what to expect from the other, the perceptions and beliefs are respectively affected. Consensus and mutual understanding refer to a psychological process by which persons reach agreement about their own perceptions (beliefs, expectations and feelings) while simultaneously incorporating others' perception of the same event (Friend et al., 1990). When others are expected to think favourably and attribute less or no blame to the person, the expectations in the interrelationship may go high. This expectation is reflected in high levels of perceived social support of HIV infected people with external onset controllability. The discrimination and devaluation that follows the label of 'HIV/AIDS', is the reason that stands behind the reduced total network of the person. These individuals are not able to maintain a vast social support network because feelings of guilt, of being a constant source of trouble and stigma to others add to the insecurity of these people which later becomes a roadblock in maintaining contacts or relationships.

It is now accepted that problem focused coping is used more when events are perceived as controllable, when problem seeking, solving active efforts to alter the situation could bring about a change in the stressful situation. Individuals infected with HIV/AIDS are already stigmatized. The person who has contracted the infection through means which he thinks were beyond his control is already frustrated for being a victim in the hand of chance. When s/he experiences discrimination in any form, the person tries to confront the situation or the person responsible by facing him, standing for one's rights and ground, by talking out with the person explaining the reasons and conditions. The HIV positive individual attributes the responsibility of his condition to external factors, which are beyond his control and so instead of just accepting things as they come, they confront them. Next they have no control over their HIV positive status but they try and control the outcome of the stressors by confronting and changing things in their direction rather than just passively accepting so that they feel a sense of control and thus power over shaping their lives.

In terms of coping strategies, HIV positive individuals with internal onset controllability differed in high usage of escape avoidance whereas those with external onset controllability used more of confrontive coping, self control, positive reappraisal, and seeking social support. Planful problem solving, distancing and accepting responsibility for both the groups remained alike despite of the factor of blame and responsibility. The similar strategies used in both groups reflect that real look of the situation is not lost on the persons blaming themselves. Though they engage more in strategies of escape avoidance, they do more conscious efforts to change the situation by focusing on how their efforts should be directed for obtaining favourable outcome. At the same time detachment or distancing is used by those with uncontrollable onset controllability because despite of active efforts like confrontation, seeking social support and positive reappraisal they also use strategies to regulate their emotion ore such as self control. Detachment is present because there is some sort of frustration and so depending on the demand of the situation either detachment or accepting responsibility is used.

Sikkema et al. (2003) found that severity of grief reaction of HIV+ men and women was associated with escape avoidance and self controlling coping strategies and depressive symptoms. In present study, those HIV+ individuals who consider themselves responsible for the infection have fewer psychosocial resources—they are target of other's hostility and stigma more and also they use escape avoidance coping strategy more often. For an internally caused event, blame is triggered towards oneself. Use of escape avoidance as a coping strategy describes wishful thinking that the situation would go away or somehow be over with. The person shows behavioural efforts to escape or avoid say by not talking to people in general, sleeping more, getting indulged in some substance-use etc.

When other people's helping judgements towards those with internal onset controllability are lesser, then these people adapt to strategy of escape or avoiding the situation instead of confronting it because they are aware and target of others hostility towards them. Confronting in ways of getting others to change the situation or using aggressive methods, others involved are expected to help less and therefore, confrontation is not considered a good technique however escape avoidance is seeking social supports also is reduced because of the very fast that they themselves and others helping judgements are influenced by the responsibility of mode of acquisition of the infection.

For those with internal onset controllability, the blame of the infection comes down fully on the person. Earlier studies have reported that depression among HIV+ individuals has been linked to internalized stigma (Lee et al., 2002), dysfunctional attitudes and maladaptive coping strategies (Gore-Felton et al., 2006; Penedo et al., 2001) major life stress and a lack of social support (McClure et al., 1996). Based on these findings, researchers have concluded that HIV status is not by itself a strong predictor of mood or anxiety disorders, but instead interacts with other psychosocial characteristics of the individual (Riggs, Vosvick and Stalling, 2007; Dickey et al., 1999).

References

Barrera, M. (1986). Distinctions between social support concepts, measures, and models. *American Journal of Community Psychology, 14*, 413-415.

Dickey, W.C., Dew, M.A., Becker, J.T., and Kingsley, L. (1999). Combined effects of HIV-infection status and psychosocial vulnerability on mental health in homosexual men. *Social Psychiatry and Psychiatric Epidemiology, 34*, 4–11.

Fleishman, J.A., and Vogel, B. (1994). Coping and depressive symptoms among young people with AIDS. *Health Psychology, 13*, 156-169.

Folkman, S., and Lazarus, R.S. (1980). An analysis of coping in a middle-aged community sample. *Journal of Health and Social Behaviour, 21*, 219-239.

Gibson K, Swartz L, Sandenbergh R. (2002). *Dealing with Change. Counselling and Coping.* Cape Town: Oxford University Press; 103-121.

Gore-Felton, C., Vosvick, M., Brondino, M., Winningham, A., Koopman, C., and Spiegel, D. (2006). Effects of quality of life and coping on depression among adults living with HIV/AIDS. *Journal of Health Psychology, 11*(5), 711–729.

Lee, R.S., Kochman, A., and Sikkema, K.J. (2002). Internalized stigma among people living with HIVAIDS. *AIDS and Behaviour, 6*, 309–319.

McClure, J.B., Catz, S.L., Prejean, J., Brantley, P.J., and Jones, G.N. (1996). Factors associated with depression in a heterogeneous HIV-infected sample. *Journal of Psychosomatic Research, 40*, 407–415.

Penedo, F.J., Antoni, M.H., Schneiderman, N., Ironson, G.H., Malow, R.M., Cruess, S. et al. (2001). Dysfunctional attitudes, coping, and depression among HIV-seropositive men who have sex with men. *Cognitive Therapy and Research, 25*, 591–606.

Riggs, S.A., Vosvick, M., and Stallings, S. (2007). Attachment Style, Stigma and Psychological Distress among HIV+ Adults. *Journal of Health Psychology, 12*, 922-936.

Russell, J.M. and Smith, K.V. (1999). A holistic view of human immunodeficiency virus-infected African American women. *Journal of Holistic Nursing, 17(4)*, 331-345.

Weiner, B. (1980a). May I borrow your class notes? An attributional analysis of judgments of help giving in an achievement oriented context. *Journal of Educational Psychology, 72*, 676-681.

Weiner, B. (1980b). A cognitive-(attribution) - emotion-action model of motivated behaviour: an analysis of judgments of help-giving. *Journal of Personality and Social Psychology, 39*, 186-200.

Weiner, B., Perry, R.P., Magnusson, J. (1988). An attributional analysis of reactions to stigmas. *Journal of Personality and Social Psychology, 55*, 738-748.

10

Neurocognitive Aspects of HIV Infection

Shahzadi Malhotra, Gaurav Rajender and T.B. Singh

HIV Infection and Central Nervous System

Acquired Immuno Deficiency Syndrome (AIDS) is the term denoting the ultimate stage of systemic infection with Human Immuno Virus (HIV). However, before the realization that the disease is caused by a virus, clinicians noted that patients complained of cognitive and mood disorders. With the advent of researches finding a viral etiology for AIDS and AIDS related disorders, investigations have also found that HIV not only is the agent of immune compromise but also may be neurotropic and neuropathogenic. The most common Central Nervous System complication is cognitive impairment so severe to lead to the diagnosis of dementia.

HIV is found in the Central Nervous System (CNS), including within the cerebrospinal fluid (CSF) and the brain. A good deal of data has suggested that the impact of HIV on the CNS may be the result of neurotoxic factors linked either directly to the virus or to infected macrohages (Grant 1990). Review of neuropsychological research reports indicates that cognitive disorders were originally believed to affect only a small proportion of HIV-infected individuals. However, studies have now reported that the prevalence and severity of cognitive impairment increase as the disease progresses (Heaton et al., 2004). Further, since the initial recognition of cognitive changes in persons who are HIV seropositive, neuropsychological research reports have documented changes in HIV –positive asymptomatic persons as well as persons with more obvious symptoms of HIV infection. Navia and Price (1987) have reported that up to 25 percent of patients with early HIV disease may present with neurological symptoms. Thus, by now HIV infection is well established to manifest with Neurocognitive Deficits (NCDs) as symptoms (Vahia, 2006). Neurological symptoms also may appear before neuroradiological detection of HIV-related CNS processes (and often before other HIV related illnesses) in up to 10 percent HIV infected individuals (Levy et al., 1985).Cognitive changes become more prevalent as HIV infection becomes more severe. For example, Saykin et al., (1988) reported no statistically significant correlations between neuropsychological test data and magnetic resonance imaging (MRI) volumetric indices.

HIV may also present with other mild deficits such as apathy, sensorimotor and gait disturbances (Dube, 2005). Intriguingly, chemotherapy for HIV also induces parallel NCD like symptoms (Hawkins et al., 2005; Miller et al., 2005) in conjunction with certain strikingly unique ones (Moreno, 2003) in a degree sufficient to impair life. It has thus, been hypothesized that neurocognitive function may provide an early indicator of CNS involvement in HIV (Scmitt et al., 1997).

At the outset of the HIV epidemic, severe cognitive decline was thought to be part of the end stage of HIV infection, associated only with AIDS (Grant et al., 1987). This cognitive disorder was found to be composed of a combination of disturbances in cognitive functioning, motor behaviour, and affective functioning, and this triad was termed as *AIDS dementia complex by* Price et al. (Brew et al.1988). Investigators also found that HIV itself produced an encephalitis or encephalopathy, which was variously termed as *subacute encephalitis, HIV encephalopathy* or *AIDS encephalopathy.* More recently, a behaviourally based set of criteria to distinguish levels of neurological and neurobehavioural impairment has been proposed by the American Academy of Neurology, which has termed these conditions as *HIV-1 associated cognitive /motor complex* (Janssen et al. 1991). These criteria mainly distinguish motor impairments from mild cognitive deficits (HIV-1 associated minor cognitive/ motor disorder) from the actual dementia.

Direct brain infection by HIV, therefore, is now widely believed to be the likely cause of related cognitive and other neurobehavioural disorders (Janssen et al., 1991). The evidence for this theory includes detection of HIV-1 in CNS, fourteen days after the initial infection (Davis et al., 1992), presence of viral nucleic acid in the brains of some patients with this disorder, direct HIV isolation from the brain and CSF (Chiodi et al., 1992), electron microscopic findings of viral particles within infiltrating macrophages (Schindelmeiser et al., 1991), and detection of viral antigens within the brains of infected individuals (Pumarola-Sune et al. 1987). Thus, this CNS neuropathology often results in cognitive changes, from mild memory impairments and cognitive slowing to a profound dementia (Everall et al., 1993; Grafe et al.1990).

Classification of Cognitive Impairments in HIV

Figure 10.1 shows the classification of HIV related brain impairments. Cognitive disorders and subtle cognitive impairment are seen throughout the spectrum of HIV infection.

Delirium occurs frequently among hospitalized HIV infected patients with reported prevalence ranging from 29-57 percent (Bialer et al., 1996). The etiology of delirium is often multifactorial in HIV infection and patients are susceptible to the development of delirium in the context of underlying HIV brain infection, common use of polypharmacy and the frequency of multiple medical complications. Evaluation and correction of the underlying medical cause of delirium is of primary importance. Prompt management of agitation due to delirium is extremely important because of the distress caused to the patient and family, potential for self harm as well the potential for exposure of HIV to others. Repeated mental status examinations, careful review of medications, thorough physical and neurological examinations, search for infections/metabolic abnormalities, neuroradiologic examination, CSF examination and EEG are essential in evaluation of delirious patients.

Figure 10.1: Classification of HIV-Related Brain Impairments

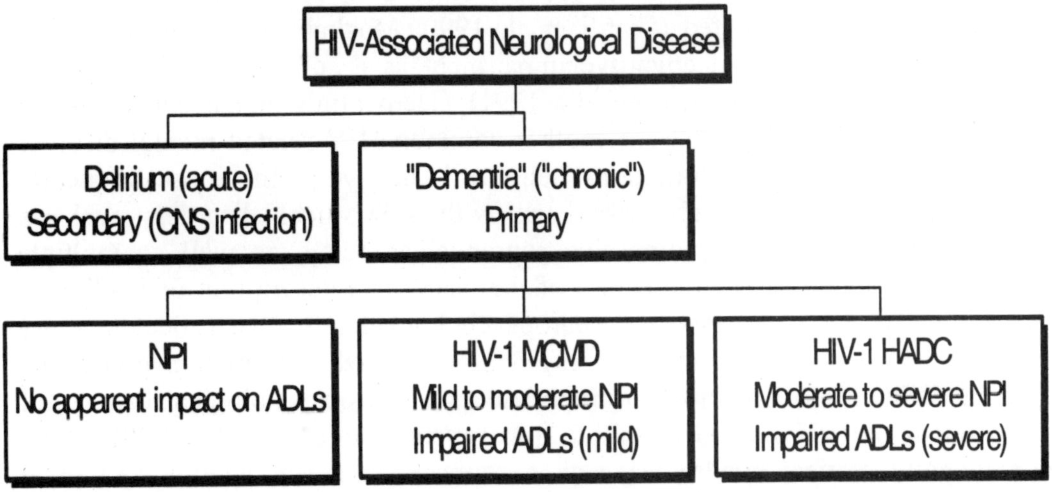

The earliest level of cognitive impairment is a subclinical cognitive inefficiency that can range in severity from a decrement in previous level of functioning in attention, speed of information processing, memory, abstraction and fine motor skills to formal test defined deficits in some of these domains. Disturbances in these functions may have no observable effects on activities of daily living or functional performance. These changes occur in more than 20 percent of HIV-1 infected individuals (Wilkie et al.1990), but the proportion of patients having these problems doubles with advanced disease (Heaton et al., 1995). More severe impairment interfering minimally with functional status is now defined by the AAN as HIV-1 associated minor cognitive/ motor disorder. Prevalence estimates of HIV-1 associated minor cognitive/ motor disorder have not yet reached a consensus, but estimates suggest that 20 percent to 30 percent of asymptomatic HIV-1 infected individuals meet formal AAN criteria for this disorder (Goodkin, 2001). Indications of early HIV-1 associated minor cognitive/motor disorder may be mild and, as such, are frequently attributed to the systemic illness or a psychosocial reaction to HIV infection. However, even under the influence of an early organic process that affects cognition, many patients will be cognizant of their own mental and physical sluggishness and personality changes, and affective changes may occur concomitantly.

Dementia is generally regarded as an acquired intellectual impairment characterized by persistent deficits in multiple areas, including memory, language, cognition, visuospatial skills, personality and emotional functioning (Cummings et al., 1984). HIV associated Dementia (HAD) has been believed to be a subcortical type of dementia affecting subcortical and frontostriatal brain processes (Brew, 1997). However, because other CNS cortical areas have been identified as being affected (Ciardi et al. 1990; Masliah et al. 1992); a strict definition of HIV related cognitive impairment as a subcortical dementia has been questioned (Poutiainen et al., 1991). Dementia's persistent cognitive impairment differentiates it from another common HIV related mental disorder due to general medical condition- delirium. The symptoms most frequently described and most closely associated with subcortical disorders such as Parkinson's disease and progressive supranuclear palsy, as well as multiple sclerosis are found in HIV infection of the CNS. The description of HAD as a subcortical process suggests that neuropsychological tests that reflect memory registration, storage, and retrieval; psychomotor speed; information processing rate; and fine motor function are important in a neuropsychological battery for assessment of HIV related cognitive impairment (Butters et al., 1990). Other traditionally cortical syndromes such as aphasia, agnosia, apraxia and other sensory perceptual functions, also can be present but usually not until later in the course of the disease and perhaps as a result of some focal opportunistic infection or neoplastic invasion of the CNS.

The prevalence of HIV-1-associated dementia (HAD) among otherwise asymptomatic subjects in United States and Europe has been estimated at 15 to 30 percent (Satishchandra et al., 2000; Ranga et al., 2004; Chandra et al., 2005). In contrast, a study from India (Satishchandra et al., 2000) documented an unusually low incidence (about 1 to 2 percent) of HAD. The low levels of HAD in economically developing societies like India are often attributed to under diagnosis, shorter life expectancy, or other factors. In an extensive follow up of earlier studies, however, six cases of HAD were found among 427 HIV-infected asymptomatic individuals (1.4 percent), indicating that the low incidence of HAD was not an artefact (Satishchandra et al., 2000) .To explain this lower incidence of HIV dementia, one of the causes hypothesized has been a compromised chemotactic function of C-Tat protein that is responsible for the monocytic chemotactic activity which has an important role in HIV dementias. It was found that the CS natural variant was defective for monocyte chemotactic activity without a loss in the transactivation property (Ranga et al., 2004). . While the CC mutant was functionally competent for both the functions, in contrast, the SC mutant was defective in both. Therefore, the loss of the C-Tat chemotactic property may underlie the reduced incidence of HAD. Although not presenting conclusive evidence, this study provided the first evidence for a potential epidemiologic phenomenon associated with biological differences in the subtypes of viruses (Ranga et al., 2004). The scenario may change in India with the early detection of HIV, prompt treatment of opportunistic infections, and HAART therapy. Better documentation and assessment of patients presenting with cognitive dysfunctions is needed to chart the occurrence, comorbidity and course of HIV dementias.

Fully developed HAD is commonly associated with significant declines in functional status. Table 10.1 and 10.2 provide a summary of signs and symptoms of HIV related neurobehavioural impairments in early and late stages of the infection. The course of HAD can steadily worsen with the development of moderate to severe cognitive deficits, confusion, psychomotor slowing, and seizures. Patients may appear mute and catatonic. Socially inappropriate behaviour, psychosis; mania; marked motor abnormalities such as ataxia, spasticity, and hyper-reflexia; and incontinence of bowel and bladder can occur.

Various meta-analysis (Reger et al., 2002; Baldewicz et al., 2004) have revealed that in the later stages of the disease, motor deficits were most prominent, with deficits also present in problem solving and other executive functions, rate of information processing, expressive language, memory and to a lesser degree, attention and concentration. The progression of cognitive decline followed a frontal subcortical pattern initially, with the areas of greatest deficit early in the disease (motor and executive functions) being subserved by these brain regions and neural circuits. In the later stages of the disease , abilities such as memory and visuospatial skills, which are less dependent on fronto-striatal circuitry also decline.

Cognitive Dysfunction in Asymptomatic HIV Infection

Neuropsychological impairment among asymptomatic HIV infected persons has been an important area of study. Several studies in India have reported neurocognitive disturbances in this group (Edwin et al., 1999; Singh et al., 2001;

Chandra et al., 1997; Sinha et al., 2003). Factors such as brain injury, malnutrition, neurological infections, alcohol and depression are all known to have a role in the causation of neurocognitive problems. All the above studies found significant deficits compared to controls, particularly in the areas of fine motor speed and information processing. One study that examined both central and peripheral electrophysiological parameters, found evidence of subtle abnormalities in clinical testing, EEG and brain stem auditory evoked responses (Sinha et al., 2003).

Table 10.1: Early Signs and Symptoms of HIV Related Neurobehavioural Impairment

Cognitive	Affective/behavioural
Memory Impairment (especially verbal, rote, episodic)	Apathy
Attention and Concentration	Depressed mood
Language comprehension problems	Anxiety
Conceptualization difficulties	Mild agitation
Problem Solving difficulties	Mild disinhibition
Visuospatial constructional Abilities	Hallucinations or misperceptions
Motor Slowing, co-ordination difficulties	
Mental tracking difficulties	
Mild frontal lobe type symptoms	
Handwriting and fine motor control difficulties	

Source: Brew, B.J., Sidtis, J.J., Petito, C.K. (1988). The neurologic complications of AIDS and HIV infection. In Advances in Contemporary Neurology. Edited by Plum, F. Philadelphia, PA, FA Davis , pp. 1-49.

Table 10.2: Late Signs and Symptoms of HIV Related Neurobehavioural Impairment

Cognitive	Affective/behavioural
Severe dementia affecting multiple cognitive areas	Severe Behavioural disinhibition
Aphasia and/ or mutism	Manic symptoms
Severe frontal lobe symptoms	Delusions
Severe psychomotor slowing	Severe hallucinations
Intense distractability	Severe agitation
Disorientation	Paranoid ideation
	Severe depression with or without suicidality

Source: Brew, B.J., Sidtis, J.J., Petito, C.K. (1988). The neurologic complications of AIDS and HIV infection. In Advances in Contemporary Neurology. Edited by Plum, F. Philadelphia, PA, FA Davis , pp. 1-49.

Specific Neurocognitive Domains Affected by HIV

The cardinal signs of HIV related cognitive impairment remain consistent by most studies (Butters et al., 1990; Collier et al., 1992; Dunlop et al., 1992; Jacobs et al., 1992., Karlsen et al., 1992, Ryan et al., 1992) and include problems with verbal memory, difficulties with attention and concentration, slowing of information processing, slowed psychomotor speed, and impairment of cognitive flexibility. In some cases the non verbal abilities of problem solving, visuospatial integration and visuospatial construction, and non verbal memory are impaired (Butters et al., 1990). Studies have also reported that psychomotor tasks, such as Digit Symbol and Block Design tests of Wechsler Adult Intelligence Scale and the Trail Making Test Part B, and memory tasks such as the Delayed visual Reproduction subtest of the Wechsler Memory Scale and the delayed recall of the Rey Osterrieth Complex Figure, were most affected in the early stages of cognitive impairment associated with the HIV infection (Van Gorp et al., 1998). Fernandez et al. (2006) found that the tasks detecting psychomotor neuromotor disturbances in HIV related neural dysfunction such as visuomotor reaction time and fine motor dexterity as measured by pegboard tasks are also sensitive measures for early detection of impairment (Dunlop et al., 1992; Karlsen et al., 1992; Nance et al., 1990).

Studies have also implicated graphomotor and manual slowing to be a major component of impairment in psychomotor tasks (Martin et al., 1992). When a memory search or reaction time paradigm was used , speed of memory search in HIV positive patients did not differ significantly from that in control subjects. This task did not assess the speed of movement but rather a cognitive reaction latency.

Other areas usually assessed by neuropsychological batteries include aphasia, apraxia, and other complex language associated functioning; verbal abstract reasoning and problem solving; and perceptual functioning of the different sensory modalities. These deficits and associated assessments have not been consistently reported to be sensitive to early detection of HIV related CNS dysfunction. Any impairment found in these neuropsychological functions may be associated with a more focal attack on the nervous system, such as HIV related infection that forms a focal abscess or a HIV related tumour. However, neuropsychological evaluations encompassing a broad range of cognitive areas (Butters et al., 1990), as are effectively implemented with other clinical entities such as head trauma or other dementias, would seem to yield adequate information about focality of involvement in the later stages of HIV disease (Kovner et al., 1989; Fernandez et al. 2006).

Clinical Relevance of Cognitive and Neuropsychological Research in HIV

The correlation between neuropsychological deficits and CD4 counts in HIV is affected by age, which exemplifies the multifactorial nature of symptoms in the CNS. An area deserving concern is the surfacing of new neuropsychological deficits such as verbal fluency (Millikin et al., 2004), verbal and spatial memory (Hinkin et al., 2002) and apathy with the potential to enhance diagnosis. Some tests such as standardized neuropsychological tests and ERP records predate the appearance of conventional HIV symptoms and hence have the potential to diagnose HIV earlier (Paul et al., 2005). Bornstein et al., (1993) showed the precedence in time of cognitive deficits over conventional AIDS symptoms. This may point to a more sensitive marker for AIDS per se rather than CD4 counts. Clinical sensitivity for identifying HIV related syndrome is contingent upon awareness of the symptoms of neuropsychological deficits. Clinical sensitivity can- in view of the recently uncovered neuropsychological deficits, be increased beyond merely detecting neuropsychological and cognitive deficits. Bornstein et al., and Wilke et al.(1990), have demonstrated early cognitive impairment in asymptomatic cases, thus, increasing the diagnostic sensitivity of HIV directly in proportion to the earliness of appearance of these symptoms. Support for such clinical sensitivity is provided by a study by Bryant et al. (2001) on Indian truck drivers where they reliably used neuropsychological deficits for correctly diagnosing HIV cases. This is further substantiated by inter rater reliability tests by Wood et al., (2004) which demonstrated high diagnostic value and consistent reproduction of the various neuropsychological deficits across varied clinical settings.

Conclusions

Neuropsychological impairment has been recognized for around two decades as a consequence of HIV infection. Deficits in neurocognitive functioning have been described at different stages of the infection. The incidence and severity of dysfunction increases, as HIV infection progresses. Primary questions concerning the natural history in the progression of neurocognitive deficits in HIV infection have been a focus of many investigations. These data suggest, at least in the short term, that the prevalence and progression of neurocognitive dysfunction in the serropositive but asymptomatic individuals is fairly rare and limited. On the other hand, data from other studies have suggested that once a person has developed a full range of dementia symptoms associated with HIV infection, there is rapid progression of symptoms leading to mortality.

Methodological issues surrounding the evaluation of the neurocognitive symptoms associated with HIV infection are also important. The search for additional risk factors that might under or over represent the occurrence of cognitive symptoms in seropositive persons remains an important area to be explored. Furthermore, documenting the nature and extent of these neurocognitive deficits is vital in patient care, particularly when it concerns decisions regarding occupational status, financial matters and daily living skills.

Questions remain, however, as to the association between neurocognitive symptoms and biological markers of HIV activity in the brain. Although work such as that by Martin et al.,(1992) is enlightening, there are a number of other potential neurotoxic processes associated with HIV infection that need to be evaluated in light of their potential contribution to neurocognitive changes in HIV disease.

References

Baldewicz t. T., Leserman, J., Silva, S.G. (2004). Changes in neuropsychological functioning with progression of HIV-1 infection: Results of an 8 year longitudinal investigation. *AIDS Behaviour*, 8; 345-355.

Bialeret PA, Wallack JJ, Prenzlauer SL, Bogdonoff L, Willets I. Psychiatric co-morbidity among hospitalized AIDS patients vs. non-AIDS referred for psychiatric consultation. *Psychosomatics* 1996; *37* : 469-75.

Bornstein, R.A. (1994). Methodological and conceptual issues in the cognitive changes in HIV infection. In Grant, I., Martin, A. eds. Neuropsychology of HIV Infections. New York: Oxford University Press, 146-160.

Brew, B.J., Sidtis, J.J., Petito, C.K. (1988). The neurologic complications of AIDS and HIV infection. in Advances in Contemporary Neurology. Edited by Plum, F. Philadelphia, PA, FA Davis , pp. 1-49.

Bryan, A.D., Fisher, J.D., Benziger, T.J. (2001).Determinants of HIV risk among Indian truck drivers. *Soc Sci Med*, 53, 1413-26.

Butters, N., Grant, I., Haxby, J. (1990). Assessment of AIDS related cognitive changes: Recommendations of the NIMH workshop on neuropsychological assessment approaches. *J Clin Exp Neuropsychol* 12; 963-978.

Chandra, P.S., Desai, G., Ranjan, S. (2005). HIV and Psychiatric disorders. *Indian Journal of Medical Research 121*, pp. 451-467.

Chandra PS, Gehlot S, Prasada Rao PSDV, Ravi V.(1997) Neuropsychological deficits in asymptomatic HIV infection. *Indian J Clin Psychol* ; *24* : 8.

Chiodi, F., Keys, B., Albert, J. (1992). HIV Type1 is present in cerebrospinal fluid of a majority of infected individuals. *J Clin Microbiol*, 30, 1768-1771.

Ciardi, A., Sindair, E., Scaravilli, F. (1990). The involvement of the cerebral cortex in HIV encephalopathy: a morphological and immunohistolochemical study. *Acta Neuropathol,* 81, 51-59.

Collier, A.C., Marra, C., Coombs, R.W. (1992). Central Nervous system manifestations in HIV infection without AIDS. *J Acquir Immune Defic Syndr*, 5, 229-241.

Davis, L.E., Hjelle, B.L., Miller, V.E.(1992).Sleep encephalogram delta frequency amplitude, night plasma levels of tumour necrosis factor α and HIV. *Neurology,*42,1736-39.

Dube, B, Benton, T, Dean, G. (2005). Neuropsychiatric Manifestations of HIV infection and

AIDS. *J Psychiatry Neurosci*, 30, 237-246.

Dunlop, O., Bjorklund, R.A., Abedelnoor, M. (1992). Five different tests of reaction time evaluated in HIV seropositive men. *Acta Neurol Scand,* 8, 260-266.

Edwin T, Nammalvar N, Sabhesan S, Ganesh R, Devarajan H. (1999) Neuro cognitive impairments in HIV infection. *Indian J Psychiatry* ; *41* : 30-6.

Everall, I., Luthet, P.J., Lantos, P.L. (1993). A review of neuronal damage in HIV infection: its assessment, possible mechanism and relationship to dementia. *J Neuropathol Exp Neurol,* 52, 561-566.

Fernandez , F., Ruiz, P.(2006). Psychiatric Aspects of Human Immunodeficiency Virus Infection /AIDS. Philedelphia, PA, Lippincott Williams and Wilkins.

Goodkin, G.M., Badewicz, T.T., Wilkie, F.L. (2001). Cognitive motor impairment and disorder in HIV-1 infection. Psychiatr Ann 31, 37-44.

Grafe, M.R., Press, G.A., Berthoty, D.P. (1990). Abnormalities of the brain in AIDS patients: correlation of postmortem MRI findings with neuropathology. AJNR Am J Neuroradiol, 11:905-913.

Grant, I., Atkinson, J.H., Hesselink, J.R. (1987). Evidence for earl central nervous system involvement in the AIDS and other HIV infections: studied with neuropsychological testing and magnetic resonance imaging. *Ann Intern Med,* 107, 828-836.

Hawkins, T., Geist, C., Young, B. (2005). Comparison of neuropsychiatric side effects in an observational cohort of efavirenz- and protease inhibitor-treated patients. *HIV Clin Trials,* 6, 187-96.

Heaton , R.K., Grant, I., Butters, N. (1995). The HNRC 500: Neuropsychology of HIV infection at various disease stages. *J Int Neuropsychol Soc*, 1, 231-251.

Heaton RK, Marcotte TD, Mindt MR, Sadek J, Moore DJ, Bentley H, *et al*. The impact of HIV-associated neuropsychological impairment on everyday functioning. *J Int Neuropsychol Soc* 2004; *10* : 317-31.

Hinkin, C.H., Castellon, S.A., Hardy, D.J. (2002). Methylphenidate improves HIV-1 associated cognitive slowing. *J Neuropsychiatry Clin Neurosci*, 13, 248-54.

Jacobs, D., Peavy, G., Velin, R. (1992). Verbal memory in asymptomatic HIV infection: evidence of subcortical dysfunction in a subgroup of patients. *J Clin Exp Neuropsychol*, 14, 101-103.

Janssen, R.S., Cornblath, D.R., Epstein, L.G. (1991). Nomenclature and research case definitions for neurologic manifestations of HIV-1 infection. *Neurology*, 41, 778-785.

Karlsen, N.R., Reinvang, I., Froland, S.S. (1992). Slowed reaction time in asymptomatic HIV positive patients. *Acta Neurol Scand* , 86, 242-246.

Kovner, R., Perecman, E., Lazar, W. (1989). Relation of personality and attentional factors to cognitive deficits in human immuno deficiency virus infected subjects. *Arch Neurol,* 46, 274-277.

Levy, R.M., Bredesen, D.E., Rosenblaum, M.L. (1985). Neurological manifestations of the acquired immunodeficiency syndrome (AIDS): experience at UCSF and review of the literature. *J Neurosurg*, 62; 475-495.

Martin, E.M., Robertson, L.C., Sorensen, D.J. (1992). Speed of memory scanning is not affected in early HIV -1 infection (abstract). *J Clin Exp Neuropsychol*, 14, 102.

Mashah, E., Achim, C.L. (1992). Spectrum of human immunodeficiency virus associated neocortical damage. Ann Neurol, 32, 321-329.

Miller , R.F., Dave, S.S., Tang, J.W.(2005). Progressive neuropsychiatric problems following institution of highly active antiretroviral therapy. *Sex Transm Infect*, 81,351-7.

Millikin, C.P., Trepanier, L.L., Rourke, S.B. (2004). Verbal fluency component analysis in adults with HIV/ AIDS. *J Clin Exp Neuropsychol,* 26, 933-42.

Moreno, A., Labelle, C., Samet, J.H. (2003). Recurrence of post traumatic stress disorder symptoms after initiation of anti-retrovirals including efavirenz. A report of two cases. *HIV Med*, 4, 302-4.

Nance, M., Pirozollo, F.J., Levy, J.K. (1990). Simple and choice reaction time in HIV seronegative and AIDS patients. Abstracts of the 6th International Conference on AIDS, Vol. 2 San Francisco, CA, p. 173.

Navia, B.A., Price, R.W. (1987). The acquired immunodeficiency syndrome dementia complex as the presenting or sole manifestation of human immuno deficiency virus infection. *Arch Neurol 44*; 65-69

Paul, R., Flanigan, T.P., Tashima, K. (2005). Apathy correlates with cognitive function but not CD4 status in patients with HIV. *J Neuropsychiatry Clin Neurosci*, 17,114-18.

Poutianen, E., Haltia, M., Elovaara, I. (1991). Dementia associated with human immunodeficiency virus: subcortical or cortical? *Acta Psychiatr Scand,* 83, 297-301.

Pumarola-Sune, T., Navia, B.A., Cordon-Cardo, C. (1987). HIV antigen in the brains of patients with the AIDS dementia complex. *Ann Neurol*, 21, 490-496.

Ranga U, Siddappa B, Ramakrishna L, Nagendran R, Mahalingam M, Mahadevan A, *et al.* Tat protein of human 465 immunodeficiency virus type 1 subtype C strains is a defective chemokine. *J Virol* 2004; *78* : 2586-90.

Reger, M., Welsh, R., Razani, J. (2002). A meta analysis of the neuropsychological sequelae of HIV infection. *J Int Neuropsychol Soc*, 8, 410-424.

Ryan, J.J., Paolo, A.M., Skarde, m. (1992). Rey auditory verbal learning test performance of a federal corrections sample with acquired immunodeficiency syndrome. *Int J Neurosci,* 64, 177-181.

Satishchandra P, Nalini A, Gourie-Devi M, Khanna N, Santosh V, Ravi V, *et al.* Profile of neurologic disorders associated with HIV/AIDS from Bangalore, south India (1989-96). *Indian J Med Res* 2000; *111* : 14-23.

Saykin,A.J., Jannsen, R.S., Sprehn, G.C., Kaplan, J.E., Spira, T.J. (1988). Neuropsychological dysfunction in HIV infection: characterization in a symphadennopathy cohort. *Int J Clin Neuropsychol*; 10; 92-97.

Schindelmeises, J., Gullotta,F. (1991). HIV-p24-antigen-bearing macrophages are only present in brains of HIV- seropositive patients with AIDS encephalopathy. *Clin Neuropathol,* 10, 109-111.

Schmitt, F.A., Mary, M.C., Stern, Y. (1997). AIDS and the Nervous system, Second Edition. Edited by Berger, J.R., Levy, R.M. Lippincott- Raven Publishers, Philadelphia.

Singh H, Sharma CS, Chakraborty PK, Sattar FA. Cognitive dysfunction in clinically asymptomatic HIV seropositive individuals. *Indian J Psychiatry* 2001; *43* : 162-70.

Sinha S, Satishchandra P. Nervous system involvement in asymptomatic HIV seropositive individuals: A cognitive and electrophysiological study. *Neurology India* 2003; *51* : 466-9.

Vahia, V.N., Bhojraj, T., Creado, D.A. (2006). Neurocognitive deficits in HIV Infected Patients: Two Case Reports: Revising AANTF guidelines in view of the recent revelation of new neurocognitive symptoms. *Indian J Psychiatry*, 48, 93-95.

Van Gorp, W.G., Satz, P., Hinkin, C. (1998). Normal ageing and the subcortical encephalopathy of AIDS: a neuropsychological comparison. *Neuropsychiatry Neuropsychol Behav Neurol,* 2, 5-20.

Wilkie,F.L., Goodkin,K., Khamiz, I. (2003). Cognitive functioning in younger and older HIV infected adults. *J Acquir Immun Deficienc Syndr,* 33, 93-105.

Woods, S.P., Rippeth, J.D., Frol, A.B. (2004).Interrater reliability of clinical ratings and neurocognitive diagnosis in HIV. *J Clin Exp Neuropsychol*, 26, 759-778.

11

Memory Impairment among HIV Infected People

Yogita Rai and Tanusree Dutta

Introduction

Human Immunodeficiency Virus (HIV) is an epidemic causing disease and death across the globe. Since it is global, HIV can be called 'pandemic'. The World Health Organization estimates that 30.6 million people are infected with HIV virus, nearly two third of whom live in Sub-Saharan Africa. Approximately 5.8 million people are infected with HIV each year and 2.3 million die of AIDS associated illness.

The Centre for Disease and Control (1993) has categorized HIV infection into three stages namely asymptomatic, symptomatic and AIDS related conditions based on the CD4 count and symptoms. The asymptomatic stage includes HIV patients with CD4 count of above 200 cell per cubic millilitre of blood, without any clinical symptom of the disease. They comprise of category A. The symptomatic category includes patients having a CD4 count between 200-500 cells per cubic millilitre of blood, along with the clinical symptoms of the disease. They comprise of category B. AIDS related conditions however include all HIV infected person who report a CD4 count bellow 200 cell per cubic millilitre of blood with the presence of onc or more AIDS related illness. They belong to category C.

Deterioration in brain functioning occurs in HIV infection when the virus infects CD4 carrying cells. Virus crosses the blood brain barrier and infects various important parts of the brain. It is important for clinicians to note that any timed testing situation can be affected by HIV infection. The earliest neurological symptoms of HIV involve cognitive slowing. In addition many anti- HIV drugs cause various neurocognitive impairments.

Neurological symptoms of HIV infected usually do not appear until late in the disease process. When they do occur, early HIV related neuropsychological symptoms cause minor functional disturbances. The most common early HIV related neurological disturbances involve slowing of mental process, motor disturbances and mild memory lapse. These symptoms rarely occur in people who have otherwise remained asymptomatic. HIV related neurological problems can occur during the long asymptomatic period of HIV infection, but disturbances are typically mild and transient.

Pajeau and Roman, (1992) reported that neuropsychological complications occur in at least sixty percent of the HIV infected patients. Bornstein, Para, Whitacre, Rosenberger, and Fass, (1993) in one of their study reported that there was a twofold increase in the cognitive impairment of asymptomatic patients and a fourfold increase in symptomatic patients. According to Zeifert, Leary and Boccellari (1995), cognitive functions that are affected in HIV patient include impairment in concentration, memory, thinking, speech, emotional expression, social behaviour, the ability to focus on specific stimuli and coordination. Grant, Atkinson and Hesselink, (1987) reported that cognitive impairment in symptomatic HIV seropositive patients and cognitive deficit in asymptomatic HIV patients are likely to have important functional consequences. For a patient infected with HIV who is otherwise asymptomatic, these deficits may result in significant morbidity, deficit in memory, attention, retrival of information, and planning which are likely to interfere with performance of daily tasks. Some studies have reported neurocognitive changes during the asymtomatic stage of infection (Grant, Marcotte, Heaton, and HNRC Group, 1999; Lunn, Skydsbjerg, Schulsinger, Parnas, Pedersen, and Mathiesen, 1991; Stern, Singer, Silva, Roger, Perkins, Hall, Vander Horst and Evans, 1992; Villa, Montelleone and Marra, 1993; Wilkie, Eisdorfer, Morgan, Loewenstein and Szapoeznik, 1990). The occurrence of cognitive impairment in clinically asymptomatic HIV seropositive persons is however controversial (Grant et al., 1999; Singh, Sharma, Chakraborty and Sattar, 2001).

Heaton, Grant, Butters and White, (1995) used a comprehensive neuropsychological test battery and found an increased rate of cognitive impairment with each successive stage of HIV infection. Studies refuting the above finding suggest that cognitive impairment does not occur until patients develop AIDS related complex (ARC) (Franzblau, Letz, Hershman, Mason, Wallace and Beksi, 1991; Janssen, Saykin, Cannon, Compbell, Pinsky, Hessol, O'Malley, Lifson, Doll and Rutherford, 1989; McArthur, Cohen, Salnes, Kumar, Cooper, McArthur, Soucy, Cornblath, Chmiel, Meicheng, Starkey, Ginzburg, Ostrow, Johnson, Phair and Polk, 1989). These HIV related neuropsychological impairment is generally mild especially in medically asymptomatic stages of the infection. However studies conducted by Damos, John, Parker and Levine (1997) and Salnes, Miller and McArthur, (1990) contradict the same and state that there are no significant difference between the cognition of uninfected and clinically asymptomatic subjects. Other studies have also reported that the majority of asymptomatic HIV positive individuals do not manifest significant neurocognitive impairment (Grant and Martin 1995; Maj, Satz, Janssen, Zaudig,

Starace, D'Elia, Sughondhabirom, Mussa, Naber, Ndetei, Schulte and Sartorius, 1994).

Cognitive disturbances resulting from HIV infection typically coincide with immune suppression, making it more vulnerable for occurrence of neurological impairment with opportunistic illness. Individual with Acquired Immunodeficiency Syndrome (AIDS) or with symptomatic Human Immunodeficiency Virus (HIV) infection have consistently exhibited neurobehavioral deficits in attention and concentration, cognitive and motor speed, learning and memory and mood state (Navia, Jordan and Price, 1986; Navia and Price, 1986; Perdices and Cooper, 1989; Perry and Joobsen, 1986). Thus it is not surprising that HIV-1 patients are often present with complaints of increased difficulty with memory and attention or other cognitive functions. Several studies have reported that cognitive complaints are associated with depressive symptomatology and not with neuropsychological impairment (Moore, van Group, Stern, Swales, and Satz, 1991; Van Group, Staz, Hinkin, Selnes, Miller, McArthur, Cohen, Paz, and the Multicenter AIDS cohort study 1991; Wilkins, Robertson, Snyder, Robertson, van der Horst, and Hall, 1991), other studies have reported that cognitive complaints are associated with specific area of neurological dysfunction particularly at the later stages of HIV illness (Beason, Hozen, Nasrallah and Bornstein, 1994; Poutiainen, Elovaara, Raininko, Vilkki, Lahdevirta, and Iivanainen, 1996; Stern et. al. 1991). Some studies have found working memory impairment in symptomatic HIV infected individuals (Bartok, Martin and Pitrak 1997; Law, Martin, Mapou, Roller, Salazar, Temoshok and Rundell 1994; Stout, Salmon and Butters 1995). Their findings suggest that a significant proportion of symptomatic subjects are compromised in their cognitive functioning. However various studies have found that a sub sample of asymptomatic individuals may have mild to moderate impairment in memory, information processing speed and some other confounding factors and are in some cases significant predictors of mortality (Wilkie, Goodkin, Eisdorfer, Feaster, Morgan, Fletcher, Blaneey, Baum, and Szapocznik, 1998).

Furthermore asymptomatic subjects without evidence of immune compromise do not appear to be at a greater risk for cognitive impairment than HIV negative control subjects, whereas for those HIV infected individuals who are immunosuppressed their seem to be an increased risk of neurological impairments (Boccellari, Dillry, Chambers, Yingling, Tauber, Moss and Osmond, 1993). Study conducted by Barbara, Giacomo, Arthuro, Elena, Sara, Paola, Mara, Adriano and Slvio (1999) in which they investigate about spatial working memory in asymptomatic HIV-infected subjects, did not find any spatial working memory impairment during the asymptomatic phase of HIV infection.

These data suggest that although structural and functional frontal sub cortical abnormalities may be found in HIV infection, they do not imply neuropsychological deficits relative to working memory during the early, asymptomatic stage of the illness.

Less consistent but prevalent in literature, are reports of sub clinical decrements on neuropsychological measures during early stages of HIV infection. These include problems with memory/cognitive and motor slowing (Grant, Atkinson, Hesselink, Kennedy, Richman, Spector, and McCutchan, 1987; Martin, et. al., 1992; Martin, Robertson and Edelstein, 1989; Poutiainen, Elovaara, Raininko, Vilkki, Lahdevirta, and Iivanainen, 1996). Low, Martin, Mapou, Roller, Salazar, Temoshok and Rundell (1994) found no evidence of memory deficits in HIV+ individuals, even in subjects with significantly slowed reaction times.

Therefore on reviewing the available literature we find that there is a lack of consensus among researches with respect to the decline of cognitive functioning among different HIV infected groups. Thus in the present study an attempt will be made to measure the memory of HIV infected people across the different stages of infection.

Methodology

Sample: The study was conducted on 80 subjects divided into three groups namely asymptomatic (n=30), symptomatic (n=30) and uninfected healthy control group (n=20). Subjects had completed at least primary education, which included reading, writing and speaking Hindi fluently. Subjects having a history of drug abuse and alcoholism were excluded. Left-handed subjects were also excluded from the study. Data of asymptomatic and symptomatic HIV infected people was collected from Voluntary Counselling and Testing Centre (VCTC), IMS, BHU, Varanasi. Subjects taking antiretroviral medicine were excluded from the study. Demographic characteristics of subject are reported in Table 11.1.

Tools: The AIIMS comprehensive neuropsychological battery (Adult Form) was used for the neuropsychological evaluation. This battery comprised of 160 items spread over 10 domains, one of which is the scale of memory, with five point scale (from 0-4) for evaluating performance. These items were credits along the dimensions of accuracy, accuracy, frequency, speed, quality and appropriateness. Subjects were asked to respond on a five point rating scale where a rating of 0 indicated normal performance, 4 indicated abnormal performance and 1-3 suggested intermediate performance.

The memory scale included recognition of bird and animals shown on the cards, items assessing remote and recent memory, immediate verbal recall of words, immediate memory for digits both forward and backward, verbal recall with homogeneous interference, verbal recall with heterogeneous interference, immediate recall of visually presented designs, nonverbal recall with heterogeneous interference. Memory scores were therefore not material- specific, but rather they reflected overall memory scores.

Table 11.1: Characteristics of HIV Positive (asymptomatic and symptomatic) and HIV Negative Subjects

Demographic characteristics	HIV positive symptomatic	HIV positive asymptomatic	*HIV negative healthy control*
Age (Mean)	29.47	29.23	*26.40*
Education			
Primary	5	-----	*4*
Secondary	7	10	*6*
Higher secondary	15	10	*8*
Above	3	10	*2*
Gender			
Male	23	13	*16*
Female	7	17	*4*
Marital status			
Married	23	25	*11*
Unmarried	-----	-----	*9*
Widow/widower	*7*	*5*	----

Procedure: This study was based on a cross sectional design. It was conducted on three group of subject's namely asymptomatic, symptomatic HIV positive and healthy control group. These three groups were administered the AIIMS comprehensive neuropsychological battery (Adult Form) to assess the memory of the subjects when they came to the Voluntary Counselling and Testing Centre (VCTC), Institute of Medical Sciences (IMS) and Sir Sunder Lal Hospital, Varanasi, India.

Result

The present study was undertaken primarily with the purpose to examine memory functioning in asymptomatic and symptomatic HIV infected patients. Accordingly, hypotheses were formulated to test the objectives. In order to find out whether there is differences in memory functioning between the healthy controls, asymptomatic and symptomatic HIV infected groups, it was hypothesized that symptomatic HIV infected group would show more memory impairment as compared to asymptomatic HIV infected and healthy control groups. As the importance of the variables like age, gender and education in influencing the test scores in neuropsychological studies is well known, formulas were evolved to determine "expected T-scores" based on age and education. If the obtained T score for any patient was higher than the expected T score, the performance was termed as abnormal, while low scores for the same denoted better performance.

Statistical analysis using one way ANOVA was used for analyzing the data. Results (Table 11.3) suggested a significant difference in the memory score of symptomatic and asymptomatic HIV positive and healthy control group (f = 18.172, df = 2, p=0.000) (Table 11.2). Memory of symptomatic was poorer in comparison to asymptomatic (p=0.004) and control group (p=0.000). Healthy control group reported better memory in comparison to asymptomatic (0.009) and symptomatic (0.000).

Table 11.2: Memory Evaluation of (a) Healthy Control, (b) Asymptomatic HIV Infected Individuals and (c) Symptomatic HIV Infected Individuals

(a) Healthy control		
Patient no.	Memory t score	Expected memory score
1	47	69
2	35	71
3	38	72
4	41	72
5	35	70
6	53	71
7	54	70
8	46	71
9	46	72
10	34	70
11	47	71
12	67	72
13	35	70
14	46	70
15	44	76
16	43	72
17	60	74
18	44	76
19	43	72

20	60	71
(b) Asymptomatic HIV infected individual		
Patient no.	Memory t score	Expected memory score
1	49	68
2	60	69
3	67	70
4	44	69
5	63	72
6	50	72
7	47	73
8	47	70
9	50	70
10	60	72
11	76*	73
12	40	72
13	104*	71
14	69	73
15	35	70
16	64	72
17	53	71
18	85*	71
19	85*	73
20	67	73
21	62	71
22	73*	72
23	54	73
24	34	70
25	34	71
26	34	69
27	46	69
28	60	71
29	41	70
30	73*	69
(c) Symptomatic HIV infected individuals		
Patient no.	Memory t score	Expected memory score
1	70	71
2	75	76
3	67	73
4	57	72
5	73	73

6	59	71
7	63	72
8	56	71
9	59	70
10	82*	71
11	80*	72
12	80*	70
13	59	71
14	92*	76
15	51	72
16	51	71
17	67	70
18	69	72
19	66	71
20	80*	76
21	66	74
22	69	73
23	101*	73
24	70	74
25	92*	76
26	83*	71
27	62	68
28	70	71
29	63	72
30	54	71

* memory impairment

Table 11.3: Summary of One-way ANOVA Showing Difference in Performance Among Healthy Control, Asymptomatic and Symptomatic HIV Infected Group with respect to Memory Function

Healthy Control	Asymptomatic HIV infected individuals	Symptomatic HIV infected individuals	F value and p value
Mean ± SD	Mean ± SD	Mean ± SD	18.172, 0.000
45.85 ± 9.155	57.80 ± 17.000	69.53 ± 12.442	

Discussion

To the best of our knowledge; this is the first study assessing the memory outcome of HIV infected people across the stages using this tool. In our finding (Table 18.2)9 symptomatic HIV infected out of 30 and 6 asymptomatic HIV infected out of 30 were found with memory impairment, however study conducted by Barbara, Giacomo, Arthuro, Elena, Sara, Paola, Mara, Adriano and Slvio (1999) in which they investigated spatial working memory in asymptomatic HIV-infected subjects and did not find any spatial working memory impairment during the asymptomatic phase of HIV infection. Remaining 21 symptomatic and 24 asymptomatic HIV positive people do not show any memory impairment during infection. However, in the present study various factors have not been taken into account in analysis such as CD4 count and education, whereas these factors influence memory significantly.

Results suggest a significant difference among symptomatic, asymptomatic HIV positive and normal healthy control group. Similar findings have been reported by Charles, David, Karen, Steven, Mona, Marta and Bryan (2002) found that HIV-infected people performed significantly worse on both the verbal and spatial working memory tasks in comparison to healthy control group. However this finding represent a contradiction with study conducted by Damos, John, Parker and Levine (1997) and Salnes, Miller and McArthur, (1990) contradict the same and state that there are no significant difference between the cognition of uninfected and clinically asymptomatic subjects. HIV positive group was significantly slower than HIV negative control on memory scale, supported by study conducted by Grant, et. al., (1987); Martin, Robertson, Sorensen, Jagust, Mallon, and Chirurgi, (1992); Martin, Robertson and Edelstein, (1989); Poutiainen, Livanaien, Elovarra, Valle and Lahdevitra, (1988). Result in the present study shows significant decline in memory among HIV infected people across the stages. It may, of course, be possible that these HIV positive subjects will go on to develop reduced memory capacity. On going longitudinal evaluation will hopefully clarify this question.

References

Barbara, G., Giacomo, G., Arturo, C., Elena, G., Sara, B., Paola, C., Mara, E., Adriano, L. and Silvio. S (1999). Spatial working memory in asymptomatic HIV infected subjects. *Journal of Neuropsychiatry and Clinical Neurosciences, 11,* 387-391.

Bartok, J.A., Martin, E.M., Pitrak, D.L. (1997). Working memory deficits in HIV-seropositive drug users. *Journal of International Neuropsychology Society, 3,* 451-456.

Boccellari, A.A., Dilley, J.W., Chambers, D.B., Yingling, C.D., Tauber, M.A., Moss, A.R., and Osmond, D.H. (1993).Immune function and neuropsychological performance in HIV-1 infected homosexual men. *Journal of Acquired Deficiency Syndrome, 6,*592- 601.

Bornstein, R.A., Nasrallah, H.A., Para, M.F., Whitacre, C.C., Rosenberger, P. and Fass, R.J. (1993). Neuropsychological performance in symptomatic and asymptomatic HIV infection. *AIDS, 7,* 519-524.

Charles H. H , David J.H., Karen I. M, Steven A.C., Mona N.L., Marta S. and Bryan Z. (2002). Verbal and spatial working memory performance among HIV-infected adults. *Journal of the*

International Neuropsychological Society, 8, 532-538.

Damos, D.L., John, R.S., Parker, E.S. and Levine, A.M. (1997). Cognitive functioning in asymptomatic HIV infection. *Archives of Neurology, 54*, 179-185.

Franzblau, A., Letz, R., Hershman, D., Mason, P., Wallace, J.I. and Beksi, J.G. (1991). Quantitative neurological and neurobehavioral testing of persons infected with Human Immunodeficiency Virus type-1. *Archive ofNneurology, 48*, 263-268.

González-Scarano, F. and Martín-García, J. (2005). The Neuropathogenesis of AIDS. *Nature Reviews Immunology* 5, 69-81.

Grant, I., Atkinson, J.H., Hesselink, J.R., Kennedy, C.J., Richman, D.D., Spector, S.A., and McCutchan, J.A. (1987). Evidence for early central nervous system involvement in the acquired immunodeficiency syndrome (AIDS) and other human immunodeficiency virus (HIV) infections. *Annals of Internal Medicine, 107*, 828-836.

Grant, I., Marcotte, T.D., Heaton, R.K. and HNRC Group (1999). Neurocognitive complications of HIV disease. *Psychological Science, 10*, 191-195.

Grant, I. and Martin, A. (1995). Neuropsychology of HIV infection. New York: Oxford University Press.

Heaton, R.K., Grant, I., Butters, N., White, D., Kirson, D., Atkinson, J.H., McCutchan, J.A., Taylor, M.J., Kelly, M.D., Ellis, R.J. and The HNRC 500 (1995). Neuropsychology of HIV infection at different disease stages. *Journal of International Neuropsychological Society, 1*, 231-251.

Janssen, R.S., Saykin, A.J., Cannon, L., Compbell, J., Pinsky, P.F., Hessol, N.A., O'Malley, P. M., Lifson, A.R., Doll, L.S. and Rutherford, G. (1989). Neurological and neuropsychological manifestation of HIV infection: Associated with AIDS related complex but not asymtomatic HIV infection. *Annals of Neurology, 26*, 259-600.

Lunn, S., Skydsbjerg, M., Schulsinger, H., Parnas, J., Pedersen, C. and Mathiesen, L.A. (1991). Preliminary report on the neuropsychological sequelae of Human Immunodeficiency Virus. *Archives of General Psychiatry, 46*, 139-142.

Law, W.A., Martin, A., Mapou, R.L., Roller, T.I., Salazar, A.M., Temoshock, L.R., and Rundell, J.R. (1994). Working memory in individuals with HIV infection. *Journal of Clinical Experimental Neueuropsychology, 16*, 173-182.

Pajeau, A.K. and Roman, G.C. (1992). HIV encephalopathy and dementia. *The Psychiatry* Clinic *of North America, 15*, 455-466.

Poutiainen, E., Elovaara, I., Raininko, R., Vilkki, J., Lahdevirta, J., and Iivanainen, M. (1996). Cognitive decline in patients with symptomatic HIV-1 infection. No decline in asymptomatic infection. *Acta Neurologica Scandanavica, 93*, 421-427.

Maj, M., Satz, P., Janssen, R., Zaudig, M., Starace, F., D'Elia, L., Sughondhabirom, B., Mussa, M., Naber, D., Ndetei, D., Schulte, G. and Sartorius, N. (1994). WHO neuropsychiatric AIDS study, cross sectional phase II. neuropsychological and neurological findings. *Archives of General Psychiatry, 51,* 51-61.

Martin, E.M., Robertson, L.C., Sorensen, D.J., Jagust, W.J., Mallon, K.F., and Chirurgi, V.A. (1993). Speed of memory scanning is not affected in early HIV-1 infection. *Journal of Clinical and Experimental Neuropsychology, 15*, 311-320.

Martin, S.I., Cano, M.R., Perez, A.P., Augayo, C.M., Coesta, F., Rodriguez, P., Pujol, L. and Llave, E. (2002). Quality of life, psychological and social aspects in patients with advanced HIV disease. *Anales de medicina interna, 19,* 396-404.

McArthur, J.C., Cohen, B., Salnes, O.A., Kumar, A.J., Cooper, K., McArthur, J.H., Soucy, G.,

Cornblath, D.R., Chmiel, J.S., Meicheng, W., Starkey, D.L., Ginzburg, H., Ostrow, D.G., Johnson, R.T., Phair, J.P. and Polk, B.F. (1989). Low prevalence of neurological and neuropsychological abnormalities in otherwise healthy HIV –1 infected individuals : Results from multicenter AIDS cohort study. *Annals of Neurology, 26*, 601-611.

Moore, L. H., van Group, W.G., Stern, M.J., Swales, T., and Satz, P. (1991). Subjective complaint versus actual cognitive deficits in predominantly symptomatic HIV-1 seropositive individual. *The Journal of Neuropsychiatry and Clinical Neurosciences, 9,* 37-44.

Navia, B.A., Jordan, B.D., and Price, R.W. (19086). The AIDS dementia complex: I, Clinical features. *Annals of Neurology, 19,* 517-524.

Navia, B.A., and Price, R.W. (1986). The acquired immunodeficiency syndrome dementia complex as the presenting or sole manifestation of human immunodeficiency virus infection. *Archives of Neurology, 44,* 65-69.

Perdices, M., and Cooper, D.A. (1989). Simple and choice reaction time in patients with human immunodeficiency virus infection. *Annals of Neurology, 25,* 460-467.

Perry, S., and Jacobsen, P. (1986). Neuropsychiatric manifestation of AIDS-spectrum disorders. *Hospital and Community Psychiatry, 7*, 135-142.

Salnes, O.A., Miller, E. and Mc Arthur, J.C. (1990). HIV-1 infection : No evidence of decline during the asymptomatic stages. *Neurology, 40*, 204-208.

Singh, H., Sharma, C.S., Chakraborty, P.K. and Sattar, F.A. (2001). Cognitive dysfunction in clinically asymptomatic HIV seropositive individuals. *Indian Journal of Psychiatry, 43,* 162-170.

Stern, R.A., Singer, N.G., Silva, S.G., Roger, H.J., Perkins, D.O., Hall, C.D., Vander Horst, C.M. and Evans, D.L. (1992). Neurobehavioral functioning in non-confounding group of asymptomatic HIV seropositive homosexual men. *American Journal of Psychiatry, 149,* 1099-1102.

Stout J C, Salmon, D. p., Butters, N., et. al. (1995). Decline in working memory associated with HIV infection. *Psychological Medicine, 25,* 1221-1232.

Van Group, W.G., Staz, P., Hinkin, C., Selnes, O., Miller, E.N., McArthur, J., Cohen, B., Paz, D., and the Multicenter AIDS cohort study (1991). Metacognition in HIV-1 seropopsitive asymptomatic individuals: Self ratings versus objective neuropsychological performance. *Journal of Clinical Experimental Neuropsychology*, 13, 812-819.

Villa, G., Montelleone, D. and Marra, C. (1993). Neuropsychological abnormality in AIDS avd asymptomatic HIV seropositive patients. *Journal of Neurology and Neurosergury Psychiatry, 56*, 878-884.

Wilkie, F.L., Eisdorfer, C., Morgan, R., Loewenstein, D.A. and Szapoeznik, J. (1990). Cognition in early Human Immunodeficiency Virus infection. *Archives of Neurology, 47*, 433-440.

Wilkins, J.W., Robertson, K.R., Snyder, C.R., Robertson, W.K., van der J Horst, C., and Hall C.D. (1991). Implication of self reported cognitive and motor dysfunction in HIV- positive patients. *American Journal of Psychiatry, 148*, 641-643.

Wilkie, F.L., Goodkin, K., Eisdorfer, C., Feaster, D., Morgan, R., Fletcher, A. M., Blaneey, N., Baum, M., and Szapocznik, J. (1998). Mild cognitive impairment and risk of mortality in HIV-1 infection. *Journal of Neuropsychiatry Clinical Neuroscience, 98*,125–132.

Zeifert, P., Leary, M. and Boccellari, A. (1995). AIDS and the Impact of Cognitive Impairment. UCSF AIDS Health Project.

12

Role of Media in Awareness of HIV/AIDS in Uttar Pradesh

Sarika Jaiswal

Introduction

HIV/AIDS is the worst epidemic humanity has ever faced. It has spread further, faster and with more catastrophic long-term effects than any other disease. Its impact has become a devastating obstacle to development. Broadcast media have tremendous reach and influence, particularly with young people, who represent the future and who are the key to any successful fight against HIV/AIDS. We must seek to engage these powerful organizations as full partners in the fight to halt HIV/AIDS through awareness, prevention, and education.

Today, 8,000 people will lose their lives to HIV/AIDS and another 14,000—10 people every single minute—will become newly infected.

The realities of today's global epidemic are graver than even the worst-case predictions of 10 years ago. AIDS killed more than 3 million people in 2003 and an estimated 5 million more became infected—bringing to some 40 million the number currently living with the virus. More than 20 million have already died since the first clinical evidence of the disease was reported in 1981.

The media have a pivotal role to play in the fight against AIDS. It is often said that education is the vaccine against HIV. Many media organizations are rising to the challenge by promoting awareness of HIV/AIDS and educating listeners and viewers about the facts of the epidemic and how to stop it.

According to national surveys conducted in the United States, 72 percent of Americans identify television, radio and newspapers as their primary source of information about HIV/AIDS, more than doctors, friends and family. Similar statistics have also been reported in the United Kingdom and elsewhere in the world.

In a survey carried out in India more than 70 percent of respondents said they had received their information about HIV/AIDS from television.

Clearly, media organizations have an enormous influence in educating and empowering individuals to avoid contracting HIV. Doing so with maximum efficiency, however, requires a clear understanding of the challenges and the obstacles to widespread and effective HIV-prevention education. AIDS has in resent years grown exponentially into a frightening worldwide epidemic. WHO estimates that more than 10 million people are currently infected with human immune deficiency virus.

The media have a pivotal role to play in the fight against AIDS. It is often said that education is the vaccine against HIV. Many media organizations are rising to the challenge by promoting awareness of HIV/AIDS and educating listeners and viewers about the facts of the epidemic and how to stop it. According to national surveys conducted in the United States, 72 percent of Americans identify television, radio and newspapers as their primary source of information about HIV/AIDS, more than doctors, friends and family. Similar statistics have also been reported in the United Kingdom and elsewhere in the world. In a survey carried out in India more than 70 percent of respondents said they had received their information about HIV/AIDS from television. Clearly, media organizations have an enormous influence in educating and empowering individuals to avoid contracting HIV. Doing so with maximum efficiency, however, requires a clear understanding of the challenges and the obstacles to widespread and effective HIV-prevention Education.

Perspectives

HIV/AIDS in News: Uttar Pradesh: U.P is considered a low prevalence state for HIV/AIDS but with its large population the problem can become serious if awareness is low.

The Backdrop

Uttar Pradesh, the most populous state of India, is a highly vulnerable region with regard to spread of the HIV/AIDS virus. The epidemic is presently low in visibility here, with the state having just 1.47 percent of the total number of AIDS cases reported countrywide Statistics for 2004 show that U.P has 10,896 people infected with HIV/AIDS. The prevalence rate is 0.8 percent in groups considered high-risk and 0.23 percent in the rest of the population. Districts with high levels of infection include Varanasi, Allahabad, Lucknow, Agra and Gorakhpur.

The Study

A content analysis of the coverage of HIV/AIDS by newspapers published from Uttar Pradesh was carried out from January 1-June 8, 2005. For a month from May 8-June 10, 2005, an intensive scan was carried out of all major print media in the state. This included 13 daily newspapers and a weekly publication. All of them either originated from the state or were national papers with editions from Lucknow.

Findings

The analysis of HIV/AIDS reportage in U.P. shows that the issue has high visibility in the press with a large number of stories. Except for a single day when no story on the subject appeared in the media during the one month intensive analysis in May/June. In fact the coverage peaked to as many as 14 articles on one particular day. An average of 3-4 articles appeared daily.

Of the 165 artricles on HIV/AIDS, an overwhelming 119 or 72 percent were news stories, 28 or 17 percent were features and four were editorials. Fifty three stories had accompanying photographs while 11 items were photographs only. Most stories (85 percent) were placed on the inside pages of newspapers, with seven stories however appearing on the front pages. Eleven stories were published in newspaper supplements.

The frame of reference of the majority of stories was equally divided between national (60 stories) and state-level (58 stories), indicating that local journalists were quite active in reporting on the situation. Thirty stories were about the global HIV/AIDS situation, 25 dealt with the community-level situation and 7 stories looked at individuals affected by the virus. Only 24 stories carried multiple perspectives of all affected parties and 19 stories were particular about maintaining the confidentiality of people living with HIV/AIDS.

On the brighter side, a considerable number of stories (48) expanded the scope of their coverage to examine HIV/AIDS linkages with migration, human trafficking, employment, poverty and gender issues. Another positive indicator was that as many as 56 stories correctly reflected the spread of the epidemic from high-risk segments to the general population. Nevertheless, some stories (30) still levelled blame for spreading the virus on particular segments of the population such as women and sex workers, men who have sex with men, injectable drug users, blood donors and truck drivers. These stories also carried covert elements of stigma and discrimination. Another 16 stories or 10 percent of the coverage served to perpetuate false notions of the epidemic by associating HIV/AIDS with behaviours such as crime, extramarital sex and multiple partners as well as sexually perverted practices. For instance, a story in Dainik Jagran headlined, "Dreaded terrorist in Doda dies of AIDS", opens with, "There is a saying that those who are cruel, and cruelly", implying that a criminal deserved to die from the virus. The article conveys a warped lesson that HIV/AIDS is just punishment for criminal action, an association that reflects negatively on others who are infected. It also informs that "blue films, local girls and virility boosting potions were found in the terrorist's hideout during police raids" indicating that sexually depraved behaviour resulted in the infection. This judgmental attitude intensifies stigma faced by people with HIV/AIDS.

Some stories (25) gave factually incorrect information on the virus. For instance, a story in Jansatta Express on a scientific breakthrough in treatment raises false hopes without providing any substantial references. It also has a sub-heading that is misleading and trivializes the infection, "*Tamatar khao-AIDS bhagao*" or "Eat tomatoes and scare away AIDS".

Creating Panic and Scare

Some alarmist news items were part of an ongoing series by their newspaper and served to evoke a feeling of doom around HIV/AIDS. The story on tomatoes and AIDS, for example, says "Everyone is afraid of death, and to top that if one's life is taken inch by inch and one has to put up with discrimination at the same time then it becomes dangerous".

A photograph of a sand sculpture depicting skulls created by an artist, ironically to promote awareness instead reinforced the fear that life ended with HIV/AIDS. This negative imagery was carried without comment by a number of newspapers.

Headlines in the media (11 stories) like "Hepatitis B not as dangerous as AIDS" and "Four members of a single family have AIDS" or "Entire family in grip of HIV", and "Youth dies of AIDS", not only selectively highlight individual infections that would be likely to lead to their social ostracism, but are based only on the fact that someone has contracted the virus. They do not carry any information on prevention and control of the infection or go into other dimensions that would give a full picture.

Words commonly used in the context of HIV/AIDS to describe its serious nature are 'bomb, genocide, dangerous disadvantage, bhayanak trasadi or fearsome tragedy' A popular description to convey the horror of the infection is til til kar marna or dying in slow agony. The terminology expresses the view that HIV/AIDS is equal to agonizing death and as destructive as a bomb. The fear thus evoked against the virus stokes revulsion against those who have it.

Comparison of Regional Language and English Press

The survey shows that there were many more articles on HIV/AIDS in the Hindi press in Uttar Pradesh as compared to the English press. While this was partly because more Hindi newspapers are published in the state and were therefore included in the survey, the Hindi press did in fact have a greater proportion of stories.

A detailed look at the coverage by the Hindi language media reveals that the two major issues it took up were HIV/AIDS awareness campaigns including those by celebrities, the other being spread of the epidemic. Some stories had a negative tone. For instance, and article on an infected woman who is described as a sex worker and a threat to military personnel in Dehradun and another article attributing an increase in HIV/AIDS infections in Bundelkhand to the growing practice of buying brides from other regions who are then blamed for spreading the virus.

The rest comprised positive reporting with some investigation, such as a story in Jansatta Express titled, "AIDS spreading from cities to rural areas," and one in Hindustan titled, "If Pepsi and Coke can reach villages then why not condoms", "Health administration lax on HIV epidemic", deals with a host of issues around the epidemic and government apathy.

In comparison to the Hindi newspaper, the English press in U.P. carried a significantly lower proportion of news on HIV/AIDS but it had a higher number of individual and community-based stories. Six of the 36 identified English stories were related to spot events. This resulted in the English press having a lower proportion of stories with a bland or neutral tone. The large majority of its articles were informative and analytical, providing a perspective to the reader. They were also better displayed.

Media Treatment of People Living with HIV/AIDS Stigma

If the issue of stigma has been raised in any of the stories, it has been done so with concern in most cases. For instance, nineteen articles discussed care as being a fundamental right of HIV positive people, many of them debunked wrong notions and provided inspiring life histories. A workshop on clinical care organized by the CCII in Lucknow with assistance from Australian experts, generated unusually extensive coverage in the local media of both languages. Five of the news reports in both English and Hindi were merely event-based reports on who spoke at the inauguration. The four positive reports focused on what had been said, using the one-day workshop as an event to explore the various dimensions of the virus and its spread in the state. There of the stories, however, raised the risk to health-care personal and their safety concerns in a manner that definitely had the potential of scaring them away from treating HIV/AIDS affected persons. In its stories titled, "AIDS : paramedics be careful", The Times of India said there is a "high danger Zone for those who are in charge of the patients. Even simple accident causes immediate infection." Similarly, a report in the Dainik Jagran sensationally headlined, "Medical workers being targeted by AIDS," warns rural health workers that they are in the direct line of fire from AIDS. Instead of reporting in a responsible manner on precautions that need to be taken, the item has the irrational advice that hospital workers who are pregnant, "should not even come near such patients" factually wrong information such as this when published in a news paper erodes hope of non discriminatory treatment infected persons.

Reporting on HIV and Gender Issues

The media has exhibited two extreme methods of treating HIV positive individuals, women in particular. A feature in The Indian Express on Veena Dhari, a positive woman from Karnataka who spoke the of overcoming social stigma and discrimination and became an inspiration for others was a sensitive story that helps reducing discriminatory reactions by- ill-informed public.

Four stories deal with the launch of a media campaign by TV actress Mandira Bedi and others on a wives being vulnerable to the infection and the need for even married couples to use condoms. An article in Sahara Samay titled, "Earning and bringing home AIDS" focused on the reasons for spread of the epidemic in eastern U.P. It brings out the risks faced by women of the region by discussing its high rate of migration for work. The feature clearly establishes the epidemics' link to poverty and unemployment in the region and analyses the availability of medical help for infected persons here and their treatment by family and society.

A similar positive role is played by an article in Hindustan titled, "28 persons have died of AIDS in kushinagar district in the past two and a half years," Despite a sensational headline the story is a meaningful investigation into eastern U.P's infection levels with special mention of the vulnerability of women. An extremely encouraging photograph carried only in Dainik jagran was that of a celebrity, Sharmila Tagore, hugging an HIV positive woman.

However, these news items are the notable exceptions. In fact, the study found 21 negative stories that could have a devastating impact on infected women, A section of the Hindi newspapers repeatedly referred in a derogatory manner to women with the virus as 'vish-kanyas" 'or poison women,'' The media adds to the stigmatization by alleging these woman were infecting "innocent victims". A report in the Swatanatra Bharat titled "The film 'Vish kanya' to raises public awareness on AIDS", is the datelined Gorakhpur and praises the movie for alerting people through its story of a women afflicted with AIDS. She establishes relationship with people that force them to a torturous death in return for just a few moments of pleasure."

A three column story in Dainik Jagran titled, "Vishkanyas are stinging the jawans," claims that infected women are being sent by terrorist to deliberately infect Indian armed forces. The article insists this is not hearsay but true reportage and that even the union health ministry was involved in countering the threat.

A series of prominently placed three column long articles in Hindustan 'exposes' for the sake of public safety, the deigns of one particular infected woman who has been 'found' in Dehradun and is allegedly spreading the epidemic by engaging in prostitution. The article dehumanizes the woman into a beast who must be kept chained for public safety.

Articles of this nature always conclude that a HIV/AIDS infected women must be a prostitute. The men involved are projected sympathetically, often as victims.

Educating and Entertaining

To be effective, messaging about HIV/AIDS must be both educational and entertaining. These two goals should not be mutually exclusive. A number of programmes have served to inform their audiences about the virus while, at the same time, achieving market success. In India, Doordarshan, the national television service, the National AIDS Control Organisation (NACO) and the BBC World Service Trust, (the international development arm of the British Broadcasting Corporation), joined forces in 2002 to launch the country's first-ever mass media campaign to increase awareness of HIV/AIDS. The campaign has been largely based on education through entertainment, with two key strands being the popular interactive detective series *Jasoos* (*Detective*) *Vijay* and the award-winning weekly 'reality' youth show, *Haath se Haath Milaa* (Let's Join Hands).

Both programmes have proved popular with audiences and *Jasoos Vijay* was voted 'Best Thriller Series' in the prestigious Indian Television Awards 2003. Viewers are therefore given information about the virus and how to protect themselves while watching an enjoyable programme at the same time. For example, according to an independent survey, 85 percent of respondents to the campaign said they had learned something new and almost a third said they had discussed messages with friends.

Putting HIV/AIDS on the News Agenda

Another key area for media involvement in AIDS education efforts is ensuring that the topic is kept at the top of the news agenda. In recent years, several leading broadcasters from around the world have found innovative ways to report on the epidemic.

The BBC World Service launched a two-week season of programming, including news reports, documentaries, and online coverage of the epidemic to mark World AIDS Day 2003. The company's high-profile interviews with several world leaders and celebrities, along with phone-ins and 'webchats' with other public figures, generated broad coverage of HIV for audiences around the world.

The Chinese national station, China Central Television (CCTV), broadcast some 230 news items on HIV/AIDS in the first 10 months of 2003.

Since 1996, Spain's Radiotelevision Espanola (RTVE) has also worked to keep discussion of the virus in the public domain. Each year, this has led to two months of special programming, aimed at raising awareness, in the lead-up to World AIDS Day.

In the US, the Time Warner network, HBO, broadcast a five-part documentary series in the summer of 2003 entitled *Pandemic: Facing AIDS*. CNN has also run a special season of HIV-related programming, which included a large news component.

The NTV Channel and the radio station Echo of Moscow (*Gazprom*) have also ensured that the virus has received widespread coverage and been kept near the top of the news agenda, whether through medical news programmes, reports about the epidemic, radio call-ins or studio discussions.

Metro TV in Indonesia has consistently broadcast HIV/AIDS-related news and featured comment and analysis about the epidemic in talk-shows and documentaries.

Mounting an effective global response to AIDS is clearly an expensive challenge, and insufficient resources have been invested in this effort to date. In ensuring that HIV remains 'headline news', broadcasters play a vital role in encouraging world leaders and policy-makers to take the epidemic seriously and provide the resources necessary to fund adequate prevention and treatment programmes.

A virtuous circle should result: the more leaders see about HIV in the news, the greater the resources they invest in anti-AIDS strategies, which in turn leads to increased media coverage of the issue and helps to sustain public awareness, which, again, has an impact on leaders' priorities.

Summary and Conclusion

While there is considerable visibility provided to the issue of HIV/AIDS in the newspapers from Uttar Pradesh, the nature of reporting needs to be focused on the epidemic in the state. Some specific findings and recommendations which emerge from the study are discussed below:

1. HIV/AIDS is no longer a theoretical threat for the state. It is a reality among the hundreds and thousands of men and woman who depend upon men to

earn a livelihood away from home. Creating a fear psychosis about the condition may not the best way to do so.

2. HIV/AIDS is often painted as being a virulent infection. Fortunately this is not so. The mere presence of the virus in the body does not lead to either debility or death. A responsible media can play a very positive role in helping individual and communities support each other through publishing stories of hope and profiles of courage.
3. The health system response to HIV/AIDS is at present very inadequate. The fact that there are many districts without safe blood banks needs to the highlighted. The media can play a very creative role in monitoring the implementation of government programmes.
4. The vulnerability of women to HIV/AIDS is an issue of grave concern in U.P. However the media constantly sensationalises the role of woman and especially in the context of sex, and this needs to change.
5. It is necessary for senior journalists and editors to put in place a clear editorial policy and guidelines for reporting on HIV/AIDS. Reporters and even stringers should also be provided with training on how to report on this sensitive subject.

The media plays a critical role in creating public opinion, in spearheading social change. In the case of HIV/AIDS a clear understanding of the nuances of the subject, a concern for human rights, capacity' building among journalists to understand and report on a such a sensitive issue, and clear editorial oversight will enable the media to play a key role in facilitating a holistic and effective response to the HIV/AIDS epidemic in the state of Uttar Pradesh.

13

Psychological Aspects of High Risk Behaviour of HIV

Sonal Sharma and Smita Jaiswal

Introduction

The HIV/AIDS epidemic is now about two decades old in India and within this short period it has emerged as one of the most serious public health problem in the country. Currently, India has the largest HIV/AIDS epidemic rates in the South Asian subcontinent (Jain, John and Keusch, 1994; FHI 2001; WHO 2001; NACO 2001; Reid and Costingan, 2002).

India is predicted to experience Significantly more infection than any other country in the world, raising tremendous concern about the future health of the Indian population and capacity of existing resources to meet long term health care needs. According to the United Nations, India is considered a high-risk country (UNAIDS, 2002). According to NACO (Annual Report, 2004), the current infection rates in India for those between 15-49 years is estimated to be at 0.98 percent. The predominant path of transmission of HIV in India is through heterosexual contact (85.69 percent). The majority of HIV infection (87.7 percent) is in the age group in 15-44 years (NACO, Annual Report, 2004).

HIV/AIDS and High Risk Behaviour

HIV/AIDS and high risk behaviour has become a priority in the current studies agenda. Risk behaviour engage people not only to needle sharing among the infection drug uses but also to unprotected sexual practices.

As observed in several studies, sexually active individuals continue to engage in unprotected sexual intercourse even after they become knowledgeable about HIV transmission (Diclemente at al, 1992; Kegeles, Adler and Lrwin, 1988; Kipke and Hein, 1990; Thurman and Frankin, 1990).

In a study by Ford (1989) the author noted that alcohol consumption made people less sexually inhibited and made sex more pleasurable. In addition, most of them reported that drinking made them likely to forget about HIV/AIDS risks and pregnancy. Sixty four percent of males and 50 percent of Female stated that they were less likely to use condoms after drinking.

Stall and his colleagues (1986) reported that 'high risk' Sexual activity amongst gay men in the USA was associated with the use of alcohol and men who used drugs with sex were at least twice as likely as other men to engage in risky activities.

The questions what are those psychological factor which are responsible for high risk behaviour in normal adults?

Studies suggest that how people think and feel it influences how they behave. Psychological aspect such as risk perception, personality characteristics psychological states are responsible for high risk behaviour. People who think AIDS is a relatively minor or remote problem are less likely to take steps to reduce their risk. In addition, people who think that they personality are not at risk for HIV infection are more likely to engage in risk behaviour.

Individual personality with risk, are more susceptible to boredom and they have a higher experience seeking behaviour than the group without risk behaviour. Patients engaging in high risk behaviour have a higher sensation seeking behaviour than the without risk group.

Antisocial personality, impulsivity, tendency to seek out new sensation etc. are related to sexual risk taking behaviour (Kalichman, 1998). Coping responses also influence risk behaviour to escape from or relieve stress. Personality factors determine sexual risk taking behaviour including high risk behaviour. High risk behaviour subjects on the whole have high sensation seeking levels. H.R.B. Subjects are more inhibited Subjects than with out High risk behaviour.

The most commonly given reasons by the subjects for engaging in high risk behaviour in rank order were, seeking pleasure, sexual dissatisfaction with spouse, lack of sex partner, as a habit, to kill loneliness, stress and worries and due to problems in the family.

Following factor have been found significant related with high risk behaviour (Chandra Prabha, Vivek Bengel, Jayashree Rama Krishna 1998).

1. Loneliness.
2. Habit/impulsivity.
3. Pleasure (Sensation Seeking).
4. Stress and worries.
5. Problem in the family.
6. Lack of Sex partner.
7. Substance abuse.
8. Peer Pressure.

Psychological States

Psychological states and disorder such as personality disorder, self destructive behaviour, hypersexuality, sexual obsession and compulsivity, depression, anxiety and negative states of mind (e.g. anger pessimism) are associated with high risk sexual behaviour with multiple partners. Which can increase HIV risk through needle Sharing and through decreasing the likelihood that safer sex practices (Such as condom use) will be used.

Some other Issues Related with High Risk Behaviour

Gender: While HIV/AIDS is a health issue, the epidemic is more of a gender issue. The gender analysis and mainstreaming strategies are contained in the gender and HIV/AIDS.

In India different attributes and roles have been assigned to males and female by society and these profoundly affect their ability to protect them selves against HIV/AIDS and to cope with its impact.

Women Often are at Greater Risk of HIV: Transmission of HIV comes mainly through heterosexual intercourse, while unsafe sex remains the main cause of infection. Many unprotected sex appears to be the norm in many societies, even when multiple partners are involved. Women are at risk for different reasons than men and there is a direct link between women's low status, the violation of their human rights and HIV transmission. Gender based violence is one of the leading factor in the increased rates of HIV infection among women. Women's restricted sexual autonomy and men's expanded sexual freedom are reflected in all studies of factor which increase women's and men's risk and vulnerability to HIV as well as several violent elements in sexual relationships. There is growing evidence that a large share of new cases of HIV infection is due to gender based violence in home, School and the work place and other social spheres. Violence against women is a world wide Phenomenon and is common in practically all societies and a major cause of death. "women are also for more likely than men to face violence, including physical, sexual abuse or psychological harm, in which they do not have control over intercourse (Turmen 2003)".

Age: Age is very important issues for HIV about half of all new HIV infection world wide or approximately 6.000 per day one quarter of total population of India (about 280 million) are young people and more them 35 percent of all reported AIDS cases in India occur among young people in the age group of 15-24 years (NACO Annual report 2004). This indicates that adolescents are a highly vulnerable group. Adolescents are not well informed about their health, sexuality or physical well-being. Knowledge is incompletes and confusing regarding the issues of health and sexuality.

Challenges for Mental Health Workers

1. To enhance HIV/AIDS education.

2. To educate people to personalize risk assessment.
3. To enhance self-management skills.
4. To enhance awareness about condom use and sterilization training.

On the basis of above mentioned studies there is an strong need of educating people about HIV. This education must involve self management skills and personalized risk assessment and training about condom use at the initial level. Unfortunately efforts which are being made are on knowledge level only, which are not sufficient for prevention in future.

To plan effective strategies, it is necessary to understand the diverse nature of the at risk groups who may very by ethnicity, gender, age, acculturation, and socioeconomic status. Operational definitions of cultural factors should move beyond merely identifying People according to researcher-defined social categories (e.g., race and gender).

References

Chandra P., Bengal V., Ramakrishna J., Krishna VAS (1998) Project founded by the National Institute of Mental Health and Neurosciences, Bangalore.

Chhabra, R., (2007) Ghosh S.N. and Sharma S.K. (2007) need assessment of an alcohol and HIV prevention education program for youth in North western Himalyas. *Journal of the Indian Academy of Applied Psychology*, January 2007, Vol. 33, No. 1, 5-14.

Diclements, R.J., Durbin, M., Siegal, D., Karsnovsky, F., Lazarus, N., and Comacho, T. (1992). Determinants of condom use among junior high school students in a minority, inner-city school district. *Pediatrics*, 89, 197-202.

Ford, N. (1989). Urban-rural variations in the level of heterosexual activity of young people, *Area*, 21, 237-248.

Jain, M.K. John. T.J. and Keuseh, G.T. (1994). A review of human immunodeficiency virus infection in India. *Joumal of Acquired Immune Deficiency Syndromes*, 7, 1185-1194.

Kalichaman, S, Cain, D., Zueben, A., and Swain, G. (2003) Sensation Seeking, sexual risk behaviour among men receiving services at a clinic for sexually transmitted infection. *Joumal of Studies on Alcohol*, 64, 564-569.

Kipke, M.D., and Hein, K. (1990). Acquired Immuno Deficiency Syndrome (AIDS) in adolescents. In M. Schydlower and M.A. Shafer (Eds), AIDS and other Sexually Transmitted Diseases. (pp. 429-449). Philadelphia : Hanley and Belfus.

NACO (2004). Annual Report (2004). Ministry of Health and Family Welfare, Government of India.

National AIDS Control Organization Survey, 2007. Government of India.

Stall, R. (1988). The prevention of HIV infection associated with drug and alcohol use during sexual activity. In: Siegal, L. (ed). AIDS and Substance abuse, New York, Harrington Park Press, pp. 73-88.

Stall, R., MC Kurick, L., Wiley, J. etal. (1986) Alcohol and Drug use during sexual activity and compliance with safe sex guidelines for AIDS : The AIDS Behavioural Research Project, *Health Education Quarterly*, 13, 359-371.

Weissman MM (2001) *Journal of Personality Disorder.* Understanding the role of personality in HIV Risk Behaviour.

World Health organization (WHO). (2005). Alcohol use and sexual risk Behaviour. A cross-cultural study in eight countries. Geneva, Switzerland: Author.

World health organization 2001, FACT SHEET School Health and Youth Health Promotion. World Health Organization, Geneva.

Zuckerman, M. (1979). Sensation-Seeking Beyond the Optimal Level of Arousal. Hillsdale, NJ: Erlbaum.

14

HIV/AIDS Awareness among Nursing Trainees

Deapti Mishra, Ranjeet Kumar, J. Mathto and S.N. Sahu

Introduction

HIV/AIDS is one of the most pressing international health problems as in the past two decades these have become a leading cause of illness and death. By the end of the year 2004, an estimated 39.4 million people worldwide were living with HIV/AIDS. More than three million people died of it in the same year. India accounts for 10 percent of global HIV burden and 65 percent of that in South and South East Asia (National AIDS Control Organization, 2003).

India has a population of one billion, around half of whom are adults in the sexually active age group. The first AIDS case in India was detected in 1986; since then HIV infection has been reported in all states and union territories. Previously it was thought that around 5 million people were living with HIV in India - more than in any other country. Better data, including the results of a national household survey, led to a major revision of the prevalence estimate in July 2007. It is now thought that around 2.4 million people in India are living with HIV (NACO, Annual Report 2002-2004).

In 2006 UNAIDS estimated that there were 5.6 million people living with HIV in India, which indicated that there were more people with HIV in India than in any other country in the world (UNAIDS, 2006). However, NACO disputed this estimate, and claimed that the actual figure was lower (NACO, 2006). In 2007, following the first survey of HIV among the general population, UNAIDS and NACO agreed on a new estimate – between 2 million and 3.6 million people living with HIV. The figure was confirmed to be 2.4 million in 2008. This puts India behind South Africa and Nigeria in numbers living with HIV (UNAIDS, 2007; UNAIDS, 2008).

In terms of AIDS cases, the most recent estimate comes from August 2006, at which stage the total number of AIDS cases reported to NACO was 124,995. Of this number, 29 percent were women, and 36 percent were under the age of 30. These figures are not accurate reflections of the actual situation though, as large numbers of AIDS cases go unreported (NACO, 2006).

The spread of HIV in India has been diverse, with much of India having a low rate of infection and the epidemic being most extreme in the southern half of the country and in the far north-east. The highest HIV prevalence rates are found in Maharashtra, Andhra Pradesh and Karnataka in the south; and Manipur, Mizoram and Nagaland in the north-east ("HIV Sentinel Surveillance and HIV Estimation, 2006", NACO, 2007). States like Chhattisgarh, Madhya Pradesh, Kerela, Haryana, Bihar, Rajasthan and Orissa had around 50,000 people living with HIV/AIDS each, in the year 2006, though prevalence in these states is low ("HIV Sentinel Surveillance and HIV Estimation, 2006", NACO, 2007).

Its spread is a major concern in India particularly in Chhattisgarh. 4 out of 5 in Chattisgarh (80 percent) have not heard of AIDS. The all-India average is 60 percent. Awareness of AIDS particularly low among women who are not regularly exposed to media and SC women, illiterate women, women living in rural area. Women who heard about AIDS — 93 percent received information about the disease from television, 47 percent from radio, 30 percent from newspapers or magazines. Women who knew about AIDS — 55 percent did not know of any way to avoid infection, whereas 21 percent of women mentioned use of condoms as a way of avoiding the disease. NFHS-2 results suggest that health personnel could play a larger role in promoting AIDS awareness. In Chattisgarh, only 4 percent of women who knew about AIDS received information about the disease from a health worker (International Institute of Population Sciences, National Family Welfare Survey, 1998-99, Mumbai, India, October 2000).

As AIDS attacks our body immune system, there is severe global deterioration in physical and mental health. HIV/AIDS infected persons suffer from various diseases leading them to hospital. Besides the family members, medical staffs particularly, nurses take care of these patients. So, Nursing students are being identified as a potential risk group for the AIDS spread. Awareness regarding AIDS in this group is crucial for AIDS management and prevention. Hospital staff and health professionals, much like the rest of the Indian population, are often unaware of the facts about HIV. This leads to unnecessary fears and, in some cases, causes them to stigmatise HIV positive people and discriminate against them. There are various misconceptions about HIV/AIDS and lack of proper information not only hampers proper treatment but health professionals can be at risk of becoming infected, too.

Active attempts are being made to create awareness about it by Government and various NGO's and improvement in the condition has been reported. Assessment is essential to the evaluation of interventions designed to increase knowledge and encourage the adoption of safer beliefs about preventing HIV/AIDS. This study was planned to serve this purpose, by assessing awareness about it in nursing trainees. It is one of the pioneer studies in this area.

Material and Methods

Tools:

1. Socio-demographic datasheet.
2. Assessment of knowledge and beliefs about HIV/AIDS among adolescents (Koopman et al., 1992).
   It consists of two sub-tests:

- Aids knowledge test and
- Safer alternatives.

These cover information in the domains of definition, risk behaviours, transmission of the virus, outcomes of the HIV infection, HIV testing and prevention and distinguishing safer from less safer behaviour.

Methodology

This was a cross sectional study in it three leading nursing colleges of Bhilai, Chhatistisgarh were contacted and permission to conduct the study was taken. All the B.Sc nursing trainees (158) were taken as the sample. Their personal details were gathered on a specially designed socio-demographic datasheet designed for the purpose. Then the 'Assessment of knowledge and beliefs about HIV/AIDS among adolescents' (Koopman et al., 1992) was administered on them to gather information regarding their awareness about HIV/AIDS. Out of 158, 6 records were considered invalid due to being incomplete. Thus the final sample consisted of 152 B.Sc nursing trainees. Data thus obtained were analyzed using appropriate statistics.

Results and Discussion

Mean age of the trainees was 18.26 (1.56 percent) years. Majority of the sample was female (78.3 percent), unmarried (98 percent), educated in convent schools (61 percent), Christians (69 percent), belonging to nuclear families (91 percent) and in the monthly income group of Rs. 5000-10,000. Most of them (64.5 percent) were in the Ist semester while 35.6 percent were final semester trainees. 31.6 percent had experience of dealing with HIV/AIDS patients, 64.5 percent had no experience while 3.9 percent didn't mention anything. Source of information about HIV/AIDS was mostly hospital (11.8 percent) and contrary to our view only 2 percent mentioned media and 86.2 percent did not mention any source.

In present study whole sample was aware of the full form of AIDS and that HIV causes AIDS. They had good information regarding transmission through blood, mother to baby, eating or swimming together. But they had poor information about transmission through oral sex, tongue kissing, semen, open cuts/wounds. They were ill informed about investigations and meaning of being 'positive' or 'negative' on testing. Though they knew about the importance of condoms, they lacked detailed knowledge about them. They also lacked information about whether: (1) HIV infection always leads to AIDS; (2) Anal sex or vaginal sex with AIDS patient is safer; (3) Drug abuse increases risk of unsafe sex; (4) Is there any preventive medicine? Many believed that they can get HIV infection by donating blood and getting tested for it.

Table 14.1: Medical Scientific Knowledge

Item	Answers					
	Right		Wrong		Not Answered	
	Frequency	Percent	Frequency	Percent	Frequency	Percent
1	152	100.0	0	0	0	0
2	4	2.6	148	97.4	0	0
3	143	94.1	9	5.9	0	0
4	149	98.0	3	2.0	0	0
5	32	21.1	119	78.3	1	.7
6	105	69.1	41	27.0	6	3.9
7	74	48.7	74	48.7	4	2.6
8	146	96.1	3	2.0	3	2.0
9	141	92.8	10	6.6	1	.7
10	144	94.7	8	5.3	0	0
11	110	72.4	42	27.6	0	0
12	125	82.2	26	17.1	1	.7
13	113	74.3	38	25.0	1	.7
14	60	39.5	89	58.6	3	2.0
15	85	55.9	67	44.1	0	0
16	107	70.4	45	29.6	0	0
17	109	71.7	41	27.0	2	1.3
18	137	90.1	12	7.9	3	2.0
19	43	28.3	106	69.7	3	2.0
20	82	53.9	53	34.9	17	11.2
21	98	64.5	52	34.2	2	1.3
22	106	69.7	42	27.6	4	2.6
Over all	102.95	67.73	46.73	30.75	2.32	1.53

These findings are in accordance with some earlier studies done in India. Kubde, Zodpey, and Vasudeo (1995), studied nursing students of Nagpur and reported that the overall knowledge regarding etiology, risk factors, transmission, treatment and prevention of AIDS was confusing among the students. However, more knowledge was found to be correlated with more positive and fearless attitude towards AIDS patients. In a recent study at Kolkata (Sibnath, 2002) findings revealed a very positive outlook of the nursing students in regard to caring for HIV/AIDS patients. Although 100 percent of the students had heard of HIV/AIDS, a good number of them had some misconceptions with regard to various aspects of the disease.

Thus it can be concluded that B.Sc. nursing students have overall good knowledge about HIV/AIDS but detailed information was lacking. There is an urgent need to include such topics in their initial and continuing training programs.

Table 14.2: Safer Alternatives

Item	Answers					
	Right		Wrong		Not Answered	
	Frequency	Percent	Frequency	Percent	Frequency	Percent
Blood giving/receiving	121	79.6	31	20.4	0	0
Contact with patient	128	84.2	23	15.1	1	.7
Vaginal/anal intercourse	52	34.2	96	63.2	4	2.6
Using used needle	81	53.3	67	44.1	4	2.6
Intercourse with drug abuser/living with AIDS Patient	124	81.6	23	15.1	5	3.3
Homosexual anal intercourse/blood transfusion	87	57.2	60	39.5	5	3.3
Unprotected sex with lesbian/bisexual men	86	56.6	64	42.1	2	1.3
Overall	98.4	63.81	52	34.21	3	1.97

Table 14.3: High Risk/Prevention Behaviours

Item	Answers					
	Right		Wrong		Not answered	
	Frequency	Percent	Frequency	Percent	Frequency	Percent
1	122	80.3	27	17.8	3	2.0
2	71	46.7	80	52.6	1	.7
3	126	82.9	24	15.8	2	1.3
4	75	49.3	74	48.7	3	2.0
5	138	90.8	14	9.2	0	0
6	59	38.8	90	59.2	3	2.0
7	117	77.0	34	22.4	1	.7
8	130	85.5	21	13.8	1	.7
9	116	76.3	30	19.7	6	3.9
10	81	53.3	69	45.4	2	1.3
11	28	18.4	122	80.3	2	1.3
12	121	79.6	27	17.8	4	2.6
13	99	65.1	52	34.2	1	.7
Overall	98.69	64.82	51.07	23.43	2.23	1.38

Table 14.4: Myths of HIV Transmission

Item	Answers					
	Right		Wrong		Not answered	
	Frequency	Percent	Frequency	Percent	Frequency	Percent
1	136	89.5	15	9.9	1	.7
2	126	82.9	26	17.1	0	0
3	99	65.1	51	33.6	2	1.3
4	97	63.8	53	34.9	2	1.3
5	138	90.8	14	9.2	0	0
6	132	86.8	20	13.2	0	0
7	145	95.4	7	4.6	0	0
8	96	63.2	55	36.2	1	.7
9	113	74.3	37	24.3	2	1.3
Overall	120.22	79.09	30.89	20.33	.78	0.59

References

"HIV Sentinel Surveillance and HIV Estimation, 2006", NACO, 2007.

International Institute of Population Sciences, National Family Welfare Survey, 1998-99, Mumbai, India, October 2000.

Kubde SS, Zodpey SD, Vasudeo ND. Indian Journal of Public Health. 1995 Jul-Sep; 39(3):109-

12.
NACO (April 2006), HIV/AIDS epidemiological Surveillance and Estimation report for the year 2005.
NACO, (August 2006), Monthly updates on AIDS.
NACO, Annual Report 2002-2004.
Programme Implementation guidelines for a Phased Scale up of Access to Antiretroviral Therapy for People Living with HIV/AIDS, National AIDS Control Organization, 2003.
Sibnath D R (2002) Attitude of nursing students of Kolkata towards caring for HIV/AIDS patients. International Conference on AIDS. Jul, 14, 7-12.
UNAIDS (2007), '2.5 million people in India living with HIV, according to new estimates', press release.
UNAIDS (2008), Report of the Global AIDS Epidemic.

15

Stigma of HIV and AIDS

Manoranjan Tripathi and S.K. Srivastava

Introduction

The continuing rise in the population of people living with HIV reflects the combined effects of continued high rates of new HIV infections and the beneficial impact of antiretroviral therapy. As of December 2008, approximately 4 million people in low and middle income countries were receiving antiretroviral therapy — a 10-fold increase over five years (World Health Organization, United Nations Children's Fund, UNAIDS, 2009).

Number of people living with HIV in 2008

- Total 33.4 million [31.1 million–35.8 million]
- Adults 31.3 million [29.2 million–33.7 million]
- Women 15.7 million [14.2 million–17.2 million]
- Children under 15 years 2.1 million [1.2 million–2.9 million]

People newly infected with HIV in 2008

- Total 2.7 million [2.4 million–3.0 million]
- Adults 2.3 million [2.0 million–2.5 million]
- Children under 15 years 430 000 [240 000–610 000]

AIDS-related deaths in 2008

- Total 2.0 million [1.7 million–2.4 million]
- Adults 1.7 million [1.4 million–2.1 million]
- Children under 15 years 280 000 [150 000–410 000]

Now that the daily cost of high quality AIDS drugs has fallen to less than one dollar a day, what would happen if the Indian government were to finance such treatment? This was the question posed to World Bank staff by an official of the National AIDS Control Organization (NACO). To answer this question, the World Bank assembled a team of Indian and international authors and asked them to estimate the costs and health benefits of three different national policy options. The result is the present study, which draws on the international literature, a set of background papers commissioned explicitly for this study and on the authors' own expertise. A first draft of this study was delivered to NACO and circulated to a limited number of people in the government in January 2003.

The three policies analyzed in this document include a minimalist policy in which the government strengthens private sector delivery, an intermediate policy of providing treatment for mothers who have AIDS and their spouses, and a generous policy of providing treatment to the poorest 40 percent of all AIDS patients. In January 2004 the Indian government adopted an AIDS financing policy which contains elements of all three of the hypothetical policies analyzed in this book. This study's projections of the total financial cost of the program and of the cost-effectiveness of the three options can help the government and its partners to plan the scale-up of the existing treatment program, to optimize the mix of components in order to improve its cost-effectiveness and to design monitoring and evaluation measures which provide feedback on program performance.

India is burdened with a larger HIV/AIDS epidemic than any other country in the world. More than 4 million Indian adults are infected with the human immunodeficiency virus (HIV), according to official government estimates, and the actual number people with HIV may be as high as 6.5 million. Among people with HIV, an unknown number—somewhere between 100,000 and 1,000,000 suffer from AIDS. The Indian government is committed to preventing HIV infection, and it has greatly expanded its efforts to prevent the disease since 1997. Although no rigorous evaluations of the effectiveness of the government's strategy have been conducted, the Behaviour Surveillance Survey (Org-Mark Quest 2002) documents moderate levels of condom use in many parts of the country, especially among people whose sexual behaviour places them most at risk.

The limited HIV surveillance system in India suggests that HIV prevalence among pregnant women may be levelling off, but the data are too sketchy, and the apparent trend too recent, to be relied on.1 Without additional data collection and more rigorous analysis, it is impossible to distinguish a true reduction in new infections from several other causes of an apparent levelling off of prevalence. For example, since HIV–infected women are less likely to become pregnant, infections among all women could be rising while the prevalence rate measured among pregnant women is levelling off. Whether or not the incidence of new infections has levelled off, the effect of existing infections on the number of new AIDS cases is predictable. In the absence of certain types of treatment, roughly 5–7 percent of people with HIV will develop AIDS every year. Given the range of values for the number of people with HIV of 4–7 million, this means that 200,000–490,000 adults with AIDS will hit the Indian health care system each year for the next 15–20 years. If India's prevention programs fail to halt the expansion of the AIDS epidemic, these numbers could double or triple over this period.

There is one, only one, cause of the AIDS crisis – the wilful refusal of homosexuals to cease indulging in the immoral, unnatural, unsanitary, unhealthy, and suicidal practice of anal intercourse, which is the primary means by which the AIDS virus is being spread through the 'gay' community, and thence, into the needles of IV drug abusers, the transfusions of hemophiliacs, and the bloodstreams of unsuspecting health workers, prostitutes, lovers, wives, children" (Buchnan, 1987, p. 23).

Similarly, an antigay activist argues: "If you think that homosexuals are largely to blame for AIDS, then you are right. It seems pretty clear if homosexuals hadn't come out of the closet and started sodomizing one another all over the world, none of this would have gotten started in the first place. It is safe to say that AIDS is the first and greatest by product of the Gay Liberation Movement" (Cameron, 1988, p. 126).

What is HIV?

HIV is a virus, like the virus which cause flu or cold. A virus is really nothing but a set of instructions for making new viruses, wrapped up in some fat, protein and sugar. Without living cells, a virus can't do anything - it's like a brain with no body. In order to make more viruses (and to do all of the other nasty things that viruses do), a virus has to infect a cell.

HIV mostly infects T-cells, also known as CD4+ cells, or T-helper cells. These cells are white blood cells that turn the immune system on to fight disease. Once inside the cell, HIV starts producing millions of little viruses, which eventually kill the cell and then go out to infect other cells.

Basics on HIV and AIDS

- **HIV is Transmitted by People with HIV:** From an epidemiological and public health perspective, people with HIV make up the most important group to address with HIV prevention strategies. A change in the risk behaviour of a PLHIV will, on an average and in almost all affected populations, have a much bigger impact on transmission of the virus.
- **Some People Living with HIV Continue to Engage in Risky Behaviours:** Following their diagnosis, many people with HIV use condoms more regularly and adopt other safer sex and drug use practices. Over time, however, many revert back to unsafe sex and intravenous drug use. Prevention interventions for positives may help people with HIV sustain healthy behaviour changes.

- **People with HIV have the Right to Live Well with HIV:** Living well with HIV includes having a healthy sex life. This means protecting people with HIV against super infection (i.e. re-infection with a different strain of HIV) and against new STIs.

What is AIDS?

- **Acquired:** Because it's a condition one must acquire or get infected with; not something transmitted through the genes.
- **Immuno:** because it affects the body's immune system, the part of the body which usually works to fight off germs such as bacteria and viruses.
- **Deficiency:** because it makes the immune system deficient (makes it not work properly).
- **Syndrome:** It's a group of symptoms caused by wide range of different diseases and opportunistic infections.

AIDS stands for 'Acquired Immuno Deficiency Syndrome'. It is a condition caused by a virus called HIV. This virus attacks the immune system, the body's "security force" that fights off infections. When the immune system breaks down, you lose this protection and can develop many serious, often deadly infections and cancers.

These are called "opportunistic infections" because they take advantage of the body's weakened defences. HIV virus by itself does not cause death. It is the opportunistic infections that cause death. AIDS is the condition that lets the opportunistic infections take hold.

Difference between HIV and AIDS

HIV weakens the body's natural ability to fight off infection. It weakens the body's immune system thus allowing infections very easily. HIV weakens the immune system that the person will become sick with types of infections known as opportunistic infections or OIs like TB, diarrhoea, Pneumonia etc. The most serious of these OIs are called AIDS defining illnesses.

When the person becomes ill with one of the AIDS defining illnesses, he or she is said to have Acquired Immunodeficiency Syndrome (AIDS). For some, it takes a long time to develop these infections. For others it takes less time. Not everyone with HIV has AIDS and AIDS is not the same as HIV.

HIV History

In July 1981, the New York Times reported an outbreak of a rare form of cancer among gay men in New York and California, first referred to as the 'gay cancer' but medically know as Kaposi Sarcoma. About the same time, Emergency Rooms in New York City began to see a rash of seemingly healthy young men presenting with fevers, flu like symptoms, and a pneumonia called Pneumocystis. About a year later, the CDC (Centres for Disease Control) link the illness to blood and coins the term AIDS (Acquired Immune Deficiency Syndrome). In that first year, over 1600 cases were diagnosed with close to 700 deaths.

Unfortunately, the AIDS epidemic continues today in Africa and much of Asia, where antiretroviral therapy is not available and health care is seriously inadequate. Over 95 percent of AIDS cases and deaths occur outside the United States. AIDS is the fourth leading cause of death worldwide, the #1 cause of death due to infectious disease, and has surpassed malaria as the #1 killer in Africa. There are more than 2.2 million AIDS cases reported worldwide, and 33.6 million people are living with HIV/AIDS. More than 16 million people have died from AIDS. It caused 2.6 million deaths in 1999. According to the National Institutes of Health more than 3 million people will die from AIDS in 2000.

Table 15.1: Number of People Living with HIV/AIDS in 2004

	Estimate [Million]	Range [Million]
Total	39.4	35.9-44.3
Adults	37.2	33.8-41.7
Women	17.6	16.3-19.5
Children	2.2	2.0-2.6

Table 15.2: People Newly Infected with HIV in 2004

	Estimate [Million]	Range [Million]
Total	4.9	4.3-6.4
Adults	4.3	3.7-5.7
Children	0.64	0.57-0.75

Table 15.3: AIDS Deaths in 2004

	Estimate [Million]	Range [Million]
Total	3.1	2.8-3.5
Adults	2.6	2.3-2.9
Children	0.51	0.46-0.60

Total number of AIDS deaths between 1981 and 2003 stood at 20 million. Total number of HIV positive people in India stood at 5.1 million.

Modes of Transmission

- Sexual intercourse (vaginal/anal) with an infected partner (heterosexual or homosexual behaviour).
- Transfusion with infected blood, blood products organ, tissue transplantation and artificial insemination.
- Contaminated syringes and needles.
- From an infected mother to her child i.e. transmission (before, during and after delivery).

HIV is not transmitted by

- Shaking hands.
- Hugging.
- Dry kissing.
- Sneezing, Coughing.
- Mosquito bites.
- Toilet sharing.
- Sharing of telephones.
- Sharing of offices.
- Sharing utensils.
- Sharing water.
- Playing together.
- Travelling together in buses and trains.
- Sharing cups or cutlery.
- Living in same room.
- Donating blood aseptically.
- Eating together.
- Insect bites.
- Masturbation.

General Terminologies in HIV and AIDS

What is STD? Sexually Transmitted Diseases (STDs) are a group of communicable diseases predominantly transmitted by sexual contact.

What is RTI? Reproductive Tract Infections (RTIs) include a variety of bacterial, viral and protozoal infections of the lower and upper reproductive tract of both sexes.

What are the Common Causes of RTI? Iatrogenic i.e. related to inadequate medical procedures during delivery, IUD, MTP, Sterilization.

Endogenous: Lack of personal, sexual and menstrual hygiene practice.

Sexually Transmitted Infections

What is OIs? Opportunistic Infections (OIs) are those infections which attacks the body taking opportunity of the weak immune system. These are some of the commonly found OIs.

A partial list of the world's most common HIV-related opportunistic infections and diseases includes:

- Tuberculosis (Pulmonary and extra-pulmonary),
- Candidiasis,
- Pneumocysitis carini,
- Toxoplasmosis,
- Cryptococcosis,
- Cryptosporidial Diarrhoea,
- Cytomegolo virus infections,
- P. Marneffea infections (a fungal infection in North Eastern part of the country) HIV-TB.

Preventing Sexually Transmitted Diseases

If you choose to have vaginal intercourse, use a latex condom to protect both you and your partner from the risk of HIV and other STDs. Studies have shown that latex condoms are very effective in when used correctly and consistently. If either partner is allergic to latex, plastic (polyurethane) condoms for either the male or female can be used.

Through Vaginal Sex: In fact, in much of the world it is the most common way the virus is transmitted. HIV can be found in the blood, semen, pre-seminal fluid ("pre-cum"), or vaginal fluid of a person infected with the virus. The lining of the vagina can tear and allow HIV to enter the body. Direct absorption of HIV through the mucous membranes that line the vagina also is a possibility.

Through vaginal sex the male is at less risk for HIV transmission than is the female. However, HIV can enter the body of the male through his urethra (the opening at the tip of the penis) or through small cuts or open sores on the penis, making infection with HIV possible. The risk of HIV infection increases if you or your partner has a sexually transmitted disease (STD).

Through Oral Sex:

What is Oral Sex? Oral sex involves giving or receiving oral stimulation (i.e. sucking or licking) to the genitalia. Fellatio (also known as a 'blow job') is the term used to describe oral sex given to a man. Cunnilingus is the term which describes oral sex given to a woman.

Is oral sex common practice? Many studies have shown that oral sex is practiced by men and women of all ages, both gay and straight. It is a very common practice and may be performed on its own, or before or after sexual intercourse.

Is oral sex safe? A number of studies have demonstrated that oral sex is not necessarily safe sex. Both giving and receiving oral sex can lead to the transmission of sexually transmitted infections or sexually transmitted diseases (also known as STIs or STDs).

Which STDs are Transmitted via Oral Sex?

The most common STD transmitted via oral sex is herpes. There are two main types of herpes simplex virus (HSV): HSV type 1 and HSV type 2. HSV type 1 usually causes cold sores around the mouth, while HSV type 2 generally causes genital herpes sores. However, oral sex can sometimes cause HSV type 1 around the mouth to be transmitted to the genital area causing genital sores in the other person. This process can also work in reverse, with HSV-2 transmitted from the genitals to the mouth of the other person during oral sex, though this is rare.

The human papillomavirus that causes genital warts can very occasionally be transmitted through oral sex, causing warts to appear around or inside the mouth in anyone who has given oral sex to an infected person.

Gonorrhoea has been shown to infect the throat of some people who have given oral sex to an infected person. This infection can then be passed on from the throat to the genitals of any future partners. The body will almost always naturally clear the throat of the bacteria that cause gonorrhoea within three months, although infections in the genital tract will usually require antibiotics to cure.

Chlamydia can also infect the throat in a similar way, although this is less common. Both infections may result in a sore throat, although many people will remain asymptomatic and unaware they are infected.

Syphilis may be passed on during oral sex if a person's mouth comes into contact with an open sore or a skin rash caused by the infection. Gastrointestinal infections and parasites may be passed on during oral contact with the anus.

The hepatitis A virus is also contained in human faeces, and may be passed on during anal-oral sex.

Hepatitis B is contained in sexual fluids and blood and may be transmitted during oral sex in a similar way to HIV.

Hepatitis C is generally only contained in blood, and will only be transmitted if there is blood present during oral sex.

Can HIV be Transmitted during Oral Sex?

HIV can pose a small risk for both the active (person giving the oral stimulation) and receptive (person receiving oral stimulation) partner.

Transmission from an HIV positive receptive partner to an HIV negative active partner may occur when the active partner gets sexual fluid (semen or vaginal fluid) or blood (from menstruation or a wound somewhere in the genital or anal region) into a cut, sore, ulcer or area of inflammation somewhere in their mouth or throat. The linings of the mouth and throat are very resistant to viral infections such as HIV, so infection is unlikely if they are healthy. Transmission from an HIV positive active partner to an HIV negative receptive partner is generally believed to be less common. This is because HIV is normally only present in saliva in very low levels that are not sufficient to cause infection. The only risk in this scenario would be from bleeding wounds or gums in the HIV positive person's mouth or on their lips, which may transfer blood onto the mucous membranes of the other person's genitals or anus, or into any cuts or sores they may have. Hepatitis C can also be transmitted this way.

What is the Risk of HIV Transmission via Oral Sex?

The risk of HIV transmission from an infected partner through oral sex is much smaller than the risk of HIV transmission from anal or vaginal sex. Because of this, measuring the exact risk of HIV transmission as a result of oral sex is very difficult. In addition, since most sexually active individuals practice oral sex in addition to other forms of sex (such as vaginal and/or anal sex) when transmission occurs, it is difficult to determine whether or not it occurred as a result of oral sex or other more risky sexual activities. Finally, several co-factors can increase the risk of HIV transmission through oral sex, including oral ulcers and wounds, bleeding gums, genital sores, genital or oral piercings, and the presence of other STDs.

When scientists describe the risk of transmitting an infectious disease, like HIV, the term "theoretical risk" is often used. Very simply, "theoretical risk" means that passing an infection from one person to another is possible, even though there may not yet be any actual documented cases. "Theoretical risk" is not the same as likelihood. In other words, stating that HIV infection is "theoretically possible" does not necessarily mean it is likely to happen - only that it might. Documented risk, on the other hand, is used to describe transmission that has actually occurred, been investigated, and documented in the scientific literature.

Various scientific studies have been performed around the world to try and document and study instances of HIV transmission through oral sex. A programme in San Francisco studied 198 people, nearly all gay or bisexual men. The subjects stated that they had only had oral sex for a year, from six months preceding the six-month study to its end. 20 percent of the study participants (39 people) reported performing oral sex on partners they knew to be HIV positive. 35 of those did not use a condom and 16 reported swallowing semen. No one became HIV positive during the study, although the small number of participants performing oral sex on HIV positive partners meant the researchers could only say that there was a less than 2.8 percent chance of infection through oral sex over a year. In 2000, a different San Francisco study of gay men who had recently acquired HIV infection found that 7.8 percent of these infections were attributed to oral sex. However, the results of the study have since been called into question due to the reliability of the participants' data. Measuring the exact risk of HIV transmission as a result of oral sex is very difficult.

In June 2002, a study conducted amongst 135 HIV negative Spanish heterosexuals, who were in a sexual relationship with a person who was HIV positive, reported that over 19,000 instances of unprotected oral sex had not led to any cases of HIV transmission. The study also looked at contributing factors that could affect the potential transmission of HIV through oral sex. They monitored viral load and asked questions such as whether ejaculation in the mouth occurred and how good oral health was. Amongst HIV positive men, 34 percent had ejaculated into the mouths of their partners. Viral load levels were available for 60 people in the study, 10 percent of whom had levels over 10,000 copies. Nearly 16 percent of the HIV positive people had CD4 counts below 200. The study, conducted over a ten year period between 1990 and 2000, adds to the growing number of studies which suggest varying levels of risk of HIV transmission from oral sex when compared to anal or vaginal intercourse.

At the 4th International Oral AIDS Conference held in South Africa, the risk of transmission through oral sex was estimated to be approximately 0.04 percent per contact. This percentage figure is a lot lower than the two American figures, because this figure is a risk per contact percentage, whereas the other figures are percentage risks over much longer time periods. Oral sex is still regarded as a low-risk sexual activity in terms of HIV transmission, but only when more work is done will we be clearer as to the risks of oral sex.

Are there any Individual Documented Cases of HIV Transmission during Oral Sex?

While it is very difficult to ever know how HIV transmission occurred, according to a fact sheet on oral sex produced by the CDC in 20005, there have been a few documented cases of transmission during oral sex. These have occurred in both receptive and active partners during fellatio, cunnilingus and anilingus.

How do I Protect myself and my Partner During Oral Sex?

The already low risk of becoming infected with HIV from oral sex can be reduced still further by using condoms. Flavoured condoms are available for those who don't like the taste of latex or spermicide. For cunnilingus or anilingus, plastic food wrap, a condom cut open, or a dental dam (a thin square of latex) can serve as a physical barrier to prevent transmission of HIV and many other STDs.

Through Anal Sex

It is possible for either sex partner to become infected with HIV during anal sex. HIV can be found in the blood, semen, pre-seminal fluid, or vaginal fluid of a person infected with the virus. In general, the person receiving the semen is at greater risk of getting HIV because the lining of the rectum is thin and may allow the virus to enter the body during anal sex. However, a person who inserts his penis into an infected partner also is at risk because HIV can enter through the urethra (the opening at the tip of the penis) or through small cuts, abrasions, or open sores on the penis.

Having unprotected (without a condom) anal sex is considered to be a very risky behaviour. If people choose to have anal sex, they should use a latex condom. Most of the time, condoms work well. However, condoms are more likely to break during anal sex than during vaginal sex. Thus, even with a condom, anal sex can be risky. A person should use a water-based lubricant in addition to the condom to reduce the chances of the condom breaking.

Blood Transfusion

Blood is a very efficient means of transmitting HIV infection. The frequency of seroconversion after transfusion of HIV-infected blood is very high, over 90 percent. Effective technology is available for prevention of HIV transmission through blood. After the HIV antibody test became available in 1985, the risk of getting HIV infection from blood transfusion was virtually eliminated in developed countries with the establishment of universal screening of blood donations. The risk was further reduced by the development of highly sensitive test kits and by such other means as donor selection, donor deferral and appropriate use of blood. In developing countries, the extent to which blood donations are screened against HIV is determined by the available resources and continuous efforts are being made to improve the coverage.

Considerable progress has been made to prevent transmission of HIV through blood in the countries of the Eastern Mediterranean Region. However, there are still a few countries which have yet to achieve universal screening of blood. This paper reviews the situation in the countries of the Region with regard to AIDS acquired through blood transmission, based upon the reports from the national AIDS programmes of these countries.

Reported AIDS Cases due to Blood

A cumulative total of 3745 AIDS cases were reported from the countries of the Region up to the end of 1995. All countries except Afghanistan have reported AIDS cases. Information about the mode of transmission is available for 3461 cases (92.4 percent). Of them, 368 (10.6 percent) cases were due to the receipt of blood or blood products. The largest number of cases due to the receipt of blood or blood products were reported from the Islamic Republic of Iran, followed by Tunisia, Morocco, Saudi Arabia, Egypt and Iraq. The proportion of cases due to receipt of blood and blood products among all cases is higher in countries such as Iraq, the Islamic Republic of Iran and Saudi Arabia than in other countries, mainly because they used much larger quantities of imported blood and blood products than did other countries.

Although the reported number of new AIDS cases has continued to rise every year, the number of cases due to receipt of blood or blood products has not risen much during the past five years. In the early stages of the epidemic, a large proportion of total AIDS cases was due to the receipt of blood or blood products. The peak was reached in 1987 when almost half of the cases were due to this mode of transmission. After the establishment of facilities for screening of blood donations against HIV, the proportion of AIDS cases due to transmission through blood or blood products started decreasing. While about 9 percent of cases were due to the transfusion of blood or blood products in 1994, the proportion decreased to 4 percent in 1995.

In spite of the establishment of screening for blood donations, AIDS cases due to blood transmission will continue to occur for some time to come. This is mainly due to the time lag between the occurrence of HIV infection and the appearance of AIDS. This has been seen in Europe and the USA. About 6000 cases of AIDS associated with transfusions were registered in 14 European countries between 1985 and 1993 and over 8000 cases in the USA between 1985 and 1992. France had the highest overall incidence of AIDS related to transfusion in Europe (3.3 per million). Incidence rates of AIDS associated with transfusion were still increasing in some southern European countries in the early 1990s. About 1300 cases of AIDS associated with transfusion had been reported in France by June 1993.

In countries where universal screening of blood donations against HIV has not been achieved, occurrence of HIV infection due to blood transfusion cannot be ruled out. Even in countries with universal screening of blood donations, a very small number of HIV infections can occur if the blood is collected during the window period, i.e. the interval between HIV infection and appearance of HIV-specific antibodies.

HIV Seroprevalence among Blood Recipients

People who receive multiple transfusions of blood or blood products, such as those with haemophilia or thalassaemia, are at greater risk of HIV infection through blood than the general population. In the early stages, HIV prevalence among such recipients was quite high; nearly 10 percent in the Islamic Republic of Iran, 3 percent in Tunisia and 1 percent in Kuwait. With the establishment of facilities for screening of blood and blood products for HIV, transmission of HIV through this means has decreased considerably over the years. This has been seen consistently in almost all countries which are carrying out surveillance among these risk groups.

Overall, the HIV seroprevalence among these risk groups has markedly decreased, from 270 per 10 000 during 1987-1989 to 7 per 10 000 in 1995. Most of the HIV infections reported lately were old infections which were only detected recently, but that a few are new infections cannot be ruled out in countries where universal screening of blood or blood products against HIV has not been secured.

Prevention of HIV Transmission through Blood

Effective technology is available to make blood and blood products safe for use. The surest means of making blood safe against HIV is by screening the blood for HIV antibodies. By this means, it has been possible to reduce HIV transmission through blood to a very low level in the developed countries. However, in many developing countries, including a few in the Eastern Mediterranean Region, lack of financial resources is still the main stumbling block to universal screening of blood. Persistent efforts are being made in these countries to improve the coverage.

In spite of screening of blood against HIV antibodies, there may be some, although very low, risk of HIV transmission from screened blood. This could happen due to: (a) a donor being in the window period of HIV infection; (b) a false-negative HIV antibody test; or c) human and operational error. No study has been reported in the Eastern Mediterranean Region on such risk but the risk has been documented elsewhere. In Thailand, 30 cases of transfusion-associated AIDS were reported during 1990-1992 and the risk of HIV from blood screened against HIV antibodies was estimated to vary from 1:3400 to 1:25 000. The risk has been estimated to vary between 1:25 641 and 1:90 909 in South Africa; between 1:210 000 and 1:1 340 000 in Vienna, Austria, and between 1:380 000 and 1:234 000 in Göttingen, Germany; and between 1:450 000 and 1:660 000 in the United States of America. Two HIV infections have been reported in the United States Army out of 700 000 blood units which had been screened for HIV antibodies. While more than 14 million units of blood and blood components are transfused yearly in the USA, only 29 documented AIDS cases have occurred in transfusion recipients who received HIV antibody-negative blood since HIV screening began in March 1985.

Any risk of HIV transmission through blood, however small it may be, must be avoided as far as possible. In addition to routine screening for HIV antibodies, other measures should be taken to improve the blood safety. These measures include proper selection of blood donors, appropriate use of blood and use of sensitive HIV tests.

Professional or paid donors are known to be associated with sexual promiscuity or drug abuse and must be avoided. Similarly, replacement or patient-recruited donors should also be avoided because they have higher HIV seropositivity rates than voluntary donors. The rate among patient-recruited donors in a Kenyan hospital was reported to be three times higher than among voluntary donors. Emphasis, therefore, should be on recruitment of non-remunerated voluntary donors. Sustained efforts including campaigns to promote voluntary donations will be required.

All potential donors should be provided with information to encourage "self-deferral" for those whose behaviour puts them at increased risk of HIV infection. Such information may be given in a written form to those who are able to read, followed by an interview which should include questions about risk behaviour. Potential donors should be examined for evidence of illicit drug use.

The larger the number of blood transfusions, the greater is the risk of HIV infection. Lackritz et al. have reported 47 percent of paediatric transfusions as inappropriate and 68 percent of adult transfusions as single unit transfusions in a Kenyan hospital. In order to improve blood safety, the aim should be to reduce the number of transfusions to the absolute minimum. The best option would be to avoid blood completely wherever feasible and to use blood substitutes.

Selection of sensitive tests also increases blood safety, by reducing the false-negative rate and by decreasing the window period. With the use of third generation ELISA tests, the window period decreases to 3 weeks from the previously reported period of 6-8 weeks. To detect HIV infection earlier, other tests such as the antigen capture test and the polymerase chain reaction (PCR) test have been suggested. The US Food and Drug Administration recommended in August 1995 that all donated blood and plasma also be screened for HIV-1 antigen, effective within 3 months of licensure of a test labelled for such use. This is expected to reduce the window period by 6 days and thus reduce the number of otherwise undetected infectious donations by approximately 25 percent per year. But these tests will have limited value in detecting early infection or in improving transfusion safety. Moreover, these tests are not affordable for developing countries.

Conclusion

HIV/AIDS has recently been predicted to the killer in the world within the next twenty years. It has already been the cause of death for millions and it there is not a decline in its numbers will continue to do so. It is not just a problem in places like Africa which is what we tend to hear most about in the media but it is a substantial problem in European countries, Canada and the United State too. It's easy to think that AIDS is something for other people to worry about and not teens. But the group most likely to contact HIV/AIDS is actually between the ages of 15 and 25, and in 2005, it was estimated that there was 2.3 million people under the age of 15 living with HIV. So it is a threat that needs to be taken seriously. To be able to protect yourself and to spread the word, you need to know the facts, and know how to avoid becoming infected. The continuing development in technology for HIV tests supplemented by efforts to reduce the risk has meant that blood safety has become a reality. Nevertheless, AIDS cases due to blood transmission will continue to occur in individuals who were infected many years ago but have not yet developed disease. Mobilizing and sustaining the resources required to ensure blood safety pose a constant challenge to the developing countries. It would be wise to use the available resources judiciously. Priorities in blood safety should include universal screening of blood for HIV antibodies using sensitive tests, promotion of voluntary no remunerated blood donations, donor deferral and appropriate use of blood. More sophisticated tests such as PCR and antigen tests are expensive and are not recommended until they become affordable.

References

Buchanan, P.J. (1987, Dec. 2). AIDS and moral bankruptcy. New York Post, p. 23.

Cameron, P. (1988). *Exposing the AIDS Scandal.* Lafayette, LA: Huntington House.

Donegan-et-al. (1990). Infection with human immunodeficiency virus type 1 (HIV-1) among recipients of antibody-positive blood donations. *Journal of Annals of Internal Medicine.* 113(21), 733-739.

Franceschi, S., Dalmaso, L. and Lavecchia, C. (1995). Trends in incidence of AIDS associated with transfusion of blood and blood products in Europe and the United States, 1985-93. *Journal of British Medical.* 311(8), 1534-1536.

Isarangkura, P. (1993). Transmission of HIV infection by seronegative blood in Thailand. *Journal of the Medical Association of Thailand.* 76(2), 106-113.

Lackritz EM (1993). Blood transfusion practices and blood-banking services in a Kenyan hospital. *AIDS. Journal of the Gay and Lesbian Medical Association.* 7(3), 995-999.

Lackritz, E.M. (1995). Estimated risk of transmission of the human immunodeficiency virus by screened blood in the United States. New England Journal of Medicine. 333(12), 1721-1725.

Lepont, F. (1995). Estimation of the size of the HIV/AIDS epidemic due to blood transfusion in France. *International Journal of Epidemiology*, 24(2), 441-445.

Roberts, C.R. (1994). Transfusion-associated human immunodeficiency virus type 1 from screened anti-body negative blood donors. *Archives of Pathology and Laboratory Medicine Journal.* 118(12), 1188-1192.

Schwartz, D.W. (1995). Risk of human immunodeficiency virus (HIV) transmission by anti-HIV negative blood components in Germany and Austria. *Journal of Annals of Hematology.* 70(4), 209-213.

Sitas, F., Fleming, A.F. and Morris, J. (1994). Residual risk of transmission of HIV through blood transfusion in South Africa. *Journal of South African Medical.* 84(3):142-4.

Sloand, E.M., Pitt, E. and Klein, H.G. (1995). Safety of the blood supply. *Journal of the American Medical Association.* 274(17), 1368-1373.

US Public Health Service guidelines for testing and counselling blood and plasma donors for human immunodeficiency virus type 1 antigen. *Morbidity and Mortality Weekly Report*, March 1, 1996; Vol. 45, No. RR-2.

Wahdan MH. *Epidemiology of acquired immunodeficiency syndrome.* Alexandria, World Health Organization, Regional Office for the Eastern Mediterranean, 1995 (unpublished document WHO-EM/GPA/014/E/L/95).

Part II

Psycho-Social and Neurological Aspects of Physical and Mental Diseases

16

Psycho-social Aspect of Elderly Women

Archana Dutta

Concept of Aging

According to ancient Indian scripture, Bhagawad Gita:

Dehino-asmin yatha dehe koumaram youvanam jara Tatha dehantar-praptir-dheerastatra na muhiyati [Chapter 2(13)]

As the embodied soul passes through childhood, youth and old age in the body, so too is its changes over to another body...the calm and wise man is not deluded by this.

This *shloka* of Bhagwad Gita explains the complete process of aging of body in a very few words but aptly. Every human being who is born on this earth is bound to go through this process. It is inevitable. All human beings possess this knowledge but everybody sees and experiences this process in different manner. Where does the difference lie? The difference lies in understanding of this truth by different people. The difference lies in knowledge and realization. If we can realize the knowledge about the reality of aging, the process will become easier for all of us.

Aging, in layman's language, means, increasing in number of years. Aging is not only a biological process but also has physical, psychological, emotional and social dimensions.

Changing Social Structure

The family is an institution that simultaneously envelops and unfolds the ideals and normative on the one hand and actual behaviour on the other (Patel T. 2005). Changing social structure is also bringing change in family structure and interpersonal relationships. The socio-economic transformation is creating permissive environment for migration for the purpose of education and work. This is directly affecting the dynamics of family values. Urbanization and industrialization combined to erode some of the traditional support systems of the elderly and to exacerbate their loss of independence (Vertinsky, 1991).

The present social structure is giving appropriate platform to nuclear structure of the family. This is affecting the life of elderly people adversely. Nuclear family structure has its own advantages and disadvantages. Itrat et al. (2008), concluded that a major change is occurring in the family systems, with most people shifting from a joint family to a nuclear family setting, despite the preference for the joint family. Due to urbanization, people need to migrate to many places and elders of the family are not very comfortable with this idea. They want to stick to their roots. This is one of the reasons for existence of nuclear families and the other is less tolerance of working women and men.

Gender-based Specification

Gender differences are prevailing in the society since ancient times and even today, after education and modernization, the society is still struggling with gender related issues. This is true that differences do exists biologically between men and women but gender roles are learned in the process of socialization. Internalization of roles starts as soon as the concept of self starts developing. The concept of self starts building up in very early age when the child starts differentiating between his own possessions and that of others. Also, this is the age when an individual start internalizing the roles and then it is reinforced by grooming style of the parents and also the society. Gender differences determine the natural order of the society.

Gender determines the differential power and control men and women have over the socioeconomic determinants of their mental health and lives, their social position, status and treatment in society and their susceptibility and exposure to specific mental health risks (World health Organization). The priorities, responsibilities and duties of both the genders are different, and so are the roles. That is the reason they show difference in various dimensions of life like physical ailments and psychological adjustment.

Kant (1986) [as cited in Balachandran, et al. 2007], observed, significant difference between males and females regarding life satisfaction, with females experiencing lower life satisfaction than men. A study by Arehaert-Triechel (2006) concluded that nearly half of the elder women had experienced at least one kind of abuse out of psychological/emotional, control, threat, physical, and sexual.

Gender issues have always remained in focus all over the world, irrespective of the fact that the country is developed or developing. Consideration of gender specific factors is very important when exploring the age group of elderly ladies as there is a stark difference between social status, life-style and problems of elderly men and women. Capoor, I. (2008), rightly mentions that it influences our access to resources and opportunities, and shapes our choices at every stage of life.

Problem Factors in Old Age

Erikson's Psychosocial Developmental Stages: According to Erikson's psychosocial developmental stages, old age brings in a core developmental conflict: *integrity versus despair*. If a person is able to achieve *integrity* of one' attitude, beliefs, motives and experiences to form a coherent whole, it will result in feeling of satisfaction with a life. Without this integrity, the older person develops a growing sense of *despair*. This can result in perceptual irritability, disgust or a sense of dissatisfaction with one's life (Morgan et al., 1993). By the time, woman reaches this stage of life's course; she has accumulated lot of experience and also wisdom from school of life. Erikson, also mentions introspection and ego integrity. Introspection is the most apt way of self analysis. Generally, at this stage of life, people introspect about their entire life, if they find it satisfying, their ego integrity is maintained and they have positive feelings for themselves. But if the person is not satisfied, there develops a feeling of worthlessness or other negative feeling about themselves.

Physical Factors: Advancing old age brings with it certain ailments as body cells starts degenerating. This includes problems related to almost all systems of the body like cardiovascular system, reproductive system, digestive system and others. Women face most of the problems related to reproductive system at post-menopausal stage. They go through hormonal changes which lead to psychological and emotional problems. They tend to reduce their physical activity due to the perception that it will further lead to illness or bodily pains.

Vertinsky, (1991), mentions that, it is a paradox that one of the main reasons given by elderly women for not being more physically active is their declining health and the perception that they are "too old," while at the same time scientific research increasingly demonstrates that one of the certain benefits of physical activity is health improvement.

Social Factors: Since the onset of industrialization women are participating with men in workforce and also are taking care of household chores. This has affected the role of women. There are numerous culturally reinforced social factors that contribute for the poor mental health of women and especially the ones in old age. These mainly include financial dependence and gender discrimination. There is a positive relationship between the frequency and severity of such social factors and the frequency and severity of mental health problems in women. Severe life events that cause a sense of loss, inferiority, humiliation or entrapment can predict depression (WHO website).

Financial aspect of elderly women is also an important factor that creates problem for their well-being. Most of the times they depend on spouse or children for financial matters. If the family is not very supportive, they have to face a lot of difficulty which further deteriorates their mental health. As the family values are changing due to various factors, family ties are weakening. Itrat et al. (2008), found that elderly people preferred staying away from the family as it keeps them away from family arguments but at the same time, they have to suffer with loneliness and boredom when staying alone.

Another important issue is role-change. Role-changes are always difficult to accept and cope with. Elderly women generally feel that they have become merely a passive participant in a family from the status of the head-of-the-family. It may have a profoundly unfavourable effect on the self-concept, thus leading to poor personal and social adjustment (Hurlock, E. B., 1981).

Psychological Factors: In a study by Hanson et al. (1987), it was found that Loneliness is related to poor psychological adjustment and to dissatisfaction with family and social relationships. It was also related to fears, expectations, and personality characteristics likely to inhibit the restoration of personal support networks after a stressful life event. Psychological adjustment is more a personal matter. Due to individual differences, everybody has different way of adjusting with environment. In old age, this environment mainly comprises family members.

Firstly, all members of the family are engaged in their work and the generation gap is another factor which reduces the communication with elders. The consequence is the loneliness of elderly ladies of the family. The feeling of being neglected slowly creeps in them and they start feeling irritated with everybody. It results in alienation from the family. A study by Balachandran, et al. (2007) concluded that aged men experience less alienation than aged women. This further results in emotional instability and depression. It is found to be more prevalent in women than men.

Coping with Problem Factors

Coping is a psychological process evoked by stress in dealing with the changes in the environment (Lazarus, 1966). Coping means how an individual perceive the problem and deals with it. Every individual have different coping style based on the personality traits. Coping style can be either problem-focused or emotion-focused. Whenever dealing with a problem, human beings are bound to struggle between logic and feelings. But problem has to be dealt with, in order to bring peace with oneself. Different people use different coping strategies based on the need of situation.

All the stages in the life of an individual have different problems and there are different ways to cope with them. The way we deal with a problem in adolescence and middle age, may not be as effective or justifiable in old age.

Coping strategies need to be changed according to the demands of advancing age. Some of the coping strategies for elder women to lead a healthy life, mentally and physically, are discussed in this section.

Maintenance of Self-identity

Assertiveness is very important in this stage of life to maintain self-identity. Generally, people make some mistakes while being assertive. When a person is showing assertiveness, it's very important to be polite and reasonable. The moment we loose the politeness and reasonability, the purpose of being assertive is defied. An elderly lady is expected to be understanding and to have an element of tolerance. As Gandhiji said, "The weak can never forgive; forgiveness is the attribute of the strong". This is the appropriate phase of life to understand the essence of this quote and implement it in daily life. At this stage, it is also very important to give space to younger generation, and then only they can respect and understand the elders. Although, generation gap exists but it is an elder who is expected to be understanding and to reduce this gap with help of their experience and knowledge. According to psychological theories, aggression has its bases in environmental and social factors but controlling aggression can solve half the problems and can make others respect you. There are few ways by which an elderly lady in the family can maintain her self-identity:

- By being assertive,
- By controlling aggression, and
- By giving space to younger generation.

Working on Perceptions and Attitudes

Our behaviour depends on our thoughts. Our thoughts are governed by our perception. We think, the way we perceive the things or situation. In the words of famous psychologist, William James, "Part of what we perceive comes from our senses and other part always comes out of our own head". This second part 'out of our own head' is our own perceptual process which is a function of individual differences or differences in attitude. Attitude is known to be guiding force for our behaviour. Most of the definitions, describe attitude as an evaluative judgment based on the information received (Bohner, G. and Wanke, M. 2002). Evaluations are expressed in terms of liking-disliking, positive-negative etc (as cited in Morgan et al., 1986). We perceive the things on the basis of these evaluations. Therefore, it is of utmost importance to evaluate the things appropriately.

When an elderly woman is staying with her children and grandchildren, she is supposed to behave most wisely without hurting feelings of other members of the family. Grandmothers are generally more interested in the activities and behaviour of grandchildren. But generation gap is also a reality. To bridge this, she needs to broaden her parameters of evaluating people and situation. Understanding others form their point of view is the key factor to earn respect from others.

Increasing Personal and Social Adaptability

It is important to understand that age will always increase every year. In the words of Charles Darwin, "it is not the strongest of the species, or the most intelligent, that survives. It is the one which is more adaptable to change." A human being needs to, first, accept the change, and then only it is possible to cope up with environmental stressors. First, women need to realize that it is a natural process and cannot be stopped and the only solution is to accept it and adjust to it. Individual differences also play a significant role in adjustment to old age.

Developing own support circle and companions in the same age group helps in personal adjustment. Elderly people share common experiences and problems. Therefore, they can easily relate to the people of the same age group. Elderly ladies should have support circle in their own age groups. Recreational activities are also a good option for both personal and social adaptability but it definitely depends on the attitude and understanding of other family members. Culture is also a significant variable as far as recreational activities are concerned.

Cultural Differences in Coping

Coping strategies differ from culture to culture. In western culture, elderly women who are alone, at times, go for remarriage. Western research studies describe marriages at this age as more tranquil and harmonious than those of most young couples. Vinick (1978) (as cited in Morgan et el, 1985) concluded that remarriage is a workable option for many older adults. But as far as eastern culture is concerned, remarriage at this stage of life is a rare option. Here, elderly ladies of the family spend most of their time in grandparenthood if they are living in a joint family. But ill-treatment of elders in these societies is as much a reality as is the respect for elders. But as the life has to go on, if people use level four defence mechanisms which are considered more mature defences, such as, sublimation and altruism, they can have better psychological states. Altruism means selfless care and love for others and getting a sense of satisfaction out of that. Sublimation is the most constructive of defence mechanisms. It redirects the psychic energy in doing something productive and of social approval.

Being Spiritual

Quality of life can be improved by understanding Vedanta, Upanishads and scriptures of any religion. They all ultimately talk about the best and the just behaviour. In the old age, when a lady is almost free from all the responsibilities, she has ample time to explore these scriptures and to find the answers related to the questions of complexities of the life. These books can help her understand the nature of humans, responsibilities and duties, the fine difference between right and wrong and good and evil. Elder lady of the family is the best agent for transmitting the culture to next generations and imbibing values in the younger ones. Spiritualism and religious observance gives a sense of relief from the routine issues and worries. Also, it is an activity reflecting social conformance and thereby enhancing social connectedness.

Pursuing Interest

It is of utmost importance to cultivate healthy habits, especially for women of this age group as she undergoes biological and psychological transition. They should also engage in some hobbies (Balachandran, et al. 2007). Some of them are listed below:

- Having nutritious food, with proper amount of roughage.
- Try to spend at least ten minutes for a morning walk.
- Yoga is a mantra of good health; some time for yoga will keep you away from many physical ailments.
- Try to nurture a hobby like gardening, cooking, reading and painting. Hobby is generally related to creativity of a person.
- Gardening is a hobby that can help you not only psychologically but also physically. Gardening gives good amount of exercise to body. It is always good to see a growing plant and a blooming flower. It gives a feel of life and beauty.
- Cooking for the family members and grandchildren gives a sense of being a member of the family and also a way of showing concern and care.
- During adulthood, a lady may not get an opportunity to realize her creative self because of responsibilities of parenthood. This is best time to convert that potentiality into something concrete. Painting and writing is a very constructive way of self-expression.

Psychological Counselling

If psychological problems still persist, it's not wrong to see a counsellor or a psychotherapist. Humanistic and existential theories of psychotherapy lay more emphasis on self-awareness, self-acceptance and self-actualization. These are client-cantered approaches. They see self as a centre of personality. This is the stage of life when a person has collected all the experience, skills and abilities and now can convert them into something productive by using their creativity. But because of some hampering variables, all of it gets suppressed and the ladies start isolating them and get alienated. Counselling programs may reduce the alienation in elderly women (Balachandran, et al. 2007). Lena, A., et al. (2009), concluded that there is a need for geriatric counselling centres that can take care of their physical and psychological needs. Counselling can be done effectively by following humanistic and existential therapies:

1. Carl Roger's client-cantered therapy: This is based on maladjustment due to discrepancy between ideal self and real self. The client-therapist relationship is designed to support the client's own understanding of the discrepancy.
2. Abraham Maslow's need theory: This is based on fulfilment of various needs, i.e., physiological needs, love and affection needs, safety needs, self-esteem needs and self-actualization needs. This is the stage of life, when a lady can actualize all her inner abilities and can fulfil higher needs of life.
3. Existential therapies: These therapists believe that a human being has control over his problems and can overcome them.
4. Gestalt therapy: These therapists believe in understanding the situation as a whole by removing all the mental and physical blocks and getting in touch with inner self.

All the above theories believe that a human being has innate potential which gets hampered when a person is not able to get in touch with his inner self due to some physical and mental blocks and these can be overcome by a human being himself.

References

Arehart-Triechel, J. (2006). *Psychiatric News*, Volume 41, Number 12, page 20 © 2006 American Psychiatric Association.
http://pn.psychiatryonline.org/cgi/content/full/41/12/20

Balachandran, M., Raakhee. A.S., and Sam Sananda Raj. H. (2007). *Journal of the Indian Academy of Applied Psychology*, July 2007, Vol. 33, No. 2, 157-160.

Bohner, G. and Wanke, M. (2002). *Attitudes and Attitude Change*. Psychological Press: UK.

Capoor, I. (2008). She too counts: Critical need for gender responsive healthcare for the elderly. Presented at the workshop organized by United Nations economic and social commission for Asia and the Pacific, Ministry of social welfare and labour, Mangolia.

Gender disparities and mental health: The Facts. Article on WHO website. http://www.who.int/mental_health/prevention/genderwomen/en/

Hansom, et al. (1987). Loneliness and Adjustment to Old Age. *International Journal of Aging and Human Development,* v .24 n. 1 pp. 41-53.

Hurlock, E. B. (1981). *Developmental Psychology: A Life-span Approach.* Fifth ed. 2005. Tata McGraw-Hill: New Delhi.

Itrat, A., Taqui, A.M., Qazi, F. and Qidwai, W., (2008). Family Systems: Perceptions of elderly patients and their attendants presenting at a university hospital in Karachi, Pakistan. *Journal of Pakistan Medical Association.* http://jpma.org.pk/ViewArticle/ViewArticle.aspx?ArticleID=1025

Kant. V (1996). Well-being and aging: An empirical analysis. *Disabilities and Impairment, 10,* 101-110.

Khetan, P. P. (2000 edition). *The Bhagavad Gita.* Sri Aurobindo Ashram Press: Pondicherry.

Lazaraus R S. (1966). *Psychological stress and coping process.* McGraw Hill: New York.

Lena A, Ashok K, Padma M, Kamath V, Kamath A. Health and social problems of the elderly: A cross-sectional study in Udupi Taluk, Karnataka. Indian Journal of Community Medicine. 2009;34:131-4.

Patel T. (2005). The Family in India: Structure and Practice. Sage Publications: New Delhi.

Vertinsky, P. (1991). Old age, gender and physical activity: The biomedicalization of aging. *Journal of Sport History*, Vol. 18, No. 1 (Spring, 1991). www.la84foundation.org/SportsLibrary/JSH/JSH1991/JSH1801/jsh1801e.pdf.

17

Life Styles of Type II Diabetics and Non-diabetics

Ira Das and Sheenu

Introduction

Type II diabetes is a serious and costly public health concern. The increase in the prevalence of this disease can mainly be attributed to increasingly sedentary lifestyle and excess energy intake, which in turn leads to overweight and obesity. These modifiable lifestyle related risk factors offer a possibility for preventive interventions, yet little conclusive evidence regarding the prevention of type II diabetes has been demonstrated.

Diabetes is a clinical syndrome characterized by hyperglycemia due to deficiency or diminished effectiveness of insulin, a disturbed chemical balance in the body. The word 'diabetes' comes from a Greek expression meaning, "Siphon" and refers to the increased urination and thirst, which often occur in newly diagnosed or uncontrolled cases. These symptoms are due to the high sugar (glucose) content in the urine and blood. Diabetes is a chronic condition of impaired carbohydrate, protein and fat metabolism that results from insufficient secretion of insulin or from insulin resistance. The cells of the body need energy to function, and the primary source of energy is glucose, a simple sugar that results from the digestion of foods containing carbohydrates. Type II (or non-insulin-dependent diabetes mellitus NIDDM) diabetes is milder than the insulin dependent type. Type II diabetes is typically a disorder of middle and old age striking those primarily over the age of 40. This type of diabetes is increasing at astronomical rates.

According to Mohan, Sandeep, Deepa, Shah and Varghese (2007), India leads the world with largest number of diabetic patients earning the dubious distinction of being termed the 'diabetes capital of the world'. Type II diabetes is the commonest form of diabetes constituting 90 percent of the diabetes population. The global prevalence of diabetes is estimated to increase from 4 percent in 1995 to 5.4 percent by the year 2025. The World Health Organization has predicted that the major burden will occur in the developing countries. There will be a 42 percent increases from 51 to 72 million in the developed countries and 170 percent increase from 84 to 228 million, in the developing countries. The countries with the largest number of diabetic people are, and will be in the year

2025, India, China and United state (King, Aubert, and Herman, 1998).

Life Style as a Determinant of Diabetes

The key to the successful control of diabetes is active self-management (Auerbach, et.al, 2001). According to studies, Type II diabetes can be completely prevented by changes in life style of high-risk individuals (Tuomilehto, et al., 2001) If the trajectory of the disease is already diagnosed, patients can be greatly improved by changes in life style. On the basis of research findings the life style factors most strongly implicated are the needs for exercise, weight loss among those that are overweight, stress management and dietary control. Life style is the way a person lives. This includes patterns of social relations, consumption, entertainment, and dress etc. A lifestyle typically also reflects an individual's attitudes or values. Having a specific "lifestyle" means engaging in a characteristic bundle of behaviours that makes sense to one self and to others at different times and place. Therefore, a life style can be used to forge a sense of self identity and to create cultural symbols for the way a person is. The behaviours and practices within lifestyles are a mixture of habits, conventional ways of doing things, and reasoned actions. Lifestyle is the accepted way of life within the majority culture or group. Sedentary life style was one of the life style of the affluent which acted as a significant factor associated with diabetes (Ramchandran, Snehalattha and Vijay 2002).

Studies show that approximately half of the 2.1 million deaths in the United States each year are due to life style factors and many deaths could be prevented if people lived in a more healthy style (McGuinnis and Foege, 1993). Unhealthy diet and activity patterns contribute the most to death in the U.S. High-calorie consumption coupled with low levels of physical activity predisposes people to over weight, diabetes, and high blood pressure. A sedentary life style is responsible for 23 percent of deaths from the leading chronic diseases. Type 2 diabetes is an increasingly prevalent lifestyle disease. It is said that diabetes is associated with being overweight: for every 20 percent increase in overweight, the chance of diabetes doubles. Improving nutrition and maintaining normal body weight can help prevent diabetes. However, it has also been observed that people who are overweight and take high calorie diet often do not suffer from diabetes. This is perhaps because of their balanced state of mind and involvement in spiritual activities.

In modern times, the life style adapted by urban people was mostly copied from western culture where capitalism prevails. This life style is usually labelled as modern life style which still prevails in Metro cities of India and is being adapted by smaller cities. Late night parties, late dinner, T.V. watching during evening and leisure time; getting up late in the morning, using modern equipments and using motor vehicles to save physical energy, avoiding walking and physical exercise, eating readymade fast food and junk food, constant visits to restaurants to satisfy taste buds and continuously sitting in front of computer for long hours to complete office works are the characteristic features of modern life style. All this is supplemented by craving for more and more money leaving no times slot in daily life for sick, elderly, or children. This creates stress in their minds. Caring for children, elderly and sick people of one's community gives a person some spiritual satisfaction. The investigator assumes that this altruistic behaviour is good for strengthening one's immune system.

It is therefore expected that improving lifestyles may reduce health problems. By controlling their weight with a diet low in saturated fats and high in fruits, vegetables, and whole grains, controlling alcohol consumption and implementing exercise activities, survivors can lead a healthy life. Exercise can also promote positive psychological and emotional wellbeing and quality of life.

Lifestyle factors, including diet and physical activity are among the strongest risk factors for type II diabetes and a key aspect of its treatment. Diet, are critical in the prevention and treatment of type 2 diabetes. Because weight gain increases diabetes risk, and even modest weight reduction reduces risk, weight management is paramount in lessening the occurrence and effects of diabetes. Diets with low glycemic index or load may have modest benefits in managing type 2 diabetes. If a diabetic patient chooses to consume alcohol, he or she should do so in moderation. Foods advocated in type 2 diabetes are similar to those that are also beneficial in reducing risk for other chronic diseases (Kathleen, 2007). Type 2 diabetes is unlikely to induce relevant eating disturbances in obese patients, apart from an increase in restraint. Abnormalities of eating attitudes and behaviour are associated with an impairment of metabolic control (Mannucci, 2002). Padmini, et.al., (2008) found that educational intervention was successful in reducing some of the obesity parameters and improving dietary patterns of individuals with pre-diabetes and diabetes. Another study by Stewart, 2003 shown that supporting patients to make changes in their physical activity and dietary habits can prevent onset of type 2 diabetes.

Physical activity plays a key role in reducing diabetes risk and can be very beneficial in promoting survival and longevity (Rewers, 1995). The risk reduction has been confirmed in many studies, The Diabetes Prevention Program Research Group (2002), Tumilehto et.al. (2001) provides one of the many major health benefits of regular physical activity is the prevention of type 2 diabetes, mediated by weight control and other mechanisms (Pan et.al., 1997, Thompson et.al. 2001, Lindstrom et.al., 2004). Given that both inactivity and obesity seem to be strongly and independently associated with diabetes and diabetes-related cardiovascular comorbidities (Sullivan, 2002), it is particularly crucial to understand how to promote physical activity in persons at high risk for diabetes. Moreover, physical activity has been shown to reduce diabetes risk in subjects with an excessive body mass index (BMI) and elevated glucose levels (Tumilehto et.al., 2001). Another study of in Native Hawaiians with or at high risk for diabetes, stage of change was found to be significantly associated with exercise behaviour (Mau, 2001). Regular physical activity reduces the risk of developing or dying from some of the leading causes of illness in the United States. According to U.S. Department of Health and Human Services, (1996), regular physical activity improves health by reducing the risk of developing diabetes, by helping to maintain a healthy weight, by promoting psychological well-being, and by reducing the risk of developing high blood pressure. It is also important for individuals who are currently at a healthy weight to strive to maintain it since both modest and large weight gains are associated with significantly increased risk of disease (Ford, etal., 1997).

Various studies (Mugrance, Allen et.al., 2002, Mansfield et.al., 2002) have reported that spirituality has been considered an important factor in chronic disease treatment with positive health outcome and improvement in quality of life with strong religious belief. This study found a significant number of people having belief on spiritual treatment, and it positive role in permanent cure, of diabetes mellitus but those who were educated found less misconceived as compared to illiterates. In review of over 1200 studies on spiritual activities and health, at least two third of them showed a significant statistical association between spiritual activity and better mental and physical health (Weaver et.al. 2003).

The researcher is therefore curious to compare the life style of type II diabetics and non-diabetics and if the difference in life style exists to determine, which particular aspect of lifestyle is more significantly different such as food intake behaviour, sleeping behaviour, physical activity, alcohol consumption and spiritual behaviour.

Method

Objective: A comparative study of lifestyle of type II diabetics and non-diabetics.

Hypothesis: There exists a significant difference in lifestyle of type II diabetics and non-diabetics.

Design: Ex post facto double matched group design.

Sample: The sample for the study has two groups. Group I consists of 200 diabetic patients in the age range of 40 to 75 years taken from the clinics of physicians. Group II was a matched group of 200 non-diabetics who were matched with group I in terms of Age, Education, Marital Status, and Socio Economic Status. The following inclusion and exclusion criteria were followed for selection of diabetics in group I:

The inclusion criteria followed were:

1. A patient, who was diagnosed by doctor to have type II diabetes and was under treatment for diabetes for at least last two years, was included in the sample of diabetics.
2. The patients in the sample were first generation diabetics.
3. Educated at least up to class XII.
4. Marital status: All diabetics and non-diabetics in the sample were married.

The Exclusion criteria followed were:

1. Person suffering from any chronic fatal disease (other than diabetes) like cancer, heart disease, asthma, arthritis and AIDS (HIV) etc was excluded from the sample.
2. Person having family history of diabetics was excluded from the sample.
3. The patients whose parents or grand parents had been diabetics were excluded from the sample.

Measures

1. Diabetes was diagnosed on the basis of doctor's (Pathologist) report obtained during last six months. If the blood sugar level after fasting was beyond the normal value of 70–100 mg/dl the person was called a diabetic.
2. Life Style Scale by Das and Chaudhary (2008): The life Style Scale consists of 45 items with maximum score= 135 and minimum score= 45. It has 5 sections.

1. **Section 1: Food Intake Behaviour:** It has total 15 items, maximum score= 45 and minimum score= 15. **Scoring:** Each item has 3 types of response: always, occasionally, and never, which were scored as 1, 2 and 3. Items 1,2,3,4,7,8,10,11,12,13,14,15 were also scored in this way. Items 5, 6, and 9 had reverse scoring and the responses were therefore scored as 3, 2, and 1. **Test-Retest Reliability** = .99.
2. **Section 2: Alcohol Consumption Behaviour:** It has total 6 items, maximum score= 18and minimum score=6. **Scoring:** Each item has 3 types of response: always, occasionally, and never, which were scored as 1, 2 and 3. Items 1, 2, 3,4,5,6 were scored in this way. No items had reverse scoring in this section. **Test-Retest Reliability** = .98.
3. **Section 3: Physical Activity Behaviour:** It has total 9 items, maximum

score= 25 and minimum score=9. **Scoring:** Each item can be responded in terms of any one of the 3 types of timing, which were scored as 1, 2, and 3. Items 1, 3, and 4 were also scored in this way. For example: in item 1, the responses 0 ≥30 min, 30min ≥1½ hour and 1½ ≥3 hour were scored as 1, 2, and 3. Items 2, 5, 6,7,8,9 had reverse scoring and the responses were therefore scored as 3, 2, and 1. **Test-Retest Reliability** = .99.

4. **Section 4: Sleeping behaviour:** It has total 7 items, maximum score= 21 and minimum score=7. **Scoring:** Each item has 3 types of response: always, occasionally, and never, which were scored as 1, 2 and 3. Items 3, 4, 5, and 6 were also scored in this way. Items 1, and 7 had reverse scoring and the responses were therefore scored as 3, 2, and 1. **Test-Retest Reliability** = .98.
5. **Section 5: Spiritual behaviour:** It has total 8 items, maximum score= 24 and minimum score=8. **Scoring:** Each item has 3 types of response: always, occasionally, and never, which were scored as 3, 2, and 1. All 8 items were scored in this way. No items had positive scoring in this section. **Test-Retest Reliability** =.69.

Results and Discussion

Table 17.1 indicates that a significant difference exists in lifestyle of type II diabetics and non-diabetics.

Table 17.1: Comparison of Mean Life Style Factors of Type II Diabetics and Non-diabetics

Measures	Type II Diabetics			Non-Diabetics			df	t
	N	Mean	SD	N	Mean	SD		
Food Intake Behaviour	200	27.72	3.64	200	34.26	3.61	398	18.06 (p<.01)
Alcohol Consumption Behaviour	200	15.38	2.91	200	15.79	2.94	398	1.4 (p>.05)
Physical Activity Behaviour	200	19.91	3.93	200	20.87	3.53	398	2.5 (p<.01)
Sleeping Behaviour	200	13.44	3.11	398	14.92	3.40	398	5.6 (p<.01)
Spiritual Behaviour	200	19.23	3.03	200	20.63	2.72	398	7.71 (p<.01)
Life style	200	99.16	12.60	200	108.01	9.97	398	6.91 (p<.01)

Table 17.1 indicates that the mean value of food intake behaviour of type II diabetics is 27.729 (SD = 3.64) and the mean value of food intake behaviour of non-diabetics is 34.26 (SD = 3.61) and the t value is 18.06 with df =398 which is significant at .01 level. This shows that there was significant difference found on food intake behaviour of type II diabetics and non-diabetics. It indicates that non-diabetics have healthier food intake behaviour, in comparison to diabetic individuals.

Mean value of alcohol consumption behaviour of type II diabetics is 15.38 (SD =2.91) and the mean value of alcohol consumption behaviour of non-diabetics is 15.79 (SD = 2.94). The t value of 1.4 with df 398 which is not significant at .05 level. This shows that there was no significant difference found on alcohol consumption behaviour of type II diabetics and non-diabetics.

Mean value of physical activity behaviour of type II diabetics is19.91 (SD = 3.93) and the mean value of physical activity behaviour of non-diabetics is 20.87 (SD = 3.53) and the t value of 2.5 with df 398 is significant at .01 level. This shows that there was significant difference found on physical activity behaviour of type II diabetics and non-diabetics. It also indicates that non-diabetics spend more time in physical activities, in comparison to diabetic individuals.

Mean value of sleeping behaviour of type II diabetics is 13.44 (SD = 3.11) and the mean value of sleeping behaviour of non-diabetics is 14.92 (SD = 3.40) and the t value is 5.6. With df =398 the t is significant at .01 level. This shows that there is a significant difference in sleeping behaviour of type II diabetics and non-diabetics.

Mean value for Spiritual Behaviour of type II diabetics is 19.23 and that of non-diabetics is 20.63 and S.D is 3.02 and 2.72 respectively. The t value of spiritual behaviour is 7.71, with df =398, the value of t is significant at .01 level. It indicates that non-diabetics spend more time in spiritual activities, in comparison to diabetic individuals.

Mean value of life style of type II diabetics is 99.16 (SD = 12.60) and the mean value of lifestyle of non-diabetics is 108.08 (SD = 9.97) and the t value is 6.91 with df 398 which is significant at .01 level. This shows that there was significant difference found on life style of type II diabetics and non-diabetics. It indicates that total life style of non-diabetics is healthier than that of diabetic individuals (Table 17.1).

Discussion

The finding clearly indicates that diabetics lead an unhealthy life style, which is also known as modern life style of the neo-rich sections of society. This includes eating fast food rich in carbohydrates and fat, eating out to satisfy taste buds and to avoid physical work (kitchen work), sitting or lying on bed for long hours without doing any physical exercise etc. When the body is not involved in any physical exercise, the body metabolism does not function properly leading to malfunctioning of pancreas resulting in diseases like diabetes. The results from previous studies by Erikson et.al. (1991), and Pan et.al. (1997) also provide evidence that changes in lifestyle is effective in preventing diabetes. These result is in agreement with the another previous findings by Feinglos and Surwit (1988), Ramachandran et al. (1992), Vishwanathan et al. (1996); Peyrot, McMurry and Kruger (1999), Bell et al. (1998), Whittemore (2000), Lager (2006), Everhart and Wright (1995), Snowling and Hompkins (2006), Preidt (2009), although these studies were not done on North Indian population.

- The food intake behaviour of diabetics has been found to be unhealthier in comparison to that of non-diabetics. Responses to items in this section indicate that diabetics have higher inclinations to eat out in restaurants etc, even if proper food is available at home. They prefer to dine out, to attend parties etc and give more importance to taste rather than hygiene factors. They are more inclined to take food which is fried, rich and heavy rather than simple balanced diet. The difference in the Mean scores of food intake behaviour of diabetics and non-diabetics has therefore been found to be significant at .01 level. Hence food intake behaviour has proved to be a serious indicator of proneness to diabetes. Studies by Daniel (2004), AMA (2003) also support this finding.
- Alcohol consumption behaviour has not been found to differ in case of diabetics and non-diabetics. The difference in Mean scores of alcohol consumption behaviour was not found to be significant even at .05 level. This means that alcohol consumption behaviour does not have much impact upon prevalence of diabetes. So alcohol consumption behaviour is not an important factor in life style which may cause diabetes.
- Another important section of life style scale is physical activity behaviour. Results have proved that diabetics had sedentary life style doing very little physical activities. Physical activity is measured in terms of amount of time spent on rigorous physical activities such as gardening, agricultural field work, cycling, fast walking, swimming etc. Results have proved that non-diabetics spend more time on rigorous physical activities in comparison to diabetics. The difference is significant at .01 level. Previous research results are also in support of these findings. Studies by Mohan et al. (2006), Ramachandran et al. (2001, 2002, and 2006), Tanasescu et al. (2003), Norman and Mills (2004), AMA (2003), Zinman (1984) have also shown the

importance of physical activities in the life style of diabetics.

- Results have also shown that type II diabetics are more involved in sleeping behaviour in comparison to the non-diabetics. The difference is significant at .01 level. No one study has been done so for compare the sleeping behaviour of type II diabetics and non-diabetics.
- Results have also shown that non-diabetics are more involved in spiritual behaviour in comparison to the diabetics. The difference is significant at .01 level. Not many studies have been done to compare the spiritual activities of diabetics and non-diabetics, except a few like that of (Mugrance, Allen, et.al., 2002, Mansfield et.al., 2002) have reported that spirituality has been considered an important factor in chronic disease treatment with positive health outcome and improvement in quality of life with strong religious belief. This study found a significant number of people having belief on spiritual treatment, and it positive role in permanent cure, of diabetes mellitus but those who were educated found less misconceived as compared to illiterates.

Conclusion

Hence it is concluded that diabetics lead an unhealthy life style in comparison to non-diabetics who lead a much healthier life style. The difference in life style mean scores significant even at .01 level. It is therefore suggested to all adults (specially to diabetics) that they should change their life style (specially their food intake behaviour and physical activities) if they want to lead normal healthy life. Even the highly educated affluent people should try to maintain a balance between their calorie intake and calorie expenditure in order to maintain a sound health. Avoiding alcohol intake and performing spiritual activities have also been proved to be helpful in maintaining normal sugar level.

Given the strong association between lifestyle behaviours and the prevention and treatment of type II diabetes, it is important that greater research attention be directed at issues related to the development of healthful eating and physical activity habits and strategies for modifying unhealthy behaviours. The focus should be on ways to change life style both from an individual perspective and a broader environmental perspective.

References

AMA (American Medical Association) (2003). American Medical Association - Complete Medical Encyclopaedia. New York: Random House.

Auerbach, S.M., Clore, J.N., Kiesler, D.J. Orr, T., Pegg, P.O. Quick, B.G., et al. (2001). Relation of diabetic patients health-related control appraisals and physician-patient interpersonal impacts to patients' metabolic control and satisfaction with treatment. *Journal of Behavioural Medicine,* 7, 322-339.

Bell,R.A., Summerson, J.H., Spangler, J.G., and Konen, J.C. (1998). Body fat, fat distribution and psychosocial factors among patients with type II diabetes mellitus. *Behavioural Medicine*, 24 (3), 138-143.

Crandall, J., Schade, D., Ma, Y., Fujimoto, W.Y., Barrett-Connor, E., Fowler, S., Dagogo-Jack, S.,and Andres, R. (2006). The influence of age on the effects of lifestyle modification and metformin in prevention of diabetes. *Diabetes Care*, 61 (10), 1075-81.

Daniel, R., Richardson, Nancy, J., and Stiles. (2004). Co morbidity and psychosocial factors in the prediction of metabolic control and self-care behaviour among older adults with type II diabetes. *Journal of Behavioural Medicine*, 45 (9), 327.

Eriksson KF, Lindgarde F. (1991). Prevention of type 2 (non-insulin-dependent) diabetes mellitus by diet and physical exercise: the 6-year Malmo feasibility study. *Diabetologia*, 34, 891-898.

Everhart, J. and Wright, D. (1995). Diabetes mellitus as a risk factor for pancreatic cancer: A Meta analysis. *Journal of the American Medical Association*, 273, 1605-1609.

Feinglos, M.N., and Surwit, R.S. (1988). Behaviour and diabetes mellitus. Kala-mazoo, MI: Upjohn.

Ford, E.S., Williamson, D.F., Liu, S. (1997). Weight change and diabetes incidence: Findings from a national cohort of US adults. *American Journal of Epidemiology* 146(3):214-22.

Frank, B. H., Jo Ann, E. M., Meir, J. S., Graham, C., Simin, L., Caren, G. S., and Walter, C. W.,(2001). Diet, Lifestyle, and the Risk of Type 2 Diabetes Mellitus in Women. *The New England Journal of Medicine*, 345, 790-797.

Gupta, B., and Mona, P.K. (2002). A study of Personality, Stress, and Socio Economic Status of Diabetics vis-à-vis their Non-diabetic Counter parts. Unpublished thesis Ph.D., Department of Psychology. Dayalbagh Educational Institute Agra.

Hu G, Lindstrom J, Valle TT, Eriksson JG, Jousilahti P, Silventoinen K, Qiao Q, Tuomilehto J. (2004). Physical activity, body mass index, and risk of type 2 diabetes in patients with normal or impaired glucose regulation. *Arch Intern Med.* 164, 892–896.

Jaana L., Johan G. Eriksson, Timo T. V., Helena H., Pirjo Ilanne-Parikka, Sirkka K.K., Mauri L., Anne L., Merja R., Virpi S., Sirkka A., Zygimantas C., Vladislav M., Martti H., Marjo M., Vesa M., Jouko, S., Matti U. (2001). Prevention of Type 2 Diabetes Mellitus by Changes in Lifestyle among Subjects with Impaired Glucose Tolerance. *The New England Journal of Medicine*, 344, 1343-1350.

Kathleen, J. M. (2007). Nutrition Review: Diet and Nutrients in the Prevention and Treatment of Type 2 Diabetes. *American Journal of Lifestyle Medicine*, 1, (5), 339-343.

King, H., Aubert, R.E., and Herman, W.H. (1998). Global burden of diabetes, 1995-2025: prevalence, numerical estimates, and projections. *Diabetes Care*, 21, 1414- 1431.

Knowler. W.C., Barrett-Connor, E., Fowler, S.E., Hamman, R.F., Lachin, J.M,, Walker, E.A. and Nathan, D.M. (2002). Reduction in the incidence of type 2 diabetes with lifestyle intervention or metformin. *The New England Journal of Medicine,* 346, (6), 393-403.

Lager, J.M. (2006). Relationship among religious coping, psychosocial factors, and quality of life in individuals with type ll diabetes. Dissertation Abstracts International, 68 (9), 115.

Mannucci, E., Tesi, F., Ricca, V., Pierazzuoli, E., Barciulli, E., Moretti, S., Di Bernardo, M., Travaglini, R., Carrara, S., Zucchi, T., Placidi, G.F. and M Rotella, C. (2002). Eating behaviour in obese patients with and without type 2 diabetes mellitus. *International Journal of Obesity*, 26,(6), 848-853.

Mansfield, C.J., Mitchell, J., and King, D.E. (2002). The doctor as God's mechanic? Beliefs in the South-eastern United States. *Social Sciences Medicine*, 54, 399-409.

Marin, M.R. (2007). Viva y arriba por major vida: Family protective factors and life satisfaction among Maxican – American elderly. Dissertation Abstracts International, 68 (10), 6972.

Mau MK, Glanz K, Severino R, Grove JS, Johnson B, Curb JD. (2001). Mediators of lifestyle behaviour change in native Hawaiians. *Diabetes Care*. 24, 1770–1775.

Mohan, V., Sandeep, S. Deepa, R., Shah, B., and Varghese, C. (2007). Epidemiology of type 2 diabetes: Indian Scenario. *Indian Journal of Medical Research*, 125, 217-230.

Mohan, V., Sandeep, S., Deepa, M., Gokulakrishnan, K., Datta, M., and Deepa, R. (2006). A diabetes risk score helps identify metabolic syndrome and cardiovascular risk in Indians-the Chennai Urban Rural epidemiology study (CURES-40). Diabetes Obes Metab (in press).

Musgrave, C.F., Allen, C.E. and Allen, G.J. (2002). Spirituality and health for women of colour. *American Journal of Public Health*, 92, 557-560.

Norman, G.J., and Mills, P.J. (2004). Keeping it simple: Encouraging walking as a means to active living. Annals of Behavioural Medicine, 28 (3), 149-151. Psychological Abstracts, 92 (3), 958.

Padmini, B., Kamalamma, N. Thakor G. P. and Ranjita M. (2008). A Community-Based Diabetes Prevention and Management Education Program in a Rural Village in India. *Diabetes Care*, 31 (6), 1097-1104.

Pan XR, Li GW, Hu YH, et al. (1997). Effects of diet and exercise in preventing NIDDM in people with impaired glucose tolerance: the Da Qing IGT and Diabetes Study. *Diabetes Care*, 20, 537-544.

Pan XR, Li GW, Hu YH, Wang JX, Yang WY, An ZX, Hu ZX, Lin J, Xiao JZ, Cao HB, Liu PA, Jiang XG, Jiang YY, Wang JP, Zheng H, Zhang H, Bennett PH, Howard BV. (1997). Effects of diet and exercise in preventing NIDDM in people with impaired glucose tolerance. The Da Qing IGT and Diabetes Study. *Diabetes Care*. 20, 537–544.

Peyrot, M., McMurry, J.F., Jr., and Kruger, D.F. (1999). A biopsychosocial model of glycemic control in diabetes: Stress, coping and regimen adherence. *Journal of Health and Social Behaviour*, 40,141-158.

Preidt, R. (2009). Lifestyle factors tied to older adult's diabetes risk. *Archives of Internal Medicine*, 14 (2), 1606-1609.

Ramachandran, A., Snehalatha, C., and Vijay, V. (2002). Burden of type 2 diabetes and complications-The Indian Scenario. Effect of urbanization. *Diabetes Resistance Clinical Practice*, 58, 55-60.

Ramachandran, A., Snehalatha, C., Dharmaraj, D., and Viswanathan, M. (1992). Prevalence of glucose intolerance in Asian Indians. Urban-rural difference and significance of upper body adiposity. *Diabetes Care*, 15, 1348-1355.

Ramachandran, A., Snehalatha, C., Kapur, A., Vijay, V., Mohan, V., Das, A.K., and Rao, P.V. (2001). Burden of type 2 diabetes and complications-The Indian Scenario. Distribution of body fat and effect of urbanization. *Ibid, 44,* 1094-1101.

Ramachandran, A., Snehalatha, C., Mary, S., Mukesh, B., Bhaskar, A.D., and Vijay, V. (2006). Indian diabetes prevention programme (IDPP). The Indian diabetes prevention programme shows that life style modification and metformin prevent type 2 diabetes in Asian Indian subjects with impaired glucose tolerance (IDPP-1). *Diabetologia*, 49, 289-297.

Ramchandran, A., Senhaltha, C., and Vijay, V. (2002). *Diabetes Research Clinical Practices*, 58, 55-60.

Rena, R.W., Michael, G.G., Kelly, J. A., Leann , L.B., John, M. J., James, F. S., Delia, S.W., Robert, W. J., and Richard, S. S. (2001). Behavioural Science Research in Diabetes: Lifestyle changes related to obesity, eating behaviour, and physical activity. *Diabetes Care* 24, 117-123.

Rewers, M., Hamman, R.F. (1995). Risk factor for non-insulin dependent diabetes. In diabetes in America. National Diabetes Data Group, Ed. Bethesda, MD, National Institute of Health, 179-220.

Snowling, N.J., and Hopkins, W.G. (2006). Effects of different modes of exercise training on glucose control and risk factors for complications in type 2 diabetic patients: A Meta Analysis. *Diabetic Care*. 29, 2518-2927.

Stewart, B. H., Robert, J. P., and Wendy, L. (2003). Lifestyle interventions for type 2 diabetes. *Canadian Famille Physician*, 49, 1618-1625.

Sullivan PW, Morrato EH, Ghushchyan V, Wyatt HR, Hill JO. (2005). Obesity, inactivity, and the prevalence of diabetes and diabetes-related cardiovascular comorbidities in the US, 2000-2002. *Diabetes Care*. 28, 1599–1603.

Tanasescu, M., Leitzmann, M.F., Rimm, E.B. et al. (2003). Physical activity in relation to cardiovascular disease and total mortality among men with type 2 diabetes. *American Heart Association*, 107, 2435-2439.

Taylor, S.E. (2006). Heart Disease, Hypertension, Stroke, and Diabetes, *Health Psychology*, 6, 367-375.

The Diabetes Prevention Program Research Group. (2002). Reduction in the incidence of type 2 diabetes with lifestyle intervention or metformin. *The New England Journal of Medicine* 346, 393–402.

Thompson, W.G. (2001). Early recognition and treatment of glucose abnormalities to prevent type 2 diabetes mellitus and coronary heart disease. Mayo Clin Proc. 2001; 76, 1137–1143.

Tuomilehto, J., Hu, G., Bidel, S., Lindstrom, J., and Jousilahti, P. (2004). Coffee consumption and risk of type 2 diabetes mellitus among middle-aged finnish and women. *Journal of Psychosomatic Research*, 291 (10), 1213-1219.

Tuomilehto, J., Lindstrom, J., Eriksoon, J.G., Valle, T.T., Hamalainen, H., Ilanne-Parikka, P., et al. (2001). Prevention of Type 2 diabetes mellitus by changes in life style among subjects with impaired glucose tolerance. *The New England Journal of Medicine*, 344, 1343-1350.

U.S. Department of Health and Human Services. (1996). Physical activity and health: a report of the Surgeon General. Atlanta, GA: U.S. Department of Health and Human Services, Centres for Disease Control and Prevention, National Centre for Chronic Disease Prevention and Health Promotion.

Viswanathan, M., McCarthy, M.I., Snehalatha, C., Hitman, G.A., and Ramachandran, A. (1996). Familial aggregation. Diab. Med., 13, 232-237.

Weaver, A., Flannelly, K., and Stone, H. (2003). Spirituality, Health, and CAM. Current Controversies Alternative Therapies in Health and Medicine, 9 (6), 42-46.

Whittemore, R. (2000). Strategies to facilitate life style change associated with diabetes mellitus. *Journal of Nursing Scholarship*, 32 (3), 225-232.

Zinman, B. (1984). Diabetes mellitus and exercise. Behavioural Medicine Update, 6 (1), 22-25.

18

Tribal and Non-tribal Employed Divorced Women: A Comparative Socio-psychological Study

Roshan Lal Zinta and Meera Manjul

Introduction

Despite socio-linguistically a giant, based on multilingualism and multiculturalism (Pandit, 1972), there exist harmony among the people of India that has tied them in single thread by forgetting their religious and cultural heritage (socioeconomic status, caste, gender, education) and presenting an ideal picture for other develop as well as developing countries across the world. But it is not always there; sometime the unity in the diversity becomes so hackneyed phenomenon that results in clashes among the communities. Although the demographic complexion of Indian people has undergone some changes after passing 59 years of Independence yet there exists social discrimination to the marginalized or disadvantaged communities, tribal populations, and females as well as with people low in socioeconomics status those preoccupies in neurotic tendencies (Misra, Srivastava and Kunwar, 1995) that forced them to resembles in psycho-physical slavery. So the literate as well as illiterate peoples from the suffering communities in general as well as the females in particular so far has not been experiencing mental freedom and still are in the path of revolution to fight against inhuman treatment such as oppression, subordinacy and social injustice from the part of men in various social sphere.

Although attained education has been proving catalytic agent for the females and marginalized sections including tribal one yet the very high education as well as lucrative profession and employment has hindered them by imposing greater threat. Although various studies (Nigam and Bhatia, 1995; Zinta, 2006, 2007, 2008; Zinta and Tiwari, 2007) pin points that the women belonging to high socio-economic status and high education with have been witnessing less strain and more positive mental health, yet it has been observed from various segments of the communities that attainment of very high education and access to lucrative professions has sown thorn to the progressing women, who suffers from cultural sophistication, social advantages and mental health problems (Bandura, 1998; Bhugra and Mastrogianni, 2004; Misra and Tripathi, 1977). The females generally a belonging to scheduled castes and scheduled tribals families has been still continuously enmeshing in such stereotypes has been suffering from social discrimination. Tribal population constitutes 8.20 percent of total population of India and their literacy rate is 47.10 with tribal men at 59.17 and tribal women at 59.17 which is very low and much less as regards the overall literacy of India, which stood at 64.84 per cent according to Census 2001.

The construct of socio-economic status may be responsible for such discrimination which is multidimensional and complex in nature (Pandey and Singh, 1985) involves socio-psychological variable such as education, wealth, occupation, employment, and income, cultural features of the home as well as neighbourhood factors such as poverty rate, unemployment, and percentage of families receiving public assistance (Bandura, 1982; Kupuswamy, 1980) and interacts with other confounding variable such as race, ethnicity and gender. According to National Institute of Health, the socioeconomic status has two aspects. First aspects deals with resources such as education, income and wealth while the second one with rank, functioning of relative position in the hierarchy e.g. social class. The business definition of socioeconomic status involves physical, social and economic conditions that influence the operation and performance of organization (McCarthy, Claibourne, Matthew, Frederick and John, 2000).

Hence the people with low socioeconomic status are prone to various types' disparities. As per theoretical part is concerned, the human differentiation on the basis of gender is a fundamental phenomenon that affects virtually every aspect of people's daily lives (Negi, 2004; Triver, 1972). Gender differentiation takes on added importance because many of the attributes and roles selectively promoted in males and females tend to be differentially valued with those ascribed to males generally being regarded as more desirable, effectual and higher status (Berscheid, 1993). Psychological oriented theories tend to emphasize the role of intra-psychic processes for governing gender development (Freud, 1905/1930; Kohlberg, 1966). These theories emphasize the cognitive construction of gender conceptions and styles of behaviour with the familial transmission model. Behaviourist theories have accorded prominence to parents in shaping and regulating gender linked conduct. The biologically-oriented theories insist on biological roles played by the males and females in reproduction underlie gender role development and differentiation (Buss, 1985; Triver, 1972). Such theories explain gender development and differentiation on the basis of ancestrally programmed (Archer, 1996; Simpson and Kenrick, 1997).

The sociologically oriented theories however have emphasized social construction of gender role mainly at the institutional level (Lorber, 1994).

Moreover, the socio-cultural and technological changes necessitate revision of pre-existing conceptions of what constitute appropriate gender conduct. Social cognitive theory of gender role development and functioning specifies how gender conception are constructed from the complex mix of experiences and operate in concert with motivational and self-regulatory mechanisms to guide gender linked conduct throughout the life course. The theory integrates psychological and socio-structural determinants within a unified conceptual structure. In this theoretical perspective, gender conceptions and roles are the product of a broad network of social influences operating interdependently in a variety of societal subsystems. People contribute to their self-development and bring about social changes that define and structure gender relationship through their agentic actions within the interrelated systems of influence (Bussey and Bandura, 1999). Social cognitive theory of gender role development and functioning integrates psychological and socio-structural determinants within a unified conceptual framework (Bandura, 1986; 1997).

According to ecological paradigm, the culture of groups and behaviour of individuals are comprehended in terms of a process of adaptation to the ecology in which it develops (Bronfenbrenner, 1979; Sinha, 1982). Ecological model of Berry, 1966, 1976 and Berry, 1987) relates the cultural and behaviour characteristics of groups and individuals to both the ecological and socio-political contexts. Despite this the gender schema theory is cantered on individual differences in gender schematic processing of information (Bem, 1981). In the words of Davar (2001) the gender has now become audible in professional circles where it was talking down attitude earlier. No significant effort in women empowerment seems to be effective for removing the oppression and threatening situation that is prevalent in the form of sexism and axiomatic disregard for the females. In the words of Vyas (2002), the women in Vedas were sovereign queen , the collectress of treasures, cognizant of supreme being, the chief of objects of worship, as such the Gods have put them in many places, abiding in manifold conditions, entering in the numerous.

There are two types of women students named as *Brahmavadinis* – life long students of theology and the second as *Sadoyovahas*, who pursued studies only till marriage. Rigveda, Upanisad, and *Kautilaya's Arthsastra* and many other writings reveal that women in India enjoyed a fair measure of equality with men in all spheres. Hence the females have been given special status by connecting the name before male e.g. Sita-Ram, Radhey-Krishan by considering the female as *Shakti* that constitute the nature. Such as concept also represent unity of male and female, which equally contribute for sustaining the reality. Common metaphor used to describe the females is *Prithvi* or Prakriti (mother earth), who upholds all the living and non-living beings. That is why the saying that "*Yatra naryastu pujyante ramanie tatra devatah*" is remarkable. But such ideology now in developed as well as developing countries has been fading and the recognition of females undergone various traumas by bearing lot of social discrimination from the site of male dominating society in this *Kaliyug*. Both illiterate as well as illiterate women are suffering a lot, even the females who avail good job after the completion of her higher degree also undergoes with various stressful discourses.

Single working woman has become a dominating phenomenon worldwide including India that involves unmarried widowed and divorced women. Their health concerns are of vital concern deserve to be given attention. Working of women outside the home, in traditional societies, where men are supposed to work outside home is closely associated with their divorce-hood and widowhood. Taking into account certain similarities between divorced and widowed women, irrespective of the mode their husbands departed from them have been noticed. Premi (2004) categorizes them collectively as the 'women-without-men' (WWM). The working conditions for widowed and divorced women have never been remained conducive for their physical, psychological and social health. Although the marriage is considered as a source of security by women, working and non-working (Hussain and Sharma, 1994; Khan and Khan, 1994), yet the death of a spouse is the most stressful and depression for them (Singh and Misra, 1987); widowhood as disaster divorce as greater wreck (Gillin et al., 1965) in women life. Pandey et al. (2000) have found that in the conditions under which women without men have to work are challenging to their mental balance.

Such a single women are prone to ischemic heart disease suffers from tension, depression (Khorana, 1989) despite this run their broken families by becoming sole breadwinner for their family (Baroota el al,1992) and themselves accompanied in numerous mental illnesses (Wig et al.,1969) such as depression , stress and anxiety (Feldman, 1990; Ruch ,1970, Singh, 1992; Srivastava and Sinha,1989). Singh (2000) concluded that in India, frequency of mental illness is higher in females than males and the genesis of mental illness is more socio-psychological than biological. The dreary aspect of depression is that it itself being an illness breeds many other sorts of health hazards by affecting physical, mental, social and spiritual wellbeing of a person (WHO, 2001). The depression disrupt normal functioning (physical and psychological) functioning by the accompanied feeling of apprehension, worthlessness, guilt, loss of appetite, sleep, sexual drive and loss of interest in pleasurable activities and behavioural changes in the pattern of movement, postural, facial apathy and change in thought content (Grinker et al.,1965; Singh,1977); causes variation in voice (Hargreaves et al., 1965); show self-negation, lack of attention, irrational thinking and some times suicidal attempts as well. Feldman (1990) in his meta-analysis on depression concluded that there has been an increase in the incidences of depression in the past years that involves change is social values. People, in the country like India, where health awareness and care are relatively low to the extent that may be termed as inadequate and miserable in case of women (India Health Report, 2006), depression play important role in it.

Biological theories assume that the cause of depression lies either in the genes or in some physiological malfunctioning that may or many not have an inherited base (Depue, 1979). In his psychoanalytic theory, Freud asserted on unconsciously harboured negative feelings toward those we love, the mourner now becomes the object of his or her own hate and anger. The mourner also resents being deserted and feels guilt for real or imagined sins against the lost person. The period of interjection is followed by the period of mourning work, when the mourner recalls memories of the lost one and there by separates himself or herself from the person who has died and loosens the bonds imposed by interjection. The grief work can go astray in overtly dependent individuals and develop in to an ongoing process of self-abuse, self-blame, and depression. The cognitive theories of depression focuses on the role of thought processes, cognitive styles and patterns characterized by logic errors, arbitrary, inferences, selective abstraction, overgeneralization, dichotomous thinking, and excessive magnification. The basic premise of the learned helplessness theory is that an individual's passivity and sense of being unable to act and control his or her own life is acquired through unpleasant experiences and traumas that the individual tried unsuccessfully to control, if failed leads to depression (Seligmen, 1975). The interpersonal theory however focuses on the deficits in interpersonal activities and negative responses they elicit from other. Life without stress, anxiety and depression is blamed for every melody thereby is an unavoidable phenomenon. According to Brown (1989) the depressions overtly and covertly affect human life in every age, sex and culture. Those who survive to these extreme conditions share certain specific personality traits such as hardy personality that appears to afford them a high degree of stress resistance. They involve various types of coping processes to adjust proper in their environment.

Coping is defined as an effort, both action- oriented and intra-psychic, to manage (i.e. master, tolerate, reduce minimize) environmental and internal demands and conflicts among them that taxed or exceed a person's resources. In nutshell, it involves any effort that seeks to preserve reality as well as conscious efforts to deal with stressful demand. According to Folkman and Lazarus (1980) coping involves all cognitive and behaviour efforts to master, reduce or tolerate demands. It seeks to alter the relationship between self and the environment or to reduce emotional pain and distress. Billings and Moos (1981) provided in their taxonomy of coping involves problem oriented and emotional oriented. Problem focused coping is directed towards source of threat and is a way to change the relationship. Emotion aroused coping regulate emotion in response to stress. Coping resource may also be personal, self esteem, self efficacy, perception of control etc. Social spot as coping sources of physical re sources include satisfactory health and adequate physical energy to meet demands. Lazarus (1993) defined coping as problem solving efforts made by an individual when the demands he faces are highly relevant to his welfare and when these demands tax his adaptive resources.

Coping styles of depressed and non-depressed person also have come under scientific scrutiny. Various scholars e.g. Coyne et al., 1981; Dise-Lewis, 1988; Kolence et al., 1990, Soloman et al., 1988 found non-significant difference between depressed and non-depressed persons. Kuyken and Brewin (1994) studied stress and coping among depressed women. The depressed subjects were found to engage in more avoidance coping and less painful problem solving or positive reappraisal than the non-depressed subjects. Desenova et al. (1994) studied way of coping among HIV-infected individuals. They assessed coping styles, depression, and physical illness in 85 HIV-infected males (aged 24-53 years). A 2-way ANOVA of questionnaire responses revealed a significant main effect for emotion focused coping on depression. Folkman (1984) study has shown that depressed people cope with recent stressful event. Chan (1995) studied depressive symptoms and coping strategies among Chinese adolescents in Hong Kong and examined the depressive symptoms of 161 Chinese adolescents. The depressive symptoms levels were found to be related to avoidant with coping strategies as well as low self-esteem and reduced social support. Hays and Zouar (1995) investigated stressors coping strategies, and mental health among 45 Tunisian women while found no statistical significant difference between the middle class village and urban students. Weinhardt et al. (1998) in their study on women with sever mental illness have found that training is assertiveness can be an asset for women's functioning. Holahan and Moos (2005) in their study on 500 women and 711 elucidated a key mechanism through which avoidance coping is linked to depressive symptoms. Geisner et al. (2006) evaluated the efficacy of a brief, mailed personalized feedback intervention designed to alleviate coping and hopelessness. The feedback was found to be more effective in reducing depressive symptoms, hopelessness and hopelessness mediated reductions in depressive symptoms.

Various studies have found that the single person accounted for more mental illness followed by married, widowed, and divorced women (Broota and Kumari,

1998; Jaco, 1980; Khorana, 1989; Mody and Murthy; 1980; Nichol, 1979; Penfold, 1981; Sharma and Verma, 1982:). But Sethi and Sharma (1981) have found non significant but inconsistent difference between the joint families of subjects with secondary depression and that of families of subjects with primary depression. Pandey and Srivastava (2000) have studies 240 career females working in various organizations and have found that work stress is positively related with the physical and psychological health. In some situations the females are quite resilient to the stressors thereby are followed with hardiness personality (Kobasa, 1979) as a constellation of personality characteristics that functions as a resistance resource for encountering with stresses. The personality disposition of hardiness involves commitment, control and challenge. Hardiness is a buffering agent in debilitating the effects of life events on illness (Kobasa, 1982).

The single women from general category in general as well as the tribal and scheduled caste category in particular suffer a lot from depressive episodes. These women are predictive of so many psychological problem like self-blaming, irritability, filling guilty their symptoms. But so far the research is lacking in this area but some indirect studies e.g. (Feldmen, 1990; Ruch, 1970 and Singh, 1977) highlights some clue among such a widowed and divorced women in terms of their socio-economic status and coping strategies. Various social scientists poses various logic to see the relationship of poor socioeconomic status to depression (Ramchandran and Saradamenon, 1980) in old age; but the study of Nandi et al. (1980) found that in each group higher socio-economic status had higher rates of mental morbidity. Khorana (1989) observed 66 percent ischemic disease in widowed women; Biswas and Rai (1991) reported tribal girls higher in neuroticism; and Singh (1992) found more hypochondria and repressive reactions among tribal people. In a cross-cultural study on the personality pattern of tribal and non-tribal adolescent girls, Manwani and Saxena (1998) found tribal and non-tribal both disclose their Self in the identical manner and observed no significant difference between tribal and non-tribal. In tune with the above studies, Nandi et al. (1975) as well as Shah and Upmayer (1977) have found that socio cultural factors determine depression among individuals similarly as well as environmental distinction influences depression to a greater extent (Bogadia et al., 1994).

Keeping in view the above review in mind, the present study has been framed to observe the relationship between socioeconomic status, depression and coping styles of employed tribal and non tribal divorced women. For surviving their families these divorced working women have been applying various efforts even by migrating from their rural native areas to the urban one. The attainment of education and vocation on the one hand although has been proving greater resources for surviving their families by selecting good profession yet it itself has also been proving equally stressful for divorced women. On the one side it has been helping in maintaining better quality of life in terms of better socioeconomic status and promotion of general wellbeing and mental health and on the other side it also has been proving as a the factor in family conflict, frustration and violence. Its reason is that in this male dominated society the expectancy of male husband and their families from the side of newly wedded female in the form of dowry has exaggerated that in turn has created turmoil and violence like situation. Although the attainment of education has been proving as a great resource for overcoming their difficulties (Zinta, 2006, 2007, 2008) yet the higher education prevalence and vocation in women itself have become problem to the qualified and employed women whose progress are not being tolerated by the men and are being tormented by their husband and family for accruing money or expectancy of dowry from them. But sometime the women facing such problem become resilient to their stressor and applying various coping styles to overcome the situation. So in the present study thrust have been given to explore the socioeconomic status, depression and coping styles of the tribal and non tribal working women for which the below mentioned methodology have been utilized.

Method

Sample: Since the study is very complex in nature and the identification of divorced women in organization involves heightened efforts. Further the identification of tribal divorcees in general and employed one in particular aggrandizes the complexities of the study and their comparison with normal divorced population further increases a great stress. Keeping in view the complexities of the study a sample of only 50 employed divorced women (25 tribal + 25 non-tribal) were selected from age ranges from 25 to 50 years from the various governmental offices from the capital of Himachal Pradesh Shimla (India) where these women have migrated to earn from the native places in order to survive their offspring and families. Hence, the study is pioneer in nature where the comparison between employed tribal and non tribal divorced population has been compared with below mentioned methodology.

Measures

Socio-Economic Status Scale (Pareek and Trivedi, 1964): In order to study the SES of the participants, SES scale (Pareek and Trivedi, 1964) was administered to the participants. The scale consists of 9 items on which objective information can be collected about an individual and his family. The items are equally weighted each having a maximum score of six. The sub items within each item are differentially weighted. The time limit for the completion of this inventory will be approximately between 15 to 20 minutes. The minimum score ranges from 4 to a maximum of 45. However, the person who scored below 13 can be put into lower socioeconomic status and the score ranges between 13-23 in lower middle; 24-32 in middle class as well as 33 to 42 in upper middle class and the people who score above 43 falls in upper class. The scale is highly reliable and the test retest reliability is r = 0.87 while the inter judge reliability in case of rank order correlation, the value of rho obtained was very high (r = 0.93). This scale is indigenous in origin hence very useful to judge socioeconomic status of the people.

Hindi Version of Beck's Depression Inventory (Beck, 1961): The scale was used for measuring attitudes and symptoms associated with depression. It is a 21-items self reporting rating inventory measuring characteristic attitudes and symptoms of depression and the total score ranging from 0 to 63. The BDI is separated to possess adequate internal consistency and test-retest reliability. Although, there have been some controversy concerning the use of the BDI yet recently it has reviewed in large number of studies. The time limit for the completion of this inventory will be approximately 10 minutes. Internal consistency for the BDI ranges from 0.73 to .92 with a mean of r = 0.86. (Charles et al., 1989). Alternate form reliability correlation between 21 items and 13 items short form have ranged from .89 to .97 indicating that the short form is an acceptable substitute for the long form.

Multidimensional Coping Inventory (Charles, 1989): Five scales of multidimensional coping inventory (four items each) measure conceptually distinct aspects of problem focused coping (active coping, planning, suppression of competing activities, restraint coping, seeking of instrumental and social support), five scales measures aspects of what might be viewed as emotion focused coping (seeking of emotional social support, positive reinterpretation, acceptance, turning to religion and denial) have been used. The respondents were told that how people respond when they face stressful event in their lives, as there are many ways to try to deal with stress by putting a tick mark on appropriate circle. Four responses choice of each question was given the weight age from 1 to 4. Each response choice that the subject responds as right was summed up for active coping, planning, and suppression of competing activities and so on for the ten sub-scales.

Results and Discussions

Results are shown in Table 18.1.

Table 18.1: Comparison between Tribal and Non-Tribal Employed Divorced Women on Some Socio-Psychological Variables (Socio-economic Status) and Coping Style

Significance Levels: ** $p < .01$; * $p < 0.05$

Tribal employed divorced women (N = 25)			Non-Tribal employed divorced women (N = 25)		
Variables	Mean	SD	Mean	SD	t-ratio
SES	21.48	3.58	18.44	2.76	3.42**
DPS	12.84	13.68	20.16	12.58	-1.968*
C S	112.60	17.49	107.52	14.98	1.103

Notations: SES: Socio-economic status; DPS: Depression; CS: Coping styles

The result revealed that there emerged significant difference between tribal and non tribal employed divorced women in socioeconomic status. The tribal employed divorced women were found significantly higher in socioeconomic status ($p = 3.42$, $p < 0.01$) as compared to their counterpart non tribal employed divorced women. This finding is supported by the study of Singh (1992) who pinpointed that socioeconomic status is influenced by the background of the people. As per the background of tribal single women are concerned, they have remained in their miserable past. The tribal families in Himachal Pradesh live in very remote areas where there are no suitable infrastructure facilities. Till today such areas are disconnected when there are heavy rain and snowfall. During those days it is not possible to maintain access in these villages. So the people of tribal areas suffer a lot during winter and rainy seasons. Beside this the position of education, health institution and other infrastructure such as road and pedestrian are not praiseworthy. But the women in general and the other men in particular from these tribal areas are quite resilient to the stressors. They apply positive emotion and hardy personality (Kobasa, 1969) to overcome their distress. The tribal females migrated from such an area to the urban are well acquainted with their miserable past reality of families from their past are now learning lesson from their apathetic state thereby generating potential energy to reduce allostatic load and learnt a lesson to live more happier and stronger life by maintaining their socioeconomic status. This is why these female perhaps have been found higher in socioeconomic status or better from non tribal females. The people once suffer; perhaps in future can learn a lesson that tribal divorced women are now practicing. These non tribal employed divorced females perhaps have been undergoing in such trauma first time and perhaps in their past they were living happier and resilient life.

Further, the second sound reason in the study for high socioeconomic status among tribal employed divorced women are that beside their employment they are also running their family business, bearing good apple orchards, other dry fruits such as Chilgoza and Neoza grown in Kinnaur as well as potatoes and pea business, and rajmah in Lahaul Spiti areas of Himachal Pradesh. The male and females belonging to tribal areas also don't hesitate to run their business related to woollen garments, shawl and topic as well as sell their domestic product by self initiative but the employed women have not sufficient time for it but they avail some incentive such as woollen cloth, handicraft and other hand made rural items. Such concept is lacking among non tribal employed women who seem to be solely dependent on their vocation and passed their life in hardship in this contemporary scenarios where inflation has touched the sky. Socio-economic status is generally considered an important variable, both in the planning of developmental programmes and in researches in the fields of education, sociology, psychology, community development, agricultural extension etc. Several studies have shown how socio-economic status influences values and norms of behaviour, social participation, pattern of leadership, motivation for improvement and communication in a community. A major concern in India today is about the methods of increasing the vertical social mobility of individuals and communities. In order to understand and help this mobility, measures of social rank and status need to be devised. Such measures of social rank are usually in terms of socio-economic status scales and indices.

Second objective in this study was to assess the prevalence of depression among tribal and non tribal employed divorced women. In this variable (depression) there emerges significant difference ($t = 1.96$, $p < 0.01$) between tribal and non tribal divorced working women. The tribal employed divorced women were found low in depression level as compared to the non tribal. The reason behind the facts again seems to be their increased socioeconomic status due to above mentioned means by which their level of depression has decreased significantly in the tribal women but its prevalence is status quo in the non tribal single working women, who themselves found helpless. The divorced working women from the tribal as well as non tribal families are experiencing greater distress since their inception or time immemorial. During in pursuing their study these women have to face various hardships to complete their higher degree or diploma by pleasing their parents to provide them school, college and university fees as well as daily expenditure for eating and clothing etc. According to Shirali and Kanwar (1987) there exists higher prevalence of mental illness e.g. somatic symptoms, neurosis and depression among women. Its frequency increases with caste, age, education, income or occupation and family structure.

In tribal families there also exists caste system that the researchers have not touched so far and the comparison is generally with scheduled caste and tribes. The scheduled castes families in scheduled tribal areas are extremely suffering due to their less holding of land and poor socioeconomic status and unemployment problem that result due to illiteracy and lifelong dominance of the elite groups. This has aggravated their depression to survive better in their environment. The concordance and prevalence rate of depression in scheduled caste females in general as well as the single working women from these marginalized families from tribal areas as well as non tribal areas are further a matter of great concern to the social scientists as well as psychologist with the suggestion they should not ignore such area rather be quite optimistic about exploring their plight. Some researches have pinpointed that lower the socioeconomic status extreme with be the maladaptive behaviour (Goldenberg and Mala, 1979; Nandi et al., 1975; and Upmayer, 1997). So the Depression is one of the major concerns for the emotional, physical, social and spiritual well being of humans.

Third variable in the present study was to evaluate coping styles of tribal and non tribal divorced employed women. There emerges non-significant difference ($t = 1.10$, $p > 0.05$) between coping styles of the triabal employed divorced women as well as non tribal divorced employed women. If we slightly pay our attention towards mean and standard deviation then we can generalize that the tribal women are applying better strategies to cope well in their environment. It is their self-efficacy that has been proving as a greater inner resource for promoting ones wellbeing. The social cognitive theory (Bandura, 1986, 2001, 2004) is directly associated with maintaining human action who view man as an agent who can happen thing intentionally. According to this theory there are complicated interaction between personal, behaviour and environmental factors. This theory states that during stressful or grim situation it is one's self-efficacy belief that work and help the affected one in surviving their environment. They show hardiness factor that involves syndrome marked by commitment, challenge and control associated with strong stress resistance. The social cognitive theory (Bandura, 1986, 2001, 2004) highlights triadic reciprocal relationship between imposed, selected and constructed environment.

Bandura talks about the social conduct that plays very important role in the human being development. The social theory however highlights role of how social or society enters into the individuals and constructs the individual's economical and political ideology (Asthana, 2002). The cognitive and social factors can contribute to maintain human health and disease (Bandura, 1998). If scheduled caste students follow the non-violence principle of *Gandhiji* wherein he talked about spiritual force (Kriplani, 1970) as well as the concept of *Dr. Bhim Rao Ambedkar* that *Self-help and Self-education* are such factors that can contribute to overall wellbeing and maintained ones status in the society (Keer, 1990). Hence, the coping pattern of ones depends upon ones own efforts and cognitive level.

Its explanation seems in accordance with the biological theories which assume that the cause of depression lies either in the genes or in some physiological malfunctioning that may or many have an inherited base (Depue, 1979). In his psychoanalytic theory, Freud asserted on unconsciously harboured negative feelings toward those we love, the mourner now becomes the object of his or her own hate and anger. The mourner also resents being deserted and feels guilt for real or imagined sins against the lost person. The period of interjection is followed by the period of mourning work, when the mourner recalls memories of the lost one and there by separates himself or herself from the person who has died and loosens the bonds imposed by interjection. The grief work can go astray in overtly dependent individuals and develop in to an ongoing process of self-abuse, self-blame, and depression. The cognitive theories of depression focuses on the role of thought processes, cognitive styles and patterns characterized by logic errors, arbitrary, inferences, selective abstraction, overgeneralization, dichotomous thinking, and excessive magnification. These females are feeling helplessness, passivities and sense of being unable to act and control his or her life is acquired through unpleasant experiences and traumas that the individual tried unsuccessfully to control, if failed leads to depression (Seligmen, 1975). Psychological oriented theories tend to emphasize the role of intra-psychic processes for governing gender development (Freud, 1905/1930; Kohlberg, 1966). These theories emphasize the cognitive construction of gender conceptions and styles of behaviour with the familial transmission model. Further the problem of ecological adaptation and individual differences as well as ones self efficacy and cognitive processing (Bandura, 1986, 2004) might play a crucial role in it.

These single women seem to be high in mental pressure due to the increase in the population, children overload as well as of society who view them with slant eyes. They have to face various types of social discrimination based on low socioeconomic state (Pandey and Singh, 1985) and Genders (Trivers). This gender differentiation and discrimination even operates at institutional level (Lorber, 1994) where the working conditions of these women are affected. On the one hand they are considered as poor and on the other hand they are considered as helpless. As a result some naughty employees in the organization in general and other people in particular from the rural as well as urban population are in a look to exploit them sexually, physically, and mentally. In the home where they live, they have to face various stagnation from their neighbour in the form cursive languages. Some consider these women (especially widows) as wretched witches and bad women who do not want to see even their face. These women are suffering from physical, mental and social level (WHO, 2001).Most of people try to seduce them for sexual pleasure, practice rape like attitude and apply their dominance. As a result these women come in contact with psychic conflict (Broota, 1992; Singh, 2000) and suffer from various types of mental and behavioural problems.

Those single women living with their families are also being tortured by their own members. One the one hand these single women have to face the workload of household activities at the other the pressure from office as well as of their own offspring for providing better education and employment. In these era where the inflation has increased a lot and the cost of every items has become very high thereby enmesh them more at cognitive level in psychopathology produce vulnerabilities by lowering resilience by such allostatic load. Some women who are not working in government sector have to stray here and there and have to face the exploitation of elite people and the bureaucrats. In such a situation they mental health are continuously affecting day by day. Some widows and divorced women are exploited even on Panchay level and their name sometime is not proposed for the pension till the satisfaction of head. Sometime the family members do not allow them to go out of home and the society see them like a prostitute even if suppose they are going for market to procure their daily needs items. So they are seen with many doubts and the illiterate people have to face a lot as compare to the literate and employed women. Their helplessness become pleasure for other but there are some judicious and pro socially active people who are clear hearted, are ready to help them without condition and even some family provide extra care for such a female. For the progress of nation it is important to the state governments that they should improve this apathetic state of the single women so as to maintain their mental health and overall functioning. Further ones own responding and self-efficacy level as suggested by Bandura (1986, 2001, 2004) can become as important source followed with attainment of education, employment and increasing livelihood sources, agriculture as well as horticulture in order to compete with the problem of unemployment. The status of confidence in education, employment and earning itself can promote ones mental health and inner capabilities that are important for overall growth of the people.

References

Archer, J. (1996). Sex differences in social behaviour: are the social role and evolutionary explanations compatible? *American Psychologist, 51,* 909-917.

Asthana, H. S. (2002). Constructionism: Some epistemic and methodological issues in psychology. In G. Misra, and A. K. Mohanty (Eds.), *Perspectives on Indigenous Psychology.* New Delhi: Concept.

Bandura, A. (1982). Self-efficacy mechanism in human agency. *American Psychologist, 37,* 122-147.

Bandura, A. (1997). *Self-efficacy: The exercise of control.* New York: W. H. Freeman.

Bandura, A. (1977). Analysis of self-efficacy theory of behavioural change. *Psychological Review, 84*, 191-215.

Bandura, A. (1998). Health promotion from the perspective of social cognitive theory. *Psychology and Health, 13*, 623-649.

Bandura, A. (2001). Social cognitive theory: An agentic perspective. *Annual Review of Psychology, 52,* 1-26.

Bandura, A. (2004). Health promotion by social cognitive means. *Health Education and Behaviour, 31*, 2, 143-164.

Brown, G.W. (1989). Depression: A radical social perspective. In K. R. Herbs and . S. Payel (Eds), *Depression: An integrative approach.* London: Heinmeman.

Buss, D. M. (1985). Psychological sex differences: origins through sexual selection. *American Psychologist, 50,* 164-168.

Bem, S. L. (1981). Gender schema theory: A cognitive account of sex typing. *Psychological Review, 88,* 354-364.

Berry, J. W. (1966). Temne and Eskimo perceptual skills. *International Journal of Psychology, 1,* 207-229.

Berry, J. W. (1976). *Human ecology and cognitive style.* New York: Sage.

Berry, J. W. (1987). The comparative study of cognitive abilities. In S. H. Irvine and S. Newstead (Eds.). *Intelligence and cognition: Contemporary frames of reference*. Dordrecht: Nijhoff.

Billings, A. G., and Moos, R. H. (1981). The role of coping, responses and social resources in attenuating the stress of life events *Journal of Behavioural medicine, 4,* 139-157.

Broota, A., George, M, Singh, A (1992). Adjustment of boys and girls from broken homes. *Journal of Personality and Clinical Studies*, 8, 81-85.

Bronfenbrenner, U. (1979). *Ecology of human development.* Cambridge Mass: Harvard University Press.

Chan, D.W. (1995). Depressive symptoms and coping strategies among Chinese adolescents in Hong Kong' Journal *of Youth Adolescence,* 24(3), 267-79.

Coyne, J. C; and Cotlib, I. H. (1983). The role of cognition in depression: A critical appraisal. *Psychological Bulletin*, 4,472-505.

Daver, B.V. (2001). *Mental health from gender perspectives. Gender and mental health: interdisciplinary perspective*. New Delhi: Sage.

Depue, R.A., and Monorol, S.M. (1978). Learned helplessness in the perspective of the depressive disorders' *Journal of Abnormal Psychology, 87*,3-20.

Dise-Lewis, J.D. (1988). The life events and coping inventory: An assessment of stress in children.' *Psychosomatic Medicine, 50* (5), 484-99.

Freud, S. (1905/1930). *Three contributions to the theory of sex*. New York: Nervous and Mental Disease Publishing Co.

Feldman, S.S, Fisher, L., Ransom, D.C, and Dimiceli, S. (1990). Sex differences in relations between adolescent coping and adult adaptation. Journal of Research of Adolescent Coping and Adult Adaptation. *Journal of Research on Adolescence,* 5(3), 333-59.

Folkman, S. and Lazarus R. (1980). An Analysis of coping in a middle-aged community sample. *Journal of Health and Social Behaviour*, 21, 219-39. Geisner, I., Markman, C. N. , and Mary E.L.(2006). A randomized clinical trial of a brief, mailed intervention for symptoms of depression. *Journal of Consulting and Clinical Psychology, 74*, 2, 393-399.

Gillin, L., Clarence, G.D., Colbert, R.J., and Kastler, N.M. (Eds). (1965): *Social problems.* Bombay: Times of India Press.

Grinker, R.R., Miller, J., Sabshin, J., Nunn, M. R., Nunnally, J.C. (1965). *The phenomena of Depression.* New York: Harper.

Hargreaves, Willow A., Starweather, J.A., K. H. Blacker (1965). Voice quality in Depression. *Journal of Abnormal Psychology*, 70, 218-220.

Holahan, J. , Rudolf H.M., Carole, K.H, Brennan, P.L. and Kathleen, K.S. (2005). Stress generation, avoidance coping and depressive symptoms: A-10 year model. *Journal of Consulting and Clinical Psychology,* 73(4), 658-666.

Hussain, A., and Sharma, T. (1994). Marital Adjustment and its correlates among working and non-working women. *Journal of Personality and Clinical Studies*, 10, 71-75.

Jaco, A. G. (1960). *The social epidemiology of mental disorders.* New York: Sage Foundation.

Keer, D. (1990). *Dr. Ambedkar's life and mission.* Bombay: Power Prakashan.

Kobasa, S. C. (1982). Commitment and coping in stress resistance among lawyers. *Journal of Personality and Social Psychology, 42,* 707-717.

Kolence, M, Hartley, D., and Murdock, N. L. (1990). The relationship of mild depression to stress and coping. *Journal of Mental Health Counselling*, 12(1), 76-92.

Kohlberg, L. (1968). A cognitive developmental analysis of children sex role concept and attitudes. In E. E. Maccoby (Ed.), *The development of sex differences.* Stanford, CA: Stanford University Press.

Khan, R.A., and Khan, N.A. (1994). A study of Security-Insecurity feeling among Women. *Journal of Personality and Clinical Studies*, 10, 83-88.

Khorana, S. A.(1989). Psychological risk factors in ischemic heart disease. *Indian Journal of Clinical Psychology*, *16,* 13-17.

Kriplani, J. B. (1`970). *Gandhi, his life and thought.* New Delhi: Ministry of Information.

Kuyken, W. , and Brewin, C. R. (1994). Stress and coping in depressed women. *Cognitive Therapy and Research*, 18(5), 403-412.

Lazarus, R. S. (1993). Coping theory and research: past, present and future. *Psychosomatic Medicine, 55,* 234-247.

Manwani, S.L. and Saxena, V.B. (1988). A study of areas of self-disclosure among tribal and non tribal youths. *Journal of Personality and Clinical Studies, 4,* 1, 31-34.

McCarthy, P., Claibourne, I. D, Matthew, W. G., Frederick , P. R., and John, I. T. (2000). Race, ethnicity, Gender, socio-economic status- research exploring their effect on child health: A subject Review. *American Academy of Paediatrics, 105,* 6, 1349-1351.

Misra, O.P., Srivastava, S.K., and Kunwar, R. (1995). Neuroticism as a function of caste and economic status in a group of Indian adolescents. In O. P. Misra, and S. K. Srivastava (Eds.), *Ecological perspectives and behaviour.* Hardwar: Gurukul Kangri University.

Mody and Murthy (1980). The study of Mental Health of children of working Mothers. *Journal of Personality and Clinical Studies,* 4 (2), 161-164.

Nandi, D.N., Jamani, S.A., Ganguli, H., Benerfee, G. Boral, G, Ghosh, A., Sarkar, S. (1975). Psychiatric disorders in a rural community in West Bengal- An epidemiological study' *Indian*

Journal of Psychiatry, 17, 87-99.

Negi, S. (2004). Effects of education on social status of tribal women of Kinnaur. *Jan Saksharta*, Bhartiya Gramin Mahilla Sangh Indore, 52, 15-22.

Nigam, S. and Bhatia, T. (1995). Role strain among working women and its relationship with age, education and status. In O.P. Misra, and S.K. Srivastava (Eds.), *Ecological Perspectives and Behaviour. Hardwar:* Gurukul Kangri University.

Pandey, S. and Srivastava, S. (2000). Coping with work stress: The role of job category, family type and job tenure. *Journal of Research and Applications in Clinical Psychology*, 3,18-21.

Pandit, P. S. (1972). India's sociolinguistic area. Pune: University of Pune.

Penfold, P. S. (1981). Women and depression. *Canadian Journal of Psychiatry*, 26(a), 24-31.

Premi, R.K. (2004). *Working Women, Living Without Men.* An unpublished *M.Phil. Dissertation*, H. P. University, Shimla (India).

Ramchandran, V. and Sarada, M.(1980). Epidemiological study of depression in old age'. In A.V. Rao and P. Devi (Eds), *Depressive illness* (Rao, pp. 59-76), Madurai: A. V.

Ruch, F. (1970). *Psychology and Life* (7th edition). Bombay: D. B. Taraporevala Sons and Co. Pvt. Ltd.

Seligman, M.E.P. (1975) *Helplessness: On Depression Development and Death*. Sans Franscio: W. H. Freeman.

Sharma, S. (1975). Self-acceptance and socio-economic status. *Journal of Education and Psychology, 32,* 205-208.

Sharma V.K., S.K. Verma (1982) ' The Aging Indian Females: A Symptomatological Investigation *Indian Journal of Psychological Medicine*, 52, 42-47.

Sing, R. A. (1992). Hypochondriasis and depression as functions of aging, sex and socioeconomic status among tribals and non-tribals of North Bihar. *Indian journal of Psychology, 67,* (3 and 4), pp. 95-103.

Singh, J.K. (2000). Psychological intervention for facilitating mental health in village: An Experimental Report' *Journal of research and Application in Clinical Psychology, 3*, 28-32.

Singh, L. B. (1977). A comparison of Expressive and non-depressive subjects on psychomotor task' *Indian Journal of Clinical Psychology*, 4,55-58.

Sinha, D. and Jha, T. (1989). Invariance of mass and number among tribal and non tribal children: a study of the influence of age, sex, culture and habituation. *Journal of Personality and Clinical Studies, 5,* 2, 105-114.

Shirali, A. and Sandhya, K. (1987). Mental illness and women: A demographic study' *Journal of Personality and Clinical Studies,* 3(2), 103-108.

Solomon, Z., Mikulincer, M., and Avitzur, E. (1988). Coping, locus of control social support and combat related post traumatic stress disorder. *Journal of Personality and Social Psychology,* 55 (2), 279-85.

Srivastava, G.P., Sinha, S. P. (1989). Stressful Life Events and Health. *Indian Journal of Clinical Psychology*, 16, 26-28.

Suchitra, D. and Devi, S. (2002). Assessing the self esteem of women employed in various occupations. *Journal of Community Guidance and Research, 19*, 3, 391-398.

Tiwari, A.K. and Zinta, R. L. (2007). Hydropower generation and economic development: A study of NJPC project in Himachal Pradesh. *Research Journal Social Sciences, 15,* 2, 136-148.

Triver, R.L. (1972). Parental investment and sexual selection. in B. Campbell (ed.). *Sexual selection and the descent of man.* Chicago: Aldine.

Wig N.N., H.C. Verma, D.K. Shah (1969) 'Parental depression and Mental illness' *Indian Journal of Psychiatry*, 11, 1-6.

WHO (2001). The world health report: 2001: *Mental Health: new understanding, new hope. Geneva:* World Health Organization.

Zinta, R.L. (2006). Effect of self-efficacy, test-anxiety and short-term intervention on problem solving: A preliminary analysis. *Social Science International, 22,* 1, 3-8.

Zinta, R.L. (2006). Is guided mastery helpful in problem solving. *Psychological Studies, 51*, 4, 323-325.

Zinta, R.L. (2006). Performance and self-efficacy of secondary students. *Journal of Indian Academy of Applied Psychology, 32,* 3, 351-360.

Zinta, R.L. and Tiwari, A.K. (2006). Impact of socio-economic status on performance among male and female secondary students of Himachal Hill State. *Nava Arthiki, 14*, 2, 1-7.

Zinta, R.L. and Tiwari, A.K. (2006). Relationship between self-efficacy, socio-economic status and performance in secondary students. *Research Journal Social Sciences, 14,* 1, 121-137.

Zinta, R.L., and Tiwari, A.K. (2007). Impact of guided mastery treatment on self-efficacy among test-anxious students. *Journal of Psychological Researches, 51,* 2, 91-101.

Zinta, R.L. (2008). Efficacy of guided mastery treatment for self-efficacy among test anxious students. *Journal of Indian Academy of Applied Psychology, 34*, 2, 233-239.

Zinta, R.L., and Tiwari, A.K. (2008). Psychological analysis on project affected and likely to be affected families of SJVN Ltd. of Himachal Pradesh. *A project Reported submitted to the Integrated Institute of Himalayan Studies,* HPU Shimla-171005.

Zinta, R.L. (2008). A comparative study of scheduled castes and non scheduled castes population in tribal areas of Himachal Pradesh. *A Research Project, submitted to the University Grant Commission, New Delhi,* India.

Zinta, R.L., and Tiwari, A.K. (2008). Socio-economic and infrastructure facilities for sustainable rural development: A factorial analysis on Himachal Pradesh. *A project Reported submitted to the Integrated Institute of Himalayan Studies,* HPU Shimla-171005.

19

Conquering Childhood Depression

S.P. Sinha and Shraddha Sharma

Introduction

Depression is the leading cause of disability as measured by Disability Adjusted Life Years (DALYs) and the 4th leading contributor to the global burden of disease (DALYs) in 2000. By the year 2020, depression is projected to reach 2nd place in the ranking of DALYs calculated for all ages and both sexes. At the end of 2003, over 50 000 children were prescribed antidepressants, and over 170 000 prescriptions a year for antidepressants were issued to people under 18 years old (Timimi, 2004). The attitude to child rearing changed from viewing relations between adults and children primarily in terms of discipline and authority to a focus on permissiveness and individual rights. Shifting economic structures also led to profound changes in the organization of family life. Suburbanization and the economic demands of successful market economies resulted in greater mobility, less time for family life, and a breakdown of the extended family. Many families (particularly those headed by young women) became isolated from traditional sources of childrearing information. The boundaries between what is considered adulthood and what is considered childhood have become blurred, and this has led to children coming to be viewed as, in effect, miniature adults.

Just as our concepts of childhood have changed, so have our concepts of childhood problems. Until the 1970s it was believed that depression to children was rare or even nonexistent (Bahls, 2002). National Institute of Mental Health in the U.S. (NIHM) officially recognized the existence of depression in children and adolescents in 1975 and the research on depression during these life phases has attracted a growing interest during the last two decades (Kazdin and Marciano, 1998; Bahls, 2002). Before this, childhood depression was viewed as very rare, and not amenable to treatment with antidepressants. Childhood depression has become a popular notion, reflecting the broader cultural changes that have taken place in individuals' view of childhood and its problems.

Sadness is a universal emotion that no one is immune from, everyone in the world feels sad in some way or another on a daily basis for various reasons. The state of feeling sad is called 'depression' and usually refers to a condition of feeling sad very often, for a prolonged period of time. Depression is a potentially serious mental illness that can have far reaching and at times devastating effects on our children. It has been found that disorders of mood increase as the child grows up. In preschool children depression is uncommon. Childhood depression is just as serious as adult depression. It affects a person's overall energy, mood, expressions of emotion and behaviour. It was generally thought that children could not become depressed. Children, like everyone else, are not immune from this insidious and dangerous disease. Because children often do not have the capacity to step back, look at themselves, and recognize that the way they are feeling is not normal for them, diagnosis and treatment of depression is more difficult than for adults.

Types of Depression

Depression in children can be categorized into various forms such as anaclitic depression, masked depression and typical depression.

Anaclitic Depression: It is an impairment of an infant's physical, social, and intellectual development resulting from absence of mothering. It occurs primarily in infants who have been separated from or lost their mothers or primary caretakers. If a child suffers from anaclitic depression there is a high risk of serious developmental problems both intellectually and physically. Anaclitic depression has been reserved almost exclusively for infants. This concept was described by Spitz and Wolf (1946) who observed that if infants are separated from mother or primary care takers then infants show some behavioural changes such as crying, sad and apprehensive physical symptoms.

Masked Depression: In it children compensate for their depressed mood by adopting behaviours that occupy their time as fully as possible such as conduct problems (hyperactivity, delinquency, aggressiveness and irritability), somatic complaints (headache, stomach ache, and enuresis) and school problems (school phobia and poor school performance). Childhood depression is divided by Frommer (1986) into three forms (a) Enuretic depressives (moody, immature, hostile and aggressive) (b) Phobic depressives (irritable, denial to feelings of depression, weepy and tense) (c) Pure depressives (weepy, sleep disturbances, appetite disturbance, anti-social behaviour, temper outburst).

Typical Depression: Some typical symptoms such as dysphoria, hopelessness, social withdrawal, psychomotor retardation, sleep and appetite changes and other depressive symptoms like adult depression were reported by Cytryn and Mcknew (1972). Typical depression is categorized as (a) Acute depression and (b) Chronic depression.

Diagnosis of Depression

DSM-III-R provides three primary diagnostic categories of depressive disorders. These three categories include: major depression, dysthymic disorder, and atypical depression. Furthermore, these categories differ in number, duration of the symptoms, and severity with major depression being the most severe and atypical depression being the least severe. Major depression includes prominent and persistent dysphoric mood or loss of interest and pleasure in usual activities (Coleman, 1986). Dysphoric mood includes symptoms of being sad, low and irritable. In addition, individuals must posses four of the following symptoms for at least two weeks: change in appetite or weight, insomnia or too much sleep, psychomotor agitation or retardation, loss of interest or pleasure in usual activities, loss of energy, feelings of worthlessness, inability to concentrate, and recurrent thoughts of death (American Psychiatric Association, 1980).

According to DSM-IV, five out of nine depressive symptoms must be present, one of which must be depressed mood or loss of interest or pleasure, for at least two weeks in order to receive a diagnosis of Major Depressive Disorder (American Psychiatric Association, 1994).

Causes of Childhood Depression

Depression does not result from one factor. There are multiple factors which affect the genesis of depression as a mass. Among them genetic factors, psychological factors, environmental factors are included.

Figure 19.1: Causes of Depression

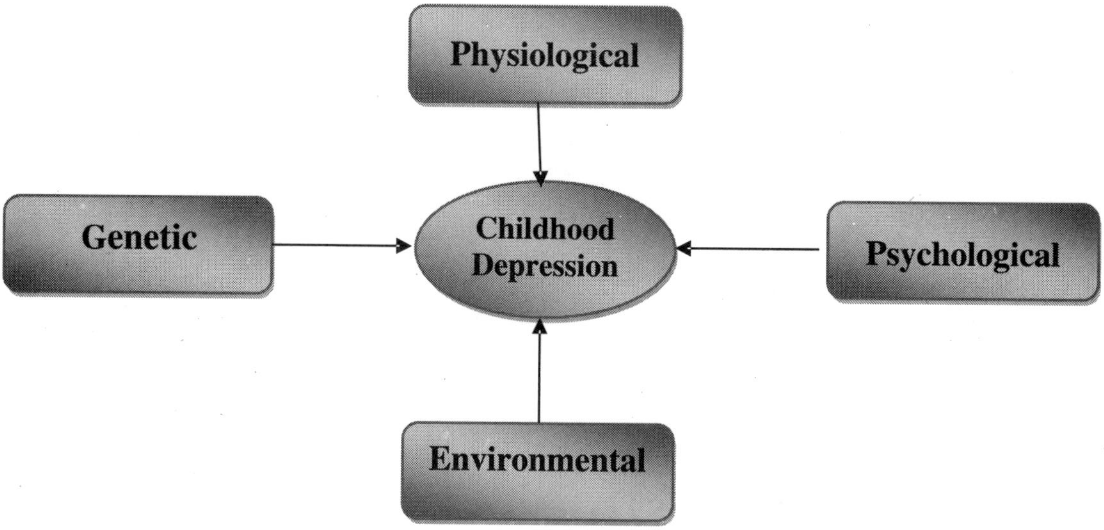

One of the reasons for depression is the biochemistry in the brain. Neurotransmitters are chemical messengers in the brain. They play a role in everything the brain regulates, including mood and emotions. Lower levels of three neurotransmitters—serotonin, norepinephrine, and dopamine have been found in people suffering from depression. This discovery is behind the chemical imbalance theory that depression is caused by deficiencies in one or all of these neurotransmitters in the brain. Deficiencies in neurotransmitters in the brain are responsible for certain symptoms of depression, including anxiety, irritability, and fatigue (Coleman, 1986). It is still a matter of debate whether the abnormalities in various neurochemical systems in the brain cause depression, or are themselves the result of depression. Anatomy of brain also influences the genesis of depressive symptoms. In a study by Steffens and Krishnan (1998) white matter hyperintensities and deep white matter intensities has been found to be associated with unipolar and biopolar disorders. Children with depressive symptoms have blunt amygdala response (decreased blood oxygen level dependent signal) to fearful and neutral facial expressions (Thomas et al., 2001). Some studies have shown the evidence of abnormal and hippocampal volumes among those who have major depression (MacMillan et al., 2003, Rosso et al., 2005).

Childhood depression is associated with a family history of mood disorders (Thapar and McGuffin, 1996) and with the existence of other psychiatric conditions. If the relative has had childhood or recurrent depression, the child is at even higher risk of developing depression. Research has shown that parents who are depressed are more likely than non depressed parents to have children with depressed symptoms (Brody and Forehand, 1986; Watkins, 2007). Furthermore, researchers (Weissman, Fendrich, Warner and Wickramaratne, 1992) found that more than 50 percent of children of depressed parents were diagnosed with depression before the age of twenty. Environmental factors play a major role in the genesis of depression. These environmental factors are very common but affect a child to a great extent. These factors lie in our day today life and unknowingly result in depression. Separation, divorce of parents or even close relatives; death of a loved one; less warm and hostile attitudes of parents (Chiariello and Orvaschel, 1995); a person or a pet; losing someone to death may cause a flood of emotions that shock children (Lewinsohn et al., 2000). Research has also been done to show that stressful events appear to precede the onset of depressive symptoms (Brown, Harris, and Peto, 1973). Lewisohn (1974) offered a model of depression in which depression develops when individuals fail to receive positive reinforcement from social interactions with others (Watson and Robinson, 1998).

A longitudinal study, involving 550 adolescent students between ages eleven and seventeen concluded that at the start of adolescence family environment is a more important predictor of depressive symptoms than stressful life events (Garrison, Jackson, McKeown and Addy, 1990). Neighbourhood quality and poverty is also associated with childhood depression (Hart, Atkins, Matsuba, 2008). Another cause of depression is psychological factors. These factors are found in child itself. Parents often are not aware that what they think as shy and introvert child may be depressed. They may develop a negative way of viewing the friends, neighbours, teachers and the whole world; social skills deficit; hopelessness, shyness and inexpressiveness etc. One of the most important causes of childhood depression is learned helplessness. Learned helplessness in children can lead to anxiety or depression, and it can be especially damaging very early in life, for the sense of mastery over one's environment is an important foundation for future emotional development. Seligman and Maier (1967) found that human motivation to initiate responses is also undermined by a lack of control over one's surroundings. Their research has shown that learned helplessness disrupts normal development and learning and leads to emotional disturbances, especially depression (Abramson et al., 1989). Seligman (1990) viewed depression as the ultimate expression of pessimism. Learning to be helpless can have dyer consequences in life. Pessimism leads to depression more easily, underachievement at work, sickness more often, less pleasurable life experiences when compared to optimists. The impact of cognitions or thinking on childhood depression has been studied by Laurent and Stark (1993).

Symptoms of Childhood Depression

Childhood depression is just as serious as adult depression (Ryan et al., 1987). Children (7-12 yrs.) resemble adults in depressed mood, incapability to experience pleasure, fatigue, concentration problems and suicidal ideation. However, it is important to recognize that children have unique signs to be aware of when recognizing and diagnosing depression.

However, it is important to recognize that children have unique signs to be aware of when recognizing and diagnosing depression. Depression in children may manifest itself in different ways and in different age groups. The younger a child is, the more difficult it is for them to understand their feelings, to identify them, and thus, to put a label to them. The younger a child is, the harder it is for them to be able to translate their feelings into thoughts and this makes it very difficult to express their feelings into words. In children ages 3 through 5, the most common emotional signs of depression are sadness, a detached or far away look, displays of anger and aggression, a timid or fearful appearance, shyness, moodiness and irritability. Young children who are depressed may have physical symptoms that are unexplainable such as headaches, stomach aches, cramps, nausea, failure to thrive, wetting the bed, asthma, tiredness, difficulties getting to sleep, and nightmares. They may display aggressive behaviours, such as hitting or fighting, or may suddenly start lying or stealing.

Table 19.1: Age-wise Distribution of Major Behavioural Symptoms

Age (Yrs.)	Anxiety	Depressive Cognitions	Mood	Recurrent Thoughts of Death
Up to 3	Separation Anxiety	-	Gaze Aversion	-
3-5	School Phobias	Low Self-esteem	Labile Mood	-
6-8	Phobias	Low Self-esteem	Prolonged Unhappiness	Death Wish
9-12	Phobias	Guilt	Sad Expression	Suicidal Ideas
13-18	Anxiety	Worthlessness	Sadness of Mood	Suicide Attempts

Depressed children may suddenly become disinterested in activities or things that they once enjoyed. They may show unusual preoccupation with morbid things, such as death or dying. They may engage in risk taking behaviours, and may be prone to accidents and injuries. The most common emotional signs of depression are irritability, moodiness, a cynical and angry attitude, continual sad mood, feelings of apathy, a gloomy or dark look, feeling of loneliness, displays of anger and hostility, low threshold for frustration, and an angry or hostile appearance. Adolescents are more likely to verbalize their negative beliefs about themselves than are younger children. The depressed adolescents may express the perception that they are not liked or accepted by their peers and they are unloved by their family. They may perceive that they are unable to fit in with their peers. Adolescents who are depressed may verbalize of physical complaints, especially headaches. They may complain of insomnia, difficulties in getting to sleep, or remaining asleep. Consequently they may have feelings of tiredness or exhaustion, and of an inability to feel rested even after a full night's sleep.

Assessment

There are a number of assessment tools available to assist in both diagnosing and estimating the severity and duration of different symptoms. The three primary measures are interviews, rating scales, and behavioural observations. However, there are several alternative methods such as Rorschach test, Thematic Apperception test, and Draw-a-Man test, to assess childhood depression.

Parents are also a good source of information because they can usually describe the child's behaviour across a variety of settings and situations. Parent interviews begin by gathering general information regarding social, medical, and academic history (Watson and Robinson, 1998). Questions are then asked about when the depressive behaviour was first noticed and in which situation the behaviour occurs. The interview consists of a set of questions about the child's activity level, appetite, and sleep patterns.

Many times depressive symptoms are not easily observed so self-report is very important method for the assessment. Self-report may be an interview session or other techniques. The child is involved in an unstructured interview followed by a structured portion where the child is asked about the duration and severity of the behaviour. This measurement is given separately to the parent and then the child. The discrepancies are then resolved to reach a consensus on the specific symptoms the subject might have according to the Diagnostic and Statistical Manual of Mental Disorders.

The most widely used self-report measure is the Children's Depression Inventory (Kovacs and Beck, 1977), which consists of items addressing cognitive, affective, and behavioural signs of depression. The Self-Rating Scale (Birleson, 1981) has also been used as self-report measures to determine the severity of a child's depressive disorders.

Rating scales can also be used as an assessment tool to gain information about the severity and duration of a child or adolescent's depressive symptoms. These assessment procedures can be used by both adults and peers in helping to identify a child's depressive symptoms. Rating scales by adults refer primarily to parents and teachers who are asked to evaluate the child's depression. Some of the measures included in the rating scales for adults are the Personality Inventory for Children, Children's Depression Inventory, and the Children's Depression Rating Scale.

Many symptoms of depression refer to observable behaviour such as diminished motor activity, slowed speech, and sad facial expressions. For this reason it is important to conduct direct observation measurement to assess the severity of depressive symptoms. Direct observation allows one to determine whether the parent and child's reports of the problem were accurate. In addition to observations in the natural setting of the subject, clinical observations and parent interaction observation are also used.

There have been several studies that have used this method of direct observation in order to obtain data on depressed children and adolescents. In one study nonverbal behaviours were assessed during an interview session in which eye contact, bodily movement, gestures, and frowning were assessed (Kazdin, Sherick, Esveldt-Dawson, and Rancurello, 1985). Direct observation was also used with inpatient children, ages 8-13 years of age. In this particular study researchers focused on behaviours that occurred during free-time periods over the course of the week. The behaviours observed were put into three categories: social activity, solitary behaviour, affect-related expression (Kazdin, Esveldt-Dawson, Sherick, and Colbus, 1985).

Management of Childhood Depression

Management of childhood depression is the most important issue. In the age of such cut throat competition it is very difficult to control all those factors which are contributing in the genesis of depression. Sometimes a single factor leads to depression when the parents are focusing on another. Certain factors are to be considered in deciding the management of childhood depression, e.g., the age of patient, developmental stage, contextual issues (family conflict, academic problems), number of prior episodes, sub types of depression (psychotic, melancholic, atypical) (Malhotra and Das, 2007). It is of great importance that parents to learn the prevention of depression at the childhood than to treating it at the adulthood. A large number of treatment strategies have been developed for the treatment of depression. There are various treatment options such as counselling, psychotherapy, supportive counselling etc. Play therapy is sometimes appropriate with younger children.

Drug Therapy: Several medications are used with adult populations. Major types include Monoamine Oxidase Inhibitors, Tricyclics and SSRIs (e.g. Prozac, Paxil, Zoloft, Serazone, Luvox), but other classes have emerged as well. These drugs are not without side effects. These drugs have been shown to be 50-70 percent more effective with adults than placebos and no other treatment. Very little is known about the safe use of antidepressants with children. A recent double-blind study found that fluoxetine reduced symptoms more than a placebo, but complete remission of symptoms was rare (Emslie et al., 1997). Sommers-Flannagan and Sommers Flannagan (1996) did an extensive evaluation of antidepressant medication treatment for children and adolescents and it was concluded that currently available antidepressant medications do not show improvement greater than a placebo. Antidepressant medications with children may have some undesirable side effects like headache, nervousness, nausea, insomnia and even seizures.

Cognitive Behavioural Therapy: Cognitive behavioural therapy focuses on the assumption that thoughts affect feelings and behaviours of individuals. This therapy is helpful in modifying children's negative thoughts into positive thoughts. Such modification in thoughts can be accomplished through story telling, artwork, puppet play or doll house play. The goals of this therapy are to challenge false negative ideas and faulty thinking that the child has about the present and future. This therapy fosters a more positive view of the self and the future, to help the child begin to process information through a more positive lens. Controlled studies of psychological treatment with depressed children have proved the effectiveness of cognitive behaviour therapy in reducing depressive symptoms.

Cognitive restructuring that is a form of cognitive therapy involves how to reinterpret ambiguous situations in less pessimistic, depressing or threatening ways (Reinecke et al., 1995). Cognitive restructuring can be done through two different ways:

Challenge Test Reward (CTR): It is the training in which the youngsters learn the skills required to challenge negative thoughts by asking themselves what the other possible interpretations of the situation are; to test less threatening outcomes: They reward themselves for testing the less negative interpretation of the situations. CTR is derived from Beck's cognitive therapy for depression and anxiety (Beck, 1976; Beck, Emery and Greenberg, 1985).

Reattribution Training: Attribution is a second strategy for reducing the impact of negative thoughts. In it the child is encouraged to consider possible alternate causes for events. It is based on the reformulated model of learned helplessness (Abramson, Seligman and Teasdale, 1978).

Play Therapy: A common therapeutic technique used with children that suffer with depression is play therapy. Soloman (1948) introduced structured play techniques. In younger children depression can be shown in a number of ways and is not typically seen with the child looking sad. Traditional "talk" therapy is not helpful in dealing with children due to their developmental level. Play therapy is a very effective means of getting a depressed child to express themselves through their play. Play therapy focuses on encouraging children to verbalize their feelings and to learn how to express those feelings to their family and others who can help them. Play is also a very effective way to assess children's issues. Through the expressive play therapist tries to reveal what is troubling the child and making him/her sad. Therapist utilizes puppets, games, colours, sand, clay or paints, dolls, or other toys in order to get child to express themselves.

Social Skills Training: Good social skills are critical to successful functioning in life. These skills enable child to know what to say, how to make good choices, and how to behave in diverse situations. The extent to which children and adolescents possess good social skills can influence their academic performance, behaviour, social and family relationships, and involvement in extracurricular activities. Social skills are also linked to the quality of the school environment and school safety. Social skills training consists of teaching children how to engage in several concrete behaviours with others such as initiating conversations, responding to others, refusing requests, making requests, etc. Children are provided with instructions, modelling by an individual or peer group, opportunities for role playing and feedback. The object of this approach is to provide the child with an ability to obtain reinforcement from others. Effective social skills programs are comprised of two essential elements: a teaching process that uses a behavioural/social learning approach and a universal language or set of steps that facilitates the learning of new behaviour. Interventions can be implemented at a school-wide, specific setting, classroom, or individual level, but at all levels the emphasis is on teaching the desired skill and not on punishing negative behaviours.

Social skills training can be imparted through three different ways: (1) Facilitate learning through normal activities: Teachers and parents must take advantage of incidental learning in which naturally occurring behaviours or events are used to teach and reinforce appropriate social behaviour. (2) Address environmental factors: In this approach the environmental factors which are affecting child' behaviour and abilities and skills are evaluated. If needed then such factors are controlled which lead child towards problematic behaviour. (3) Address individual factors: Some children need more intensive and personalized training because of individual factors such as a disability. These interventions might be aimed at children experiencing a specific difficulty or those who have previously been identified as at risk for behaviour problems. Studies have proved the effectiveness of a focus on enhancing overt social behaviours by such techniques as assertion and social skills training (Lewinsohn and Gotlib, 1995).

Exercise: Depression is particularly responsive to exercise. Engagement in physical activities, work and exercise not only release tension from body but also enhance the blood circulation in the brain, stimulate the autonomic nervous system, and trigger the release of various hormones. An individual is never too old or too young to exercise. The important is to choose something appropriate to own abilities. Effects of aerobic exercise program were studied in a research by Holmes (1984). In this study he randomly assigned one third subjects into a group of mildly depressed female college students who received an aerobic exercise program, another third to a program of relaxation therapies, and the final third to a no-treatment condition (the control group). Ten weeks later, the subjects in the exercise group reported the largest decrease in depression. Thus, aerobic exercise can also be effective adjunct to counselling or other forms of psychotherapy in decreasing anxiety, improving self-esteem, and reducing depression (Hinkle, 1992). The types of exercise seem in part to determine its benefits. As far as particularly children are concerned their participation in games and sports should be motivated by parents as well as by teachers. Now a days so many types of video games are available for children and children are used to spend long hours in playing them even without break. Parents have to be aware about the harmful results of such games.

Supportive Therapy: As the name suggests in this therapy, therapist tries to give support to the child and make him/her assure that he/she is not alone to face the problems. A feeling of security is provided to him/her. This therapy focuses on building trusting relationships with child. It is also assured to the child that conversation would be confidential and he/she has his/her privacy. Child also needs to feel respected, cared for, and listened to. In this therapy efforts are made to develop a therapeutic relationship between child and therapist and on accurately assessing what the child is communicating about their experience. Supportive therapy with the child can be very productive when it is accompanied by education about the illness (Weller and Weller, 1999).

Family Therapy: In this therapy other family members are also included in the treatment process. This therapy focuses on pattern of interaction among family members, their relationships, attitude towards child who is facing problems etc. This therapy emphasizes that environmental factors play a crucial role in the development of depression (Cole and Turner, 1993). This approach points out the importance of teaching the young persons how to cope up with the interpersonal stress via more effective overt behaviour- for example, interacting more effectively with others and being appropriately assertive with overbearing peers. Kaslow and Thompson (1998) recognized the importance of family involvement in dealing with depression.

Interpersonal Therapy: Some modifications in interpersonal therapy are found to be required and effective on children such as focus on peer pressures, separation from parents and authority issues (Moreau et al., 1992: Mufson et al., 1994).

Role of Parents

Parents have to play a very crucial role in the prevention of depression in child because a child is often attached to their parents than others. If parents observe day to day behaviour of child then they may prevent depression at early stage before it becomes fatal. For parents, there are some tips which may be helpful in developing their child mentally healthy and happy:

- Make sure that child takes any prescribed medicines and encourage healthy eating too, as this may help improve mood and outlook.
- Make sure that child stays active. Physical activity has been shown to help alleviate the symptoms of depression. Incorporate physical activities, such as bike rides or walks, into your family's routine.
- Remind the child that they are there, that they love and care about him/her and want to hear what he/she has to say, even if it isn't pleasant. Although these things may be difficult for the child to believe yet it is important for parents to say them.
- Accept the situation and never tell the child to "snap out of it." Keep in mind that it\ isn't laziness causing the child's inability to get out of bed, complete chores, or do homework. He or she simply doesn't have the desire or the energy. However, parents can still praise and reward their child for making extra effort.
- Watch for warning signs, and make sure the prescribed treatment is followed, whether it is medication, therapy, or both. Many parents dismiss their concerns, thinking they will go away, or avoid acting because they may feel guilty or prefer to solve family problems privately.

Childhood depression is an important issue to be considered. Depression is onc of the leading causes of ,poor school performance, learning problems, dropping out of school, delinquency, drug and alcohol abuse, phobias, panic disorder, eating disorders, excessive risk taking behaviour, violence and suicide (Iannelli, 2009). Children of today will be saviour of tomorrow so it is important for the saviours to be healthy physically as well as mentally. Successful parenting does not mean to achieve high even at the cost of child's happiness. Parents should have to understand that a child perceives the world from their eyes and feels what they make his/her feel so they have understand him/her and would have to feel what the child is feeling. It is the duty of teachers also that child may learn from them how to deal with the ups and downs of life. If a child is found depressed then it does not mean that he/she is abnormal or unable to spend a normal life.

References

Abramson, L., Seligman, M., and Teasdale, J.C. (1978). Learned helplessness in humans: Critique and reformation. *Journal of Abnormal Psychology, 87*, 49-74.

Abramson, L.Y., Metalasky, G.I., and Allay, C.B. (1989). Hopelessness depression: A theory-based subtype of depression. *Psychological Review, 96*, 358-372.

American Psychiatric Association. (1980). *Diagnostic and statistical manual of mental disorders* (3rd ed.). Washington, DC: Author.

American Psychiatric Association. (1994). *Diagnostic and statistical manual of mental disorders* (4th ed.). Washington, DC: Author.

Bahls, S.C. (2002). Epidemiology of depressive symptoms in adolescents of a public school in Curitiba, Brazil. *Revista Brasileira de Psiquiatria, 24*(2), 63-67.

Beck, A.T., Emery, G., and Greenberg, R. (1985). *Anxiety disorders and phobias.* New York: Basic Books.

Beck, A.T. (1976). *Cognitive therapy and the emotional disorders.* New York: International Universities Press.

Birleson, P. (1981). The validity of depressive disorder in childhood and the development of a self-rating scale: A research project. *Journal of Child Psychology and Psychiatry, 22,* 73-88.

Brody, G. H., and Forehand, R. (1986). Maternal perceptions of child maladjustment as a function of the combined influence of child behaviour and maternal depression. *Journal of Consulting and Clinical Psychology, 54,* 237-240.

Brown, G. W., Harris, T.O., and Peto, J. (1973). Life events and psychiatric disorders. Part II: Nature of causal link. *Psychological Medicine, 3,* 159-176.

Campbell, M., and Cueva, J.E. (1995). Psychopharmacology in child and adolescent psychiatry: A review of the past seven years. Part I. *Journal of American Academy of Child and Adolescent Psychiatry, 34* (9), 1124-1132.

Chiariello, M.A., and Orvaschel, H. (1995). Patterns of parent-child communication: Relationship to depression. *Clinical Psychology Review, 15,* 395-407.

Cole, D., and Turner, J., Jr. (1993). Models of cognitive meditation and moderation in child depression. *Journal of Abnormal Psychology, 102,* 271-281.

Coleman, M. C., (1986). *Behaviour disorders: Theory and practice* (2nd ed.). Needham Heights: Prentice Hall.

Cytryn, L., and Mcknew, D. (1972). Proposed classification of childhood depression. *American Journal of Psychiatry, 129,* 149-155.

Emslie, G.J., Rush, J., Weinberg, W.A., Kowatch, R.A., Hughes, C.W., et al. (1997). A double-blind randomized placebo-controlled trial of fluxetine in children and adolescents with depression. *Archives of General Psychiatry, 54,* 1031-1037.

Frommer, E.A. (1986). Depressive illness in childhood. *British Journal of Psychiatry, 2,* 117-136.

Garrison, C.Z., Jackson, K.L., McKeown, R.E., and Waller, J.L., and Addy, C.L. (1990). Incidence of major depressive disorder and dysthymia in young adolescents. *Journal of American Academy of Child and Adolescent Psychiatry, 36(4),* 458-465.

Hart, Daniel, Atkins, Robert, Matsuba, M. Kyle. (2008). The association of neighbourhood poverty with personality change in childhood. *Journal of Personality and Social Psychology, 94* (6), 1048-1061.

Hinkle, J.S. (1992). Aerobic running behaviour and psychotherapeutic implications for sports, counselling and psychology. *Journal of Sport Behaviour, 15,* 263-277.

Holmes, D.S. (1984). Meditation and somatic arousal reduction: A review of the experimental evidence. *American Psychologist, 8,* 10-39.

Iannelli, Vincent. (2009). *Treatment of resistant depression in adolescents.* Retrieved from http://pediatrics.about.com/cs/mentalhealth/a/depression_stdy.htm.

Kaslow, N.J., and Thompson, M.P. (1998). Applying the criteria for empirically supported treatment to studies of psychosocial interventions for child and adolescent depression. *Journal of Clinical Psychology, 27,* 146-155.

Kazdin A.E., and Marciano, P.L. (1998). Childhood and adolescent depression. In: E. Mash, and

R. Barkley, (Eds). *Treatment of childhood disorders*. New York: The Guilford Press.

Kazdin, A.E., Esveldt-Dawson, K., Sherick, R.B., and Colbus, D. (1989). Assessment of overt behaviour and childhood depression among psychiatrically disturbed children. *Journal of Consulting and Clinical Psychology, 53*, 201-210.

Kazdin, A.E., Sherick, R.B., Esveldt-Dawson, K., and Rancurello, M. D. (1985). Nonverbal behaviour and childhood depression. *Journal of the American Academy of Child Psychiatry, 24,* 303-309.

Kovacs, M., and Beck, A.T. (1977). An empirical-clinical approach toward a definition of childhood depression. In J. G. Schulterbrandt and A. Raskin (Eds.), *Depression in childhood: Diagnosis, treatment, and conceptual models*. New York: Raven.

Laurett, J., and Stark, K. (1993). Testing the cognitive content-specificity hypothesis with anxious and depressed youngsters, *Journal of Abnormal Psychology, 102*(2), 226-237.

Lewinsohn, P.M., Rohde, P., Seeley, J.R., Klein, D.N., and Gotlib, I.H. (2000). Natural course of adolescent major depressive disorder in a community sample: Predictors of recurrence in young adults. *American Journal of Psychiatry, 157 (10)*, 1584-1591.

Lewinsohn, P.M. (1974). Clinical and theoretical aspects of depression. In K. S. Calhoun, H. E. Adams, and H.M. Mitchell (Eds.), *Innovative treatment methods of psychopathology.* New York: Wiley.

Lewinsohn, P.M. and Gotlib, I.H. (1995). Behavioural and cognitive treatment of depression. In E.E. Becker and W.R. Leber (Eds.), *Handbook of Depression.* New York: Guilford Press.

Malhotra, Savita and Das, Partha Pratim. (2007). Understanding childhood depression. *Indian Journal of Medical Research. 125*, 115-128.

Moreau, D., Mufson, L., Weissman, M.M., and Klerman, G.L. (1992). Interpersonal psychotherapy for adolescent depression: Description of modification and preliminary application. *Journal of the Academy of Child and Adolescent Psychology, 30*, 642-651.

Mufson L., Moreau, D., Weissman, M.M., et al. (1994). Modification of interpersonal psychotherapy with depressed adolescents (ITP-A): Phase I and Phase II studies, *Journal of American Academy of Child and Adolescents Psychiatry, 33,* 695-705.

Reinecke, M., Dattilio, F., and Freeman, A. (1995). *Cognitive therapy with children and adolescents*. New York: Guilford Press.

Ryan, N.D., Puig-Antich., J., Ambrosini, P., Rabinovich, H., Robinson, D., Nelson, B., Iyengar, S., and Twomey, J. (1987). The clinical picture of major depression in children and adolescents. *Archives of General Psychiatry*, *44*, 854-861.

Seligman, M.E., and Maier, S.F. (1967). Failure to escape traumatic shock. *Journal of Experimental Psychology*, *74,* 1–9.

Seligman, M. (1990). *Learned optimism: How to change your mind and your life*, New York: Pocket Books.

Soloman, J.C. (1948). Play techniques. *American Journal of Orthopsychiatry*, *18,* 402-413.

Sommers-Flannagan, J., and Sommers-Flannagan, R. (1996). Efficacy of antidepressant meditation with depressed youth: What psychologists should know. *Professional Psychiatrists, 27* (2), 145-153.

Spitz, R.A., and Wolf, K.M. (1946). Anaclitic depression. *Psychoanalytic Study of the Child, 2,* 313-347.

Thapar, A., and McGuffin, P. (1996). The genetic etiology of childhood depressive symptoms: A developmental perspective. *Developmental Psychopathology*, *8* (4), 751-760.

Timimi, S. (2004). Rethinking childhood depression. *Journal of Behaviour Modification*, *29*,

1394-1396.

Watkins, Carol E. (2007). Depression in children and adolescents. Retrieved from http://www.ncpamd.com/cadepress.htm.

Watson, T.S., and Robinson, S. L., (1998). A behaviour analytic approach for treating depression. In T.S. Watson, and F. M. Gresham (Eds.), *Handbook of child behaviour therapy*. New York: Plenum Press.

Weissman, M., Fendrich, M., Warner, V., and Wickramaratne, P. (1992). Incidence of psychiatric disorder in off-spring at high and low risk for depression. *Journal of American Academy of Child and Adolescent Psychiatry, 31,* 640-648.

Weller, E.B. and Weller, R.A. (1999). Mood disorders in prepubertal children. In Wiener, J.M. (Eds.), *Text Book of Child and Adolescent Psychiatry* (II Edition), Chennai: All India Publishers.

20

Preventing Inhalant Abuse among Children

Surila Agarwala and Satya Satvir Singh

Introduction

Health is a resource for everyday life, not the objective of living. Health is a positive concept emphasizing social and personal resources, as well as physical capacities. Health psychology is concerned with the application of psychological knowledge and techniques to health, illness and health care. Its primary objective is to understand and to help improve the well-being of individuals and communities. WHO (1948) defined health as "a state of complete physical, mental, and social well-being and not merely the absence of disease or infirmity." Health is a positive multi-dimensional state that involves three domains: physical health, psychological health and social health. Abuse of any substance has negative effects on physical, psychological and social health of substance abuser.

Humans have used substances for thousands of years, to cure diseases, alleviate pain, and relieve mental suffering. Despite the often-devastating consequences of taking such substances into the body, their initial effects are usually pleasing, a factor that is perhaps at the root of substance abuse.

Inhalant Abuse is a lesser-known form of substance abuse, but is no less dangerous than other forms. The inhalants are a class of substances that include a broad range of chemicals found in hundreds of different products, many of which are readily available to the general population. These chemicals include volatile solvents (liquids that vaporize at room temperature) and aerosols (sprays that contain solvents and propellants). Examples include glue, gasoline, paint thinner, hair spray, lighter fluid, spray paint, nail polish remover, correction fluid, rubber cement, felt-tip marker fluids, vegetable sprays, and certain cleaners. The inhalants share a common route of administration— that is, they are all drawn into the body by breathing. They are usually taken either by breathing in the vapours directly from a container (known as "sniffing"); by inhaling fumes from substances placed in a bag (known as "bagging"); or by inhaling the substance from a cloth soaked in it (known as "huffing"). Inhalants take effect very quickly because they get into the bloodstream rapidly via the lungs. The "high" from inhalants is usually brief, so that abusers often take inhalants repeatedly over several hours. This pattern of abuse can be dangerous, leading to unconsciousness or even death.

The latest revision of the Diagnostic and Statistical Manual of Mental Disorders published in 2000 (also known as DSM-IVTR), lists inhalant dependence and inhalant abuse as substance abuse disorders. The DSM-IV-TR specifies that one or more of the following symptoms must occur at any time during a 12-month period (and cause significant impairment or distress) in order to meet diagnostic criteria for inhalant abuse:

- Interference with role fulfilment. The person's use of inhalants frequently interferes with his or her ability to fulfil obligations at work, home, or school. People may find they are unable to do chores or pay attention in school because they are under the influence of inhalants.
- Danger to self. The person repeatedly uses inhalants in situations in which their influence may be physically hazardous (while driving a car, for example).
- Legal problems. The person has recurrent legal problems related to using inhalants (such as arrests for assaults while under the influence of inhalants).
- Social problems. The person continues to use inhalants despite repeated interpersonal or relationship problems caused by or made worse by the use of inhalants. For example, the affected person may get into arguments related to inhalant use.

Inhalant abuse has been showing a rising trend all over the world. Inhalants are one of the few substances more commonly abused by younger children rather than older ones. It has been estimated that 10 percent–20 percent of youths aged 10–17 have tried inhalants (Fendrich et al., 1997). About 6 percent of the United States population admits to having tried inhalants prior to fourth grade (American Academy of Paediatrics, Committee on Substance Abuse and Committee on Native American Child Health, 1996). The peak time for inhalant abuse appears to be between the seventh and ninth grades (Balster, 1998; Bennett, 2000; Joseph, 2005). Inhalants are sometimes referred to as "gateway" substances, which means that they are one of the first substances that people try before moving on to such other substances as alcohol, marijuana, and cocaine. Males generally abuse inhalants more frequently than females. However, a National Household Survey on Drug Abuse has shown no gender differences in rates of inhalant use in youths between the ages of 12 and 17. Children younger than 12 and adults who use inhalants, however, are more likely to be male.

The most common abusers of inhalants are young children. Factors that are associated with inhalant abuse include curiosity; fatigue and boredom; poverty; a history of childhood abuse; poor grades; and dropping out of school (Tenenbein et al., 1999; Brouette and Anton, 2001). The latter two factors may simply be a result of inhalant abuse, however, rather than its cause. The abuse of inhalants is highly likely to be influenced by peers. Inhalants are often abused by children because inhalants are readily available, inexpensive and easy to access (Basu et al., 2004).

Inhalant abuse is one of the most burning problems of the world. Most inhalants produce a rapid high that resembles alcohol intoxication with initial excitement, then drowsiness, disinhibition, lightheadedness and agitation. Short term effects include headache muscle weakness, abdominal pain, severe mood swings and violent behaviour, slurred speech, numbness and tingling of hands and feet, nausea, hearing loss, limb spasms, fatigue, and lack of coordination (Meadows and Verghese, 1996; Fendrich et al., 1997; Beauvais, 2002). Long term effects include central nervous system or brain damage. Serious effects include damage to the liver, heart, kidneys, blood oxygen level depletion, unconsciousness and death (Maruff et al., 1998; Williams, 2004).

Inhalant abuse leads to many psychological problems in children like- conduct disorders, anxiety disorders, learning disorders, bipolar tendencies and low level of self-esteem (Hanna et al., 2000).

Self-esteem is the disposition to experience oneself as being competent to cope with the basic challenges of life and of being worthy of happiness. Self-esteem is how we feel about ourselves, and our behaviour reflects those feelings. The term Self-esteem refers to the evaluation a person makes and customarily maintains with regard to him or herself. Self-esteem is a ratio or relationship between our achievements and our aspirations (James, 1890). Self-esteem is an evaluative measure of one's self image (Coopersmith, 1967). Self-esteem includes a person's subjective appraisal of himself or herself as intrinsically positive or negative to some degree (Sedikides and Gregg, 2003).

Healthy self-esteem is a child's armour against the challenges of the world. A person with high self-esteem is fundamentally satisfied with the type of person he is, yet he may acknowledge his faults while hoping to overcome them (Rosenberg and Owens, 2001). Greater levels of self-esteem can affect many aspects of children's lives, such as improving school performance and efforts toward achieving goals (Guest and Biasini, 2001). People with high self-esteem report more positive attitudes, feelings and life satisfaction and less anxiety, hopelessness and depressive symptoms (Crocker, 2002).

In contrast low level of self-esteem has been linked to behavioural problems and poor school performance (Raj and Agarwala, 2003). Lower self-esteem in childhood can lead to the development of a variety of emotional disturbances and an increased risk of suicide (Thompson, 2005). Low self-esteem can actually trigger higher levels of stress, anxiety, sleeplessness and many other health-depriving symptoms (Vonk et al., 2006).

It is hard to fight inhalant abuse among children, but it can be done. Young children are more intelligent than we often give them credit for being. If we talk with them about specific inhalants and their negative effects, it will go a long way towards winning the battle against child inhalant abuse.

Objectives

The study was undertaken with the objectives of comparing the self-esteem among inhalant abusers and non-abusers and to study the effectiveness of behaviour intervention in reducing inhalant abuse and in enhancing self-esteem of children.

Hypotheses

- Inhalant abusers have lower self-esteem than non-abusers.
- Behaviour intervention is effective in reducing inhalant abuse.
- Behaviour intervention is effective in enhancing self-esteem.

Method

The study was conducted in two parts. In part 'A', effect of inhalant abuse upon self-esteem was studied. To study the effect of inhalant abuse upon self-esteem, self-esteem of inhalant abusers and non-abusers was compared. In part 'B', of the study effectiveness of behaviour intervention in reducing inhalant abuse and in enhancing self-esteem of children was studied.

Sample

In part 'A' of the study sample consisted of two groups. Group I comprised 10 inhalant abusers (all males) and Group II comprised 10 non-abusers. The age range of these subjects was 10-15 years. All the subjects were taken from different schools of Agra city. The inhalant abusers comprised those subjects, who had been abusing inhalants at least for last one year. The non-abusers consisted of subjects who did not abuse inhalants or any other substance. The information regarding the identification of inhalant abusers was partly gathered from the students in the school, during a preliminary investigation. Once few students were identified and they agreed to participate in the study. They helped in the identification of other such cases in the school. In part 'B' of the study 10 inhalant abusers from part 'A' of the study was included in the sample.

Design

In part 'A' of the study matched group design (matching by pairs) was used. Group I and group II was matched in terms of age, sex, and education. In part 'B' of the study pre and post design was used.

Measure

Self-esteem Inventory (SEI) developed by Coopersmith (1975) was used to measure self-esteem of inhalant abusers and non-abusers. Its school form was used in the present research. Retest reliability for the SEI was reported by Coopersmith to be 0.88 and by Bedeian et al. (1977) as 0.80 for males and 0.82 for females. Kokens (1974) reported and confirmed the SEI's construct validity. In the present study Hindi translation of school form of the measure (done by the researcher) was used. The English and Hindi versions showed a correlation of 0.96 ($n = 100$).

Procedure

In part 'A' of the study SEI was administered on the sample of 20 subjects (10 inhalant abusers and 10 non-abusers), out of which 10 subjects (inhalant abusers) were selected for behaviour intervention in part 'B' of the study. Behaviour intervention for 2 months was given to subjects included in the sample for the purpose of reducing their inhalant abuse and for enhancing their self-esteem. Baseline inhalant abuse behaviour of subjects was measured. For this purpose, a self-monitoring chart was given to each subject and they were asked to keep this chart with them and put a tally in the appropriate column when they abuse inhalants or feel the urge for abusing inhalants. This chart was monitored by the researcher.

Self-Monitoring Chart

Name				
Day	Date	No. of time inhalants abused	Urge for inhalant abuse	Signature of the researcher

Frequency of inhalant abuse was obtained from self-monitoring chart and also from peer group reports. The average frequency of inhalant abuse of one week was taken as a baseline measure. Self-monitoring was continued throughout intervention period as was done during baseline period. After establishing the baseline, intervention was started. Behaviour intervention for 2 months was given to subjects included in the sample. Behaviour intervention included Behaviour Self-control Training (BSCT). In BSCT following strategies were included.

Environmental Strategy

In environmental strategy times, places or situations where subjects experience inhalant abuse behaviour, was changed. The peer group or group of senior students with whom subjects socialize, was also changed. Situations or settings where inhalant abuse behaviour is more likely to occur, was monitored. The situations or settings, in which subjects usually took inhalants, were-while coming to school, while coming back from school to home and in free periods in school. To monitor these situations researcher took the help of parents and teachers. Teachers were requested to engage such children in sports, cultural and other competitive and creative activities during free periods in school. It was also suggested that they should try not to put them in the group of those students with whom they abuse inhalants. It was suggested to parents to observe/escort their children when they are going to school and coming home from school. Thus, efforts were made to keep subjects away from the situations in which thcy abused inhalants.

Behavioural Strategy

In behavioural strategy the antecedents and consequences of behaviour was changed. Social or familial support for subjects was increased. It was suggested to family members to give extra attention and care to their child, encourage the child for creative and constructive activities, to keep the friendly atmosphere of the family so that child may express his problems, tensions and anxieties freely. Family members should listen their problems carefully and try to solve their problems.

Reinforcers for engaging in constructive/creative activities and negative reinforcers for engaging in inhalant abuse behaviours were developed. When the child does the creative/constructive activities positive reinforcement was given and for inhalant abuse behaviour, negative reinforcement was given. The use of punishment is unethical so the positive approach that is negative reinforcement was given. Prepotent behaviour of the subjects was used for negative reinforcement.

Cognitive Strategy

In cognitive strategy cognitive restructuring was included. Subject's thoughts or beliefs about inhalant abuse were changed. The researcher discussed the negative effects of inhalant abuse with subjects e.g. how inhalant abuse negatively affects the academic achievement, family life and social life of an individual. If they use that time in creative/constructive activities, and to develop their talent they may achieve success in life and they may develop physical and mental health.

During two months intervention period BSCT was given in daily sessions for one week, in sessions on alternate days for another week, and then twice a week. Subjects were assured that researcher was available to help them. If they face any problem in reducing inhalant abuse, they may ask for help from the researcher.

For the enhancement of self-esteem a behaviour intervention program was designed by the researcher. Initial measures of self-esteem of subjects served as baseline. Behaviour intervention for 2 months was given to subjects for the purpose of enhancing their self-esteem. It includes the following steps.

Initially Parents/guardians of each subject were told that they should give extra attention and care to their child, encourage the child by helping and praising and behave in a friendly manner with the child, so that the child can freely express himself. Other family members of each subject were also told that they should give extra attention and care to their child, and encourage the child.

All the teachers teaching the subjects were given a list of these subjects. Teachers were requested to give special/extra attention to those subjects in the class, encourage them, give them maximum opportunities for participation in the class room activities and give them proper and immediate feedback for their performance/activities.

The researcher also met each subject and talked to the subject about his performances and achievement, praised and encouraged the subject for still better results.

The above intervention was continued for two months. After behaviour intervention post measure of inhalant abuse behaviour and self-esteem was done. Frequency of inhalant abuse was obtained from self-monitoring chart and peer group reports and self-esteem of subjects was measured with the help of SEI. The measurement conditions maintained during pre-measure were maintained during post measure also.

Analysis of Data and Results

In part 'A' of the study, the self-esteem of inhalant abusers and non-abusers was compared. To compare the self-esteem of inhalant abusers and non-abusers, Wilcoxon Mann-Whitney *'U'* test was used. Results are presented in result table 20.1.

Table 20.1: '*U*' Value for the Self-esteem of Inhalant Abusers and Non-abusers at 0.01 Level of Significance

Groups	N	'*U*'	Level of Significance	Result
Inhalant abusers	10	3	0.01	**Significant**
Non-abusers	10			

It can be observed from Result Table 20.1 that obtained value of '*U*' has been found significant at 0.01 level of significance, which proves one of the underlying hypothesis that inhalant abusers have lower level of self-esteem than non-abusers.

Figure 20.1: Comparison among Self-esteem Scores of Inhalant Abusers and Non-abusers

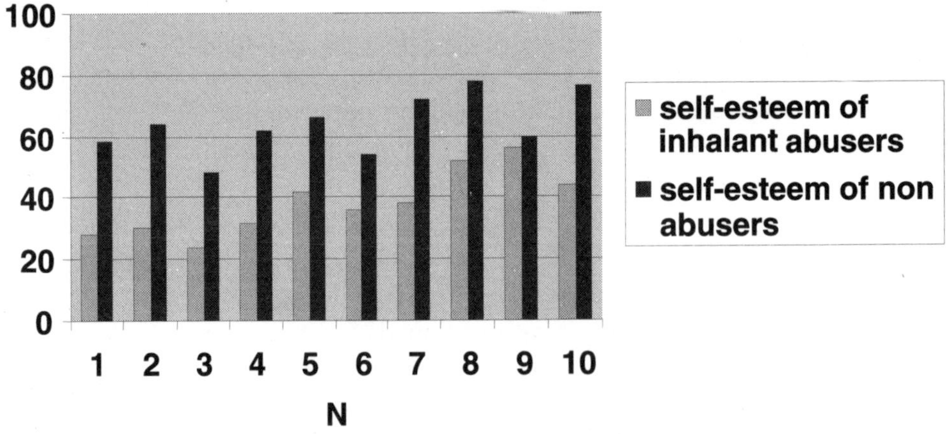

Figure 20.1 represents the difference between self-esteem of inhalant abusers and non-abusers. Graphical presentation shows that level of self-esteem among inhalant abusers is within the range of low self-esteem and medium self-esteem. Though some inhalant abusers have medium level of self-esteem, their level of self-esteem is lower than the level of self-esteem among non-abusers.

In part 'B' of the study it was hypothesized that behaviour intervention is effective in reducing inhalant abuse. Wilcoxon *T* test was applied to test the significance of difference between pre and post intervention behaviour of inhalant abuse. Results are presented in result Table 20.2.

Table 20.2: Value of '*T*' for Pre- and Post-measure of Inhalant Abuse Behaviour

Group	N	Sum of ranks with positive signs	Sum of ranks with negative signs	T
Subjects (inhalant abusers) received behaviour intervention for reducing inhalant abuse	10	0	55	0

It can be observed from Results Table 20.2 that $T = 0$. According to Appendix Table, with N = 10 subjects, T must be less than or equal to 5 (on one tail test at $\alpha = 0.01$) in order to accept the hypothesis. $T_{observed}$ (0) is less than the table value of T, and it proves that there is significant difference between the pre-intervention and post intervention behaviour of inhalant abuse. The results are shown with the help of figure also.

Figure 20.2: Showing Pre- and Post-intervetion Frequencies of Inhalant Abuse

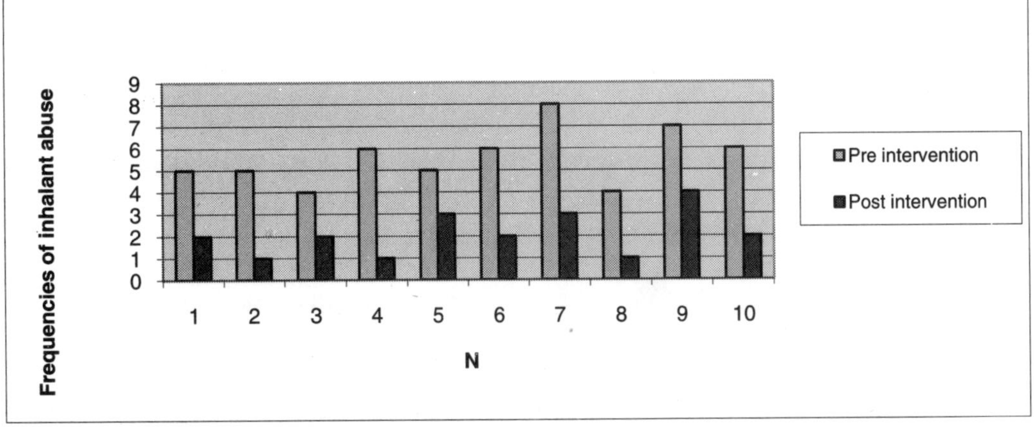

In figure 20.2 pre-intervention and post-intervention frequencies of inhalant abuse are compared to show the effect of behaviour intervention on inhalant abuse and it can be observed that as the effect of behaviour intervention, post intervention frequencies of inhalant abuse are lower than the pre intervention, in case of each subject. Behaviour intervention reduces not only inhalant abuse behaviour but it is helpful in reducing urge for abusing inhalants also. It is represented in figure 20.3 that after behaviour intervention subject's urge for abusing inhalants has also been reduced. Results are significant statistically as well as clinically. It is the representative of the fact that behaviour intervention is effective not only on one particular individual but on all those who abuse inhalants. It can be observed that effectiveness of behaviour intervention varies in relation to each subject. Effectiveness of behaviour intervention varies due to individual differences.

Figure 20.3: Showing Pre- intervention and Post-intervention Frequencies of Urge for Abusing Inhalants

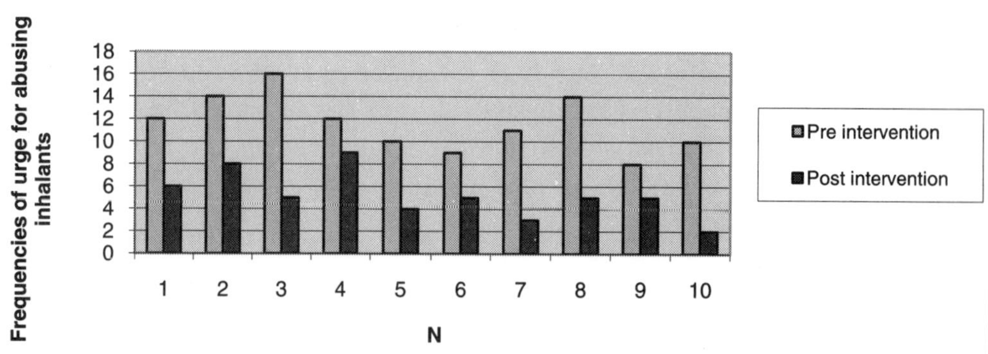

In part 'B' of the study it was also hypothesized that behaviour intervention is effective in enhancing self-esteem. Wilcoxon *T* was applied to test the significance of difference between pre and post measures of self-esteem. Results are presented in result Table 20.3.

Table 20.3: Value of '*T*' for Pre- and Post-measure of Self-esteem

Group	N	Sum of ranks with positive signs	Sum of ranks with negative signs	**T**
Subjects (inhalant abusers) received behaviour intervention for reducing inhalant abuse, and for enhancing self-esteem	10	55	0	0

Results presented in result Table 20.3 reveal that obtained *T* value is 0 and it has been mentioned above that according to appendix, with N = 10 subjects, *T* must be less than or equal to 5 (on one tail test at $\alpha = 0.01$) in order to accept the hypothesis. *T* observed (0) is less than the table value of *T*, and it proves that there is significant difference between the pre and post-test scores of self-esteem. So, we conclude that behaviour intervention is effective in enhancing self-esteem. The results are shown with the help of figure also.

Figure 20.4: Showing Pre and Post Test Scores of Self-Esteem

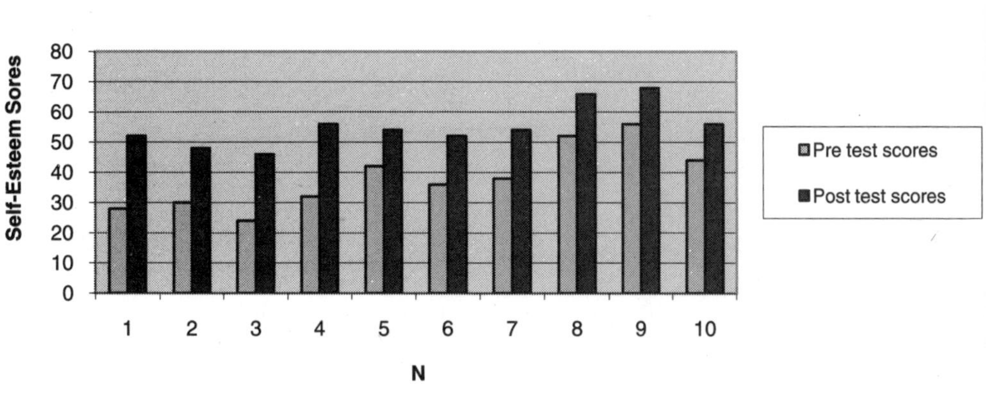

Figure 20.4 represents the pre and post test scores of self-esteem of inhalant abusers. It is shown that when behaviour intervention is given inhalant abuse reduces. Reduction in inhalant abuse leads to enhancement in level of self-esteem. Thus results are not only statistically significant but they are clinically significant also.

Discussion

Results of part 'A' of the study showed that inhalant abusers have lower self-esteem than non-abusers. Childhood is a time for trying new things. Children abuse inhalants for many reasons, including curiosity, because it feels good, to reduce stress, to feel grown up or to fit in. As the result of inhalant abuse the condition of social withdrawal, feeling of insecurity, fear of failure arises and one's self-esteem level goes down. A child who abuses substance may exhibit a low tolerance for frustration, giving up easily, blame others for his own shortcomings, feel or pretend to feel emotionally indifferent, put down his own talents and abilities, and be easily influence (Rosenberg and Owens, 2001). All these situation leads to the low level of self-esteem to a great extent.

The results of part 'B' of the study revealed that behaviour intervention is effective in reducing inhalant abuse and in enhancing self-esteem. The abuse of inhalants can lead to serious health consequences. The heavy metals in certain inhaled products can cause irreversible damage to the brain, kidneys, liver and central nervous system (Maruff et al., 1998; Bennett et al., 2000). Low self-esteem has been identified as a risk factor for aggression, delinquency, depression, poor school performance and so forth (Crocker, 2002; Thompson, 2005). Hence there is a need to reduce inhalant abuse and enhance self-esteem of children.

The important way is to boost people's self-esteem by being accepting and approving of them. If parents, family members, teachers or others create an atmosphere that is characterized by acceptance and freedom from anxiety, which tends to promote and encourage curiosity and exploratory behaviour, children would learn to honour their strength and maintain their high self-esteem. Building self-esteem in children requires collaboration between parents, family members, school personnel and the child (Elliot and Dweck, 1988; Wells et al., 2002).

Inhalant abuse is a treatable disease and inhalant abuse can be stopped. A child can overcome this with the help of parents, and the help of support groups, psychotherapy, medication, treatment programs and family counselling (Futterman and Sapadin, 2006).

Inhalant abuse harms everybody and does good to none. Government, society, families, and the individual inhalant abuser - all suffer because it is a social problem. Children of today are the future of tomorrow. Issue of inhalant abuse among children has become so troubling that if something is not done urgently about it, our future may be reduced to rubbles. If we wish for healthy and prosperous future, we should check inhalant abuse. It is necessary to treat this behaviour in beginning so that it may not be severe. There is also a need to enhance the self-esteem of children because healthy self-esteem is a child's armour against the challenges of the world. Reduction of inhalant abuse and enhancement of self-esteem among children is of great importance from individual as well as social point of view.

Conclusions

The result of part 'A' of the study leads to the following conclusion: Inhalant abusers have lower self-esteem than non-abusers and result of part 'B' of the study leads to the following conclusion: Behaviour intervention is effective in reducing substance abuse and in enhancing self-esteem.

References

American Psychiatric Association. Diagnostic and statistical manual of mental disorders. 4th ed. Washington, D.C.: American Psychiatric Association, 2000:239, 257-60.

Balster RL. (1998). Inhalant abuse in pregnancy. *Obstet Gynecol Clin North Am, 25,* 153-67.

Basu D., Jhirwal O.P., Singh J., Kumar S., and Mattoo S.K. (2004). Inhalant abuse by adolescents: A new challenge for Indian physicians. *Indian Journal of Medical Sciences 58,* 245-249.

Beauvais, F., Thurman, P., Plested, B., and Helm H. (2002). A survey of attitudes among drug user treatment providers toward the treatment of inhalant users. *Substance Use Misuse, 37,* 1391-410.

Bedeian, A.G., Geagud, R.J., and Zmud, R.W. (1977). Test-retest reliability and internal consistency of the short form of Coopersmith's Self-Esteem Inventory. *Psychological Reports, 41*, 1041-1042.

Bennett, M.E., Walters, S.T., Miller, J.H., and Woodall, W.G. (2000). Relationship of early inhalant use to substance use in college students. *Substance Abuse, 12,* 227-40.

Brouette, T., and Anton R. (2001). Clinical review of inhalants. *Addict, 10,* 79-94.

Coopersmith, S. (1967). *The Antecedents of Self-Esteem.* Palo, Alto, CA: Consulting Psychologists Press, Inc., 3-10.

Coopersmith, S. (1975). *Developing Motivation in Young Children.* Palo Alto, CA: Consulting Psychologists, Press, Inc.

Crocker, J. (2002). Self-esteem that's based on external sources has mental health consequences. *Journal of Social Issues, 58* (3), 16.

Elliot, E.S., and Dweck, C.S. (1988). Goals: An approach to motivation and achievement. *Journal of Personality and Social Psychology, 54,* 5-12.

Fendrich, M., Mackesy, M.E., Wislar, J.S., and Goldstein, P.J. (1997). Childhood abuse and the use of inhalants: differences by degree of use. *Public Health, 87,* 765-769.

Futterman, R., and Sapadin, K. (2006). Transferring psychological technology into inhalant abuse treatment: Inhalant abuse as a psychiatric illness. *Addiction Research and Theory, 14*(3), 265-274.

Guest, K.C., and Biasini, F.J. (2001). Middle childhood, poverty and adjustment: Does social support have an impact? *Psychology in the schools, 38*(6), 549-560.

Hanna, E.Z., Hsaio-Ye, Y., and Dufour, M. (2000, June). *The relationship of drinking alone and other substance use alone and in combination to health and behaviour problems among youth aged 12-16: Findings from the Third National Health and Nutrition Examination Survey (NHANES III).* Paper presented at the 23rd Annual Scientific Meeting of the Research Society on Alcoholism, Denver, CO.

Inhalant abuse. American Academy of Pediatrics, Committee on Substance Abuse and Committee on Native American Child Health. *Pediatrics 1996, 97,* 420-423.

James, W. (1890). *The Principles of Psychology, 1,* New York: Holt.

Joseph, D., and Parker, S. (2005). "Inhalants" *Drugs of Abuse.* United States Drug Enforcement Administration.

Kokenes, B. (1974). Grade level differences in factors of self-esteem. *Developmental Psychology, 10*, 954-958.

Maruff, P., Burns, C.B., Tyler, P., Currie, B.J., and Currie J. (1998). Neurological and cognitive abnormalities associated with chronic petrol sniffing. *Brain, 21,* 1903-1917.

Meadows, R., and Verghese, A. (1996). Medical complications of glue sniffing. *South Medical*

Journal, 89, 455-62.

Raj, P., and Agarwala, A. (2005). Enhancing self-esteem and controlling behavioural problems. *National Academy of Psychology, 50* (4), 348-351.

Rosenberg, M., and Owens, T.J. (2001). Low self-esteem people: A collective portrait. In T.J. Owens, S. Stryker, and N. Goodman (Eds.), *Extending self-esteem theory and research: Sociological and psychological currents* (pp. 400-436). New York: Cambridge University Press.

Sedikides, C., and Gregg, A.P. (2003). Portraits of the self. In M.A. Hogg and J. Cooper (Eds.), *Sage Handbook of Social Psychology* (110-138). London: Sage Publications.

Tenenbein, M., Young, S.J., and Longstaffe, S. (1999). Inhalant abuse and the abuse of other drugs. *Drug Alcohol Abuse, 25,* 371-376.

Thompson, A.H. (2005). The relative age effect and the development of self-esteem. *Educational Research, 46*(3), 313-320.

Vonk, R., Jolij, J., and Boog, I. (2006). *Effects of unconditional positive regard and self-reflection on self-esteem.* Manuscript in preparation.

Wells, D., Miller, M., and Clanton, R. (2002). Using a psycho-educational approach to increase the self-esteem of adolescents at high risk for dropping out. *Psychological Abstracts, 89,* 31678.

Williams, J. (2004). Responding to petrol sniffing on the Anangu Pitjantjatjara Lands : A case study. *Social Justice Report 2003.* Human Rights and Equal Opportunity Commission.

21

Emotional Work and Mental Health

A.V.S. Madnawat and V.K Bhardwas

Introduction

Emotion work i.e. emotional labour is defined as emotional regulation required while displaying organizationally-desired emotions by the employees. Emotional labour involves managing emotions so that they are consistent with organizational or occupational display rules, regardless of whether they are discrepant with internal feelings. Emotion work includes: (1) the requirement to display positive emotions; (2) the requirement to display negative emotions, (3) the requirement to be sensitive to clients' emotions; (4) emotional dissonance: the expression of emotions that are not actually felt. It has received increased attention because it is relevant in the service industry where social interactions with customers, clients, or patients are a significant part of the job.

In most economic societies service work plays an important role now. In the European countries, for example, more than 50 percent of the workforce comprises service workers (Paoli, 1997). Consequently, the psychological analysis of service work has received increased attention in recent years (Nerdinger, 1994; Zeithaml and Bitner, 2000). One of the core aspects of service work is the social interaction with customers or clients where the requirement to efficiently and effectively regulate one's emotions plays a central role. Hochschild (1983) coined the term ''emotional labour'' for this requirement. She investigated the work of flight attendants and showed that a substantial part of the job was dealing with the passengers and their emotions.

Based on qualitative findings, Hochschild (1983) argued that high emotional demands had negative effects on psychological and physical health. Whereas most but not all empirical studies so far were able to demonstrate such negative effects of emotional labour, the empirical findings with regard to positive effects were much more inconsistent. In some studies, the frequency of emotion display was positively related to well-being; in others it was not. In particular, it has been argued that the display of positive emotions has positive consequences.

Emotional labour or emotion work (Zapf, 2002) is an important aspect of employee – client interactions. ''Client'' refers to any person who interacts with an employee, for example, patients, children, customers, passengers, or guests.

Expressing appropriate emotions during face-to-face or voice-to-voice interactions is a job demand for many employees in the service industry. Service workers are required to manage their emotions as a part of their job. Certainly, service workers cannot be assumed to be always in a good mood. Rather, they may sometimes be bored and they may all more or less frequently encounter situations eliciting negative emotions such as anger, fear, or disappointment. Emotion work as part of the job, however, implies the display of organizationally desired emotions even in these unpleasant situations. Accordingly, emotion work has been defined as the psychological processes necessary to regulate organizationally desired emotions as part of one's job (Grandey, 2000; Hochschild, 1983; Rafaeli and Sutton, 1987; Zapf, 2002).

Hochschild (1983) argued that carrying out emotion work for long hours would overtax the service providers' abilities to show the desired emotions. They would go on smiling, but they would not feel the expected emotions. This discrepancy between displayed and felt emotions she called ''Emotional Dissonance''. She maintained that showing emotions not actually felt at that moment would lead to the alienation of one's feelings in the long run, which would cause psychological ill health. In her qualitative interviews with flight attendants, she found a variety of negative health consequences of emotion work such as psychosomatic symptoms, and alcohol and sex problems. Other studies, however, did not uniformly find these negative effects, and some even found positive effects of emotion work. Therefore, researchers started to develop models differentiating various dimensions of emotion work.

According to Hochschild, jobs involving emotional labour are defined as those that: (1) require face-to-face or voice-to-voice contact with the public; (2) require the worker to produce an emotional state in another person; (3) allow the employees to exercise a degree of control over their emotional activities.

Display rules refer to the organizational rules regarding the kind of emotion to express on the job.

Emotion regulation refers to the process of modifying one's own emotions and expressions. These are the processes by which individuals influence which emotions they have, when they have them, and how they experience and express these emotions.

There are two kinds of Emotion regulation:

1. Antecedent-focused emotion regulation, which refers to modifying initial feelings by changing the situation or the cognitions of the situation;
2. Response-focused emotion regulation, which refers to modifying behaviour once emotions are experienced by suppressing, faking or amplifying an emotional response.

3. Employees can display organizationally-desired emotions by acting out the emotion. Such acting can take two forms:

- Surface acting, involves "painting on" affective displays, or faking; Surface acting involves an employee presenting emotions on his or her "surface" without actually feeling them. The employee in this case puts on a facade as if the emotions are felt, like a "persona".
- Deep acting wherein they modify their inner feelings to match the emotion expressions the organization requires.

Though both forms of acting are internally false, they represent different intentions. That is, when engaging in deep acting, an actor attempts to modify feelings to match the required displays, in order to seem authentic to the audience ("faking in good faith"); in surface acting, the alternative strategy, employees modify their displays without shaping inner feelings. They conform to the display rules in order to keep the job, not to help the customer or the organization, ("faking in bad faith"). Deep acting is argued to be associated with reduced stress and an increased sense of personal accomplishment; whereas surface acting is associated with increased stress, emotional exhaustion, depression, and a sense of inauthenticity.

Most of these models comprised dimensions referring to the frequency of emotion display and/or emotional dissonance (Brotheridge and Grandey, 2002; Grandey, 2000; Morris and Feldman, 1996, 1997; Schaubroeck and Jones, 2000). Moreover, applying Hackman's (1969) distinction of job analysis approaches followed the behaviour requirement approach, thus focusing on the situational job requirements (Diefendorff and Richard, 2003; Schaubroeck and Jones, 2000) rather than on the individual work behaviours or emotion regulation strategies (Brotheridge and Lee, 2002; Morgan, 2002; Glomb and Tews, 2004). Others differentiated between various dimensions of emotion work requirements (Zapf, Vogt, Seifert, Mertini, and Isic, 1999): (1) the requirement to display positive emotions (abbreviated as ''positive emotions''), (2) the requirement to display and handle negative emotions (''negative emotions''), (3) the requirement to sense the emotion of the interaction partner (''sensitivity requirements''), and (4) the dissonance between felt and displayed emotions (''emotional dissonance'').

In line with most empirical studies (Adelmann, 1995; Brotheridge and Lee, 2003; Morris and Feldman, 1997) the frequency of emotional display was considered to be an important aspect of emotion work. Factor analyses (Zapf, Vogt et al., 1999) demonstrated the necessity of distinguishing between being required to show positive and negative emotions. This is so because the necessity to display positive and negative emotions is not uniformly high or low across occupations. Rather, it depends on specific job requirements. For a call centre agent, the requirement to show negative emotions will be relatively infrequent (Zapf, Isic, Bechtoldt, and Blau, 2003). In contrast, a frequently cited example for a job comprising a frequent requirement to show negative emotions is the case of a bill collector (Sutton, 1991). The requirement to display negative emotions should not be mistaken for letting out one's negative emotions in an uncontrolled manner. Rather, the controlled expression of anger may be used to make clear that one is seriously affected by something or that one is taking something very seriously. For example, a nurse may use controlled anger to make clear that she does not want to be touched by a patient. Whereas there are some studies which also included the requirement of positive emotions display (Diefendorff and Richard, 2003; Schaubroeck and Jones, 2000), the requirement to express negative emotions has been considered in qualitative studies (Stenross and Kleinman, 1989; Sutton, 1991) but only rarely in quantitative studies.

Empirical studies found equivocal effects on psychological well-being which indicates that emotion work is a multidimensional construct with dimensions having both positive and negative health effects. Although it has often been presumed that jobs involving "people work" (e.g., nurses, service workers) are emotionally taxing (Maslach and Jackson, 1984), seldom is the emotional component of these jobs is explicitly studied. Maslach et al. (1984) compared two perspectives of emotional labour as predictors of burnout beyond the effects of negative affectivity: job-focused emotional labour (work demands regarding emotion expression) and employee-focused emotional labour (regulation of feelings and emotional expression). Significant differences existed in the emotional demands reported by five occupational groupings. The use of surface-level emotional labour, or faking, predicted depersonalization beyond the work demands. Perceiving the demand to display positive emotions and using deep-level regulation were associated with a heightened sense of personal accomplishment, suggesting positive benefits to this aspect of work. These findings suggest new antecedents of employee burnout and clarify the emotional labour literature by comparing different conceptualizations of this concept.

The expression of organizationally-desired emotions is not an end in itself. Emotions are shown to have an influence on clients (Kruml and Geddes, 2000; Pugliesi, 1999). Expressing emotions is one possible way to influence the clients' feelings. To be able to influence the clients' emotions, their accurate perception is an important prerequisite. In social interactions, information provided by the emotion display of the interaction partner is used to guide one's own response (Elfenbein, Marsh, and Ambady, 2002). Therefore, sensitivity requirements as the necessity to be sensitive and to consider the emotions of clients is another aspect of the emotion work concept (Zapf, Vogt et al., 1999). Sensitivity requirements are low if there are no or only few interactions with clients or if an employee can display organizationally-desired emotions independent from the clients' feelings, for example, in the case of highly scripted interactions. Sensitivity requirements are high, if knowledge of the clients' emotions is a prerequisite for one's own emotional reaction.

Closely associated with emotion work is the concept of emotional dissonance (Abraham, 1998; Kruml and Geddes, 2000; Morris and Feldman, 1996, Nerdinger, 1999; Zapf, Vogt et al., 1999; Zerbe, 2000). Emotional dissonance occurs when an employee is required to express emotions which are not genuinely felt in the particular situation. A person may feel nothing when a certain emotion display is required, or the display rule may require the suppression of undesired emotions and the expression of neutrality or a positive emotion instead of a negative one. Emotional dissonance was found to be resulting from external demands rather than being a reaction to emotion display or a behavioural strategy (Zapf, Vogt et al., 1999). It is assumed that surface acting which is a response-focused strategy to express an emotion which is not felt (Grandey, 2000; Hochschild, 1983), is an adequate and probably the most frequently used emotion regulation strategy to respond to emotional dissonance as a situational demand, e.g., if the situational demand is to be friendly to an arrogant customer. However, the service provider may also not be willing to put on the expected friendly face. Rather he or she may look neutral or even angry, thus showing emotional deviance (Rafaeli and Sutton, 1987) as another possible response. In cases, the service provider may even try to overcome his or her negative inner feelings, which corresponds to the concept of deep acting (Hochschild, 1983).

With the approaching two decades milestone of Arlie Russell Hochschild's classic book, *The Managed Heart* (1983), the study of emotion work continues to be advanced by scholars from diverse disciplines and of varied perspectives. Emotion work seems to be the over-arching term emerging from the literature, and is defined as the paid and unpaid work that involves the use of emotions to facilitate work-related tasks required in and outside of a workplace, as well as, the management of the workers' own emotions in the workplace. All emotion work "typically necessitate contact with other people external to or within the organization, usually involving face-to-face or voice-to-voice" (Steinberg and Figart, 1999).

The gendered nature of emotion work rises resolutely from the literature. Almost all of the articles make some reference to women's work; feminization of emotion work; gender roles and expectations; women and emotion work of all kinds; and especially to caring labour and work. "Emotion work is depicted as a form of exploitation which involves the subordination of women's emotional needs to those of others" (Firth and Kitzinger, 1998), Diane Perrons in a very serious article "Care, paid work, and leisure: rounding the triangle" states that "the current distribution of paid and caring work is inequitable". She argues that "in practice, distinctions between work, care and leisure are blurred. Correspondingly the division of women's labour and time needs to be spread more evenly between these activities". Rutman maintains "care-giving most often is women's work - regardless of whether the care is provided to children or to elders, whether the labour is paid or unpaid, or whether the care is delivered in home or in institutional or centre environments."

Paid work and unpaid work are also intrinsically different. There is much discussion about the distinction between paid and unpaid work, and whether caring work can be monetarily compensated for (Steinberg and Figart 1999). Caring labour, paid work that involves dealing with the feelings of others and an assumption that the worker cares about the feelings of others, is the most prevalent subset of emotion work. Many of the case studies on caring labour examine home care support workers, nursing, social workers, child care workers, counsellors, and teachers. Studies looking at emotional labour, the paid work that requires the worker to manage their emotions to create an encrypted scenario for clients, are also widely researched. Methodologically, emotion work has mostly been studied through case studies. Case studies of unpaid emotion work include: women (Erickson, 1993; Fioze, 1996), and family workers (Erickson, 1993). Case studies of paid emotion work include: professors (Acker, 1999; Bellas, 1999; Brown, 1997), service industry (Leidner, 1999; Tolich, 1993; England, 1999), counsellors (Austin, 1993), educators (Cameron, 1998; Chin, 2000; Crawford, 1993;), social service workers (Anderson, 2000; Ashforth, 1993; Ebenstein, 1998), and health care professionals (Davies, 1995; Deary, 1996 and Fagin, 1996).

Emotion Work Learning

The information and discussions about emotion work learning is shallow and unexplored. The processes, structures, theories, ideas, and procedures that explain and consider the learning workers do to negotiate their emotion work is ignored, glazed over and/or left out.

Allusions to learning found in the literature are grouped into eight themes - training and formal schooling; memorizing and indoctrination; socialization /natural abilities; cultural norms/intuitively understood; talking with peers or professional socialization; employee recruitment; role playing/imagination; and experiential learning. Training and formal schooling is featured in a number of articles (Steinberg and Figart 1999; Ebenstein, 1998 and Leidner, 1999). "Service workers may, for example, be trained to greet customer in a certain way, to smile, make eye contact, thank customers, and close a transaction with 'Have a nice day' (Steinberg and Figart, 1999).

While memorization and indoctrination are two very different teaching tactics, they have similar outcomes (Steinberg and Figart 1999, and Leidner 1999). "Insurance sales agents learn very specific and detailed scripts for handling the patterned responses they are likely to receive as they knock on people's doors (Steinberg and Figart 1999). Leidner maintains that "once employees are hired, organizations use a variety of techniques to instil organizationally-favoured attitudes and to teach new staff how to do their jobs and comply with organizational rules. An important component of orientation programs and of ongoing employee relations efforts in many workplaces is indoctrination with company culture." (Leidner, 1999).

Most often exploited or denounced as a learning tactic, is the concept socialization or natural abilities (Steinberg and Figart 1999; England and Folbre 1999; Bellas, 1999; Steinberg and Figart 1999). Some authors suggest that people are 'meant' for their jobs. Most often what is actually being said is that women are 'meant' to be in their caring role. James states, "the supposed 'naturalness' of women's caring role is central to the significance, value and invisibility of emotional labour". Or "despite the skills involved in effective teaching, like so much of so-called women's work, teaching appears to draw on natural abilities" (Bellas, 1999).

Similar to socialization as a learning process, are cultural norms and intuitively understood as learning tactics (Steinberg and Figart 1999; and Ebenstein, 1998). Steinberg and Figart (1999) claim that "cultural norms" influence the selection of an appropriate person to perform a particular job. Gender is implicated within these social norms, which vary by culture. Ebenstein (1998) declares about home care workers that "they intuitively understood that stimulation increased alertness and strengthened connections to the outside world".

Talking with peers and professional socialization are also learning processes alluded too Bellas (1999). DeVault in her discussion about lesbian parents suggests that parents "contact other parents to discuss issues that arise in their children's friendships". Bellas (1999) suggests that "professors learn these feeling rules through professional socialization and explicit organizational or occupational codes of conduct".

Employee recruitment is another apparent process by which people learn emotion work in their jobs (England and Folbre 1999; Steinberg and Figart, 1999; and Leidner, 1999). England and Folbre, (1999) highlight this process, "The process of learning a skill often goes hand in hand with developing a preference for exercising that skill, so that by selecting people with the skills for a job, employers unwittingly select more of those who would take the job for lower pay than others".

Steinberg and Figart (1999), blatantly state, "Understanding the role that emotion plays can help organizations recruit properly socialized employees". Ebenstein (1998) and Lois (2001) both make reference to role-playing and imagining as ways of learning to do emotion work. Of a home care worker's learning technique explains that "imagining how the world looked through their client's eyes helped a worker understand the client's needs and reasons for behaviour that may have at first appeared unreasonable". Jennifer Lois (2001) highlights one way that a rescuer worker learns their emotion work. "Preparing for edgework by imagining numerous different scenarios gave them some sense of control of the unpredictable future, and through such planning; they were able to manage their uncomfortable anticipatory feelings about the unknown".

And the final allusion to learning in the literature is experiential learning (Bellas, 1999). As Nelson and Barley state, for seasoned emergency medical technicians "being skilled, therefore, meant more than having formal knowledge of what to do.

Although the experience of work is saturated with emotion, research has generally neglected the impact of everyday emotions on organizational life. Further, organizational scholars and practitioners frequently appear to assume that emotionality is the antithesis of rationality and, thus, frequently hold a pejorative view of emotion. This has led to four institutionalized mechanisms for regulating the experience and expression of emotion in the workplace: (1) neutralizing, (2) buffering, (3) prescribing, and (4) normalizing emotion. In contrast to this perspective, it is argued that emotionality and rationality are interpenetrated, emotions are an integral and inseparable part of organizational life, and emotions are often functional for the organization (Zapf, 1999). What and how learning takes place for managers is inextricably emotional. The traditional cognitive approach to management learning has obscured the presence and role of emotion. The conceptual positioning of emotion is reviewed, illustrated though 'competencies' and 'business ethics'. It is concluded that more explicit frameworks are desperately needed, derived the wilder organizational literature on emotion, to place emotion as both a product and process of learning. Special attention is required to the growth of corporate emotion engineering, 'flexible' work structures and 'virtual' managing. These areas raise challenging technical and moral questions for learning theorists and practitioners.

Emotion Work and Burnout

The positive and negative effects of emotion work are investigated with regard to burnout (Schaufeli and Enzmann, 1998). This concept was introduced as an individual reaction to high emotional demands in human service work. It can be understood as an indication that employees are no longer able to manage their emotions adequately when interacting with clients. Burnout is a syndrome consisting of three aspects: emotional exhaustion, depersonalization, and reduced personal accomplishment (Maslach and Jackson, 1986). Emotional exhaustion measures one's feeling of being burnt out, frustrated, and perceiving working with people to be demanding. Depersonalization comprises the tendency to treat clients like objects and to become indifferent and apathetic with regard to clients. Personal accomplishment includes the feeling of having the competence to do things and of being able to meet one's aspirations in one's job.

Explanations for the positive and negative effects of emotion work on burnout can be given at two different levels. First, at the interaction level, the emotion work aspects can be seen as indicators of positive or negative social interactions with clients. Second, explanations at the conceptual level of emotion regulation relate to processes and mechanisms inherent in the emotion work concept (Grandey, 2000; Zapf, 2002). The potential positive and negative effects of the emotion work aspects on burnout both at the level of social interactions and the level of emotion regulation need to be discussed. Starting with the negative effects, studies consistently found correlations between emotional dissonance (or variables which share some features with emotional dissonance such as suppressing negative emotions or surface acting) and psychological strain (Abraham, 1998; Brotheridge and Grandey, 2002; Grebner et al., 2003; Heuven and Bakker, 2003; Lewig and Dollard, 2003; Morris and Feldman, 1997; Nerdinger, 1999; Schaubroeck and Jones, 2000; Zapf, Vogt et al., 1999; Zerbe, 2000). In particular, relations between emotional dissonance and emotional exhaustion were found in the studies of Heuven and Bakker (2003), Lewig and Dollard (2003), Morris and Feldman (1997), Nerdinger (1999); Zapf, Vogt et al. (1999), and Zerbe (2000). Similar results were found for emotional dissonance and depersonalization (Dormann and Zapf, 2004; Dormann, Zapf, and Isic, 2002; Zapf, Vogt et al., 1999). A variety of explanations exists for this result. An explanation at the interaction level is that emotional dissonance is related to emotional exhaustion because it is a sensitive qualitative indicator of unpleasant and stressful interactions with clients. Clients may be aggressive, they may confront the service provider with disproportionate expectations, or they may behave in an uncivil manner. These behaviours have been related to psychological strain (Ben-Zur and Yagil, 2005; Dormann and Zapf, 2004; Duffy, Ganster, and Pagon, 2002; Spector, 1997) and emotional dissonance may be a good indicator to cover these different kinds of negative social interactions with clients or customers.

Moreover, at the level of emotion regulation, Gross and colleagues (Gross, 1998; Gross and John, 1997; Gross and Levenson, 1997) argued that emotion regulation as any process of self-regulation (Muraven, Tice, and Baumeister, 1998) has its psychological costs. Emotional dissonance often means the suppression of negative emotion and there is evidence that emotion suppression is related to the sympathetic activation of the cardiovascular system (Gross and Levenson, 1997) which has been shown to be associated with poor health, adjustment, and coping responses (Pennebaker, 1990). Finally, Brotheridge and Lee (2002) suggested that surface acting which is one way to react if the required emotions do not conform to the emotions actually felt, may threaten one's authenticity (Erickson and Wharton, 1997). This comes close to Hochschild's (1983) notion that emotional dissonance generates feelings of estrangement from the self, which is supposed to be related to psychological strain. Emotional dissonance may also lead to the chronic detachment of other people's feelings which may be related to depersonalization. Thus, based on these explanations both at the interactional and the conceptual level and in line with previous research, it is hypothesized that emotional dissonance is positively related to emotional exhaustion and depersonalization.

With regard to the frequency of being required to display emotions, contradictory hypotheses exist. Some authors proposed that these requirements have negative health effects (Hochschild, 1983; Morris and Feldman, 1996); others (Schaubroeck and Jones, 2000) proposed a positive effect for the requirement to display positive emotions. Overall, it is assumed that emotional job requirements, i.e., the requirement of the job to display positive or negative emotions and to sense the emotion of the client, depend on the existence of display rules (rules for the expression of emotions), the frequency and the duration of service interactions as well as on the quality of these interactions, i.e., whether the clients are behaving positively or negatively (Grandey, 2000; Morris and Feldman, 1996; Zapf, 2002). It is further assumed that there is a positive relation between emotional requirements and health outcomes as long as these requirements are matched by the personal prerequisites of the service provider. On a qualitative level, Tolich (1993) described supermarket clerks who enjoyed showing prescribed emotions in the form of jokes or entertainment of customers who chose their checkout lines.

Empirically, findings with regard to positive effects are inconsistent. Wharton (1993) found a positive relation between emotional labour and job satisfaction. Morgan (2002) was able to demonstrate a causal effect of expressing positive emotions on job satisfaction in a longitudinal study. Morris and Feldman (1997) found positive effects of duration on emotional exhaustion and job satisfaction, but similar negative effects of the frequency of interaction. However, these effects all disappeared in multiple regressions where emotional dissonance was included. Lewig and Dollard (2003) did not find any positive effect. Brotheridge and Grandey (2002) and Diefendorff and Richard (2003) found a positive effect of the requirement to express positive emotions on job satisfaction. Schaubroeck and Jones (2000) found a respective negative effect instead of the hypothesized positive effect on physical symptoms.

These are the interactions in which service providers automatically show the required emotions. If, however, the required emotions are not automatically shown, then the person may respond with deep acting to bring the felt emotions in line with the required emotions. When using deep acting as an emotion regulation strategy, an individual actively tries to experience the required emotion (Grandey, 2000; Hochschild, 1983). This may have similar effects as if the emotions were displayed automatically. Accordingly, Brotheridge and Grandey (2002) reported positive relations between deep acting and personal accomplishment in their studies. Alternatively, the required emotion may not be spontaneously felt, but will be displayed. This corresponds to the definition of emotional dissonance. Thus, it is hypothesized that the emotional job requirements to display positive or negative emotions related to emotional dissonance. There is no direct effect of the emotion work requirement variables on emotional exhaustion and depersonalization, but these effects are mediated by emotional dissonance.

Moreover, if sensitivity requirements are too high, they may overtax the employees' abilities to be sensitive because of the continuous necessity to concentrate and process information while communicating with the client. In recent years, stress researchers started to control stressor – strain relationships for negative affectivity (NA). NA has often been equated with neuroticism (Burke, Brief, and George, 1993; Watson and Clark, 1984), and it has been interpreted as a general dimension that lowers the threshold to experience negative emotions. Some authors have argued that NA represents a nuisance variable that directly affects stressor – strain relations (Burke et al., 1993). According to this view, individuals high in NA tend to view both their working conditions and their health conditions more negatively than individuals low in NA, thus producing an artificial correlation between the variables. At the theoretical level, it can be argued that individuals high in NA tend to experience negative emotions more frequently. They will be more often exposed to emotional dissonance because the display of positive emotions is typically required in most service interactions. Moreover, applying the ''stressor creation mechanism'' (Spector, Zapf, Chen, and Frese, 2000) to the present context implies that individuals high in NA tend to create or contribute to social conflicts with clients thus creating or contributing to a negative quality of this interaction in which negative emotions are experienced instead of the positive ones frequently required by the organizational display rules.

Studies show that the burnout dimensions are associated with NA or neuroticism (Schaufeli and Enzmann, 1998). Moreover, although individuals with a tendency to experience negative emotions should report more occasions where positive emotions are required but negative emotions are felt (emotional dissonance), it is hypothesized that these mechanisms do not substantially decrease the relation between emotional dissonance and emotional exhaustion and depersonalization. This result from the fact of the emotional dissonance measure in the present study is intended to describe aspects of the work situation rather than subjective reactions. Usually, such measures are only little affected by NA as a nuisance factor (Spector et al., 2000). NA does not affect the emotional requirements because these are mainly determined by the display rules and the frequency and duration of service interactions. Moreover, the instrument used in this study aimed at measuring the work environment thereby trying to minimize the influence of individual cognitive and emotional processing in the measurement process (Frese and Zapf, 1988). There is evidence that under these circumstances, the effects of NA on stressor-strain relations are only small in terms of Cohen's effect size criteria (Spector et al., 2000). So far, several studies on emotion work included neuroticism or NA. Brotheridge and Grandey (2002) and Diefendorff and Richard (2003) found an effect on demands to suppress negative emotions. In contrast, Schaubroeck and Jones (2000) found a relatively strong effect of trait negative effect on demands to suppress negative emotions ($r = .48$).

Although some degree of convergence exists regarding the definition of burnout, emotional labour has been conceptualized in two main ways. First, job-focused emotional labour denotes the level of emotional demands in an occupation. This has been measured as occupational titles such as service jobs that are thought to represent "people work" (Hochschild, 1983; Wharton, 1995), work demands such as frequency of interactions with customers (Morris and Feldman, 1996, 1997), and job expectations to express certain emotions (Schaubroeck and Jones, 2000; Wharton and Erickson, 1995). Second, employee-focused emotional labour denotes employee process or experience of managing emotions and expressions to meet work demands. This has been measured as emotional dissonance - when expressions differ from feelings (Abraham, 1998; Morris and Feldman, 1997) and as emotion regulation processes when one attempts to modify expressions to meet work demands (Brotheridge, 1998; Grandey, 2000; Hochschild, 1983; Pugliesi, 1999).

As is well known from the stress literature, both job characteristics and individual characteristics contribute to the reported levels of stress. To pursue the emotional characteristics of the job that predict burnout, the burnout and emotional labour literatures as well as both the occupational type and the reported interpersonal demands and emotional control required by the job were taken into account. These variables can be configured onto Karasek's (1979) demands—control stress theory. In contrast to previous applications of this theory (Pugliesi, 1999), the construct of "demands" refers exclusively to demands inherent in employee-customer interactions, and the construct of "control" refers to the perception that one has autonomy over one's emotional expressions at work. In considering the aspects of the employee that predict burnout, the literature of emotion regulation was drawn (Gross, 1998) to propose how employees modify expressions for organizational purposes. These two approaches to determine the extent to which the emotional quality of the job and the employee's emotion management process contribute to burnout were considered.

The occupational perspective views occupational grouping as being relevant in and of itself, such that workers employed in the categories of "high emotional labour" jobs (Hochschild, 1983) and "high burnout" jobs (Cordes and Dougherty, 1993) report significantly higher levels of employee stress than do other workers. This study examined how emotional demands differ for employees in people work. Occupational differences in burnout do exist. It has been commonly assumed that there is something unique about health care, social service work, teaching, and other "caring" professions that make their occupants more likely to experience burnout (Cherniss, 1993; Jackson et al., 1986; Leiter and Maslach, 1988; Schaufeli et al., 1993). Researchers have demonstrated differences in dimensions of burnout for different service and caring professions (Singh et al., 1994) and have developed taxonomies of "high-burnout" jobs based on their frequency of interactions (Cordes and Dougherty, 1993) and the emotion control needed while interacting with the public.

In the emotional labour literature, the focus is customer service, where interactions are less spontaneously "emotional," yet high emotional control is needed to maintain positive relations with customers across time and situations (Hochschild, 1983; Van Maanen and Kunda, 1989). Hochschild (1983) proposed a list of "emotional labour jobs" that involve frequent customer contact and emotion displays controlled by the organization. However, comparing the occupations on Hochschild's list to non-emotional labour jobs has not been very effective in predicting stress and burnout (Schaubroeck and Jones, 2000; Wharton, 1993; Wharton and Erickson, 1995). In other words, employees in the "high emotional labour" grouping do not report significantly higher levels of emotional exhaustion than do those in the "low emotional labour" grouping. This may be because emotional labour is not a dichotomous variable; there may be a range of emotional labour demands, and many jobs have some level of these demands (Morris and Feldman, 1996; Pugliesi, 1999).

Occupational Differences in Job-Focused Emotional Labour

The main focus of the study was to explore the emotional nature of "people work." If the job focused view of emotional labour is accurate, then there should be higher levels of emotional demands for persons in service occupations. Using Hochschild's (1983) criteria for emotional labour jobs, the study measured the perceived interpersonal work demands and lack of emotion control. These demands across five occupational categories: human service workers, service/sales, managers, clerical workers, and physical labourers were compared. Interpersonal demands, such as the intensity and frequency of client interactions and the expectations for positive displays, were expected to be much greater for customer service representatives (Hochschild, 1979, 1983) and for human service workers than for other employees (Cordes and Dougherty, 1993; Hawthorne and Yurkovich, 1994; Rafaeli and Sutton, 1989; Smith, 1991). Managers, clerical workers, and physical labourers have been studied less often within the emotional labour or burnout literatures, although recent studies have included broader job categories (Leiter and Schaufeli, 1996; Schutte, Toppinen, Kalimo, and Schaufeli, 2000). The research on emotional intelligence suggests that managers have emotional demands and a high need for emotional control (Goleman, 1995). One study reported that affective requirements were higher for clerical workers than for service professionals and faculty (Pugliesi and Shook, 1997), although to be that the actual differences were quite small. Physical labourers, by nature of their jobs, should report less frequent and less emotionally laden interactions with the public.

The differences between service work (prototypical emotional labour job) and caring work (prototypical burnout job) were tested in an exploratory way. Likewise, differences in employee-focused emotional labour were explored and not proposed. Job-Focused Emotional Labour Predicting Burnout, in different occupational categories differs in mean level of interpersonal work demands.

However, employee perceptions of emotion work demands across jobs may be more predictive of burnout levels than their occupational categories; more differences may exist within a specific occupational category than between categories. Regardless of their occupational category, the perception of work demands and control over the personal expression of emotions may engender stress (Hochschild, 1983; Karasek, 1979).

Interpersonal Work Demands

The frequency or quantity of interactions has been considered a main cause of burnout (Cordes and Dougherty, 1993). Likewise, the expectations for long interactions with clients and the level of intensity and variety of emotional expressions needed have also been proposed as defining dimensions of emotional labour and predictors of burnout (Cordes and Dougherty, 1993; Morris and Feldman, 1996). Indeed, Maslach (1978) found that employees who had less emotionally charged interactions with clients reported less emotional exhaustion than did those whose interactions were more intense. However, in a sample of human resource professionals, the interpersonal demands of frequency, duration, and intensity were not significant predictors of emotional exhaustion (Cordes, Dougherty, and Blum, 1997). Likewise, Morris and Feldman (1997) did not find support for frequency and duration as predictors of emotional exhaustion, and Bulan, Erickson, and Wharton (1997) found that frequency of public contact was unrelated to feelings toward work for bank and hospital employees. This lack of support has raised the question of whether emotional demands are actually stressful. Multiple occupations were examined to clarify these mixed findings.

Emotion Control: Perceived Display Rules

Emotion control for organizational purposes has also been referred to as display rules (Ekman and Friesen, 1975; Rafaeli and Sutton, 1989; Wharton, 1993), which remove emotional autonomy from the employee. These display rules refer to the degree to which showing and hiding emotions is seen as an expected part of employee performance (Wharton and Erickson, 1995). Hochschild's (1983) view—that organizational control of emotional displays is inherently stressful—has received mixed support in both qualitative (Leidner, 1999; Tolich, 1993) and quantitative research. In one study, the requirement to hide negative emotions was positively associated with burnout. Similarly, the perceived requirement to express positive emotions and hide negative emotions was related positively to physical symptoms for employees in one organization (Schaubroeck and Jones, 2000). A study with a bank and hospital employees found that the requirement to be friendly was unrelated to feelings about work

(Bulan et al., 1997). The current study attempted to clarify these mixed results by using a broader occupational sample and testing hypotheses consistent with the emotional labour literature and Karasek's demand–control perspective. Thus, it is proposed that higher levels of interpersonal work demands and lower levels of autonomy of emotional expression will predict burnout.

Employee-focused Emotional Labour

Predicting burnout emotional labour may also be viewed as an individual process in which employees' emotion management processes predict burnout levels (Hochschild; 1979, 1983). Emotional demands and display rules are stressful because they create the need to manage emotional states for the organizational goals, and this emotion work is the more proximal predictor of stress (Grandey, 2000). Hochschild's (1979, 1983) research suggested two main processes of emotional labour—surface acting and deep acting—that represent how employees manage emotions to meet work role demands. This perspective expands studies that have focused on emotional dissonance, a state of tension, as emotional labour (Abraham, 1998). This internal approach to emotional labour is congruent with general emotion regulation theories that can be used to make predictions (Brotheridge, 1998; Grandey, 2000; Gross, 1998).

Employee-focused Emotional Labour: Surface Acting

In surface acting, employees modify and control their emotional expressions. For example, employees may enhance or fake a smile when in a bad mood or interacting with a difficult customer. The inauthenticity of this surface-level process, showing expressions discrepant from feelings, is related to stress outcomes (Abraham, 1998; Brotheridge, 1998; Erickson and Wharton, 1997; Pugliesi, 1999; Pugliesi and Shook, 1997) due to the internal tension and the physiological effort of suppressing true feelings (Gross and Levenson, 1997; Morris and Feldman, 1997; Pugliesi, 1999). Hochschild (1983) argued that acting inauthentic over time may result in feeling detached not only from one's true feelings but also from other people's feelings, suggesting a relationship with the dimension of depersonalization. Feeling diminished personal accomplishment is also likely if the employee believes that the displays were not efficacious or were met with annoyance by customers (Ashforth and Humphrey, 1993; Brotheridge, 1998). Thus, surface acting is expected to relate to all three dimensions of burnout.

Employee-focused Emotional Labour: Deep Acting

Deep acting is the process of controlling internal thoughts and feelings to meet the mandated display rules. Emotions involve physiological arousal and cognitions, and deep acting works on modifying arousal or cognitions through a variety of techniques (Baumeister, Heatherton, and Tice, 1994; Folkman and Lazarus, 1991; Gross, 1998; Lazarus, 1991; Totterdell and Parkinson, 1999). Hochschild (1979, 1983) argued that doing "emotion work" was a way of decreasing a state of emotional dissonance and may also result in a feeling of accomplishment if the performance is effective. Thus, deep acting might not relate to emotional exhaustion because it minimizes the tension of dissonance. Deep acting is related to lower depersonalization and more personal accomplishment because deep acting involves treating the customer as someone deserving of authentic expression, the positive feedback from the customer may increase a sense of personal efficacy. Employee-focused emotional labour in relation to each burnout dimension beyond job-focused emotional labour was examined (e.g., frequency, display rules).

Conclusions and Ideas for Further Research

Emotion work as a field of study has grown extensively, and is increasingly becoming visible to researchers in a wide range of disciplines, as well as to employers and the general public. While scholars are looking at a wide range of issues relating to emotion work, and various forms of emotion work, there are a number of gaps and critical issues. This brings us back to the central question of the annotated bibliography - What is the literature saying about how workers learn to do the emotion work required of them? After completing an extensive literature search and analyzing numerous articles we can fairly say that scholars have not fully explored the ways in which diversely situated individuals and groups learn to do emotion work.

From these conclusions, further research suggestions obviously include empirically studying emotion work learning in general and specifically. How do workers learn to do the emotion work involved in their paid or unpaid jobs? This could be done through a case study of a profession that does caring or emotional labour, or a number of case studies in a wide range of professions, or by interviewing unpaid caring or emotional workers, or by following up on any or all of the learning processes alluded to in the literature or by comparing the learning processes and theories between paid and unpaid caring and emotion workers. In studying emotion work learning, insights on equity, inconsistencies, availability, accessibility, power relations and much more could be unearthed, emphasized and addressed.

References

Abraham, R. (1998). Emotional dissonance in organizations: Antecedents, consequences, and moderators. Genetic, Social, and General Psychology Monographs, 124(2), 229–246.

Acker, S. (1999). Caring as work for women educators. In S. A. Elizabeth Smyth, Paula Borne and Alison Prentice (Ed.), Challenging Professions: Historical and Contemporary Perspectives on Women's Professional Work. (pp. 277-295). Toronto: University of Toronto Press.

Adelmann, P. K. (1995). Emotional labour as a potential source of job stress. In S. L. Sauter and L. R. Murphy (Eds.), Organizational risk factors for job stress (pp. 371 – 381). Washington, DC: American Psychological Association.

Anderson, D. G. (2000). Coping strategies and burnout among veteran child protection workers. Child and Neglect, 24(6), 839-848.

Ashforth, B. E., and Humphrey, R. H. (1993). Emotional labour in service roles: The influence of identity. Academy of Management Review, 18(1), 88–115.

Austin, B.L. (1993). Women's experience of becoming a counsellor: a phenomenological inquiry. , University of Victoria, Victoria.

Baumeister, R.F., Heatherton, T.F., and Tice, D.M. (1994). Losing control: How and why people fail at self-regulation. San Diego: Academic Press.

Bellas, M. L. (1999). Emotional labour in academia: the case of professors. The Annals of American Academy, 561(1), 96-110.

Ben-Zur, H., and Yagil, D. (2005). The relationship between empowerment, aggressive behaviours of customers, coping, and burnout. European Journal of Work and Organizational Psychology, 14, 81 – 99.

Brotheridge, C.M., and Grandey, A.A. (2002). Emotional labour and burnout: Comparing two perspectives of "people work". Journal of Vocational Behaviour, 60, 17 – 39.

Brotheridge, C.M., and Lee, R.T. (1998). On the dimensionality of emotional labour: Development and validation of the Emotional Labour Scale. Paper presented at the First Conference on Emotions in Organizational Life, San Diego.

Brotheridge, C.M., and Lee, R.T. (2002). Testing a conservation of resources model of the dynamics of emotional labour. Journal of Occupational Health Psychology, 7, 57 – 67.

Brotheridge, C.M., and Lee, R.T. (2003). Development and validation of the Emotional Labour Scale. Journal of Occupational and Organizational Psychology, 76, 365 – 379.

Bulan, H.F., Erickson, R.,and Wharton, A. (1997). Doing for others on the job: The affective requirements of service work, gender, and emotional well-being. Social Problems, 44(2), 235–256.

Burke, M.J., Brief, A.P., and George, J.M. (1993). The role of negative affectivity in understanding relations between self-reports of stressors and strains: A comment on the applied psychology literature. Journal of Applied Psychology, 78(3), 402–412.

Cameron, N.E. (1998). Teaching from the water: soul as the source of care in nursing education. , University of Western Ontario, London, Ontario.

Cherniss, C. (1993). The role of professional self-efficacy in the etiology and amelioration of burnout. In W. B. Schaufeli, C. Maslach, and T. Marek (Eds.), Professional burnout: Recent developments in theory and research (pp. 135–149). Washington, DC: Taylor and Francis.

Chin, T. (2000). 'Sixth grade madness': parental emotion work in the private high school application process. Journal of Contemporary Ethnography, 29(2), 124-163.

Cordes, C.L., and Dougherty, T.W. (1993). A review and an integration of research on job

burnout. Academy of Management Review, 18(4), 621–656.
Cordes, C.L., Dougherty, T.W., and Blum, M. (1997). Patterns of burnout among managers and professionals: A comparison of models. Journal of Organizational Behaviour, 18, 685–701.
Crawford, M.J. (1993). The lived experience of nurse educators: caring experience with students in clinical teaching. , University of Manitoba, Winnipeg.
Davies, C. (1995). Competence versus care? Gender and caring work revisited. Acta Sociologica, 38(1), 17-31.
Deary, Ian .J., Agius, R.M. and Sadler A. (1996). Models of job-related stress and personal achievement among consultant doctors. British Journal of Psychology, 87(Feb), 3-29.
Diefendorff, J.M., and Richard, E.M. (2003). Antecedents and consequences of emotional display rule perceptions. Journal of Applied Psychology, 88, 284 – 294.
Dormann, C., and Zapf, D. (2004). Customer related social stressors and burnout. Journal of Occupational Health Psychology, 9, 61 – 82.
Dormann, C., Zapf, D., and Isic, A. (2002). Emotionale Arbeitsanforderungen und ihre Konsequenzen bei Call Center-Arbeitspla¨tzen (Emotional job requirements and their consequences in call centre jobs). Zeitschrift fu¨r Arbeits- und Organisationspsychologie, 46, 201 – 215.
Duffy, M.K., Ganster, D.C., and Pagon, M. (2002). Social undermining in the workplace. Academy of Management Journal, 45, 331 – 352.
Ebenstein, H. (1998). They were once like us: learning from home care workers who care for the elderly. Journal of Gerontological Social Work, 30(3-4), 191-201.
Ekman, Paul, and Friesen, Wallace V. (1975/1984): Unmasking the face. Englewood Cliffs, NJ: Prentice-Hall. (Reprinted by Consulting Psychologists Press, Palo Alto, CA.).
Elfenbein, H.A., Marsh, A., and Ambady, N. (2002). Emotional intelligence and the recognition of emotion from the face. In L. Feldman Barrett and P. Salovey (Eds.), The wisdom of feelings: Processes underlying emotional intelligence (pp. 37 – 59). New York: Guilford Press.
England, P., and Folbre, N. (1999). The cost of caring. The Annals of the American Academy of Political and Social Science, 561(Jan), 39-51.
Erickson, R. J. (1993). Managing emotions on the job and at home: understanding the Academy of Management. Academy of Management Review, 18(3), 457-486. Brown, R. B. (1997). Emotion in organizations: the case of English university business school academics. Journal of Applied Behavioural Science, 33, 247-262.
Erickson, R.J., and Wharton, A.S. (1997). Inauthenticity and depression: Assessing the consequences of interactive service work. Work and Occupations, 24(2), 188–213.
Fagin, L., Carson, J., Leary, J., and al. (1996). Stress, coping and burnout in mental health nurses: findings from three research studies. International Journal of Social Psychiatry, 42(2), 102-112.
Folkman, S., and Lazarus, R.S. (1991). Coping and emotion. In A. Monat and R. S. Lazarus (Eds.), Stress and coping: An anthology (pp. 207–227). New York: Columbia Univ. Press.
Frese, M., and Zapf, D. (1988). Methodological issues in the study of work stress: Objective vs. subjective measurement of work stress and the question of longitudinal studies. In C. L. Cooper and R. Payne (Eds.), Causes, coping, and consequences of stress at work (pp. 375 – 411). Chichester, UK: Wiley.
Frith, H. A., and Kitzinger, C. (1998). 'Emotion work' as a participant resource: a feminist analysis of young women's talk-in-interaction. Sociology, 32(2), 299-320.

Glomb, T.M., and Tews, M.J. (2004). Emotional labour: A conceptualization and scale development. Journal of Vocational Behaviour, 64, 1 – 23.

Goleman, D. (1995). Emotional intelligence: Why it can matter more than IQ. New York: Bantam Books.

Grandey, A. A. (2000): Emotion regulation in the workplace: A new way to conceptualize emotional labour. Journal of Occupational Health Psychology, 5(1), 95–110.

Grebner, S., Semmer, N.K., Lo Faso, L., Gut, S., Ka¨ lin, W., and Elfering, A. (2003). Working conditions, well-being, and job-related attitudes among call centre agents. European Journal of Work and Organizational Psychology, 12, 342 – 365.

Gross, J.J. (1998). Antecedent- and response-focused emotion regulation: Divergent consequences for experience, expression, and physiology. Journal of Personality and Social Psychology, 74(1), 224–237.

Gross, J.J., and Levenson, R.W. (1997). Hiding feelings: The acute effects of inhibiting negative and positive emotions. Journal of Abnormal Psychology, 106, 95 – 103.

Hackman, J. R. (1969). Toward understanding the role of tasks in behavioural research. Acta Psychologica, 31, 97 – 128.

Hawthorne, D., and Yurkovich, N. (1994). Caring: The raison d'etre of the professional nurse. Canadian Journal of Nursing Administration, 7(4), 35–55.

Heuven, E., and Bakker, A. B. (2003). Emotional dissonance and burnout among cabin attendants. European Journal of Work and Organizational Psychology, 12, 81 – 100.

Hochschild, A.R. (1979). Emotion work, feeling rules, and social structure. American Journal of Sociology, 85(3), 551–575.

Hochschild, A.R. (1983). The managed heart. Berkeley, CA: University of California Press. Jo¨ reskog, K.G., and So¨ rbom, D. (1996). LISREL 8: User's reference guide. Chicago: Scientific Software, Inc.

Hochschild, A.R. (1983). The managed heart: The commercialization of human feeling. Berkeley: Univ. of California Press.

Jackson, S.E.; Schwab, R.L. and Schuler, R.S. (1986). Toward an understanding of the burnout phenomenon. Journal of Applied Psychology, 71(4), 630–640.

Karasek, R.A. (1979). Job demands, job decision latitude, and mental strain: Implications for job redesign. Adm. Sci. Q., 24, 285-308.

Kruml, S.M., and Geddes, D. (2000). Catching fire without burning out: Is there an ideal way to perform emotional labour? In N. M. Ashkanasy, C. E. J. Hartel, and W. J. Zerbe (Eds.), Emotions in the workplace: Research, theory and practice (pp. 177 – 188). Westport, CT: Quorum Books.

Leidner, R. (1999). Emotional labour in service work. In R. J. Steinberg and Figart (Eds.), The annals of the American Academy of Political and Social Science (pp. 81–95). Thousand Oaks, CA: Sage.

Leiter, M.P. and Maslach, C. (1988). Impact of interpersonal environment on burnout and organizational commitment. Journal of Organizational Behaviour, 9, 229 – 243.

Leiter, M.P., and Schaufeli, W.B. (1996). Consistency of the burnout construct across occupations. Anxiety, Stress, and Coping, 9, 229–243.

Lewig, K.A., and Dollard, M.F. (2003). Emotional dissonance, emotional exhaustion and job satisfaction in call centre workers. European Journal of Work and Organizational Psychology, 12, 366 – 392.

Lois, J. (2001). Peaks and valleys: the gendered emotional culture of edgeworkers. Gender and

Society, 15(3), 381- 406.

Maslach, C. (1978). The client role in staff burn-out. Journal of Social Issues, 34(4), 111–124.

Maslach, C., and Jackson, S.E. (1984). Patterns of burnout among a national sample of public contact workers. Journal of Health and Human Resources Administration, 7, 189–212.

Maslach, C., and Jackson, S.E. (1986). Maslach Burnout Inventory (2nd ed.). Palo Alto, CA: Consulting Psychologists Press.

Morgan, L.M. (2002). A longitudinal analysis of the association between emotion regulation, job satisfaction, and intention to quit. Journal of Organizational Behaviour, 23, 947 – 962.

Morris, J.A., and Feldman, D.C. (1996). The dimensions, antecedents, and consequences of emotional labour. Academy of Management Review, 21(4), 986–1010.

Morris, J.A., and Feldman, D.C. (1997). Managing emotions in the workplace. Journal of Managerial Issues, 9(3), 257–274.

Muraven, M., Tice, D.M., and Baumeister, R.F. (1998). Self-control as a limited resource: Regulatory depletion patterns. Journal of Personality and Social Psychology, 74, 774 – 789.

Nerdinger, F. W. (1994). Zur Psychologie der Dienstleistung (On the psychology of service). Stuttgart, Germany: Scha¨ ffer-Poeschel.

Nerdinger, F.W., and Ro¨ per, M. (1999). Emotionale Dissonanz und Burnout. Eine empirische Untersuchung im Pflegebereich eines Universita¨ tskrankenhauses (Emotional dissonance and burnout: An empirical examination in the nursing sector of a university hospital). Zeitschrift fu¨r Arbeitswissenschaft, 53, 187 – 193.

Paoli, P. (1997). Second European survey on the work environment 1995. Dublin, Ireland: European Foundation for the Improvement of Living and Working Conditions.

Pennebaker, J. W. (1990). Opening up: The healing power of confiding in others. New York: Morrow.

Pugliesi, K. and Shook, S. (1997). Gender, jobs, and emotional labour in a complex organization. Social Perspectives on Emotion, 4, 283–316.

Pugliesi, K. (1999). The consequences of emotional labour: Effects on work stress, job satisfaction, and well-being. Motivation and Emotion, 23(2), 125–154.

Rafaeli, A. and Sutton, R.I. (1989). The expression of emotion in organizational life. In L. L. Cummings and B. M. Staw (Eds.), Research in organizational behaviour (Vol. 11, pp. 1–42). Greenwich, CT: JAI.

Rafaeli, A., and Sutton, R.I. (1987). Expression of emotion as part of the work role. Academy of Management Review, 12(1), 23–37.

Schaubroeck, J., and Jones, J.R. (2000). Antecedents of workplace emotional labour dimensions and moderators of their effects on physical symptoms. Journal of Organizational Behaviour, 21, 163–183.

Schaufeli, W. B., and Enzmann, D. (1998). The burnout companion to study and practice: A critical analysis. London: Taylor and Francis.

Schaufeli, W.B.; Maslach, C. and Marek, T. (1993). The future of burnout. In W. B. Schaufeli, C. Maslach, and T. Marek (Eds.), Professional burnout: Recent developments in theory and research (pp. 253–259). Washington, DC: Taylor and Francis.

Schutte, N., Toppinen, S., Kalimo, R., and Schaufeli, W. (2000). The factorial validity of the Maslach Burnout Inventory–General Survey (MBI-GS) across occupational groups and nations. Journal of Occupational and Organizational Psychology, 73, 53–66.

Singh, J.; Goolsby, J.R. and Rhoads, G. K. (1994). Behavioural and psychological consequences of boundary spanning burnout for customer service representatives. Journal of Marketing

Research, 31, 558–569.

Spector, P.E. (1997). The role of frustration in antisocial behaviour at work. In R. A. Giacalone and J. Greenberg (Eds.), Anti-social behaviour in organizations (pp. 1 – 17). Thousand Oaks, CA: Sage.

Spector, P. E., Zapf, D., Chen, P. Y., and Frese, M. (2000). Why negative affectivity should not be controlled in job stress research: Don't throw out the baby with the bath water. Journal of Organizational Behaviour, 21, 79 – 95.

Stenross, B., and Kleinman, S. (1989). The highs and lows of emotional labour. Journal of Contemporary Ethnography, 17(4), 435–452.

Sutton, R. I. (1991). Maintaining norms about expressed emotions: The case of bill collectors. Administrative Science Quarterly, 36(2), 245–268.

Tolich, M.B. (1993). Alienating and liberating emotions at work: Supermarket clerks' performance of customer service. Journal of Contemporary Ethnography, 22, 361 – 381.

Totterdell, P., and Parkinson, B. (1999). Use and effectiveness of self-regulation strategies for improving mood in a group of trainee teachers. Journal of Occupational Health Psychology, 4(3), 219–232.

Van Maanen, J., and Kunda, G. (1989). "Real feelings": Emotional expression and organizational culture. Research in Organizational Behaviour, 11, 43–103.

Wharton, A. (1993). The affective consequences of service work: Managing emotions on the job. Work and Occupations, 20(2), 205 – 232.

Wharton, A. S., and Erickson, R. J. (1995). The consequences of caring: Exploring the links between women's job and family emotion work. Sociological Quarterly, 36(2), 273–296.

Zapf, D. (2002). Emotion work and psychological strain: A review of the literature and some conceptual considerations. Human Resource Management Review, 12, 237 – 268.

Zapf, D., Isic, A., Bechtoldt, M., and Blau, P. (2003). What is typical for call centre jobs? Job characteristics, and service interactions in different call centres. European Journal of Work and Organizational Psychology, 12, 311 – 340.

Zapf, D., Vogt, C., Seifert, C., Mertini, H., and Isic, A. (1999). Emotion work as a source of stress: The concept and development of an instrument. European Journal of Work and Organizational Psychology, 8, 371 – 400.

Zeithaml, V.A., and Bitner, M.J. (2000). Services marketing: Integrating customer focus across the firm (2nd ed.). Boston: McGraw Hill.

Zerbe, W.J. (2000). Emotional dissonance and employee well-being. In N. M. Ashkanasy, C. E. J. Ha¨ rtel, and W. J. Zerbe (Eds.), Emotions in the workplace: Research, theory and practice (pp. 189 – 214). Westport, CT: Quorum Books.

22

Vulnerability to Sexually Transmitted Infections (STIs) in Adolescents

Anubhuti Dubey and Dhananjay Kumar

Introduction

Increasing trends of both communicable and non-communicable diseases are very high worldwide and the long-term consequences of STI are potentially severe. Adolescence is one of the most vulnerable and turbulent period of growth and development and little attention has been paid on the health requirements of adolescents (Troop and Green, 1997).

Adolescents comprise of more than 23 percent (about 230 million) of India's population. More than 22 percent of India's population is in the adolescent age group of 10–19 years; 12 percent are in the 10–14 year age group and 10 percent in the 15–19 year age group. Around 35 percent of all reported HIV/AIDS infections in India occur amongst young people in 15-24 years age group (National Behavioural Surveillance Survey, 2001, NACO and UNICEF). According to the United Nations, adolescence is defined as the stage of life during which individuals reach sexual maturity; it is the period of transition from puberty to maturity (United Nations, World Population Monitoring 1996). The National Population Policy (2000) has recognized adolescents as an underserved vulnerable group that need to be served especially by providing reproductive health information and services.

According to Sigmund Freud, adolescents are in a stage marked with egos that leads to some level of superiority complex and inferiority complex as well. Children arrive at adolescence with the capacity to make "rational" choices. Nonetheless, adolescents frequently make risky choices. It is not only a time of opportunity but also of vulnerability to risk behaviours, which can have lifelong consequences, especially for health. The risk of acquiring sexually transmitted infections (STIs) is one of the most significant and immediate risks to the health and well-being of adolescents. STIs are those infections transmitted via the mucous membranes and secretions of the sexual organs, throat, and rectum. They are relatively easy to contract, and so it is important to know what they are, what they look like, and what one needs to do to get them treated. There are an estimated 333 million new cases of sexually transmitted diseases (STDs) every year worldwide (WHO, 1995). Causes of the increased rates of STIs/HIV in young people are complex; however, the main reasons include biological factors, risky sexual behaviour patterns (e.g. early initiation of sex, premarital sex, bisexual orientation and multiple sexual partners), transmission dynamics and treatment-seeking behaviour (Harms, et.al., 1998). Adolescents STI risk behaviour tend to cluster with other risk behaviours like emotional disorder, lack of parental monitoring and parental communication, violence, substance abuse, delinquency etc. Community based information on problems of adolescents, their self-esteem, sexuality and perception about reproductive health are inadequate as the adolescents out of school are difficult to trace and reach.

Lack of Knowledge of Sexual Health and STI

Generally, adolescents are perceived relatively healthy segment of the population; therefore, their health related needs are ignored or overlooked. However, the young people are central to the HIV pandemic; their sexual and reproductive health requires needful attention and action. Many behaviours developed during adolescence may have long lasting effects. Providing knowledge and education about reproductive health will equip young people to explore their beliefs, opinions, values, attitudes regarding sex and sexual health that may in turn make them less vulnerable to contract any STI/HIV infection. A KAP (knowledge, attitude and practice) study conducted in Nepal on more than two thousands adolescents reported that only 30.0 percent of adolescents heard of reproductive tract infections (RTIs). More than three quarters (77.0 percent) heard of sexually transmitted infections (STIs), particularly HIV/AIDS. They cited multiple sex partners (78.4 percent) and commercial sex workers (52.7 percent) as sources of STI (UNFPA, 1999). A study from UP India reiterates the similar results. It highlights that only 13.5 percent of Adolescents (15-22 Years old) had heard about STIs while 19.6 percent heard of AIDS (Singh, et al., 1998). A study conducted in Madhya Pradesh of India points out that less than half of students were able to correctly define puberty, wet dreams and ages of secondary growth changes.

Only 38 percent understood why menstruation occurs. Some rural students even simply took it as a curse from god. Only a quarter (25.5 percent) knew that AIDS could spread through non-sexual contact as well. Only 39.6 percent of the students know what the acronym STD stands for. Less than this percentage could name STDs other than AIDS (Pathak, et. al., 2001). McManus and Dhar (2008) in a cross sectional study in south Delhi on 15-19 years old found that more than one third of students in this study had no accurate understanding about the signs and symptoms of STIs other than HIV/AIDS. About 30 percent of respondents considered HIV/AIDS could be cured, 49 percent felt that condoms should not be available to youth, 41 percent were confused about whether the contraceptive pill could protect against HIV infection and 32 percent thought married women should only take it. However, Singh et. al. (2005) reported that the proportion of young women who knows different ways to prevent STI was significantly lower than those who know about prevention of HIV/AIDS.

In all countries, young women are the group facing the highest risk of HIV infection through heterosexual contact (Ferguson, Quinn, Eng and Sundellowski, 2000: Newmann, et. al., 2000). Globally, nearly 45 percent of all new HIV infections (about 2.4 million per year) occur among 15-24 years olds, and in several settings, the rate is equal to or more than that estimated among adults (UNICEF, UNAIDS and WHO, 2002). KAP study (UNFPA, 1999) on sexual and reproductive health in Nepal stated that before their first sexual intercourse, about 53.1 percent of males and 23.2 percent of females claimed to know about sex mostly from friends. The gap in knowledge, attitude and practice has been evident in many findings. Sanches and Selig (2004) demonstrated that students with excellent knowledge of HIV transmission mechanisms do not translate into adoption of safe sex practices. They have poor perception of personal vulnerability to HIV. Gender-based violence, including violence between intimate partners, is a factor in the spread of HIV/STI. Traditional expectations associated to masculinity is often related with behaviours that increase the risk of HIV/STI infections among boys

Perception of Vulnerability

Vulnerability outlines a set of factors whose interaction increases or decreases the chances for a person to be infected. Research evidences suggest that just like adults, adolescents also perceive themselves as less vulnerable to contract with STIs than people around them. Both adults and adolescents do not differ in their degree of personal risk perception for negative events such as having a STI (Cauffman, Steinberg and Woolard, 2002; Byrnes, 2003). Gender differences are also evident in this perception of vulnerability. Burger and Burns (1988) found that sexually active young women had rated themselves as less vulnerable than others of unintended pregnancy. The magnitude of this *'illusion of invulnerability'* was found to be associated with the use of contraception, as those who reported highest levels of invulnerability were less likely to use effective ways of birth control and their tendency to underestimate personal risk leads resistant to change (Weinstein and Klein, 1995). At the level of information adolescents may consider unprotected sexual intercourse as dangerous for physical, social and mental health but not for them because they usually underestimate (Weinstein, 1998; Weinstein and Klein, 1995). Adolescents have the limited capacity to follow the connection between present actions and its long-term outcomes. Generally, adolescents are more oriented towards the '*here and now*' phenomena and, are less likely to involve in healthy protective behaviours and more likely to engage in risky health behaviour (Hall and Fong, 2003). They may be strongly influenced by immediate anticipated positive outcomes of engaging in unprotected intercourse, like, physical sensation, feelings of spontaneity, feelings of self worth and sexual gratification and outweigh the consequences as risk of STI/HIV contraction or unintended pregnancy.

High Risk Behaviour in Adolescents

Jessor and his colleagues described risk behaviour as "*conditions or variables associated with a lower likelihood of positive or socially desirable outcomes and a higher likelihood of negative consequences*" (Jessor, Turbin, and Costa, 1998). Adolescents' attitudes about sex and sexual behaviour are shaped by family values and cultural proscriptions as well as personal experiences. There exist great variations between different cultures. Studies have shown that adolescents in the South Asian countries rarely discuss sexual matters such as sexual intercourse, sexuality and sexual preferences, menstruation etc. explicitly with their parents or with other significant adults. Most information on these subjects comes either from their peers, who may be equally uninformed or misinformed and/or from the media, which tend to represent either sexual and gender stereotypes or extremes. Due to such a situation, the adolescents are not prepared mentally or psychologically to cope with physical and sexual changes (Mehta et. al., 1998). Indian studies shows that significant proportion of young men and women report both premarital and extramarital sexual activities (Verma and Lhungalim, 2004). Many adolescents have sex without protection (both in and out of marriage), the proportion of unplanned and unwanted births to the adolescents and young people is relatively high. The reasons for risky sexual behaviour as reported in a study by male participants are fun, curiosity, friendship and under the influence of alcohol (Thomas, Chandra, Selvi, and Swaminathan, 2009).

Early marriage being a reality of the South Asian region hence, sexual activities start at very early age. The Indian data supporting this reality indicates that in India, one-half of all young women are thought to be sexually active by the time they are 18, and almost one in five are sexually active by the time they are of fifteen years (Gupta, 2003). The data suggest approximately 10 million pregnant adolescents and adolescent mothers throughout India at any given time. This reality results in adolescents facing high risk of acquiring STIs. The studies reveal that pre-marital sex is also not very uncommon. It is higher among males than females and higher in urban than in rural areas.

A study conducted on the boys and girls from the selected colleges of Mumbai revealed that a large percentage of boys and girls reported engaging in non-penetrative sexual experiences (e.g., kissing, hugging, touching sexual organs), but only 26 percent of boys and 3 percent of girls reported that they had experienced sexual intercourse (Leena Abraham, 2001). Another study in Chennai found that 13 percent of male school-going adolescents and 10 percent of female school-going adolescents clearly approved of premarital sex,14 percent of the students, both boys and girls, stated that premarital sex is allowable for males only (Sirur, 2000).

Adolescents living in stressful environmental conditions are generally more likely to take sexual risks. Poverty is the most consistent correlates of STIs. Sometimes sex may be bartered for money and/or drugs (Lown et. al., 1995). Associations have been found in family SES and adolescents' sexual activity in lower family income (Upchurch et. al., 1999) and lower parental educational attainment (Sieving, McNeely and Blum, 2000). These associations may reflect differences in perceived life opportunities and available social roles.

Less availability of parental figures in the family was directly associated with risky sexual behaviour and is associated with poorer parental monitoring (Metzler, Noell, Biglan, Ary, and Smolkowski, 2002). The socialization model postulates that youth's problem behaviour and risky sexual behaviours are learned within the friendship network where deviancy training can occur (Boislard et. al., 2009).

Adolescent Women and Risk of STI

Cultural and social gender norms prevailing in our culture often restrict adolescent girls' access to basic information and knowledge and prescribe an unequal and passive role in sexual decision-making. Not all sexual intercourse is voluntary, particularly for girls. Both biological and social factors tend adolescents' girls at risk of acquiring STIs. Women, have a higher incidence of STIs than men because of their greater biological susceptibility (UNFPA, 2004). Adolescent girls are more susceptible to STI because of their protective hormonally driven mechanisms have not yet fully developed and the inadequate mucosal defence mechanism and the immature lining of the cervix provide poor barriers against infections. They are also less able to refuse sex and/or less able to insist on adequate protection. Social factors, like early marriage, early pregnancy, high maternal mortality rate, domestic violence and deprivation of educational benefits, compound the vulnerability. The adolescent girls usually have no say in the decision about whom to marry or when to marry, whether or not to have sexual relations, and when to bear children. On the contrary, married adolescents face tremendous social pressure to prove fertility immediately after marriage, and in many settings, bearing sons is the only means by which young women can establish social acceptance and economic security in their marital homes. Lack of autonomy within their marital homes often means that married girls have limited alternative life choices, and are constrained by non-egalitarian gender norms and expectations. They have limited mobility, decision-making power and control over their own reproductive and sexual rights. Young girls and women within marriage are often powerless to make reproductive decisions (Thapa, Davey, and Waszak, 2000; Patel, Capoor, and Joshi, 2000).

Pregnancy during adolescent phase is risky and younger the girls the higher the risk. Early childbearing has resulted in adverse health consequences, including damage to the reproductive tract, maternal mortality, pregnancy complications, peri natal and neonatal mortality and low birth weight (Kulkarni, and Bott, 2003). They were less likely to have been allowed a major role in the decision, more likely to have been coerced into an abortion, and conversely, more likely to have faced opposition from their families. Females were more likely to be infected by the treatable STIs and HIV, despite risky behaviour being more common among males. Unemployment, little formal education, the presence of bacterial STIs and post-coital bleeding or a bad smell from the vagina was highly associated with the risk for HIV in females. The higher prevalence of STIs, including HIV, among adolescent girls cannot be explained by sexual behaviour only, as boys reported more risk behaviour and are still less affected by STIs. Biological and social factors are definitely of importance (Rassijo, Mirembe and Darj, 2006).

Sexual abuse and sexual crime against minors and adolescent girls are rising. The acute consequences of sexual abuse especially female victims include physical injury, sexually transmitted infections (STIs), and psychological trauma. There is the added danger of unwanted pregnancy, injury, and the chronic complications of STI related vaginal discharge, dysmenorrhea and pelvic pain. Adolescent girls, who have been abused often have difficulty differentiating between sexual and affectionate behaviours, and have a higher incidence of teenage pregnancy and STI/HIV infection than in their non-abused peers. It is an established fact that sexual abuse has long-term effects on the sexual and reproductive health of adolescents and young people. Victims of sexual abuse are often incapable of undertaking self-protective behaviour, because the personal skills needed to prevent STIs and unintended pregnancy are exactly those life skills stunted by sexual abuse. They may be unable or unwilling to make and follow through on decisions that will reduce abuse or remove them from harmful situations. Sexual abuse can also result in low self-esteem, causing victims to seek acceptance through sex.

Avenues for Psychological Researches

The gamut of contributors in adolescents STI/HIV risk behaviour may incorporates cognitive, family, social, and/or environmental factors. Perception of the threat posed by STIs is one of the most important cognitive factors that have an effect of STIs protective behaviour among adolescents. Perceived threat is a psychological construct composed of perceived susceptibility and severity. Threat perception of STI means that the adolescent believe that he/she may be infected and the consequences of infection are very severe. Adolescents at high risk of HIV infection do not perceive personal susceptibility to HIV or other STIs (St. Lawerence et. al., 1999b).

Parental communication and monitoring are two very pertinent antecedents. Open communication with at least one parent especially with mothers has been associated with adolescents' report of engaging in sex less frequently (Dutra, Miller and Forehead, 1999; Dilorio, Kelly and Hockenberry-Eaton, 1999). Similarly, adolescents receiving less parental monitoring have been engaged in more high-risk behaviour and are more likely to acquire an STI (Small and Luster, 1994, DiClemente, et. al., 2001c). Parent child relationships, parental control and parent child communication have been implicated in adolescents' sexual behaviour. Better parent child relationships are associated with postponing intercourse, fewer sex partners and less risk taking. Poor parent child relationship may enhance susceptibility to peer influence or increase the propensity to associate with deviant friends (Whiteback, Conger and Kao, 1993). Adolescents' perception of parental disapproval of sex is associated postponing intercourse (NcNeely and Blum, 2000).

Understanding of the social context of risk behaviour including gender dynamics that affects common sexual behaviour patterns and characteristics remains critical to the development of preventive strategies. Gender role differences contribute to unequal power in adolescents relationships. Older male partners may be resistant to protective behaviour, leaving less assertive females vulnerable to unprotected sex (DiClemente et. al., 2002). Adolescents' ability to communicate their sexual desires and intentions to their sex partners is an important antecedent to their sexual risk behaviour. High assertive communication skills, high self-control over condom use and perceived high control over their partner's use of condoms, each independently predicted consistent condom use by females (Wingood and DiClemente, 1998b).

Feelings of sexual desire and love collide with social prescriptions create restraint, and set the stage for psychological conflict and behavioural inconsistency. Both sexual ideation and activity increases over the adolescent period (Halpern et. al., 1993). Teenagers engage in a spectrum of sexual behaviours ranging from fantasy and self-stimulation to various forms of intercourse. A substantial body of theoretical and experimental literature supports the notion that affect or mood is related to risk behaviour; fewer empirical studies have been conducted to examine directly the associations, particularly in adolescents. What studies have been done so far suggest that both positive and negative mood are correlated with sexual interest, the occurrence of coitus, safer sex behaviours such as condom use (Fortenberry et. al., 2003; Wills, 1999) and degree of substance use (Isen, 2002).

Research indicated that attitudes, outlooks, norms and beliefs around sexual behaviour determine the intended sexual behaviour of young people (Green, Rubin and Hale, 1995). Attitudes, norms and motivational factors are crucial elements in the decision making process of adolescents around engaging in risky behaviours (Whitt, 1995). Gender-based attitudes and behaviour are powerful social institutions that influence attitudes toward sex and the way people talk about it, sexuality, risk-taking behaviour and gender roles. These distinctions place males and females at risk for different reasons. Behaviour change in adolescents and youth is influenced by the environment in which they live, study and work. A favourable family environment is essential to achieve sexual health. When looking at reasons for risk-taking behaviours, it is critical to understand that adolescents behave differently according to the culture to which they have been exposed (Weden and Zabin, 2005) as well as the multiple contexts in which youth live, work, and play (Graber, Brooks-Gunn, and Galen, 1998).

The Information, Motivation, and Behavioural Skills (IMB) model was examined in preventing STI/HIV (Boyer, Pollack, Becne, Jennifer, Shafer, 2008). This model offers a framework for better understanding of how knowledge and psychosocial factors influence sexual risk behaviour. Developed specifically to understand and explain human immunodeficiency virus (HIV) risk behaviour, the IMB model integrates psychological theories of health and behaviour, including the theory of Reasoned Action (Ajzen, and Fishbein, 1980), Efficacy theory (Bandura, 1997) and the Health Belief model (Rosenstock, Strecher and Becker, 1988). Specifically, the model asserts that information regarding transmission and prevention is a prerequisite of risk reduction behaviour. Motivation (i.e., the willingness to act on one's knowledge of the transmission and prevention of HIV) is a second primary determinant of HIV preventive behaviour. Motivation is a function of one's attitudes and beliefs toward prevention behaviour. Behavioural skills are the third primary determinant in that they affect whether a knowledgeable and motivated person will engage in prevention. Behavioural skills include the ability to communicate with one's sexual partner about safe sex, refusal to engage in unsafe sexual behaviour.

Intervention Programmes

The behavioural intervention programs are one of the most promising prevention strategies for STI prevention among adolescents. The behavioural intervention programs may design to minimize the factors contributing to sexual risk behaviour and consequently reducing the probable exposure to STI. Psychology offers a variety of learning techniques and theoretical frameworks to develop a diverse range of behavioural interventions for adolescents vulnerable to STIs and HIV. The intervention may include knowledge-based approaches to sexual communication, skill based approaches, with life skills approaches. The STI behavioural intervention programs for adolescents so far are delineated with emphasis on implying interactive learning, peer facilitation, fostering peer norms support of safer sex behaviour, culture and gender specific methodologies and developmentally appropriate skill based instructions (Kirby, 2000; Wingood and DiClemente, 1996). Greater intervention efficacy was observed in studies that specifically targeted African American females used gender- or culture-specific materials, used female deliverers, addressed empowerment issues, provided skills training in condom use and negotiation of safer sex, and used role-playing to teach negotiation skills (Crepaz, 2009). The avenues for delivering such intervention programs may be clinics, communities and schools. A Meta analysis of community based sexual risk reduction intervention studies demonstrated the significant impact with regard to increasing condom use, decreasing unprotected sex and decreasing number of sexual partners and the practice of abstinence to avoid STI (Jemmott and Jemmott, 2000). Bridging the gap between knowledge and practice (particularly with respect to the use of condoms) has emerged as a major behaviour change communication challenge to reduce adolescents' vulnerability to STIs and unwanted pregnancies (Goyal, 2005).

Conclusion

Adolescents are demographic force, economic force, change agents. Therefore, this significant resource to be nurtured trained and developed into productive citizens and leaders of tomorrow. When adolescents acquire knowledge, attitudes, values and life skills, they benefit in a variety of ways.

These Life Skills help adolescents to make informed decisions, solve problems, think critically and creatively, communicate effectively, build healthy relationships, empathize with others and cope with and manage their lives in a healthy and productive manner. The present dearth of STI education in India is a major concern, particularly in schools. Information about behaviour, attitudes, and knowledge through regular surveys is essential to better understand the dynamics of the STI epidemic. This information is also important in assessing changes over time because of prevention efforts.

Often students are confused or misinformed due to erroneous information received from these sources. Therefore, evidence-based sex education must be a major strategy in school-based programs, with user-friendly resources readily available to students.

References

Abraham, Leena (2001).Understanding Youth Sexuality: A Study of College Students in Mumbai City. The Indian Journal of Social Work, 62(2).

Ajzen, I., and Fishbein, M. (1980). Understanding attitudes and predicting social behaviour. Englewood Cliffs, NJ: Prentice-Hall.

Bandura, A. (1997). Self-efficacy: The exercise of control. New York: Worth Publishers.

Bott S et al., 2003, Towards Adulthood: Exploring the Sexual and Reproductive Health of Adolescents of South Asia. Geneva: WHO.

Boyer, C.B., Pollack, L., Becne, I., Jennifer, M.A. Shafer, M. (2008). Relationships among Sociodemographic Markers, Behavioural Risk, and Sexually Transmitted Infections in U. S. Female Marine Corps Recruits, Military Medicine, November.

Burger, J.M. and Burns, L. (1988). The Illusionary unique invulnerability and the use of effective contraception. Personality and Social Psychology Bulletin, 14, 264-270.

Byrnes, J.P.(2003). Changing view on the nature and prevention of adolescents risk taking. In D. Rorner (ed.) Reducing Adolescents Risk: Toward an Integrated Approach, (pp.11-17)Thousands Oaks, Calif: Sage Publications.

Cauffman, E., Steinberg, L. and Woolard, J. (2002). Age differences in psychosocial capacities underlying competence. Stand trial program and abstracts of the biannual meetings for the Society for Research on Adolescence, April 11-14, New Orleans, Louisina.

Crepaz, N., Marshell, K.J., Latrina, P.H., Aupont, W., Jacobs, E.D., Mizuno, Y., Kay, L.S., Jones, P., McCree, D.H., and O'Leary, A. (2009). The efficacy of HIV/STI behavioural interventions for African American females in the United States: A Meta –Analysis. American Journal of Public Health, Vol, 99, No. 11, 2069-2078.

DiClmente, R.J., Wingood, G.M., Crosby, R.A., Sionean, C., Cobb, B.K, Harrington, K. Davies, S.L. Hook, E.W. and Oh, M.K. (2002). Sexual risk behaviour associated with having older sex partners: A study of African American female adolescents. Sexually Transmitted Diseases, 29 , 20-24.

DiClmente, R.J., Wingood, G.M., Crosby, R.A., Sionean, S., brown, L., Rothbaum, B., Zimand, E., Cobb, B.K. Harrington, K. and Davies, S. (2001c). A prospective study of psychological distress and sexual risk behaviour among African American adolescent females. Pediatrics, 108 (5), 1-6.

DiIorio, C., Kelley, M. and Hockenberry-Eaton, M. (1999). Communication about sexual issues: Mothers, fathers and friends. Journal of Adolescents Health, 24, 181-189.

Dutra, R., Miller, K.S. and Forehand, R. (1999). The process and content of sexual communication with adolescents in two-parent families: Associations with sexual risk taking behaviour. AIDS and Behaviour, 22, 21-34.

Ferguson, Y.O., Quinn, S.C., Eng, E. and Sundlelowski, M. (2000). The gender ratio imbalance and its relationship to risk of HIV/Aids among African American women of historically black colleges and universities. AIDS Care, 18, 323-31.

Fortenberry, J., Temkit, M.H., Tu, W., Katz, B., Orr, D. (2003). Mood, mood change, sexual activity and condom use among adolescents women, Journal of Adolescent Health,, 32, 157-166.

Gupta, A., Mehta, S., Ghate, M., Reynolds, S., Sahay, S., Godbole, S. (2004). Same sex behaviour, sexually transmitted infections (STI) and HIV risks among men attending STI clinics in Pune, India, 1993-2002. Abstract no. WePeC6109. XV International AIDS Conference: Bangkok, Thailand.

Goyal R.(2005) Socio-psychological Constructs of Premarital Sex Behaviour among Adolescent Girls in India. Jaipur: Indian Institute of Health Management Research, India.

Greene K, Rubin D, Hale J. (1995).Egocentrism, message explicitness, and AIDS messages directed toward adolescents: an application of the theory of reasoned action. Journal of Social Behaviour and Personality. 10:547–570.

Graber J. A., Brooks-Gunn, J., and Galen, B. R. (1998). Betwixt and between: Sexuality in the context of adolescent transitions. In Jessor, R. (Ed.), New perspectives on adolescent risk behaviour (pp. 270-316). New York: Cambridge University Press.

Harms G, Corea A, Iyambo S, Radebe F, Fehler H, Ballard R.(1998). Perceptions and patterns of reproductive tract infections in a young rural population in Namibia. 2nd European Congress on Tropical Medicine. Liverpool, UK.

Isen, A.M.(2002) Missing in action in the AIM: positive affect's facilitation of cognitive flexibility, innovation, and problem solving. Psychological Inquiry,13 :57 65.

Jemmott, J.B. III and Jemmott, L.S. (2000). HIV behavioural interventions for adolescents in community settings. In J.L. Peterson and DiClemente (Eds.) Handbook of HIV prevention (pp.103-128). New York: Plenum Press.

Jessor, R., Turbin, M. S., and Costa, F. M. (1998). Protective factors in adolescent health behaviour. Journal of Personality and Social Psychology, 75(3), 788-800.

Kirby, D. (2000). School based interventions to prevent unprotected sex and HIV among adolescents. In R.J. DiClemente and J.L. Peterson (Eds.) Handbook of HIV prevention (pp 83-102). New York: Plenum Press.

Kulkarni, S . (2003).Thc rcproductive health status of married adolescents as assessed by IIPS, ORC MACRO, India.

Lown, E.A., Winkler, K., Fullilove, R.E., and Fullilove, m.T. (1995). Tossin' and tweakin': Women's consciousness in the crack culture. In A. Aauire (ed.) Women and AIDS: Psychological perspectives (pp. 90-106). Thousand Oaks, CA: Sage.

Marie;Aude Boislard, P., Poulin, F., Keisner, J., Dishion, T.J.(2009). A longitudinal examination of risky behaviours among Canadian and Italian adolescents: Considering individual, family and friend characteristics. International Journal of Behavioural Development, Vol. 33, No. 3, 265-276.

McManus, Alexandra and Dhar, Lipi (2008). Study of knowledge, perception and attitude of adolescent girls towards STIs/HIV, safer sex and sex education: (A cross sectional survey of urban adolescent school girls in South Delhi, India), BMC Women's Health. 2008; 8: 12.

Mehta, S., Groenen, R. and Francisco, R. (1998). Adolescents in changing times: issues and perspectives for adolescent reproductive health in the escape region.

Metzler, C.W., Noell, J., Biglan, A., Ary, D., and Smolkowski, K. (1994). The social context for risky behaviour among adolescents, Journal of Behaviour Medicine, Vol. 17, No. 4, 419-38.

NACO (2002). National Baseline High Risk and bridge population Behavioural Surveillance Survey.

NACO. Monthly Updates on AIDS. 2005.

National Population Policy (2000). Department of Health and Family Welfare, Ministry of Health and Family Welfare, Government of India.

Newmann, S., Sarin, P., Kumaraswamy, N., Amalraj, E., Rogers, M., Madhivanan, P. et. al. (2004). Marriage, monogamy and HIV: A profile of HIV infected women in South India. International Journal of STD/AIDS, 11, 20-3.

Patel, P., Capoor, I., Joshi.U. Barge, S., and Uttekar, V. (2000).Knowledge, Awareness, Beliefs and Practice on sexuality and Reproductive Health of adolescents, in slums of Ahmedabad, Gujarat, India.

Rassijo, E.B., Mirembe, F.M. and Darj, E. (2006). Vulnerability and risk factors for sexually transmitted infections and HIV among adolescents in Kampala Uganda. AIDS Care, Vol. 18, No. 7, 710-716.

Rosenstock, I.M., Strecher, V.J. and Becker, M.H. (1988). Health Belief Model, Health Education Quarterly, Summer; 15(2):175-83.

Sanches, K. and Selig, L. (2004). Adolescents vulnerability to STI/HIV/AIDS. International conference on AIDS, Jul 11-16. Federal University of Rio de Janerio, Brazil.

Singh, S.K., Lhungdim, H., Chattopadhya, A and Roy, T.K.(2005). Women's vulnerability to STI/HIV in India: Findings of the CHARCA Baseline Survey. International Institute for Population Sciences, Deonar, Mumbai.

Singh, M. et al. (1998). A study of adolescent learners' knowledge, attitude, and behaviour regarding gender equality, small family norms, reproductive health, and reproductive rights. Lucknow: State Resource Centre, U.P. – Literacy House, p. 97..

Sirur, Rajni R. (2000). Reproductive and Sexual Health Education for Adolescents: Need Assessment. New Delhi: Discovery Publishing House.

Small, S.A. and Luster, T. (1994) Adolescents sexual activity: An ecological, risk factor approach. Journal of Marriage and the Family, 56, 181-192.

St. Lawrance, J.S., Crosby, R.A., O'Bannon III, R O. (1999b). Adolescents risk for HIV infection: Comparison of four high risk samples. Journal of HIV/AIDS Prevention and Education for Adolescents and Children, 3(3), 63-86.

Thapa, S., Davey J, and Waszak C. (2000). Reproductive Health Needs of Adolescents and Youth in Nepal: Results from a Focus Group Study. Kathmandu, Family Health International.

Troop, P. and Green, S. (1997). The Health of the Nation four years on: What have we done, what must we do? British Journal of Hospital Medicine, 57, 81-2.

UNFPA. (2004). Sexually Transmitted Infections: Breaking The Cycle of Transmission. New York: United Nations Population Fund.

United Nations- 1996, World Population Monitoring : Selected Aspects of Reproductive Rights and Reproductive Health (United Nations publication, Sales No. E.97.XIII.5).

UNFPA (1999) Valley Research Group. Reproductive health awareness, attitudes and behaviour of adolescents in Nepal. Kathmandu:. 110 p.

WHO (2002). AIDS Epidemic update. http://www.who.int/hiv/an/

Wills, T.A., Sandy, J.M., Shinar, O., Yaeger, A. (1999). Contributions of positive and negative affect to adolescent substance use: Test of bi-dimensional model; in a longitudinal study. *Psychology of Addictive Behaviour,* 13, 327-338.

Wingood, G.M. and DiClmente, R.J. (1998b). Partner influences and gender- related factors associated with non-common use among young adult African American women. American Journal of Community Psychology, 26 (1), 29-51.

Verma, R.K.and Lhungalim, H. (2004). Sexuality and sexual behaviour in rural India: Evidence from a five state study. In Sexuality in the times of AIDS: Contemporary perspectives from communities in India (pp156-76). New Delhi: Sage Publications.

Weden, M.M., and Zabin, L. S. (2005). Gender and ethnic differences in the co–occurrence of adolescent risk behaviours. Ethnicity and Health, 10(3), 213-234.

Weinstein, N.D. (1998). Accuracy of smokers' risk perceptions. Annals of Behavioural Medicine, 20, 135-140.

Weinstein, N.D. and Klein, W.M. (1995). Resistance of personal risk perceptions to debasing interventions. Health Psychology, 14, 132-140.

Whitt, J.K.(1995) Current research on children's and adolescents' HIV/AIDS-related knowledge, attitudes, and behaviour. Journal of Paediatric Psychology. 20:37–40. doi: 10.1093/jpepsy/20.1.37.

Wingood, G.M. and DiClemente, R.J. (1996). HIV sexual risk reduction interventions for women: a review. American Journal of Prevention Medicine, 12, 209-217.

23

Type-A Behaviour, Emotional State and Sleep Pattern of Diabetics

Smita Jaiswal

Introduction

Diabetes is a chronic disorder of the endocrine system in which the body is not able to manufacture or properly utilize insulin. Insulin is the hormone secreted by the pancreas that controls the movement of glucose into cells and glucose metabolism. When there is an insulin dysfunction, there is an excess of glucose in the blood, and this is discharged into urine. This is how diabetics acquired its name: diabetes mellitus, the scientific name, literally "honey passing through", referring to the high sugar content of the urine. It is most common chronic illness in this country and one of the leading causes of death.

Control of diabetes is important. It is very essential to keep blood sugar under strict control. Diabetes if not controlled properly, can over the long-term lead to a number of physiological as well as psychological complications.

Diabetes and Depression

The rate of depression is much higher among diabetics than in the general population. Diabetics with major depression have a very high rate of recurrent depression episodes within the following five years. A depressed person may not have the energy or motivation to maintain good diabetic management. Depression is frequently associated with unhealthy appetite changes.

Recent studies on western sample have suggested that effective treatment of depression can improve diabetic control. In a study by Lustaman and colleagues (1997), glucose levels were shown to improve as depression lifted.

Research indicates that people with diabetes are twice as likely to experience depression as those without diabetes. Approximately 15-20 percent of adults with diabetes suffer from depression. Women with diabetes suffer more from depression than men with diabetes.

The changes of becoming depressed increase as diabetes complications worsen. A person with depression is less likely to follow medication or healthy eating plans.

The reasons for the increased risk of depression for people with diabetes are not yet fully understood. Possible explanations include the daily demands of diabetes self-care, the stress of dealing with diabetes complications, and the perhaps the physical effects associated with the disease, such as chemical and blood-flow changes in the brain.

Depression can have major implications for diabetes including:

- Increased blood glucose levels, and therefore higher risks of long-term complications.
- Reduced social activity and quality of life.
- Decreased physical activity and increased likelihood of obesity.
- Greater likelihood of smoking or alcohol abuse.

Diabetes and Stress

Being diagnosed with diabetes is a major life stress (Lustman, P.J. Griffith, L.S. Freedland, K.E. and Clouse, R.E., 1997). It requires a large number of physical and mental accommodations. The individual must learn about a complex system of dietary and medical interventions. Life style, work and social schedules may have to be altered. This can consume a lot of energy for both the individual and his or her family. Just as important, are the psychological adjustments. One must adjust to a new view of oneself. For those who liked to see themselves as invincible, this may be particularly difficult.

Each person has a somewhat different response to stress. When one experience stress body tends to respond as if were under attack. This can be regardless of whether stress is physical or psychological. The body responds to stress by preparing itself to take action. This is called the "fight-or-flight" response. In the fight-or-flight response, the levels of many hormones rise. These hormones include adrenaline, growth hormone and glucocorticosterorides.

Diabetes and Anxiety

Anxiety and stress can also cause large jumps in blood glucose levels. Panic attacks may resemble hypoglycemic episodes and vice versa. People respond differently to stressful situations. Given the same subjective level of stress, one diabetic may have a different glucose response from another. Because of this, one should monitor blood glucose more frequently during periods of stress. One the positive side, a conscientious diabetic may have unique barometer of stress unavailable to the general population.

Adults with diabetes are considerable more likely to experience, anxiety and other disorders that cause serious psychological distress than those without diabetes.

In Indian context only a few studies have been found. Mishra A., Mishra S., Srivastava A.K. (2005) compared the diabetics and non diabetics on life events and found that non-diabetics differed significantly on 17 stressful life events out 51 stressful life events. Mona and Gupta (2001) have supported that type A-behaviour pattern plays an important sole in causing diabetes. Diabetic were found more aggressive.

Diabetes and Sleep Pattern

Sleep deprivation in healthy man has been experimentally found to result in disturbance in glucose metabolism ands in sympathovagal imbalance. Research on sleep pattern has resolved significant relationship between quality of sleep and physical and mental health. In precious studies Ataharin, Terttu (1983), Kates, Joyce and others (1984), Kronhalm and Hyyppa (1985), Reynolds, Charles (1986), Kerkhofs, Myraim (1988) and man, David, Silve and others (1990) have found that high depression and anxiety determine the pattern of sleep. Studies on diabetic persons have shown high incidence of sleep disturbance. Nilson et. Al. (2004) have suggested that sleep disturbance is associated with an increased risk of diabetes 9.3 percent diabetes reported either difficulties in falling asleep or regular use of hypnotics and 2.4 percent subjects reported both of these. L. Mallon, J-E Brown and J. Helta (2005) have reported high incidence of diabetes in men with sleep complaints or short sleep duration.

Related literature has also revealed that too much or too little sleep raises the diabetics risk. According to diabetes care (March 2006) a longitudinal study of 15 years on more than 1000 men found that those getting less than six or more than eight hours of sleep at night had a significant increased diabetes risk. The risk was roughly twice as high for those sleeping relatively shorter periods, and more than three times as high for those who slept for longer periods. Those who slept for seven to eight hours a night were at the least risk. Knulson K.L., Ryden A. M., Mander B.A. and Cauter E.V. (2006) have reported a positively significant relationship between role of sleep duration on quality in the risk and severity of type two diabetes mellitus. Speegal K., Knutson K., Leproult R., Tasali E. and Cauter E.V. (2005) have reported sleep loss a novel risk factor for insulin resistance and type-2 diabetes.

Diabetes and Type A Personality

Personality Type is associated with development of illness. The person identified as Type-A personality typically a pattern of behaviour, which includes easily aroused hostility, excessive competitiveness, and a pronounced sense of time urgency. Type A Personality typically displays hyperactive to stressful situations. By contrast, the less driven type-B personality does not display the hostility, competitiveness and time urgency of the type-A personality. In various studies it has been found that type-II (no-insulin dependent) diabetics appear too sensitive to the effects of type-A behaviour (Lazarus, 1974; Cohen et. al. 1979; Goldband et. al. 1979)

Studies indicate that type-A diabetics experiencing high level of stress show poorer blood glucose control that type-B diabetics under control (Halford et. al., 1990). This may occur because type-A individuals react more strongly to threats to personal control, which elicits active and often stressful efforts to cope, hereby elevating sympathetic nervous system activity and, correspondingly, glucose levels (Rhodewalt and Macraft, 1988)

A high positive correlation was found between psychological coronary risk factors (type-A behaviour, exhaustion and depression) and serum insulin, and c-peptide and blood glucose concentrations (Raikkonen et. al. 1994).

Karlberg (1998) evaluates the effects of an intervention on hostility and time pressure in primary health care patients. Results revealed that the intervention group changed global type A behaviour, hostility and time pressure significantly more than the control group.

Objectives

- To compare the type AB behaviour pattern of diabetics and non-diabetics.
- To compare the mood and emotional states of diabetics and non-diabetics.
- To compare the sleep pattern of diabetics and non-diabetics.

Hypothesis

- There is no significant difference in type A behaviour pattern of diabetics and non-diabetics.
- There is no significant difference in mood and emotional status of diabetics and non-diabetics.
- There is no significant difference in the sleep pattern of diabetics and non-diabetics.

Methods and Procedures

1. Population: The present study was conducted on Diabetic and Non-diabetic Patients of Distt. Jalaun (U.P.).
2. Sample: The total sample of the study consisted of 82 subjects 41 diabetic and 41 non-diabetic males from the age group of 40 to 55 years. Both the groups

were matched in terms of age, sex, education level, marital status and duration. Patients, suffering from any other serious mental or somatic disorder sere excluded from sample. All the subjects were clinically tested.

3. Design: Ex-post facto research design was used to test the hypothesis.
4. Tools:

- A B B P S (A B behaviour pattern scale) developed by Upindher Dhar and Manisha Jain.
- 8 S Q (Eight state questionnaire) developed by Sh. Malay Kapoor and Dr. Mahesh Bhargava. Description of the States measured by the 8 S Q are, Anxiety, Stress, Depression, Regression, Fatigue, Guilt, Extraversion, and Arousal.
- Sleep Pattern Scale (developed by Dhamija S.C. (1994) was administered.

5. Statistical Analysis - Results were statistically analyzed by t-test.

Data Analysis and Discussion

The result obtained are presented in following tables:

Table 23.1: Mean, Standard Deviation and t-value of Diabetics and Non-diabetics on Type-A Behaviour

Sample	N	Mean	S.D.	t
Diabetic Patients	41	59.38	8.83	2.23
Non-Diabetic Patients	41	55.22	7.01	< .05

Table 23.1 reveals that the mean type-A behaviours scores (M=59.38) of diabetic patients are higher than mean type-A behaviour scores (M=55.22) of non-diabetic patients. The t value (2.23) is statistically significant at .05 level. The results are showing that Diabetics are having tendency towards type-A behaviour. There is a clear difference in the personality of Diabetics and Non-diabetics. Diabetics have much more impatience, aggressiveness, and a sense of time urgency and desire to achieve recognition and advancement, a hyper awareness of time, they walk, eat and perform most activities rapidly and perfectly than Non-diabetic. Similar findings have been reported by Mona P. K. and Gupta B. (2001).

Studies indicate that type-A diabetics experience high level of stress show poorer blood glucose control that type-B diabetic under control (Halford et al. 1990). This may occur because type-A individuals react more strongly to threats to personal control, which elicits active and often stressful efforts to cope, there by elevating sympathetic nervous system activity and correspondingly, glucose level (Rhodewalt and Macraft, 1988).

Table 23.2: Mean Standard Deviation and T-Value of Diabetics and Non-diabetics on 8 S Q

8 S Q Factor	Diabetic (N=41)		Non-Diabetic (N=41)		t value
	Mean	S. D.	Mean	S. D.	
Anxiety	20.26	4.51	15.73	4.97	4.33**
Stress	20.76	4.18	15.85	4.69	5.00**
Depression	18.82	2.95	15.78	3.92	3.97**
Regression	19.38	3.20	16.73	3.54	3.56**
Fatigue	18.94	4.88	15.07	5.12	3.50**
Guilt	18.44	4.86	16.20	4.41	2.19*
Fatigue	21.56	3.73	17.51	3.81	8.86**
Extraversion	22.32	2.93	17.22	3.49	4.17**

d. f. 80 □ .01** level 2.64
□ 0.5* level 1.99

Table 23.2 reveals that mean anxiety score of diabetics (M=20.26) is higher that non-diabetics (M=15.73). The t value (4.33) is statistically significant at .01 level. This finding shows that diabetics have more anxious emotional state than non-diabetics.

Recent studies on diabetics have reported that anxiety is associated with decreased functioning and quality of life. Generalized anxiety disorder was present in 14 percent and elevated symptoms of anxiety is 40 percent of patients with diabetics (Grigspy A. B. et al. 2002).

Table 23.2 also reveals that mean stress scores of diabetics (M=20.76) are higher than mean stress score of non-diabetics (M=15.85) the t value (5.00) is statistically significant at .01 level. The finding shows that diabetics feel more stressful than non-diabetics.

People while fighting with life stresses need higher glucose level (energy) to cope. In return secretion of high insulin increases the glucose level. Being diagnosed with diabetes is a major life stress. It requires a large number of physical and mental accommodations. The individual must learn about a complex system of dietary and medical interventions. This can consume a lot of energy for both the individual and his or her psychobiological adjustments. One must adjust to a new view of oneself for those who liked to see themselves as invincible, this may be particularly difficult. (Carol E.W., 2006). Another explanation of present finding may be that diabetic's have low stress tolerance and get pursued easily.

That is why they have reported more stress is compression to non-diabetics. Probably a pre and post study on diabetes may provide better explanation.

Table 23.2 reveals that mean depression score (M= 18.82) of diabetics is higher the non-diabetics (M=15.78). The t value (3.97) is statistically significant at .01 level. The result shows that diabetics feel more depression than non-diabetics. Review of literature reports similar findings of depression. In diabetics it is much higher than in general population (Carol E. W. 2006) Diabetics with major depression have a very high rate of fallowing five years (Lustman et. al. 1977). Recent studies have suggested that effective treatment of depression can improve diabetic control. In a study by Lustman and colleagues, glucose levels were shown to improve as depression lifted (Lustman 1977).

Table 23.2 reveals that mean regression score (M=19.38) of diabetics is higher than mean regression score of (M=16.73) of non-diabetics. The t value (3.56) is statistically significant at .01 level. This shows that diabetics are more confused, unorganized, have poor concentration and difficulty in coping they also have great suggestibility.

Table 23.2 reveals that mean fatigue score (M=18.94) of diabetics is higher than mean fatigue score (M=15.07) of non-diabetics. The t value (3.60) is significant at .01 level. This finding shows that diabetics get tired easily, they are easily exhausted and need rest.

Table 23.2 reveals that mean guilt score (M=18.44) of diabetics is higher than mean guilt score (M=16.20) of non-diabetics. The t value (2.19) is statistically significant at .05 level. This finding shows that diabetic patient feel more guilt in them self. They are regretful and concerned about own misdeeds and they are also dissatisfied with self.

Table 23.2 reveals that mean extraversion score (M=21.56)of diabetics is higher than mean extraversion score (M=17.61) of non-diabetics. the t-value (4.17) is statistically significant at .01 level. This finding shows that diabetic patients are more sociable outgoing adventure some and enthusiastic in comparison to non-diabetics.

Table 23.2 reveals that mean arousal score (M=22.32) of diabetics is higher than mean arousal score (M=17.22) of non-diabetics. The t-value (7.77) is statistically significant at .01 level. This finding shows that diabetic patients are easily aroused, excited and stimulated easily.

Table 23.3 reveals that mean score of sleep pattern of diabetic (M=7.9) is higher than mean score of non-diabetic (M=6.80). The t-value (1.92), is not statistically significant. However on the basis of mean scores it can be observed than diabetics have more problems in falling asleep, and feel disturbance in sleep at night. A large sample will be needed to confirm the present findings.

Table 23.3: Mean Standard Deviation and T-Value of Diabetics and Non-diabetics on Sleep Pattern

Sample	N	Mean	S.D.	t
Diabetic Patients	41	7.91	2.54	1.92
Non-Diabetic Patients	41	6.80	2.41	> .05

Sleep deprivation in healthy man has been experimentally found to result in disturbance in glucose metabolism and in sympathovagal imbalance. Research on sleep pattern has resolved significant relationship between quality of sleep and physical and mental health.

Related literature has also revealed that too much or too little sleep raises the diabetics risk according to diabetes care (March 2006) a longitudinal study of 15 years on more than 1000 men found that those getting less than six or more than eight hours of sleep a night had a significant increased diabetes risk. The risk was roughly truce as high for those sleeping relatively shorter periods, and more than three times as high for those who slept for longer periods. Those who slept for seven to eight hours a night were at the least risk.

On the basis of above mentioned findings it may be concluded the diabetes significantly effects the person's mental condition also. While treating diabetes physician should also pay attention to the patient's mental condition. Programmes on self managements skills can also provide good results.

References

Carol E. Watkins; (2006) Diabetes, Depression and Stress, Northan County Psychiatric Associates.

Dhamija S.C. and Sapna Kashyap; (1994) Effect of depression and anxiety on sleep pattern; *Ecological Perspective and Behaviour*, 146-148.

Faludi and Gabor, (1982). ABO blood groups and the Therapeutic response of Schizophrenics to antidepressants Medicate 14(6), 889-892.

Fraindis and Lambert (1980). Handbook of Cross-cultural Psychology Perspective Vol. I pp. 149-155.

Goldband, S.; Katkin, E. and Morrel, M. (1979). Stress and Anxiety, 6, 351-370.

Halford, W.K.; Cuddihy, S. Mortimer, R.H. (1990) Psychological stress and blood glucose regulation in type-I diabetic patients, *Health Psychology*, 9: 516-528.

Jogawar, V.V. (1984). Personality correlates of human blood groups. *Indian Journal of Clinical Psychology,* 11(2), 5-8.

Karlberg, L.: Krakau, I. And Und, E.A. (1998). Type A behaviour intervention in primary health care reduces hostility and time pressure: a study in Swedan. Soc. Sci. Med. 46(3): 397-402.

K.L. Knutson, A.M. Ryden, B.A. Mander and E. Van Cauter. September 18 (2006); Role of sleep duration and quality in the risk and severity of type 2 diabetes mellitus. Archives of internet medicine, 166(16): 1768-1774.

K. Spiegal, K Knutson, R. Leproult, E. Tasali and E.V. Cauter. (Nov. 2005) Sleep Loss: A novel and type-2 diabetes. *Journal of Applied Physiology*, 99(5) 2008-2019.

Lazarus, R.S. (1974). Int. J. Psychiatry Med. 5, 321-333.

Lustman, P.J. Griffith L S, Clouse, R E et al. (1997); Effect of Nor-tryptiline on depression and glycemic controlling diabetes: results of a double blind, Placebo controlled trail. Psychosomatic Medicine, 59(3) 241-250.

Lustman, P.J. Griffit, L.S. Freedland, K E Clouse R E; (1997). The course of major depression in diabetics. Gen Hosp Psychiatry 19(2), 138-143.

Mallon L., Bromab J.E., Helth J. High incidence of Diabetes in men with sleep complaints in men with sleep complaints or short sleep duration : A-12 year follow-up study of a middle aged population diabetes care, no. 2005-28(1) 27622767.

Manosevix, M. Lindzey, G. Thirrach D.D. (1969). Behavioural Genetics, Methods and research, pp. 649-655.

Mishra A., Mishra S. Srivastava A.K.26-28 Fev.(2005),A comparative study between diabetics and non-diabetics on various life events. International Conference on Applied and Community. Psychology Trends and Directions Hardware.

Montejo, L. Feradez, A. Lajusentse, R. (1985). ABO blood groups and unipolar affective disorder. 12(7), 395-400.

Nilson P.M., Mattias R., Gunnar E.; Bo Hedblad B.; Goran B. Diabetes care 2004, 27: 2464-2469.

Owen, Dawn M.; Hastings, Richard P. (2004) Life events as correlates of problem behaviour and mental health is a residential population of adults with developmental disabilities. Research in developmental disabilities, (Jul-Aug), Vol 25(4), 309-320.

P.K. Mona Gupta B (2001); A study of personality type among diabetics, Prachi journal of Psycho-cultural dimensions, Vol. 17 No. 1 23-26.

Panday, Janak (1988) Organizational Behaviour and Mental Health Vol. III. Sage Publications. New Delhi.

Rinieris, P., Rabavilas,: Lykouras, E. Stefanis, C. (1983). Neurosess and ABO blood groups types. Neuropsychobiology 9(1), 16-18.

Rhodewalt, F. and Marcraft; M. (1988). Type A behaviour and diabetic control: Implications of psychological reactance for health outcomes. *Journal of Applied Social Psychology* 18(2): 139-159.

Singh, A.K. and Thapa, K. (1989) Type A behaviour pattern and Coronary heart diseases. *Indian Journal of Clinical Psychology*, 16, 9-12.

Singh R.N. and Sharma Rachna (2002), Advanced Applied Psychology, Atlantic Publishers and Distributors, New Delhi, p.. 351-357.

Singh, V.P. (2002) A study of personality of drugger's relation to their value and mental health. 21-32.

Srivastava, J.P. and Sinha, S.P. (1989) Stressful life events and Health. Indian Journal of Clinical Psychology, 16, 26-28.

24

Effects of Examination Stress on Adolescents' Health

Kailash Chandra Barmola and S.K. Srivastava

Introduction

We may think of stressful events as unpleasant ones, such as losing a job or having difficulties at home or at school. But changes for the better can also cause stress, like a new baby, a wedding, and a new house. In an ideal world, maybe we could get away from stressful situations, or change them. Examinations and interviews are undoubtedly situation, which call for stress. Every child goes through such situations and learns to cope up with stress arising out of them. They are also learnt by imitation of the parents or parent figures. Appearing for examination is one of very common situation, which an adolescent finds difficult of cope up with. Right approach and right coping strategies may stimulate an adolescent to over come anxiety and maximize own performance in the examination.

Stress is the specific and non-specific response of the body to any kind of physiological pressure or unwanted forces due to environmental or peripheral effects. Stress acts in different axes including hypothalamus-pituitary–adrenal (HPA) axis, hypothalamus–pituitary–gonads (HPG) axis, and hypothalamus–pituitary–thyroid (HPT) axis. In addition, there are autonomic responses by sympathetic nerve system to the stressful condition i.e. the activation of sympathetic nerve system and the activation of the above axes especially HPA occur, simultaneously. Many kinds of different stress need the responses of endocrine glands, for example responses to the stress of temperature, hypoglycemia, surgery, pain, occupations, or decreasing energy, are mediated by different endocrine glands. Individual differences in cardiovascular and neuroendocrine responses to stress are cardiovascular complication (hypertension and increasing heart beat), gastric ulcer, migraine headache, and asthma. Among neuroendocrine stress reactions the releasing of catecholamine, adrenaline and nor adrenaline play a key role in human adjustment to environmental demands, for example, augmentation of the peripheral catecholamine level is accompanied by a series of changes in cardiovascular and metabolic function which facilitate adaptation to a wide range of stimulus conditions.

Human studies suggest that cardiovascular responses to stress are sex-dependent and in females differ during the menstrual cycle. Women usually have lower blood pressure and adrenaline in responses to stress than do men, suggesting that determinants of women's stress responses may differ from men's responses. It has been shown that pre menopausal and postmenopausal women differed in physiological responses to behavioural stressor.

Most of the studies in different responses to stress carried out in middle age men and women, and there were not many reports that investigated the effects of stress on the young university students. The examination stress was accounted as an acute physiologic stress in some subjects. Examinations are anecdotally viewed as extremely stressful to Singapore school children. Patients with acne may experience worsening of the disease during examinations. A study in Netherlands on PhD students showed that although the blood pressure did not change significantly by the examination stress, but peripheral benzodiazepine receptor density, allopregnanolon, and cortisol concentration were significantly increased during examination.

Stress among Various Age Groups

Stress is not only for people occupied with work but it is among all age groups:

Stress in Children: Recent researches show that persons who had experienced traumatic events during childhood are more susceptible to stress during adulthood and some of the experiences are the reminiscence of the childhood trauma. Some of the events which act as trigger for stress in children are Loss of parents. Ill treatment by step parents Physical abuse - 'The Battered baby' Sexual abuse, Sibling rivalry, Inability to adjust with friends and peers Educational stress, Bullying at the school. If adequate support is given to the affected child, chances of recovery are good. If not, the child becomes more susceptible to further stress during rest of life.

Stress in Teens: The teen age or the adolescence is the link between the childhood and adulthood. The person gets released from the clutches of parents and become independent. Hormonal changes resulting in puberty occurs, Attraction towards opposite sex starts, Aggressiveness is more, Friendship develops, Get more chances for experimenting different things including substance of abuse. Stress in teens could be due to Pubertal Changes, Changing relationship with peers, New demands in the school, Safety issues in their neighbourhood, Responsibilities to their families, Negative thoughts and feelings, Separation or divorce of parents, Death of a loved one, Chronic illnesses,

Changing schools, Financial problems.

Stress in Adults: Adults are exposed everyday to different persons, stimulus and situations. Some of these can prove to be hostile resulting in stress. Moreover if the person has had a stressful childhood the chances are still higher. The triggers could be: Misunderstanding with the spouse, Death of the spouse, children or parents, Workplace stress including bullying by colleagues, inability to perform well, Accidents and arguments with strangers in the traffic, financial insecurity, and job insecurity. The age group may be different. The stress factor may not be similar. But the effects of stress are the same. Due to the effects of stress on the body, the physical and the mental health get affected and the affected person finds difficult to lead a normal life.

Adolescents' Stress

It can cause adverse effect in future. Stress can affect anyone from children to adolescents to adults. The causes of teen stress are totally different and they need somewhat different stress management. Teen stress is similar to the adult stress in terms of the signs and symptoms. But the causes of teen stress are totally different and they need somewhat different stress management programs for dealing stress. It is estimated that teens form 20 percent of the total population. Yet they are a neglected group of the population. The adolescent group is the intermediate group between the dependent childhood and the independent adulthood. This transition from childhood to adulthood is never so easy. This group is a vulnerable group to both physical and emotional stress. There are problems everywhere for them—problems at home with their parents and siblings, problems in the school with their friends and education. Adolescent medicine is a new concept in the field of medicine. The adolescents cannot be treated as either adults or kids because their problems are totally different. In this a lot of physical and emotional changes occur during this period, which are very significant in the shaping a person. There are two kinds of changes mainly.

1. **Physical Changes:** The physical changes include, Increase in the weight, Increase in the height, Change in voice, Development of secondary sexual characters, Menarche (beginning of menstruation) in girls.
2. **Mental Changes:** These are equally significant which include, Feeling of independence, Attraction towards opposite sex, Aggressive behaviour, Experimenting new things including substance of abuse.

Surveys conducted shows that one third of the teenagers suffer at least one episode of stress every week. Though stress has the same kind of response in all the age groups, the stress factors are different. Stress in teens could be due to, Pubertal Changes, Changing relationship with peers, New demands in the school,

Safety issues in their neighbourhood, Responsibilities to their families, Negative thoughts and feelings, Separation or divorce of parents, Death of a loved one, Chronic illnesses, Changing schools, Financial problems, Holiday stress. In a study conducted on the stress and related problem of teens in the city of Baltimore showed that the following figures. The Biggest Causes of Stress: School work (78 percent), Parents (78 percent), Romantic relationships (64 percent), Problems with friends (64 percent), Siblings (64 percent).

What's stressful for you may be quite different from what's stressful to your best friend, your spouse, or the person next door. For example: Some people enjoy speaking in public; others are terrified. Some people are more productive under deadline pressure; others are miserably tense. Some people are eager to help family and friends through difficult times; others find it very stressful. Some people feel comfortable complaining about bad service in a restaurant; others find it so difficult to complain that they prefer to suffer in silence. Some people may feel that changes at work represent a welcome opportunity; others worry about whether they will be able to cope. People react to stress in different ways. Once you identify your own signs of stress, they can serve as your personal early warning system. Think of yourself as a car that's equipped with lights and gauges to warn you if any problems are developing. If you keep an eye on the gauges and catch the trouble early, the problem may be easy to fix. If you ignore the warning signs, you may be in for a major repair job. You should assess yourself for four types of stress signs: Changes in body functions and physical health, Changes in emotions and feelings, Changes in behaviour, Changes in thoughts.

To understand what stress does to us, imagine you lived tens of thousands of years ago, at a time when humans were threatened by hungry animals such as sabre-toothed tigers and wolves. Our caveman ancestors had to be able to react instantly, either by fighting the beasts or running away. So humans evolved the ability to respond to a stressful situation instantly, by preparing the body for "fight or flight." Under sudden stress, you will get a burst of exceptional strength and endurance, as your body pumps out stress hormones: Your heart speeds up, Blood flow to your brain and muscles increases up to 400 percent, Your digestion stops (so it doesn't use up energy that's needed elsewhere), Your muscle tension increases, You breathe faster, to bring more oxygen to your muscles.

Sometimes we can still benefit from this "fight or flight" response - like the case of a mother whose child was pinned under a concrete slab during a tornado. Under stress, she found the strength to lift the huge slab with her bare hands, even though it later took three men to move it. But much of the time in modern life, the "fight or flight" response won't help. Yet those stress hormones still flood your system, preparing you for physical action. And if you are under stress frequently, it can harm your physical health.

Once you know how to "tune in" to your signs of stress, you will be better able to analyze the situations that are stressful to you. These "stressors," as they are called, could be either external or internal.

1. **External Stressors:** are things and events outside your body that can make you feel threatened or out of control. For example: Physical irritants like noise, pollution, heat, or humidity, Work demands or conditions, Frightening events, like narrowly escaping a traffic accident, Social or family demands, changes, or problems.
2. **Internal Stressors:** result from one's own attitudes and thinking patterns. For example: Do you always talk to yourself with words like "should, must, and ought?" Do you feel like a failure if you are late, or if things don't go as planned? Do you have "me last" syndrome, feeling you have to look after everyone else's needs before you think of your own? Do you feel worthless unless everyone likes you all the time? Are you guilty of "awful-izing," which means always expecting the worst? For example, if family members are late, do you often imagine they are injured or dead?

It has been estimated that two-thirds of all visits to physicians are for stress-related problems. Recent evidence indicates that the physical changes associated with stress may contribute to the leading causes of death - heart disease and cancer. The effects of stress include the following: Stress can cause chronic fatigue, digestive upsets, headaches, and back pain. Stress can affect the blood cells that help you fight off infection, so you are more likely to get colds and other diseases. Constant stress can increase blood pressure and can increase the risk for stroke. Stress can increase the danger of heart attacks, particularly if you are often angry and mistrustful. Stress can make an asthma attack worse. Stress triggers behaviours that contribute to death and disability, such as smoking, alcoholism, drug abuse, and overeating. Stress can lead to diminished sexual desire and an inability to achieve orgasm. Stress makes it harder to take other steps to improve health, such as giving up smoking or making changes in diet.

Now next question arises that how can we come to know that a student is under examination stress. There are many research findings which may help us to know these symptoms. These findings suggest following reactions as a symptoms of examination stress:

1. **Common Physical Reaction During Exam Preparations:** Muscular tension, indigestion, sleeping difficulties, repaid, uneven or pounding heartbeat, frequent urge to pass urine, fast/shallow breathing, chest discomfort, change in appetite, constipation or diarrhoea, backache etc.
2. **Psychological Reaction to Stress:** Feeling under pressure, frustration and

aggression, feeling tense and unable to relax, feeling mentally drained out, fussy, gloomy or suspicious being constantly frightened or irritable, inability to concentrate or complete the task.

Stress Management

The teen stress should be dealt with both at home and outside home in school. There is a wrong notion among adults that there is no earthly reason for stress in teens. This should be avoided. The first step in tackling teen stress is to identify the signs and symptoms of stress in the teens. The teens should be allowed to talk freely about their problems. Parents and teachers should teach them stress relief methods. They should set only reasonable goals in both curricular and extra curricular activities. There are several treatment models to help the teens cope up with stress. The steps of one such model—Ask the teenager to define stress taking an example of an incident. Ask the teens about their response to that stressful event. Explain to the teens about normal stress response and ways of tackling stress. Identify the source of stress in teens and help them understand that the same event incites different responses in different persons. Teach the teen the best stress relieving techniques. Advise them to avoid unhealthy methods of tackling stress like aggression, avoidance etc.

Examinations and interviews are undoubtedly situation, which call for stress. Every child goes through such situations and learns to cope up with stress arising out of them. They are also learnt by imitation of the parents or parent figures. Appearing for examination is one of very common situation, which an adolescent finds difficult of cope up with. Right approach and right coping strategies may stimulate an adolescent to over come anxiety and maximize own performance in the examination. Stress is the body's response to any unpleasant situation. Anything can cause stress as long as it is perceived as unpleasant. However, some stressful event, such as a close contest in sport, can bring out the best in the people.

Eating Healthy: Balancing food choices over time is what counts, Breakfast provides the energy needed through an active morning, Children who skip breakfast may have trouble concentrating, Fast food supply more fat, salt and calories that good nutrition, Fast food is moderation won't ruin a healthful diet, especially when consumed with green salads, Replace finger chips with an apple, Add roughage to your diet - Dalia, Corn etc. will help prevent stomach discomfort and you will feel lighter, The golden rule for food safety is to keep hot foods hot and cold foods cold, Parents should teach good habits by example.

Good Sleep-Good Exam: Insomnia (The inability to fall or stay asleep) Can be caused by Stress and anxiety of Exam, Disturbances of 'sleep- wake' cycle during exams, If sleep struggles continue, talk them over with your doctor.

Exercise and Physical Activity: Walk or cycle 15 minutes a day at least thrice a week, Avoid sitting cross-legged on the ground because this is bad for your knees, Avoid being a couch potato, Cut out junk food and control your weight, Swim or play a sport at least twice a week.

Mind Games to Play and Think about: Develop systematic problem - solving skills. How do you do that ?, Identify the stressful situation, Define it as an objective, a problem that can be solved, Brainstorm solutions - think of all the possible options but don't evaluate them. Anticipate the possible outcomes of each solution. Choose a solution and act on it.

The Must Do's for Students: Know your concentration span, Study with breaks, Work out best time for concentration, Group study for difficult subjects, Do Not let pervious results discourage you-identify your weak areas from previous exams and work on them, Time Management plan must be made for all subjects, Choose a study place with minimum distractions and auto suggest to your self about your resolution, Try to coincide study time with the time, you would be giving an exam, In case of average achievers, master what you know and are comfortable with, for low achievers, master the essential information first, Prioritize the workload. Give your best concentration time to the toughest subject, Repeat your learnt work so the recall in exam is easy. Work not repeated or revised is easily forgotten; try to plan your revision time by drawing up a timetable. Build in time for the things you enjoy—like watching your favourite TV programme, going out with your friends, or going to play football in the park, Give yourself a few treats - pamper yourself with a long hot bath, or listen to your favourite CD for an hour after you have finished your revision, Relax with what you know before entering the exam hall, Do not get anxious about the result—cross that bridge when you come to it—options await.

Active-Study Strategies: when studying you can Recite You could, Describe or explain aloud any topic in your own words, Teach or explain the information to someone else (or record into a tape recorder) or, Engage in simulation or role play. When studying, you can write you could, Make a chapter study Review Card (Use an index card, include special vocabulary, main ideas, examples, key events and people, causes, result and so on), Make and use a set of flashcards (vocabulary and definition, math problems and solutions, questions and answers and so on), Make list of related information by categories (causes results, important event or concepts, main ideas examples, key people and so on and recite them, Draw a diagram, map a sketch, or a chart; do this from memory and check your notes or books for accuracy, Write questions you think will be on the test and recite the answers, Create a mnemonic to remember, information (such as please excuse my dear aunt sally, used for order of operations in solving an equation - parenthesis - exponent - multiply - divide - add - subtract) Graphic Organizers: Graphic organizers and semantic maps (word maps) which offer a visual representation of ideas. When students organize and design these maps, they apply important analytical skills as they think about how ideas are interrelated. Abstract information is put into concrete and visual form which can be pictured in one's mind and more readily retrieved later. When studying, you can visualize you could-Your eyes and "picture in your mind" any chart, diagram, word, map event, time period, scene, experiment or character (from a story) that you are trying to remember.

The Must DO's for Parents: Student can fail to do well if they fail to cope with stress. Parents should guide their children in planning, organizing and setting a time-table. To Avoid a Stress situation for the child the parents must provide right kind of motivation and a conducive environment. Help the child to develop self - discipline, self-direction, self - confidence and a sense of achievement. Just good schooling and tuition are not substitutes for emotional cushioning. Help the child in maintaining his confidence especially when he seems discouraged by his dropping marks or grades. Do not displace your anxiety on the child. The achievement goals should be realistically set according to the child's capability. Do not mix academic issues with family conflicts. Praise your child when he does well. Encourage child's performance with positive statements like, "well done" "you can do better" rather than saying "that was not enough". Work out our child's schedule with him instead of nagging him. There could be learning problems. Do not harp on previous failures or results. Under achievement may be due to some children believing it is safer not to try than to try and fail. If achievement expectations are high then some children would prefer to be criticized for being lazy than being considered not good enough. Humour relieves tension so be light and humorous with the child. Try to gain your child's confidence and discuss his problems with him, help him to find a solution. Exams are not the end of the world. Accept that expectation for everyone to do well is unrealistic as many won't pursue this for long.

Key Messages

The 5 "A's" for Controlling the Exam Stress: Acknowledging, Appreciating, Alleviating, Altering and Avoiding.

1. **Acknowledge:** the stress and strain because every one faces it. In everyday life, stress manifests as mental or physical tension, which you would rather not have, recognize stress as inevitable.
2. **Appreciating:** What causes your stress? Then, instead of blaming yourself or

failing of cope; you end up pinpointing the real problem and tackling that.

3. **Alleviating:** the pressures is all about resorting to simple stress-busting techniques. Perhaps you have a calming visual to look at when you need a mental escape from your surrounding. Or you may relax your muscle before you go to sleep.
4. **Altering:** your lifestyle is the next step towards Exam Stress. Once you've seen the benefits of relaxation, it will encourage you to develop more permanent ways of reducing stress. If stress continues to be persistent, either you haven't tried the major stress alleviating formulae or alternately your haven't kept them up long enough to deliver the needed result.
5. **Avoiding**: last step is the toughest but also the most beneficial. You have to start avoiding stress building habits and burnouts. Avoid smoking - a serious stress builder exercise briefly but regularly, make an effort to maintaining a normal weight, eat regular balanced meals and get adequate sleep.

Objectives

There are following objectives.

1. To explore the effect of examinations stress on adolescents health.
2. To review the studies related to examination stress on adolescents health.
3. To estimate the effect of examination stress on adolescents health.

Current Studies on Exam Stress

Jernelov, Hoglund, Axelsson, Axen, Gronneberg, Grunewald, Stierna and Lekander (2009), have studied the effects of examination stress on psychological responses, sleep and allergic symptoms in atopic and non-atopic students: Atopic students were worse off in aspects of psychological well-being and sleep, but displayed only partly stronger responses to a stressor compared to non-atopic students. In spite of a broad negative response to examination, allergic symptoms were not affected.

Uskun, Kisioglu and Ozturk (2008), have studied the stress and its effects on depression and anxiety among undergraduates: The findings provide information regarding the stress factors in students during the years of study at university. Awareness of stress and depression existing among young people and of its causes can give adults ideas for solving such problems.

Macht, Haupt, and Ellgring (2008), have studied the academic stress, power motivation, and decrease in secretion rate of salivary secretory immunoglobulin: The s-IgA secretion rate was significantly lower in high-stress than low-stress periods for the whole group. In addition, personality characteristics differentiated patterns ofs-IgA secretion rates. Students characterised by a great need to establish and maintain warm personal relationships secreted more s-IgA at each point than did all other subjects. The s-IgA secretion rates of those with a high inhibited need for power continued to decline through the final low-stress period rather than recovering as in all other subjects.

Rafiq, Ghazal, and Farooqi (2007), have examined the test anxiety in students: Semester vs. Annual System: Results indicate no significant difference in anxiety among students studying under the two educational systems. Implications for implementation of semester system are being discussed.

Aggarwal, Prabhu, Anand, Kotwal (2007), examined the stressful life events among adolescents: The comparison showed a strong positive correlation with CBCL scores with a model fit ($r^2 = 0.32$) and a weak positive correlation with parental stress (Pearson's coefficient = 0.011) due to life events. Thus, a life event scale for adolescents was especially adapted to the Indian conditions.

Lofta, Thomasb, Petriea, Boothb, Milesc and Vedharad (2007), have examined the examination stress results in altered cardiovascular responses to acute challenge and lower cortisol: The exam group exhibited significantly higher HR reactivity following the CO2 inhalation test and slower systolic blood pressure (SBP) recovery compared with the non-exam group. The exam group also reported higher perceived stress and higher stress scores were related to higher HR reactivity following CO2 inhalation. Female students across both groups exhibited significantly lower SBP reactivity compared with male students. Salivary cortisol levels were consistently lower in the exam group. These findings indicate that ongoing natural stress alters cortisol secretion and cardiovascular responses in the face of an acute stress challenge.

Gibson, Myers, Jane (2006), studied the perceived stress, wellness, and mattering: A Profile of First-Year Citadel Cadets Journal of College Student Development Overall, wellness scores were negatively skewed. Although there were no differences in perceived stress or mattering between the citadel cadets and a comparison group of cadets at west point, the citadel cadets scored higher than available norm groups on both scales. Implications for wellness programs at military colleges and counselling for beginning cadets are explored. In addition, applicability of the results for non-military college students is discussed.

Oaten and Cheng (2005), have asserted the academic examination stress impairs self–control: Perceived stress, emotional distress, and regulatory behaviour were assessed by questionnaire. During the exam period, the exam–stress group showed impaired performance on a lab task (Stroop) following thought suppression, a form of self–regulatory activity. They also reported significant increases in perceived stress and emotional distress; they also reported an increase in smoking and caffeine consumption; a decrease in healthy eating, emotional control, frequency and duration of physical activity, maintenance of household chores and self–care habits, attendance to commitments, and monitoring of spending; and a deterioration in sleep patterns and study habits. The control group showed no systematic changes in the lab task, perceived stress, emotional distress, or regulatory behaviour across sessions. The results are discussed in relation to the effect of real-world stress in decreasing self–control strength.

Eskiocak, Gozen, Yapar, Tavas, Kilic and Eskiocak (2005), examined the Glutathione and free sulphydryl content of seminal plasma in healthy medical students during and after exam stress: This study demonstrated that glutathione and free sulphydryl levels in seminal plasma decreased in subjects undergoing examination stress. Furthermore, poor sperm quality may be due to loss of glutathione and free sulphydryl content of seminal plasma.

Wang, Fen and Chang (2005), studied stress, coping, and psychological health of vocational high school nursing students associated with a competitive entrance exam: Two-way analyses of variance (2-way ANOVA) revealed that problem-focused coping had a positive main effect of alleviating psychological distress. A significant interaction was observed between stress perceived and problem-focused coping used for psychological health. Further examination of the interaction effect showed that problem-focused coping behaviours were potentially more adaptive in relation to psychological health at the lower and moderate stress levels (25-75 percent) than that at the extreme stress level (> 75 percent). Conversely, emotion-focused coping had a negative main effect or impairing psychological health. No interaction effect was found between stress perceived and emotion-focused coping used, suggesting that the relationship between emotion-focused coping and psychological distress was consistent across various stress levels.

Koçkar and Gencoz (2004), have examined the Personality, social support, and anxiety among adolescents preparing for university entrance examinations in Turkey: The total sociotropy score and the total social support score predicted anxiety for females, whereas for males, anxiety was predicted by four variables, namely, achievement expectancy, concern over approval, social support from family, and social support from friends. Implications of these results were discussed.

Khaksari, Mahmoodi, Rezvani, Sajjadi, Karam and Hajizadeh (2004), studied the differences between male and female students in cardiovascular and endocrine responses to examination stress: These data suggest that, the responses to physiology examination stress are different between two sexes.

Shaikh, Kahloon, Kazmi, Khalid, Nawaz, Khan and Khan (2004), have asserted students, stress and coping strategies: The prevalence of perceived stress seems to be high among medical students, which tends to affect not only their academic performances but also all aspects of health. Review of academics and exam schedules, more leisure time activities, better interaction with the faculty and proper guidance, advisory services and peer counselling at the campus could do a lot to reduce the stress.

Lumley, Mark, Provenzano, Kimberly (2003), studied Stress management through written emotional disclosure improves academic performance among college students with physical symptoms: Students rated their mood before and after writing each day, and transcripts provided GPAs for the baseline and subsequent semesters. Compared with the control condition, disclosure led to significantly better GPAs the next semester. Among disclosure students, but not control students, improved mood from the first to last writing days predicted improved GPA. Writing about general life stress leads to improved academic functioning, particularly among those who become less distressed over writing days.

Chiu, Susan, Chon, Alexa, and Kimball (2003), asserted the changes in the severity of acne vulgaris as affected by examination stress: Patients with acne may experience worsening of the disease during examinations. Furthermore, changes in acne severity correlate highly with increasing stress, suggesting that emotional stress from external sources may have a significant influence on acne.

Verma, Sharma and Larson (2002), this study examines the influence of school demands on the daily time use and subjective states of Indian young people: These adolescents were found to spend one third of their waking time in school-related activities, with girls spending more time than boys. Schoolwork generated negative subjective states as reflected in low affect state, below-average activation levels, lower feeling of choice, and higher social anxiety. These negative states were most frequent during homework. The trade-off faced by Indian adolescents were evident in the findings that those who spent more time doing homework experienced lower average emotional states and more internalising problems, while those who spent more time in leisure experienced more favourable states but also reported higher academic anxiety and lower scholastic achievement.

Hong and Lewis (2002), examined antecedents of state test anxiety: Female students reported higher trait test anxiety and statistics course anxiety than did males. Math ability had a positive relationship with statistics achievement. Students with low math ability perceived statistics courses as difficult, which in turn strongly influenced their level of statistics course anxiety. Trait worry had a significant direct effect on state worry but not on state emotionality, and the same pattern occurred with trait–state emotionality. Trait worry, but not trait emotionality, was positively related to statistics course anxiety. Students reporting high statistics course anxiety perceived the final exam as difficult; however, neither statistics achievement nor state test anxiety was influenced by statistics course anxiety. Students' perception of statistics course difficulty had an impact on their perception of test difficulty, which in turn had significant direct effects on both state worry and emotionality. As expected, achievement on statistics midterm exams had a direct effect on state worry but not on state emotionality.

Lacey, Zaharia, Griffiths, Ravindran, Merali and Anisman (2000), have examined a prospective study of neuroendocrine and immune alterations associated with the stress of an oral academic examination among graduate students: Although, graduate students did not differ from controls with respect to perceived stress and feelings of mastery, they reported more frequent malaise (e.g. headaches, sore throat, fatigue) than did controls. The present findings suggest that during the course of lengthy anticipatory periods preceding a scheduled stressor, different stress-sensitive, situation-dependent biological processes may be engendered. It is further suggested that cortisol release is most closely aligned with immediate threats, while the immune alterations are sensitive to more distal events, or are subject to adaptation in response to a protracted stressor.

Folkman, Susan, Lazarus, and Richard (1985), examined a study of emotion and coping during three stages of a college examination: Results show that for Ss as a whole, there were significant changes in emotions and coping (including the use of social support) across the 3 stages. Some Ss experienced seemingly contradictory emotions and states of mind during every stage of the encounter; Ss experienced both threat emotions and challenge emotions, reflecting ambiguity regarding the multifaceted nature of the examination and its meanings (especially during the anticipatory stage). Ss used combinations of most of the available forms of problem-focused coping and emotion-focused coping at every stage. Problem-focused coping was more prominent in the anticipatory stage and distancing more prominent during the waiting stage. An analysis of selected appraisal and coping values, taking GPAs into account, explained about 48 percent of variance in threat and challenge emotions at the anticipatory stage. Including grade, 57 percent of the variance in positive emotions at outcome and 61 percent of negative emotions at outcome were explained.

Conclusions

Present study has the main objective to know the effect of examinations stress on adolescents' health. This study has adopted theoretical approach to explore the effect of examination stress. As present study states that examination stress is a psychological and physiological pressure among adolescents and discuss various psychological and physical causes of stress and also describes about psychological and physical reactions of the stress on adolescents health. This paper throws light on various coping strategy to manage examination stress. To estimate the effect of examination stress many related studies have been analysed. This paper findings states that the main effect of examination stress are lower performance in academic examinations, increases in perceived stress and emotional distress, in smoking and caffeine consumption, a decrease in healthy eating, emotional control, frequency and duration of physical activity, maintenance of household chores and self–care habits, attendance to commitments, and monitoring of spending, and a deterioration in sleep patterns and study habits, aspects of psychological well-being, biological changes like in immune system, secretion of hormones etc. Review of this paper suggests academics and exam schedules, more leisure time activities, better interaction with the faculty and proper guidance, advisory services and peer counselling at the campus could do a lot to reduce the stress.

References

Aggarwal Shilpa, Prabhu H.R.A, Anand Aalok, Kotwal Atul (2007). Stressful life events among adolescents. *Indian Journal of Psychiatry,* 49(2), 96-100.

Chiu Annie, Susan, Chon Y., and Kimball Alexa B. (2003). Changes in the severity of acne vulgaris as affected by examination stress. *Arch Dermatol,* 139, 897-900.

Eskiocak S., Gozen A.S., Yapar S.B., Tavas F., Kilic A.S. and Eskiocak M. (2005). Glutathione and free sulphydryl content of seminal plasma in healthy medical students during and after exam stress. *Human Reproduction,* 20(9), 2595-2600.

Folkman, Susan, Lazarus and Richard S. (1985). Study of emotion and coping during three stages of a college examination. *Journal of Personality and Social Psychology,* 48(1),150-170.

Gibson, Myers Donna M., Jane E. (2006). Perceived stress, wellness, and mattering: A profile of first-year citadel cadets. *Journal of College Student Development*, 47, 647-660.

Hong Eunsook and Lewis Karstensson (2002). Antecedents of state test anxiety. *Contemporary Educational Psychology,* 27(2), 348-367.

Jernelov Susanna, Hoglund Caroline Olgart, Axelsson John, Axen Jennie , Gronneberg Reidar, Grunewald Johan, Stierna Pontus and Lekander Mats (2009). Effects of examination stress on psychological responses, sleep and allergic symptoms in atopic and non-atopic students. *International Journal of Behavioural Medicine, 16(4)*, 305-310.

Koçkar Aylin Ilden and Gençoz Tulin (2004).Personality, social support, and anxiety among adolescents preparing for university entrance examinations in Turkey. *Current Psychology,* 23,138-146.

Khaksari Mohammad, Mehdi Mahmoodi, Rezvani Mohammad E., Sajjadi Mohammad A., Karam Gholamreza. Asadi, and Hajizadeh Sohrab (2004). Differences between male and female students in cardiovascular and endocrine responses to examination stress. *International*

Journal of Behavioural Development, 29(10),1341-4.

Lumley, Mark A., Provenzano, Kimberly M.(2003). Stress management through written emotional disclosure improves academic performance among college students with physical symptoms. *Journal of Educational Psychology,* 95(3), 641-649.

Lacey K., Zaharia M.D., Griffiths J., Ravindran A. V., Merali Z. and Anisman H. (2000). A prospective study of neuroendocrine and immune alterations associated with the stress of an oral academic examination among graduate students. *Psychoneuroendocrinology*, 25(4), 317-420.

Lofta Patricia, Thomasb Mark G., Petriea Keith J., Boothb Roger J., Milesc Jeremy, Vedharad Kavita (2007) Examination stress results in altered cardiovascular responses to acute challenge and lower cortisol. *Psychoneuroendocrinology*, 32, 367–375.

Macht Michael, Haupt Christine and Ellgring Heiner (2008). Academic stress, power motivation, and decrease in secretion rate of salivary secretory immunoglobulin. *The Lancet*, 321(8339), 1400-1402.

Oaten Megan and Cheng Ken (2005). Academic examination stress impairs self–control. *Journal of Social and Clinical Psychology*, 24, 254-279.

Rafia Rafiq, Ghazal Saima and Farooqi Yasmin N. (2007). Test anxiety in students: semester vs. annual system. *Journal of Behavioural Sciences,* 17, 1-2.

Sikri Arpit (2005). Exam stress: Natural feeling learn to deal with it. *Education and Career Articles.*

Shaikh Babar T., Kahloon Arsalan, Kazmi Muhammad, Khalid Hamza, Nawaz Kiran, Khan Nadia A and Khan Saadiya (2004). Students, stress and coping strategies: *A Case of Pakistani Medical School Education for Health*, 17(3), 346 – 353.

Uskun E., Kisioglu and Ozturk M. (2008), The stress and its effects on depression and anxiety among undergraduates. *International Journal of Behaviour Development,* 38, 196-201.

Verma Suman, Sharma Depali, Larson Reed W. (2002). The influence of school demands on the daily time use and subjective states of Indian young people. *International Journal of Behavioural Development*, 26, (6), 500-508.

Wang, Fen Huey Yeh, and Chang Mei (2005). Stress, coping, and psychological health of vocational high school nursing students associated with a competitive entrance exam. *Journal of Nursing,* 13(2).

25

Coping Mechanisms for People Suffering from Life Threatening Diseases

Priyanka Behrani and Nitu Singh Bhadouria

Introduction

A life threatening disease can be viewed as a major stressful event which is starting of stressful conditions characterized by a large number of minor events with strong negative consequences of well being. The way such acute and chronic stressors are coped, affects health and well being expressed in terms of suffering, adaptation, recovery, coping and quality of life. (Agarwal and Pandey, 1998; Tripathi and Agarwal, 2003; Agarwal, Mona and Gupta, 2002). Kohli and Dalal (1998) assert that the acceptance of suffering is the first step toward its cognitive reconstruction and a process of healing. In context of chronic illness ,perceived control, future orientation, positive life orientation, family support are associated with greater feeling of wellness and life satisfaction. (Agarwal, 2003, Agarwal, and Dalal, 1993). These kinds of studies provide some insight about the possible mechanism though which positive thinking and support influence recovery process. These psychosocial measures are of great value to the persons suffering from life threatening disease because their treatment is often concerned with improving their quality of life.

Coping is a process by which people try to manage the perceived discrepancy between the demands and resource they appraise in a stressful situation. We cope with stress through our cognitive and behavioural transactions with environment coping process are not a single event. Because coping involves ongoing transaction with the environment, the process is best viewed as a dynamic series of continuous appraisal and reappraisals of the shifting person- environment relationships. .

Functions of Coping

According to Richard Lazarus and his colleagues, (1987) coping can serve two main functions. It can alter the problem causing stress or it can regulate the emotional response to the problem.

Emotion-focused coping. It is aimed at controlling the emotional response to the stressful situation. People can regulate their emotional responses through behavioural and cognitive approaches.

People tend to use emotion focused coping when they believe they can do nothing to change the stressful conditions (Hackett and Weistman, 1985).

Problem-focused Coping

It is aimed at reducing the demands of the stress situation or expanding the resources to deal with it. People tend to use problem-focused approaches when they believe their resources or demands of the situation are changeable. (Greenglass and Nogachi 1996). The predominance of one type of strategy over another is determined by personal style and also by the type of stressful event; for example, people typically employ problem-focused coping to deal with potential controllable problems such as work- related problem and family-related problem, whereas stressors perceived as less controllable, such as certain kinds of physical health problems, prompt more emotion-focused coping (Billings and Moos, 1981).

An additional distinction that is often made in coping literature is between active and avoidant coping strategies. Generally speaking, active coping strategies, whether behavioural or emotional, are thought to be better ways to with stressful events, and avoidant coping strategies appear to be a psychological risk factor or marker for adverse responses to stressful life events (Holahan and Moss, 1987). The study examined the emotions, stress experienced by the patients suffering from life threatening disease that is cancer, renal failure and AIDS as well as study coping techniques used by them.

Method

Sample: Sample was randomly selected, i.e. on the availability irrespective of their age, gender, education or occupation. Sample consisted of fifteen patients five from each of the life threatening diseases, viz. cancer, HIV+ and kidney failure.

Table 25.1: Details of Participants in the Study

S.N	Diseases	No. of males	No. of females	Total
1.	Kidney failure	4	1	5
2.	Cancer	3	2	5
3.	HIV+	2	3	5

Research Sites: Data was collected from Sir Sayajirao Gaekwad Hospital, Vadodara, for HIV+patients. Premiere hospital in Vadodara, for Kidney failure patients Muni Seva Ashram in Goraj for cancer patients .All the patients taken for study were undergoing treatment in respective units.

Tools: COPE Questionnaire: The COPE is a multidimensional coping inventory having 28 items developed by Carver, C.S. (1997) incorporating 14 conceptually distinct scales which were developed on theoretical grounds or chosen on the basis of previous work which demonstrate their role in facilitating or impending adaptive coping in different context.

Test• retest reliabilities for the dispositional version were obtained from samples of subjects over six and eight week periods and ranged from 0.42 to 0.89 for different scales. This indicates that the coping tendencies measured by COPE are reasonably stable.

Explanation of the 14 Dimensions Used in Cope Scale

1. **Active Coping**: Active coping over here means taking action and exerting efforts, to remove or lessen the distress that one would face.
2. **Planning:** In planning person would start thinking about how to confront the stressor, it is planning one's active coping effort.
3. **Seeking Instrumental Social Support:** In seeking instrumental social support person would try to cope by seeking information, assistance or advice about what to do. Here one would ask otters in similar situation what they did or will take advice from others what to do.
4. **Seeking Emotional and Social Support:** Here person would try to get sympathy or emotional support from someone, and would discuss their feeling and distress that they are going through.
5. **Self Distraction:** In this particular coping mechanism one would start suppressing their attention to other activities in which one might engage, in order to concentrate more completely on dealing with stressor.
6. **Turning to Religion:** In this coping technique there will be increase of engagement in religious and spiritual activities. Over here one would comparatively pray more than usual and would try to find comfort in their religion.
7. **Positive Reframing:** Positive reinterpretation and growth means making the best of the situation by growing from it, or viewing it in a more favourable light.
8. **Acceptance:** Accepting the fact that stressful event has occurred and is real. Here patient accept the fact that he is suffering from life threatening disease.
9. **Focus on and Venting of Emotions:** An increases awareness of the ones emotional distress and a tendency to discharge those feeling.
10. **Denial:** An attempt to reject the reality of the stressful event. Thus, over here

patient is not able to believe that he has life threatening disease.

11. **Behavioural Disengagement:** Giving up or withdrawing from the attempt to attain the goal with which the stressor is interfering.
12. **Alcohol/Drug Use:** Use of alcohol or drug like sleeping pill, anti depressant etc for coping.
13. **Humour:** Taking things lightly and to laugh at situation for coping.
14. **Self Blame:** blaming one's ownself for whatever happened and feeling responsible for the result.

Semi Structured Questionnaire

A semi structured questionnaire was prepared with leading questions, for the convenience of the researcher the questionnaire and semi structured interview was translated to local language and contextualized and back translated to make the patients more comfortable.

Procedure: The data was obtained by Semi-structured interview and COPE questionnaire. The tools used studied emotions, anxiety experienced, techniques used by them to cope with theirs stress. Semi-structured interview was conducted for acquiring the information for patients' emotional reaction, belief system, and social support. There was no pre-conceived hypothesis; rather interview proceeded with information, obtained through observations and respondent responses. This gives information about what, how and why aspect of various psychological and emotional aspect of respondent's coping mechanism. The data was collected by seeking permission from the authorities and finding the willingness from the patients to be the part of study and got the consent form signed. The interviews were conducted at the convenience and comfort of the patient.

Results and Discussion

The results were analyzed through SPSS where descriptive statistics of mean and standard deviation and one way ANOVA was used to compare the coping mechanisms of patients of three different life threatening diseases shown in table 25.2. And qualitative data was put to content analysis and based on that the responses were categorized and percentages were calculated.

Graph profile represent coping patterns of cancer, HIV positive and kidney failure patients on coping dimensions on COPE. It indicates that religion is the most important and generally used by patients having life threatening diseases. While least used dimensions is humour and substance use as all patients suffering from life threatening disease believed that how anybody could make fun of their illness.

Table 25.2: Mean, Standard Deviation and f of Cancer, Kidney Failure and HIV Positive

S.N	Dimensions	Cancer		Kidney Failure		HIV+		F
		Mean	SD	Mean	SD	Mean	SD	
1	Self Distraction	5.40	1.517	5.40	1.342	5.80	1.483	.127
2	Active Coping	6.40	2.191	6.60	2.191	5.60	1.949	.313
3	Denial	3.20	2.168	4.20	1.643	5.00	2.236	.984
4	Substance Use	2.00	.000	2.00	.000	3.40	1.949	2.579
5	Use of Emotional Support	7.00	1.414	6.40	1.342	4.80	2.168	2.282
6	Use of Instrumental Support	3.80	1.304	3.40	1.140	5.40	2.408	1.909
7	Behaviour Disengagement	3.00	1.732	5.60	1.817	6.20	1.643	4.822*
8	Venting	4.20	2.049	4.40	1.517	4.60	2.074	.056
9	Positive Reframing	4.80	1.643	5.60	2.074	4.60	1.673	.429
10	Planning	4.20	1.304	4.40	2.302	4.80	1.483	.152
11	Humour	2.40	.894	2.00	.000	2.20	.447	.600
12	Acceptance	5.60	.894	5.60	1.140	6.20	1.095	.545
13.	Turning to Religion	5.80	1.483	5.20	1.924	6.80	.837	1.485
14	Self Blame	5.40	2.074	4.80	2.168	5.00	2.236	.100

HIV positive patients use self distraction techniques more than cancer and kidney failure patients. HIV positive patients hardly suffer from any physiological problems and are efficient enough to carry out with their daily routine. So they can easily get involved in activities that distract them from stress and anxiety experiences due to illness. Kidney failure patients use active coping more than cancer. Kidney patients suffer from various physiological difficulties and pain. To reduce it, they undergo treatments and take various steps which may help them to overcome. This indirectly helps them overcome their emotional distress produced due to illness. While HIV positive patients use it less than kidney failure patients and cancer patients as HIV positive patients can hardly able to talk about their illness with others. So it is difficult for them to find the ways which may be helpful to overcome with their disease. Denial, instrumental support, planning, behavioural disengagement, substance use and acceptance are used more by HIV positive patients than compare to kidney patients and cancer patients. Whereas kidney failure patients use active coping, positive reframing and self blame the most and more than cancer and HIV positive patients.

Graphical Profile of Coping Dimensions Used by Patients Having Life Threatening Diseases

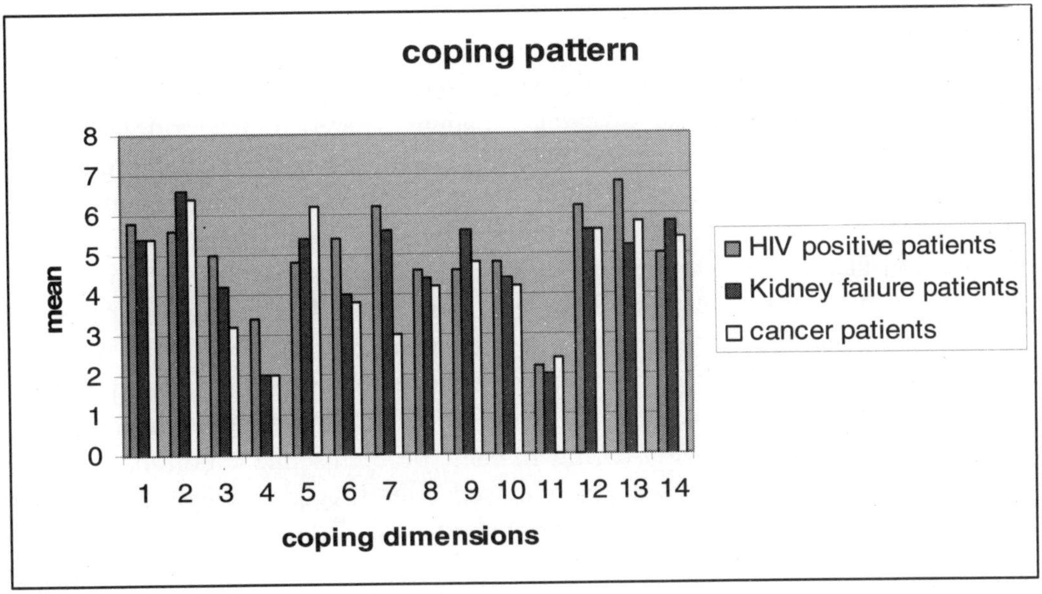

While cancer patients use emotional support more compare to kidney patients and HIV positive patients. To see the differences in the coping mechanisms of patients suffering from cancer kidney failure and HIV+, one way ANOVA was done shown in Table 25.2 which did not show any significant differences with relation to the three types of life threatening disease, accept for the dimension of behaviour disengagement where cancer patients differ from HIV+ and Kidney failure patients.

This gives a clear understanding that the patients suffering from life threatening diseases do not differ in coping mechanisms so it is clear whatever may be the disease there is no significant difference in the way patients try to cope up with the trauma of the disease and its painful treatment procedures (Miyazki, Bodenhorn 2008). Qualitative analysis was segregated to different categories based on responses received from the respondents.

Patient's Reaction Response on Knowing about the Disease

All the patients experienced anxiousness and nervousness. They were tensed and worried about their future. One of them even cried for two days as she was afraid about other's reactions on her illness and also worried about future. ("I cried for almost 2 days I was blank about future. I was only thinking what will happen now, every body will hate me") 2 of them were afraid from treatment procedure as it is long and painful especially chemotherapy.)

Sharing of Emotion as Coping Mechanism

Over all 60 percent of the participants used sharing of emotion as a coping technique. In case of cancer, 2 among 3 patients shared their emotions to their closed and dear ones. "I share my experience with her as I feel communication makes life easier and happier." While 4 out of 5 HIV positive participants shared their feelings only with their close ones especially their spouse and avoided exposure of fact of illness to others. "Why to tell others, what they will be able to do...how can I say this to them. How will they react? I only share my feelings with my husband. Only we are there to understand each other." While one who was unmarried hardly shared his emotions. He used other coping techniques such as religion and instrumental support to cope up with their distress. Whereas 3 of 5 kidney failure patients avoid sharing of their problems and emotional distress with others as they didn't wish their closed ones to get worried and stressed because of them. "By telling to wife or anybody else, I don't want to make them more worried and sad. But I tell them when pain is intolerable." Some patients shared their every feeling they experienced and every thought with which they are occupied with others to extreme level. "Yes, tell even a small problem I have, even a little pain or swelling in any part of body, to my mother and to father as well. I only share to my parents not to anybody else."

Spiritualism as Coping

Overall, 73 percent of the participants used spiritualism as a coping technique. For cancer and HIV Positive all participants used spiritualism as major coping mechanism. Belief in God helped to build hope in towards their life and also helped to overcome their stress, directly or indirectly. Most of them involved themselves in spiritual activities such as going to religious places regularly, performing rituals, reading holy books, etc. as reported "God is there, he has given me the disease, he will only help'', "faith on god gives me the strength, I feel good by performing prayer and rituals."

In kidney failure, only one patient showed faith on God and he goes to the temple and chat mantras daily to relieve his stress, while others refused to have faith on God and complained Him for cursing them with such illness. "If God would be there why this would have happened to me. My mother has faced lots of problem throughout her life and worked hard, she always pray to god and did whatever is possible. When it is their turn to get rest and peace, this happened. They are again suffering due to me, working hard to arrange money, serve and take care of me 24 hours."

Active Coping

Overall, 53 percent of participants used active coping as a coping mechanism. This coping technique is used less by cancer patients (Lazarus and Folkman, 1984). Only one cancer patient has collected information about the illness, their causes, treatment procedure and its progress. He used to take care of himself by taking medicine on time, taking appointments and talking to physicians. "I have to keep record of myself. I myself manage everything." While others who belonged to low socio-economic background hardly showed their interest in collecting information regarding their illness. They are partially or fully dependent on their spouse or other family members. "Yes I take care of my schedule but usually my wife does it for me. So I don't have to take care about it." In case of HIV positive interviewees active coping is not found to be major coping techniques. 2 out of 5 kidney failure patients preferred to take care of themselves while 3 were totally or partially depended on others to take their care, remember the time of medicine, doctor's appointment. Cognitive orientation is very useful coping mechanism (Schwarzer and Schwarzer, 1996).

Positive Reframing

47 percent of participants used positive reframing as a coping mechanism. They had wishes which they wanted to fulfil. One of the patient said I am confident and positive .I have seen worst cases then me. If they are surviving, why will not me. I want to see my younger son's marriage. They were satisfied with their lives. 2 out of 5 cancer patients had faith on doctor while one patient had great faith on Guru which ultimately helps him to build positive attitude to face the situation. Whereas one has developed hope and positive attitude by observing other cases that were extremely critical but still surviving. "I have seen many people even more critical then me; they are cured now so I will also be cured." In case of kidney failure patient, 3 of 5 were satisfied with their life as they fulfilled their roles and duties towards their family.

Family Support/Social Support

In all cases, social support was found to be essential and vital mechanism to overcome their mental distress. 87 percent of the participants used it as a coping mechanism. This finding is much with coordination to other studies conducted in this area (Tondon and Mehrotra 2007, Wethington and Kessler1986) 4 out of 5 cancer patients consider their family support as major strength which helps them overcome with their distress. All the patients considered family support, love and care as a factor which helped them to overcome their mental distress. "Family member are always ready to serve me and take care of me. My son stands by me 24 hours in my service. He handles business and me too. My son is so attached to me that he cries for me. He is so helpful, (saying that, he had tears in his eyes). In others house who care so much. Now none of son is so caring in today's world. So many things I think of him and feel bad" In case of kidney failure patients, all 5 patients considered family support as a major strength helping them to deal with their critical situation, whereas, 4 out of 5 HIV positive patients also thought the same.

Self Blame

Overall, 27 percent of the participants used self blame as a coping mechanism. 3 of 5 cancer patient who were male considered their habit of chewing tobacco to be responsible for their illness. "My Smoking and drinking habit has led me to this disaster. I have been smoking and taking alcohol since 3-4 year."

While in case of kidney failure and HIV, this technique is hardly noticed. "My in-laws took me in government hospital for delivery as it is free there. Hospital did not take proper care .it was unhygienic. So during that time I got infected. All because of my in-laws".

Use of Instrumental Support as Coping Mechanism/Self Distraction

60 percent of the participants keep themselves busy in other activities such as listening music, doing household chores, chatting and wandering with friends; so that they can avoid thinking of their illness. One of the participant reported "I try to keep busy myself among friend, chatting with them, wander here and there with them on bike. I mostly remain out of the house almost for whole day only come for meal and sleep."

3 out of 5 patients of cancer, kidney failure and HIV positive involved themselves in other activities such as watching TV, listening music etc. "I see TV whole day and sometime whole night. I hardly talk to other very much."

Acceptance

100 percent of the participants have accepted the fact of their illness and

considered it as their destiny. "One gets according to one deed (karam). I must have done something wrong either in this life or previous birth .nothing can be done against Gods will, everything happen." They do accept the philosophy of death. One of the kidney failure patient quoted a line from film which tells his level of acceptance "sabko mukamil jahan nahi milta, kisi ko zamin kisi ko aasma nahi milta" Mindfulness approaches focusing on concepts such as acceptance and living in the moment (Kabat-Zinn et al., 1992; Kaplan, Goldenberg, and Galvin-Nadeau, 1993) appear to be promising avenues for improving coping.

Behaviour Disengagement

33 percent of participants used this as a coping technique because they hardly had any further wishes because they avoid thinking or formatting any further new wishes or desires in life. They do not show interest initiating any new job. "I do not have further desire. I don't think of that.... I don't feel to initiate new things." 2 out of 5 HIV positive and kidney failure patient showed behaviour disengagement whereas only one cancer patient used behaviour disengagement as coping.

Conclusion

The study examined the emotions, stress experienced by the patients suffering from life threatening disease that is cancer, renal failure and AIDS as well as study coping techniques used by them. The research indicated that religion is the most important and generally used coping mechanism by patients having life threatening diseases, while the least used dimension is humour and substance use. Other coping strategies included their spiritual belief system, family and social support, acceptance of fate and cognitive appraisal. The study will help to form an intervention for patients suffering from life threatening diseases to develop effective coping strategies as well as and enhance their mental well being. It will also help to see that as a professional what kind of professional help can be given to them to cope in the better way.

The researcher also had some difficulties working with the patients of life threatening like it was very difficult to convince the patients for the interview as they were already suffering from emotional distress. Doctors were not permitting for the conduction of interview as they believed that the feelings of the patient of such patients may be hurt. Sometimes the patients got so emotional that they avoid replying to the questions. The research would have been more effective if the sample size was taken more than the present study.

References

Aldwin, C., B Revenson. T. (1987). Does coping help? *Journal of Personality and Social Psychology*, 53, 337-348.

Bolger, N. (1990). Coping as a personality process : A prospective study. *Journal of Personality and Social Psychology*: 59, 525-537.

Bradshaw.J . and Lawton, D. (1978). Tracing the cause of stress in families with handicapped children. *British Journal of Social Work*, 8, 181-192.

Breslau, N, Staruch, K., Mortlmer, E. (1982). Psychological distress in mothers of disabled children, American Journal of Diseases of Childhood, 136, 682-686.

Carver CS, Scheier MF, Weintraub JK. Assessing coping strategies: a theoretically based approach. *Journal of Personality and Social Psychology*. 1989;56(2):267–283.

Folkman, S., and Lazarus, R.S. (1980). An analysis of coping in a middle-aged community sample. *Journal of Health and Social Behaviour*, 21, 219-239.

Folkman, S and Lazarus, R. 1985. if it changes it must be a process : Study of emotion and coping during 3 stages of a college examination. *Journal of Personality and Social Psychology*, 48 (1): 150-170.

Folkman, S., Lazarus, R.S. Dunkel-Schetter, C., DeLongis, A., and Gruen, R.J. (1986). Dynamics of a stressful encounter: Cognitive appraisal, coping, and encounter outcomes, *Journal of Personality and Social Psychology*, 50, 992-1003

Kabat-Zinn J, Massion AO, Kristeller J, Peterson LG, Fletcher KE, Pbert L, et al. Effectiveness of a meditation-based stress reduction program in the treatment of anxiety disorders. *American Journal of Psychiatry*. 1992;149:936–943..

Landis BJ. Uncertainty, spiritual well-being, and psychosocial adjustment to chronic illness. *Issues in Mental Health Nursing*. 1996;17:217–231.

Lazarus, Folkman *Stress, appraisal, and coping*. Springer; New York: 1984.

Peaslin, L.I., Schooler, C. (1978). The structure of coping. *Journal of Health and Social Behaviour*; 19, 2-21.

Tondon S and Mehrotra S.(2007) Encounters with cancer Illustrating the process of psychological adaptation. *Psychological Studies*, 42(1):54-61.

Turnbull, A.P., B Turnbull, H.R. (1990). Families, professionals, and exceptionality: A Special Partnership (2nd ed.). Columbus, OH: Merrill.

26

Understanding and Treatment of Social Phobia in Youth

Namitesh Gupta

Introduction

Social phobia, a common problem in children and adolescents, has recently gained serious attention in clinical practice and research. Social phobia is defined as "a marked and persistent fear of social or performance situations in which embarrassment may occur" (according to the Diagnostic and Statistical Manual (IV) of the American Psychiatric Association, 1994, p. 411). Children or adolescents with social phobia become so disabled by the fear of other people's reactions and expectations that they avoid situations in which they fear that evaluation by others might occur.

Diagnosing Social Phobia in Children and Adolescents (DSM-IV)

A diagnosis of social phobia requires that (1) an individual, when exposed to the feared social situation, must invariably experience anxiety and must recognize that this anxiety is excessive or unreasonable, (2) the individual experiences intense distress while in the feared situation or avoids it, (3) the social phobia interferes significantly with the person's normal routine, social activities, or occupational/academic functioning, and (4) the fear or avoidance of social situations cannot be due to the direct physiological effects of a substance or general medical condition or be better accounted for by another mental disorder.

The diagnosis of social phobia in children emphasizes the following important developmental differences between children and adults:

1. A child with social phobia must show the capacity for age-appropriate social relationships with familiar people, and his or her anxiety must occur in peer contexts, not just with adults.
2. The anxiety brought on by social situations may be evidenced in children by crying, tantrums, freezing, or shrinking from social situations with unfamiliar people.
3. Due to limitations of cognitive and perceptual skills in young children, children with social phobia need not recognize that their fear in social

situations is excessive or unreasonable.

4. Under the age of 18 years, there must be evidence of the social fears existing for a minimum of six months.

Prevalence

Studies estimate rates of social phobia in youth at approximately 1-9%, depending on the age and gender. While studies have reported cases of social phobia in children as young as 8 years, it is more frequently diagnosed in adolescents. One study found that the average age of onset of social phobia falls between 11.3 and 12.3 years. Thus, social phobia appears to be a common problem that typically emerges in pre-adolescence; early recognition offers an opportunity for prevention and treatment.

Developmental Pathways to Social Phobia

Normative Developmental Factors: Children as young as 6 months through 3 years of age commonly show anxiety in the forms of stranger and separation anxiety. Some young children, when confronted with a new social situation, throw tantrums, cling to a familiar person, avoid contact, refuse to take part in group play, and become overly vigilant. By late childhood and early adolescence, children's fears of social evaluation of academic and social performance are forefront. Although at some point during their adolescence all youth will experience some level of anxiety about being judged in school or social situations, obviously not everyone goes on to develop pathological levels of social anxiety (i.e., social phobia).

Temperamental Factors: A predisposition to timidity and nervousness has been believed to be a matter of inborn temperament. The majority of recent research in the role of temperamental factors in the development of social phobia focuses upon behavioural inhibition (BI). BI refers to a temperamental style that is characterized by reluctance to interact with and withdrawal from unfamiliar settings, people or objects. In infants, BI is typically manifest as irritability, in toddlers as shyness and fearfulness, and in school age children as cautiousness, reticence and introversion. BI includes reactions that can be seen in behaviour, such as interrupting of ongoing behaviour, ceasing vocalization, comfort seeking from familiar persons, and retreat from and avoidance of unfamiliarity. BI also includes reactions that are physiological, such as stable high heart rate, acceleration of heart rate to mild stress, pupillary dilation, and increased salivary cortisol. Overall, evidence to date suggests that a behaviourally inhibited temperament may predispose a child to the development of high social anxiety, although BI has yet to be definitively identified as a necessary precursor to the development of the clinical syndrome social phobia.

Physiological Factors: Researchers have just begun to explore the physiology of social phobia, and studies have been primarily conducted with adults. When facing phobic situations, socially phobic individuals commonly experience such symptoms as blushing, racing heart, sweating, and increased respiration, all of which are reactions associated with the autonomic nervous system (ANS). However, the few studies that have examined ANS functioning in socially phobic individuals have provided mixed results.

Other research has examined the function of the amygdala, a small region in the forebrain involved in the output of conditioned fear responses, e.g., freezing up behaviour, blood pressure changes, stress hormone release, and the startle reflex. Hypersensitivity in the neural circuitry that centres on the amygdala may be responsible for behavioural inhibition in children. The application of currently developing neuroimaging technologies to children and adolescents may prove to be especially useful in elucidating the continuities and differences between social phobia in youngsters and in adults.

Genetic Factors

Twin Studies: Taken as a whole, studies using twins to determine whether genetics play a significant part in the development of social phobia are inconclusive. Some twin studies have examined the heritability of shyness and social fears rather than the clinical disorder social phobia. Overall, these studies suggest that genetics play a modest to moderate role in the development of symptoms and temperamental traits associated with social phobia.

Family Studies: Studies examining the rates of social phobia in the offspring or in other first-degree relatives of socially phobic individuals show that social phobia rates in relatives are higher than in the relatives of individuals with other anxiety disorders or no disorder. Overall, these studies suggest that social phobia is at least moderately familial and possibly specific in its transmission. However, family studies cannot specifically sort-out the relative contributions of genetic influences and family environmental influences on the development of a disorder. Thus, the mechanisms behind this familial connection in social phobia still need clarification.

Parenting/Family Environment Factors: Research indicates that parent characteristics and family environment, through such mechanisms as modelling of avoidant responses and restricted exposure to social situations, are likely to have at least a moderate effect on the development of social phobia in children and adolescents. It appears likely that if the parent's own anxiety is communicated to the child, a cycle is established in which parent and child reinforce each other's anxiety. Controlling/overprotecting and less affectionate parenting styles have been found to be associated with social phobia in adult offspring, although the cause and effect relationship between these characteristics and social phobia is unclear. A major gap in this area is research that uses children with social phobia or children at high risk for social phobia, and this needs to be filled before the developmental impact of parental and family factors can be specified.

General Subtypes of Social Phobia

The current diagnostic system specifies two types of social phobia : (1) "Generalized," if the individual's fear encompasses most situations, and (2) "Non-generalized" social phobia, sometimes also described as "discrete," "circumscribed," "limited," or "performance," when social anxiety is limited to a few specific contexts (e.g., eating in front of others, writing, public speaking etc.) In order to differentiate between subtypes, a thorough assessment of an individual's anxiety in many different types of social situations is necessary.

Sub-types in Children and Adolescents: Two studies provide preliminary evidence for distinct social phobia subtypes in adolescent and young adult populations. These studies specifically found that generalized socially phobic adolescents (those who experience anxiety across many social situations) appear to be distinguishable from those who have non-generalized social phobia (experience anxiety in only one or two social contexts) by earlier age of onset, greater level of impairment, greater risk for developing co-morbid disorders, greater parental psychopathology, separation difficulty during childhood, and behavioural inhibition. However, further studies are needed not only to validate these findings but, also, to see if subtypes exist in preadolescents with social phobia.

Relationship of Social Phobia to Other Problems

Consistent findings of research focused on youth with social phobia are high rates of co-existence among social phobia and other anxiety disorders, mood disorders, ADHD, and substance abuse disorders. Social phobia often precedes the development of coexisting conditions. However, research suggests that individuals who develop major depression prior to the onset of social phobia have a significantly better chance of recovery than do those who report an onset of depression following the social phobia. Overall, studies suggest that youth with social phobia and co-existing disorders are significantly compromised by a disabling psychiatric pattern that can extend into adulthood.

Consequences of Social Phobia

Children and adolescents with social phobia fear a range of situations and activities including speaking, eating, writing, or performing in front of others, initiating or maintaining conversations, attending parties and after-school activities, speaking to authority figures, acting in an assertive manner, and informal social situations. Additionally, affected youth suffer from high levels of dysphoria, loneliness, and general anxiety. Children with social phobia (ages 7 to 14 years) are found to have impaired social skills relative to non-anxious controls. Both adolescent males and females reporting high levels of social anxiety feel less accepted and supported by peers, and also less romantically attractive to others. Overall, findings suggest that social anxiety may interfere specifically with the development of close interpersonal relationships, especially for girls.

Although work done with shy adolescents (not diagnosed) indicates that shy youth are at risk for suicide attempts, the relationship of social phobia to suicidal ideation or attempts in youth has not yet been directly studied. Social phobia in adults is associated with increased suicide attempts.

Over the long term, social phobia is associated with a number of personal costs for affected individuals and their support systems, including impairments in role functioning and quality of life. As with other severe psychiatric conditions, social phobia is associated with failure to complete high school in females, and failure to enter and complete college in males and females. Beyond costs at the individual level, truncated educational attainment is associated with a number of adverse life-course and societal consequences including less training of the workforce, decreased participation and functioning in civic activities, and greater demands on the social welfare system. Thus, the potential consequences of the disorder are broad, impacting the emotional, occupational and social functioning of the individual over the long term, with individuals suffering functional impairments in the areas of school, social relations, family life, and employment.

Treatment of Social Phobia in Youth

Cognitive Behavioural Treatment: Treatment from the cognitive-behavioural perspective assumes that social anxiety is a normal and expected emotion. Social anxiety becomes problematic when it exceeds expected developmental levels and results in significant distress and impairment at home, school, and in social contexts. Anxiety is assumed to comprise of physiological, cognitive, and behavioural components. Cognitive behavioural treatment (CBT) involves specific psychoeducation, skills training, exposure methods, and relapse prevention plans for addressing the nature of anxiety and its components.

Psychoeducation provides corrective information about anxiety and feared stimuli; somatic management techniques target autonomic arousal and related physiological responses; developmentally appropriate cognitive restructuring skills are focused on identifying maladaptive thoughts and teaching realistic, coping-focused thinking; exposure techniques involve graduated, systematic, and controlled exposure to feared situations and stimuli; and, relapse prevention methods focus on consolidating and generalizing treatment gains over the long term. Social phobia (or social anxiety disorder) consists of a marked and persistent fear of social or performance situations. Affected individuals fear that they will be evaluated negatively or that they will act in a humiliating or embarrassing way.

Exposure to social or performance situations invariably leads to panic or marked anxiety, and such situations therefore tend to be avoided or endured with extreme distress. Social phobia is the third most common mental disorder in adults worldwide, with a lifetime prevalence of at least 5% (depending on the threshold for distress and impairment). There is an equal gender ratio in treatment settings, but in catchment area surveys, there is a female preponderance of 3:2. Individuals are more likely to be unmarried and have a lower socio-economic status. Although common, social phobia is often not diagnosed or effectively treated. There have, however, been a number of developments in our understanding and treatment of social phobia over the past decade, and these are the focus of this article.

Modifying Post-Interaction Ruminations: Those affected by social phobia often engage in 'postmortems'. Here, the therapist helps the patient to identify the content of the event (not the feelings) and review what actually happened by shifting to external processing and constructing an alternative data log of information that is normally disregarded or distorted.

Therapy would normally take between 8 and 20 out-patient sessions, depending on the severity and chronicity of the phobia. Patients with very severe phobia, who are housebound or dependent on alcohol, might do better on an intensive programme of CBT as either day-patients or in-patients in the right setting.

Pharmacotherapy

Medication is indicated if it is the patient's first choice, CBT has failed, there is a long waiting-list for CBT or there is significant comorbidity of depression. The treatment of choice in social phobia is a selective serotonin reuptake inhibitor (SSRI). The SSRIs, only paroxetine is licensed and marketed in the UK for social phobia, although there is no reason why other SSRIs may not be as effective. Most affected individuals can tolerate a normal starting dose of an SSRI, as they do not usually experience an 'activation syndrome' (as in panic disorder). The starting dose is used for 2–4 weeks and then increased as necessary. The onset of action is usually within 6 weeks and an adequate trial period is 8 weeks. The full response may occur after up to 12 weeks. About 50% of patients relapse on discontinuation of an SSRI and treatment is therefore continued for a minimum of 12 months. Once in remission, the dose may be reduced slowly (e.g. a 25 percent reduction every 2 months). If a patient fails to respond to an SSRI, then some evidence exists for the efficacy of a monoamine oxidase inhibitor (MAOI) (e.g. phenelzine, 45–90 mg daily) or a reversible monoamine oxidase inhibitor (RIMA) (e.g. moclobemide, 300–900 mg daily). Allow 2 weeks between discontinuing an SSRI (5 weeks if fluoxetine) and commencing an MAOI or RIMA. Although there are no evidence-based guidelines on the treatment of patients who have failed to respond fully to an SSRI or an MAOI, expert opinions suggest the adjunctive use of betablockers (e.g. propranolol, starting dose 20 mg daily, gradually increased to 60 mg, or atenolol 50–100 mg daily) to augment the response. Similarly, clonidine may augment the response for symptoms of blushing when used as an adjunct to an SSRI. The use of benzodiazepines (especially short-acting ones) is not recommended, because side-effects at a higher dose can include sedation, forgetfulness, impaired concentration and disinhibition, especially when used intermittently. Benzodiazepines are especially contraindicated for patients with comorbidity of depression and/or a history of alcohol or substance misuse.

Which Treatment for Whom?

Only one trial has compared later versions of CBT with an SSRI (Clark et al., 2003), and it found CBT to be superior to fluoxetine. No trials have yet compared later versions of CBT with a combination of CBT and another SSRI, especially in the long term and after discontinuation of the active treatment. As always, treatment will depend upon patient choice and availability of therapy, but in common with other anxiety disorders, CBT is the initial choice of treatment for social phobia, as it is usually more acceptable and has a reduced risk of relapse. As always, the main problem is user choice and access to CBT in a timely manner.

In addition to general CBT programs for anxiety, two promising and developmentally appropriate programs have been developed specifically to treat social phobia in children and adolescents. Social Effectiveness Therapy for Children (SET-C) is appropriate for youth ages 8 through 12 and involves 24 treatment sessions held over a 12-week period. Each child participates in one group social skills training session and one individual exposure session each week, with structured homework assignments serving to promote generalization of the within session experience to the child's real life. Based upon the success of Cognitive Behavioural Group Treatment for adult social phobia, Albano and colleagues adapted the protocol (CBGT-A) for adolescents ages 13 through 17. CBGT-A involves 16 group sessions incorporating psychoeducation, skills training (cognitive, social, and problem solving), and behavioural exposures.

Pharmacotherapy: Attention is just turning to the evaluation of pharmacologic agents for the treatment of social phobia in youth. Selective serotonin reuptake inhibitors (SSRIs) are demonstrating the most promise in treating anxiety in youth. Only two studies directly addressed social phobia or its variant, selective mutism.

In response to the dearth of controlled pharmacologic trials, the National Institute of Mental Health has established the Research Units in Pediatric Pharmacology (R.U.P.P.), a division focused on the controlled evaluation of psychotropic medications for use in children younger than 18 years of age. R.U.P.P. investigations focus on testing the efficacy of specific compounds for the range of emotional and behavioural disorders in youth. At present, the R.U.P.P. is evaluating the efficacy and safety of medications such as the SSRIs for the treatment of social phobia and related anxiety disorders in youth. Results of these trials are forthcoming.

In general, most pediatric psychiatrists will agree that treatment of anxious youth should begin with cognitive behavioural therapy or that CBT should be included in the treatment plan. It is unusual and not recommended for medication to be considered as the sole treatment for anxious youth.

Conclusion

Social phobia, once called the "the neglected anxiety disorder," is a chronic and debilitating condition that onsets early and can extend into adulthood. Exciting and essential research efforts are under way, bringing together researchers from different yet interrelated disciplines to understand the psychological and physiological contributants to social phobia. Through such research we are developing a better understanding of the risk and protective factors of social phobia in children and adolescents, which will ultimately lead to improvements in primary prevention and intervention efforts for children at serious risk for long-term problems with education, employment, social relationships and independent adult functioning.

References

Albano AM, Marten P, Holt C, Heimberg R, and Barlow, D (1995) Cognitive-behavioural group treatment for social phobia in adolescents: A preliminary study. *The Journal of Nervous and Mental Disease*, 183, 649-656.

Anne Marie Albano, Ph.D., is the Recanati Assistant Professor of Child and Adolescent Psychiatry, NYU School of Medicine.

Arntz, A. and Weertman, A. (1999) Treatment of childhood memories: theory and practice. *Behaviour Research Therapy*, 37, 715–740.

Ballenger, J. C., Davidson, R.T., Lecrubier, Y., *et al.* (1998) Consensus statement on social anxiety disorder from the International Consensus Group on Depression and Anxiety. *Journal of Clinical Psychiatry*, 59, 54–60.

Beidel DC and Turner SM (1988) Shy Children, Phobic Adults: Nature and Treatment of Social Phobia. Washington, DC: American Psychological Association.

Bogels, S. M., Mulkens, S. and De Jong, P. J. (1997) Task concentration training and fear of blushing. *Clinical Psychology and Psychotherapy,* 4, 251–258.

Chichester: John and Wells, A. (1995) A cognitive model of social phobia. In *Social Phobia–Diagnosis, Assessment, and Treatment* (eds R. G. Heimberg, M. R. Liebowitz, D. Hope, et al.), pp. 69–93.

Clark, D. M. (2001) A cognitive perspective on social phobia. In *International Handbook of Social Anxiety: Concepts, Research and Interventions Relating to the Self and Shyness* (eds W. R. Crozier and L. E. Alden). pp. 405–430.

Connor, K.M., Davidson, J.R.T., Churchill, L.E., *et al.* (2000) Psychometric properties of the Social Phobia Inventory (SPIN). *British Journal of Psychiatry,* 176, 379–386.

Davidson, J.R.T., Potts, N.L.S., Richichi, E.A., *et al.* (1991) The Brief Social Phobia Scale. *Journal of Clinical Psychiatry*, 52, 48–51.

Gilbert, P and Andrews, B. (1998) *Shame: Interpersonal Behaviour, Psychopathology, and Culture*. New York: Oxford University Press.

Hackmann, A., Clark, D.M. and McManus, F. (2000) Recurrent images and early memories in social phobia. *Behaviour Research and Therapy,* 38, 601–610.

Heimberg, R. G, Dodge, C. S., Hope, D. A., *et al.* (1990) Cognitive behavioural group treatment for social phobia: Comparison with a credible placebo control. *Cognitive Therapy and Research*, 14, 1–23.

Liebowitz, M. R. (2002) Social phobia. *Modern Problems in Pharmacopsychiatry,* 22, 141–173.

New York: Guilford. Ehlers, A., Hackmann, A., *et al.* (2003) Cognitive therapy vs. fluoxetine plus self exposure in the treatment of generalized social phobia (social anxiety disorder): A randomised placebo controlled trial. *Journal of Consulting and Clinical Psychology*, in press.

Olivia N. Velting, Ph.D. is an Associate Research Scientist at the NYU School of Medicine.

Index

Index

D

E

F

G

H

I

W